Charles Brockden Brown's
Revolution and the
Birth of American Gothic

Charles Brockden Brown's Revolution and the Birth of American Gothic

PETER KAFER

PENN

University of Pennsylvania Press

Philadelphia

10   9   8   7   6   5   4   3   2   1

Published by
University of Pennsylvania Press
Philadelphia, Pennsylvania 19104-4011

Library of Congress Cataloguing-in-Publication Data

Kafer, Peter
   Charles Brockden Brown's revolution and the birth of American Gothic /
Peter Kafer
      p.   cm.
   ISBN: 0-8122-3786-2 (cloth : alk. paper)
   Includes bibliographical references (p.) and index.
   1. Brown, Charles Brockden, 1771–1810—Criticism and interpretation.
2. Horror tales, American—History and criticism. 3. Gothic revival (Literature)—
United States. 4. Literature and history—United States. 5. United States—History—
Revolution, 1775–1783—Literature and the revolution. I. Title
PS1137 .K34   2004
813′.2—dc22   2003066581

Frontispiece: *Charles Brockden Brown,* attributed to Ellen Sharples after James Sharples, c. 1810. National Park Service, Independence National Historic Park.

To the Memory of my Father

Contents

Oh! my friend, to expire in such torments! to die amidst curses and execrations! to bear the insults of an exasperated mob! to be exposed to all the mortifications of shame and infamy! who can reflect without horror on such a doom? Let me then exult in my exchange. I have sold distant and uncertain happiness for present and secure. I have preserved a life, which otherwise I had lost in torture; and I have obtained the power of procuring every bliss which can make that life delicious! The infernal spirits obey me as their sovereign; by their aid shall my days be passed in every refinement of luxury and voluptuousness. I will enjoy unrestrained the gratification of my senses; every passion shall be indulged even to satiety; then will I bid my servants invent new pleasures, to revive and stimulate my glutted appetites! I go impatient to exercise my newly-gained dominion.
I pant to be at liberty.

—*Matthew G. Lewis*, The Monk

Introduction

At the age of twenty-seven Charles Brockden Brown invented the American Gothic novel with a story in which a father dies by spontaneous combustion and the son, a onetime deist, goes crazy and strangles his wife and five children, seeks to murder (and perhaps rape) his sister, and commits suicide. Brown then sent a copy of his novel to the vice president of the United States, announcing himself "a stranger to the person, though not the character of Thomas Jefferson" and hoping that *Wieland; or the Transformation, an American Tale* "is capable of affording you pleasure." To Thomas Jefferson: a deist who designed his Monticello home as the American epitome of classical proportion, who got a violent headache when he stood atop Virginia's Natural Bridge and looked down "into the abyss," who would seek to have David Hume's *History of England* purged of its disturbing *un*republican elements, and whose favorite novel was Laurence Sterne's sentimental *Tristram Shandy*. What *was* he thinking?[1]

It's a safe bet that Jefferson had never read any of *Wieland*'s English precursors, or at least had never read one *through*. Certainly he would not have read *The Castle of Otranto*, the novella by Horace Walpole that initiated the Gothic literary genre in 1764. This book was objectionable on political grounds alone, for its author was the son of the prime minister Sir Robert Walpole, a politician reviled by Jefferson and all good country Whig republicans for what they deemed his corrupt use of patronage to undermine the British constitution. But even if Horace Walpole had carried an acceptable ideological pedigree, the plot and style of his novella would have sufficed to induce in Jefferson another headache.[2]

For thus *Otranto*: A haunted castle with plenty of subterranean vaults and passageways. An ancient prophecy *that the castle and lordship should pass from the present family whenever the real owner should be grown too large to inhabit it*. A usurper prince with a son who is to marry the daughter of a marquis. A giant helmet—"an hundred times more large than any casque ever made for human being"—smashing down out of nowhere to crush the son to death on his wedding day. A peasant stepping forward to observe that "the miraculous helmet" is exactly like that on a statue of a beloved former prince buried in the church graveyard. News arriving that that graveyard statue is bizarrely missing its helmet. Prince imprisoning peasant under the giant helmet. (Peasant subsequently escaping from the giant helmet with the help of the prince's daughter.) Prince deciding to send his own wife to a convent so he can marry his son's fiancée, the marquis's daughter. Marquis's daughter being horrified by the incestuous prospect. Marquis's daughter fleeing this fate through subterranean passages. Prince stopping at nothing to get the marquis's daughter back in his control. Marquis's daughter falling in love with the peasant. Three drops of blood dripping from the graveyard statue's nose. Fleshless skeleton with hollow eye sockets showing up in a hermit's cowl. Prince accidentally stabbing his own daughter to death (when what he meant to do was stab the marquis's daughter because she, the woman he desired, was in love with the peasant). Claps of thunder, castle walls shaking and collapsing, and a gigantic figure arising out of the ruins—the beloved prince of yore from the graveyard—to announce that the peasant is not a peasant, that he is the true heir of the castle. Usurper prince abdicating to "peasant"/true prince, who marries the marquis's daughter. Proper order and legitimacy restored to the principality of Otranto.

In short, *The Castle of Otranto* was a consummately anti-Jeffersonian production, and nowhere more so than in its explicit moral "that *the sins of fathers are visited on their children to the third and fourth generation.*" Not that Jefferson would have quibbled with Walpole's depiction of a corrupt European princely family that needed uprooting. Jefferson had seen enough of these during his years as American minister in France in the 1780s. It's just that Jefferson's whole life was dedicated in principle to creating a world in which the *sins of fathers* would not matter to the children. His own "self-evident" credo was "*that the earth belongs in usufruct to the living*; that the dead have neither powers nor rights over it." In *Otranto*, by contrast, the aristocratic corruption is remedied not by the creation of a republican New Order of the Ages, but when a peasant appears who is not a peasant, who is in fact by hereditary blood a rightful noble heir. Jefferson certainly wasn't about to plow through a surrealistic tale with giant helmets and bleeding statues for *that* payoff. His tastes were too rational and classical and republican and his time too precious.[3]

The latter consideration alone would have steered him clear of Ann Radcliffe's four-volume *The Mysteries of Udolpho* (1794). More sentimental in its aesthetics and less fantastic in its plotting than *Otranto, Udolpho* still offered its share of supernatural gimcracks (floating shrouds, spectral figures, and the like), though its author is at pains to provide, in due course, rational explanations for each and every one of these. But Thomas Jefferson was not about to wade through volumes of melodramatic prose to learn that the "horror" that causes the heroine/victim Emily St. Aubert to drop senseless on the floor in chapter 6 of volume 2 is not the corpse she thinks it is, but a waxwork figure.

Matthew Gregory Lewis's *The Monk* (1796) would have repulsed on other grounds. A sensationalist exposé of the Catholic Church—and in particular, the perversions attendant upon the monastic lifestyle—*The Monk* accorded well with Jefferson's own opinions about hierarchical and authoritarian institutions grounded in "superstition." (Especially since Jefferson, in Paris, had sent his two daughters to a convent school with the stern American republican intention of keeping them walled off from the sexual mores of French high society, only to have the eldest announce to him two years later that she wanted to become a nun.) But though the political message of Lewis's novel was congenial, its manner was most un-Jeffersonian, for it was "Monk" Lewis who put *horror* into the Gothic novel, along with doses of the truly disgusting and a saturating prurience that bordered on the pornographic. Within the developing Gothic genre, that is to say, *The Monk* was a breakthrough achievement. It imagined—and duly exploited—the *not-to-be-imagined*.[4]

The novel begins tamely enough in the *Otranto* and *Udolpho* style. A curse about retribution. An ominous setting. A dream of "a monster" and "a crumbing cathedral." Subsidiary tales about Bleeding Nuns and the Wandering Jew. There is a bit more explicit sexual material than in Walpole's and Radcliffe's novels—dreams about naked breasts; a sexual relationship between the protagonist and a temptress who lives within the monastery disguised as a novice—but for the most part *The Monk*, for its first half, follows their lead. Until Lewis has his hero/villain, the monk Ambrosia, cast his sights on the pure and beautiful Antonia.

To this point in the story Ambrosia's dealings have been with monastery insiders, with people already tainted by the inbred culture of the place. Antonia comes from outside the order. Her mother is dying and she seeks a priest "whose wise and pious consolations may soften the agonies of my parent's death-bed." Ambrosia has never met anyone so "sweet," so "harmonious," so "heavenly." *So innocent.* Lewis has his monk reflect:

> She is lost to me; by marriage she cannot be mine: and to seduce such innocence, to use the confidence reposed in me to work her ruin—Oh! it would be a crime, blacker than yet the world ever witnessed! Fear not, lovely girl! your virtue runs no risque from me. Not for Indies would I make that gentle bosom know the tortures of remorse.

This is to lay out the proper boundaries. But Lewis has shifted into a new gear. He virtuously conjures the things that cannot be done *precisely for the purpose of having his hero/villain DO THEM*, in titillating and sensational detail.[5]

Lewis's repertoire includes a magic mirror that enables his monk to turn Peeping Tom ("She was undressing to bathe herself. The long tresses of her hair were already bound up. The amorous monk had full opportunity to observe the voluptuous contours and admirable symmetry of her person . . ."), special sleeping potions to facilitate rape, forays into grossness ("my hand rested upon something soft: I grasped it, and advanced it towards the light. Almighty God! What was my disgust. . . . In spite of its putridity, and the worms which preyed upon it, I perceived a corrupted human head . . ."), scenes of incest and parricide, and an underlying pagan ethic ("Let us . . . despise the world's prejudices" and move beyond "Shame and remorse," let us "dare to be happy") that leads not to the grandiosity of Goethe's Faust or Nietzsche's *Übermensch* but to the desiccated psychotic world of *The Silence of the Lambs*' Buffalo Bill. ("Compose yourself, Antonia. . . .You are imagined dead; society is for ever lost to you. I possess you here alone; you are absolutely in my power, and I burn with desires which I must either gratify or die.")[6]

Of course Monk Lewis was hardly the first European novelist to explore forbidden territory. John Cleland published his pornographic classic, *Memoirs of a Woman of Pleasure*, better known as *Fanny Hill*, in 1748–49, allowing himself to illustrate the progressive Enlightenment principle that the natural instincts are good. And in France, the great philosophe Denis Diderot, when not writing articles on agriculture and the production of steel for the *Encyclopédie*, was writing half-philosophical, half-pornographic novels like *The Indiscreet Jewels*, in which female genitalia are allowed their epistemological say, and *The Nun*. (Jefferson should have read this before committing his two daughters to the convent school of Panthémont.) And after 1789 and the fall of the Bastille, its former inmate the Marquis de Sade began to publish his unrivaled *oeuvre*—again, for the high Enlightenment purpose of illustrating just precisely what "nature" was capable of—about which the historian Simon Schama has written: "If there ever was a justification for the Bastille, it was the Marquis de Sade."[7]

Monk Lewis's literary discovery was how to indulge the subversive imagination and still credibly package and sell the product as a paean to "virtue." He could write *The Monk* and remain socially respectable, a member of Parliament in good standing, and have his novel pass through multiple editions in England and Ireland, so that it could readily find its way into the hands of the stolid Philadelphia Quaker matron Mrs. Henry Drinker. "It is a horriable work," she recorded in her diary. (And by this she meant, presumably, "a work in the horror genre.") "It shews great genius and a luxuriant fancy, pity 'twas not used to better purpose." But she—unlike Thomas Jefferson, we can be sure—read it all the way through![8]

In sending the vice president his own "horriable work" in December 1798, Charles Brown's stated wish was that "Mr. Jefferson will be induced to open the book that is here offered him; that when he has begun it he will find himself prompted to continue, and that he will not think the time employed upon it tediously or uselessly consumed." Beyond this there was the very practical calculation that the vice president might see fit to recommend the book to others, and thereby "diffuse the knowledge of its author, and facilitate a favorable reception to future performances."[9]

The Gothic formula requires hero/villains, innocent victims, places of haunting, historical pasts weighing upon the present, and an author's willingness to write to excess. Horace Walpole found his necessary elements in "Otranto," a thirteenth-century Italian principality. Ann Radcliffe's "Udolpho" is situated in the lawless Apennine Mountains of sixteenth-century Italy. *The Monk*'s action unfolds in a Capuchin church in Madrid. All share a continental Roman Catholic frame, and all thereby exploit longstanding English stereotypes about non-Protestant *outsiders*: lecherous priests and monks, perverse nuns, corrupt/libertine French and Italian aristocrats. But the frame is not without its contemporary eighteenth-century English application, for England had its own share of corrupt and useless aristocrats, and questions about their social and political privileges were the order of the day—and never so glaringly so as after the fall of the Bastille.

The Monk in particular was perfectly tuned for popular success. Its very title carried allusions to the homegrown "Medmenham Monks," a notorious libertine "order" of rakes and blasphemers whose meetings took place in the cells of a Cistercian abbey, whose motto was "Fay ce que voudras" ("Do what you want," not so far from *The Monk*'s "dare to be happy"), and whose membership included the prince of Wales, the fourth earl of Queensberry, the fourth earl of Sandwich, a son of the archbishop of Canterbury, and select special commoners like the M.P. John Wilkes and the artist William Hogarth (he of *The Rake's Progress* series). Lewis set his story in the religious orders of distant Spain, but the *frisson* of his tale—which culminates in a mass revolt: "the populace besieged the building with persevering rage: they battered the walls, threw lighted torches in at the windows, and swore that by break of day not a nun of St. Clare's order should be left alive"—necessarily bore down on an English audience that had been reading reports of French Revolutionary "terror" and wondering if the horrors would stop at the Channel's edge.[10]

In the America of Charles Brockden Brown, however—or more precisely, in the America *before* Brown—such types and concerns were not part of a cultural terrain where corrupt castellated nobles like Otranto's Manfred and Udolpho's Montoni and libertine cloistered monks like Ambrosia simply didn't exist. Nor were archbishops' rakish sons or world-class scandalous demagogue politicians to be found. (There was Aaron Burr, but he had not yet come into his prime.) Instead, a generalized Protestant moralism seemingly encompassed high, low, and middling alike, and nowhere more pressingly than in Brown's hometown, Quaker Philadelphia. Where was extremity, *intensity* in this world? Where could models for hero/villains be found? Where was the weight, the guilt, of history? How could such a place—the home of William Penn and Benjamin Franklin—give birth to and nurture the Gothic imagination?

Fiction in the new American republic reflected this social and cultural landscape. The first American novels were exercises in either the Samuel Richardson seduction or Henry Fielding picaresque modes. William Hill Brown's *The Power of Sympathy* (1789), for example, dedicated to "the Young Ladies, of United Columbia," amounted to a sermon on "the fatal consequences of SEDUCTION." Hannah Webster Foster pursued the same theme from a feminine perspective in *The Coquette* (1797). Both are compressed epistolary novels set in the drawing rooms of Congregational /Presbyterian New England. Royall Tyler's picaresque *The Algerine Captive*, self-described as a "homespun history of private life," combined a coming-of-age in Puritan New England satire with a North Africa captivity tale, and in the crossover delivered a democratic condemnation of slavery in the American South. Hugh Henry Brackenridge's *Modern Chivalry* (the first four volumes appearing in 1792, 1793, 1797) dramatized contemporary political debates about "democracy" by setting loose an Americanized Don Quixote and Sancho Panza—"Captain Farrago" and "Teague O'Regan"—among the town, village, and backwoods social types of Pennsylvania. And then in 1798 appeared *Wieland*, with its oddness, its fierceness, its perversity, its patently uncertain morality. It was, to borrow a phrase from Melville, a "hell-fired book"—the American republic's first in what would be a long, characteristic line. Where had it come from?

Charles Brockden Brown's Revolution offers my answer to that question, though like any self-respecting Gothicist I will not trot out my *horrors* until the time is ripe. But by way of introduction to this eighteenth-century Philadelphia Quaker's achievement, I would like to contemplate a *Wieland* avatar that appeared 179 years after the original.

Stephen King's *The Shining*—published in 1977—carries an explicit homage to Edgar Allan Poe's "The Masque of the Red Death." It is Poe's tale about an obscene self-deluding revel in the midst of an all-devouring plague that King uses to inform the political moral of his modern-day horror story—a story in which the imperial history of twentieth-century America lies most heavily on the present and on the fate of a father, mother, and son.

The setting is a grand hotel in the Colorado Rockies. It is winter. The Overlook Hotel is closed and inaccessible to the outside world due to massive snowfalls. Its only residents are the caretaker, Jack Torrance, his wife Wendy, and their son Danny, who is "five going on six."

The Torrance family has been through a terrible year. Jack, a writer, had had a good job teaching at a New England boarding school, but a problem with alcohol and a violent incident led to his dismissal. This was during a period for Jack of heavy drinking and sporadic violent outbursts, when on one occasion he had struck his wife, and on another he had—maybe inadvertently, maybe not—broken his son's arm.

Jack—the hero/villain of the story—has his demons, and they derive from his own alcoholic and bullying father. When he was a kid his father would get drunk and beat him and his brothers. When Jack was nine, his father, after a boozing weekend, had battered his mother with a cane and put her into the hospital. Like father like son.

The winter in the Rockies was a time for the family to heal. Jack had stopped drinking, and he was going to finish writing a play that would rehabilitate his career prospects. He was going to find personal redemption, and from this would follow his family's redemption. But at the hotel Jack starts hearing voices, and one of these—that of his father—tells him to kill his son and wife.

As Jack has a haunting past, so does the hotel. It was built in the early 1900s and had been the scene of many revels among the rich and powerful and famous. Nelson Rockefeller had stayed there in 1950. Henry Ford and family in 1927. Jean Harlow in 1930. Clark Gable. Carole Lombard. Hollywood mogul Darryl F. Zanuck in 1956. President Warren Harding in 1922. Other presidents had stayed there too, along with assorted millionaires and gangsters. And there was the night of August 29, 1945, when the hotel had hosted a costume party, a masked ball, to celebrate simultaneously its reopening and America's victory over the Japanese.

As Jack goes progressively insane, his history, the hotel's history, and America's history bleed into each other. They are all equally rotten. Jack's history is one of a physically abusive father; the hotel's history is of corrupt, greedy, philandering men whose money came from munitions and chemical factories, bootlegging, Las Vegas gambling casinos, and who use the luxurious site for their playground; and America's history is of too much wealth and the arrogance of power. Jack himself remarks that the hotel's history "forms an index of the whole post-World War II American character," and it bodes unwell for the Torrances when Wendy announces to Danny that "*The Overlook has gotten into your daddy.*" *It* has indeed, and "the thing" is driven to destroy the most precious and innocent treasures in Jack's life: his son and wife.[11]

Central to *The Shining* is an interplay of visions, dreams, and imagined voices. Danny possesses "precognition": the ability "to shine." He can read other people's thoughts, and he knows things he hasn't actually experienced—including future things. Sometimes he sees and hears these on his own; sometimes an imaginary friend, "Tony," pops up to tell him. Jack, for his part, hears voices, the first of which, his dead father's voice, speaks to him in a half-dream. But he comes to hear other voices too: among these the voice of the hotel itself and the voice of a former caretaker who had murdered *his* wife and children there.

And now my point: This is *Wieland* redivivus. The American Gothic formula

Charles Brockden Brown devised in 1798 is alive and flourishing in 1977. Haunted setting? In *Wieland*, it's a Pennsylvania wilderness community called Mettingen; in *The Shining*, it's the wilderness retreat in the Rockies called the Overlook. Hero/villain? In both stories it is a "good" middle-class family man who cracks because of a family history in which fathers pass destructive propensities unto sons. Innocent protagonist victim? In *Wieland*, it is Clara who undergoes two horrors, one when she is six (her father's death by spontaneous combustion), the other when she's in her mid-twenties and her brother turns lunatic murderer; in *The Shining*, Danny is "five going on six" and Wendy is in her mid- to late twenties when Jack takes up his bloody mallet. Also among the Gothic devices facilitating the two stories: both feature a hero/villain who hears *voices* telling him "to kill." In *Wieland*, furthermore, there is a ventriloquist who projects mysterious voices, one of which periodically warns Clara about entering dangerous places. In *The Shining*, "Tony" periodically warns Danny about dangers. And both novels use dreams and visions to set up the suspense. Clara dreams about assaults to come; while Danny "shines" the gory horrors ahead.

In both novels, too, American history plays a weighty part. The history that hangs over *The Shining* is crystal clear to the reader. It is Nixon. Vietnam. The corruption of post-World War II America. King flags this again and again. Early in the novel a character observes: "Federal government's into everything these days, ain't it? FBI openin mail, CIA buggin the goddam phones . . . and look what happened to that Nixon. Wasn't that a sorry sight?" Later Jack, who has been looking through the hotel's dusty records and discovered the role that Las Vegas sharpers and dummy corporations and mafiosi had played in its past, exclaims about the tenor of guests who had stayed in the presidential suite: "Great place. . . . Wilson, Harding, Roosevelt, Nixon, and Vito the Chopper, right?" And among the odd events in the hotel's annals, there was the night in August 1974 when "a man who had won the Bronze and Silver Stars in Korea (that man now sat on the boards of three major corporations . . .) unaccountably went into a fit of screaming hysterics on the putting green." This is "unaccountable" only if the reader forgets that Nixon resigned from office in August 1974. Finally there is the most explicit flag waving in the novel, when Jack comes across an old invitation to that masked ball of August 29, 1945. On the card is printed *"Dinner Will Be Served At 8 P.M. Unmasking And Dancing At Midnight."*

Jack's mind goes to work.

Dinner at eight! Unmasking at midnight!
He could almost see them in the dining room, the richest men in America and their women. Tuxedos and glimmering starched shirts; evening gowns; the band playing; gleaming high-heeled pumps. The clink of glasses, the jocund pop of champagne corks. The war was over, or almost over. The future lay ahead, clean and shining.

America was the colossus of the world and at last she knew and accepted it. And later, at midnight . . . "Unmask! Unmask!" The masks coming off and . . . (*The Red Death held sway over all!*) He frowned. What left field had that come out of? That was Poe, the Great American Hack. And surely the Overlook—this shining, glowing Overlook on the invitation he held in his hands—was the farthest cry from E. A. Poe imaginable.[12]

But of course that *is* Stephen King's point. The Overlook Hotel—and post-World War II America—was not a far cry from Poe. It was, it is Poe. Exactly.

Which, as the critic Mark Edmundson has argued, is the historical subtext for all of contemporary American Gothic—when there is a subtext behind the gore and titillation. *The Fog. Nightmare on Elm Street. Halloween. Eyes Wide Shut. The* (old) *Oprah Winfrey Show.* Anything by Oliver Stone. What's the problem? Our institutions and authority figures are corrupt and rotten, and our elders, when not complicit with the evil about us (see *Rosemary's Baby*), are clueless as to what's really going on. Meanwhile our loving, well-meaning parents (God bless 'em) abet the evil/hypocrisy by mindlessly mouthing and practicing the establishment's shibboleths. Thus in *Nightmare on Elm Street* (for Edmundson, "a work of lowbrow genius"), the alcoholic mother puts metal bars on all the windows of the house in hopes of protecting her daughter, when the point is that Freddy Krueger *already lives inside.*[13]

The past hangs over and corruption suffuses the world of *Wieland,* but not quite in the ways of modern Gothic. For one the novel lacks our cynicism. The horror—the evil—is not assumed. Its manifestation comes out of the blue, as a genuine shock. And the history—which is crushing in its weight—is anything but crystal clear. It is covert, which is precisely the way Brown intended it.

I mean to be a bit mysterious here, for the case of Charles Brockden Brown presents an intriguing biographical and historical mystery. In an American Revolutionary world populated by Franklin and Adams and Washington and the Thomases Paine and Jefferson, and Mrs. Henry Drinker, he was the lone subversive Gothicist. There was no one like him.

So, again, why did he send that copy of *Wieland* to Thomas Jefferson? Well to whom else could he have sent it? Benjamin Franklin?

Philadelphia's most famous citizen was the American republic's most successful writer and its most accomplished prose stylist. A lover of novels, Franklin had been the first American to print Richardson's *Pamela*—a work idolized by Brown. But Franklin was no longer around in 1798 (he had died in 1790), and in any case he was a problematic figure for Brown, seeing as Brown's people, the Quakers of Philadelphia, didn't much like or respect Benjamin Franklin. (See Chapters 1 and 2 below.)

How about Alexander Hamilton? He sought to establish a powerful and rich nation where writers, among other interests, could flourish. In his 1791 *Report on Manufactures* he even called for a 10 percent tariff on imported books as a way to encourage the domestic publishing industry and, thereby, native authors. He was as well the ideological founder of the Federalist political party that Brown would spend his last years serving in a partisan capacity. But Charles Brockden Brown would never have sent his book to Hamilton, and not least because, when Brown was six years old, there's a very good chance Hamilton broke into his house and stole food and blankets. He certainly stole food and blankets from the Browns' Quaker friends and neighbors. Hamilton called what he was doing "distraining" military necessities. But to young Charles it would have felt like violation and robbery. (See Chapters 1 and 3 below.)

Then what about President John Adams? He was a prolific writer and published author of note. Moreover, his middle son was a friend of Brown's. Yet Brown would never have sent his book to him, because John Adams had once put Brown's father's name on a list that could have been his father's death warrant. (See Prologue and Chapter 3 below.)

Which leaves, among the cultural luminaries in 1798 America, the author of the Declaration of Independence. *Thomas Jefferson*: a man of exquisite tastes and broad learning, who was now vice president of the United States, who had a good chance of soon becoming president of the United States . . . *and who had a dark secret.*

The first rumors about *that* side of Jefferson began to swirl in the late 1790s. Jefferson's Virginia neighbors had noticed the close physical resemblance between the master of Monticello and a number of his slaves, and local gossip had taken it from there. These rumors would make their way into partisan print in 1802, but they first made their way up to Philadelphia along with the nation's political leaders. Dozens of French émigrés lived in Philadelphia too, some of whom had known the famous American Revolutionary in Paris in the 1780s, where his household exotically included the two black slaves he had brought with him from Virginia: one to learn the art of French cuisine, and the other—a remarkable teenage beauty—to take care of his youngest daughter, who spent most of her time in a convent school.[14]

Now what if a young novelist interested in true revelations of "domestic history" and "the moral life"—as was Brown—observed Jefferson walking the streets of Philadelphia. Here was a man in his fifties, a widower of almost two decades, who wrote passionate words about liberty, whose accomplishments proclaimed his strenuous morals and ideals, and who was a large slaveholder. As secretary of state in Philadelphia in the early 1790s, Jefferson had had with him James Hemings, his slave trained as a chef in Paris. Jefferson had manumitted this man in 1796, and Hemings—light skinned, attractive, fluent in French—now lived in the city as a free man. Did he have siblings? A sister? One only had to ask. What was the great man's life like back at Monticello, back in the part of America—the only part—that had aristocrats anything like those in *The Castle of Otranto* and *The Mysteries of Udolpho?* What might a novelist, in the Richardsonian "seduction" mode, make of this?[15]

Now what if the young novelist was of a Gothic turn, interested in the weight of history and how *the sins of fathers are visited on their children to the third and fourth generation* and beyond. Then a series of additional questions would necessarily crop up. Monticello and the vice president's other properties? How had they come into the family? And what had happened to their aboriginal possessors? Whatever it was, it wasn't that long ago; the consequences were still palpable. And the vice president's hundred-plus slaves? Where had they come from? (James Hemings, who was the vice president's father-in-law's son and therefore his deceased wife's half brother, could have told quite a tale here.) And where, after the master of Monticello's death, would they—some of them perhaps *his* own children—go?

Needless to say, Brown never told *this* tale. But he was equipped to, for he was the only man or woman in 1790s America with the requisite Gothic imagination to sense the dark histories already weighing down on the American republic. Instead, with *Wieland,* he began to tell the tale of his own family's extended American saga, and he proudly sent this novel to the author of the Declaration of Independence who wanted to believe that *the dead have neither powers nor rights over the living.*

Whatever he was thinking, Charles Brockden Brown was a most curious individual, and this book tells his tale, starting with a season of American Revolutionary horrors that predated Stephen King's *The Shining* by two hundred years precisely, and that were but the most extreme in a succession of historical horrors that had shadowed the Brown family ever since the 1650s and 1660s, when, in the Midlands of England, they first turned to the *light* that was Quakerism.

Philadelphia, 1777

Philadelphia, Summer 1777–Summer 1778: "the Horrors of the night"

On August 28, 1777, John Adams, as one of three members of the Continental Congress's ad hoc Committee on Spies, helped make up a list with eleven names on it. All were Philadelphia Quakers. The list was then handed over to the "governing authority" of Pennsylvania, the Supreme Executive Council, along with Congress's *recommendation* that "all persons . . . notoriously disaffected, forthwith . . . be disarmed and secured, until such time as they may be released without injury to the public cause." The Council responded to the "recommendation" by expanding the list. For the purpose it asked four individuals—David Rittenhouse, William Bradford, Sharp Delany, and Charles Willson Peale—to identify additional persons "dangerous to the State who ought to be arrested." They contributed thirty more names, about half of whom were Quakers, the rest Anglican Tories. On August 31 the Council, list in hand, issued a general warrant for the arrest of forty-one citizens, and on September 2, 3, 4, and 5 the arrests took place. First to be rounded up, at 11 A.M., was the Tory doctor William Drewet Smith. At noon the Quaker artisan Thomas Affleck and Quaker merchant Thomas Gilpin were picked up, along with Tories William Lenox, Alexander Stedman, and Charles Stedman. In the afternoon some of Philadelphia's most prominent citizens were forcibly taken into custody, including Israel and John Pemberton, Thomas Wharton, and Miers Fisher. By the end of day one, nineteen men were imprisoned in the Freemason Lodge, eleven of them Quakers. On September 3, two more Quakers were arrested—one the wealthy merchant Henry Drinker—and on September 4, James Pemberton, John Hunt, and Samuel Pleasant were apprehended. The final arrest took place at noon on September 5: a thirty-seven-year-old Quaker retail merchant, Elijah Brown.[1]

All in all, of the forty-one names on the list, twenty-six were actually jailed. Seventeen of these were Quakers. The fifteen who avoided incarceration did so by taking the test oath (or affirmation) of allegiance to the Revolutionary state of Pennsylvania, or—if they were deemed "men of reputation" by the Council—by giving their word, their "parole," that they would "remain in their dwellings ready to appear on demand of Council, and meanwhile to refrain from doing anything inimical to the United States of

America, by speaking, writing, or otherwise." None of the Quakers, on principle, would take the test oath or give his parole. And they insisted that they had done nothing "inimical" for which they had to give security.[2]

On September 9, when the Supreme Executive Council formally ordered the prisoners banished to the Virginia frontier town of Staunton, twenty-two men remained in jail. The prospect of banishment encouraged two more non-Quakers to give their parole, so that on September 11 twenty unwilling Philadelphians were loaded into wagons and, under the command of two light-horse captains and a contingent of the City Guards, carted west. Seventeen of these were Quakers, including all eleven men on the Committee on Spies original list. No trial, no hearing before any authority, had taken place. Indeed, no formal charges had ever been brought. The twenty men were to be exiled because, according to the Council's banishment order, they "manifested by their general conduct and conversation a disposition highly inimical to the cause of America." Or to put the case another way, they were to be exiled because they were on a list made up by seven men, John Adams among them.[3]

For these Quakers, names were a crucial part of this outrageous episode, and in a "Journal of the transactions" they kept a record of who did what. Thus they recorded that it was John Galloway, William Hollingshead, Eman Eyres, William Tharpe, and John Lile who carried out the first arrests; and it was Paul Cox, John Purviance, William McCulloch, William Hevsham, Joseph Marsh, Charles Willson Peale, William Bradford, Joseph Blewer, Matthew Erwin, James Loughead, William Will, and James Kerr who, cumulatively, arrested the Quaker grandees and searched their houses. Elijah Brown was arrested, and his house searched, by James Loughead and James Kerr.[4]

Specifically unmentioned in the Quaker prisoners' "Journal"—but screaming out of it all the same—is the fact that most of these names were Scots-Irish Presbyterian; as was the name of the individual "in power" who signed the general arrest warrant, George Bryan, vice president of the Council; as was the name of the person authorized by the warrant to carry out the arrests, Colonel William Bradford. The name on the Council's subsequent banishment order, dated September 9, was Timothy Matlack, secretary of the Council. Not a Presbyterian, Matlack was perhaps something even worse (by the Quaker prisoners' way of thinking). He was an angry, violent, renegade Quaker.[5]

While it was the Continental Congress's initiative and impetus that induced the arrests, the Quaker prisoners did not blame Congress for what they deemed their unjust incarceration, for without a doubt Congress had a crisis on its hands. A massive British fleet had been sighted in the upper Chesapeake Bay on August 22, and on August 25 General Howe's 18,000-man army landed at the Head of Elk, sixty-five miles from its obvious destination: Philadelphia. Also on August 25 the American general John Sullivan had forwarded to Congress "papers" he had captured during a raid in New York—papers purported to have been written by the Quaker meeting at Spanktown on Staten Island. These papers, in their concern about Continental Army troop movements and in their information, dated August 19, about Howe's landing in the Chesapeake, were clearly treasonous. They certainly suggested the need for Congress, in military areas, to crack down on those Quakers who might be in sympathy with the British cause and who were positioned to lend aid to the enemy. The only problem with this conclusion was that there was no Quaker Spanktown Meeting. Nor could anyone on Staten Island on August 19 have known that General Howe's force—which had been at sea for over five weeks—would disembark in Maryland on August 25. The captured papers, then, as Philadelphia's Quakers were quick to aver, appeared to be blatant forgeries.[6]

Of course Congress, with Howe's army staring it in the face, was not in a position to investigate the logical niceties of the matter, and so it ordered its Committee on Spies on August 28 to draw up a list of unreliable Philadelphians. This step, too, the Quaker prisoners had no problem with. Under the dire circumstances, it was certainly prudent. Their problem, rather, was with what came *next*. For the Committee on Spies—John Adams, Richard Henry Lee, and William Duer—were strangers to Philadelphia. True, John Adams at least had had some personal contact with the city's Quaker leaders: back in 1774, when, at a meeting concocted for the purpose, perhaps fifty Friends, "with their broad brimmed Beavers on their Heads," and led by Joseph Fox, James Pemberton, and especially Israel Pemberton, had harangued him and his fellow Massachusetts delegates for, among other injustices, their Puritan ancestors' abuse of Quakers. (All three chief haranguers ended up on the Committee's list—though Fox's name was subsequently removed, owing to his infirm condition.) But for the most part, the Committee's knowledge of who in Philadelphia was "disaffected" and "dangerous" came through conversations with local political associates.[7]

In a published *Address to the Inhabitants of Pennsylvania*, the Quaker prisoners—or "Those FREEMEN, of the CITY of *Philadelphia*, who are now confined in the MASON'S LODGE, BY VIRTUE OF *A GENERAL WARRANT* SIGNED in COUNCIL BY THE VICE PRESIDENT OF THE COUNCIL OF PENNSYLVANIA," as they styled themselves—explained their plight, and in particular they honed in on this *local* dimension of the affair. They had been arrested, "in pursuance of a recommendation of Congress," under the authority of a "General Warrant, specifying no manner of offence against us, appointing no authority to hear and judge, whether we were guilty or innocent, nor limiting any duration to our confinement!" This "extraordinary Warrant," moreover, gave to its enforcers—its "messengers"—"the powers . . . to break, and search not only our own, but all the houses their heated imaginations might lead them to suspect." Under these circumstances, then, the Quakers had been arrested and their houses searched. Subsequently, all their remonstrances and appeals to the Council and its president, and to Congress, went unanswered. In the name of "American Liberty," rights guaranteed to them by "the fundamental rules of justice, by our birthright and inheritance, the laws of the land," and most recently by articles 9 and 10 of the Revolutionary Pennsylvania Constitution of 1776, were to be denied—but *just to them.* Indeed, they had heard the alarming story that when one of the city magistrates had inquired of the Council about the cause of the confinements, he had been told by the vice president of the Council—George Bryan—"that we were to be sent to Virginia UNHEARD." And how had this entire concatenation, this perversion of justice, this masking and shirking of responsibility, come about? Here was the key point the Quaker prisoners wanted the Pennsylvania public to contemplate:

You will observe, that the President and Council, who know our characters, and to whom (but for their prejudice, and want of candor in this instance) we could have appealed for the innocence of our *conduct and conversation*; they have not undertaken to charge us with any offence, but rely as a foundation for their proceedings, on the information contained in a recommendation of Congress, to whom the greater part of us are scarcely known but by name, and who must have formed the hard judgment they pronounced against us *unheard*, from reports whispered by our enemies.[8]

This, for the Quaker prisoners, was the real context of the affair. Behind the arrests, the searches, the terrorizing, were the maneuverings of "our adversaries," of whom the Continental Congress was not part. With its "recommendations" and aura of authority, the Congress had been but a facilitator of this local "set of men" with their "personal animosities."[9]

On September 11, eight of the prisoners tried one last tactic, applying to the chief justice of the state supreme court for a writ of habeas corpus. They needn't have bothered, though, for the wheels of banishment were rolling inexorably; and their fate was in fact already sealed. At five o'clock on that afternoon of the eleventh, the seventeen Quakers and three Tories "were compelled some by actual force, and others by force being admitted to take seats in a number of waggons, and were drove through Third Street to the upper part of the City and from thence to the falls of Schuylkill." As they moved, they observed expressions of "Grief" in the faces of onlookers, and, except for "very few of the lower class," no "marks of approbation"—"untill we had crossed Vine Street, where a rabble consisting for the most part of boys . . . threw some stones at one or two of the carriages."[10]

The first night out of Philadelphia the prisoners were permitted to stay in the houses of Quakers who lived near the falls of the Schuylkill, and the second night they boarded at Pottsgrove. Here, "with much difficulty," they prevailed upon their "conductors" to hold up, pending the arrival of a baggage wagon. This delay proved short-lived, however, for a rumor spread that the prisoners and their guards were being forcibly detained at Pottsgrove by the Potts family, who sympathized with the plight of the exiles. So on September 13 a special force of Berks County militiamen was sent to the village to, in effect, liberate the hostage train and goad it on its way. In the meantime, two messengers arrived from Philadelphia with writs of habeas corpus signed by the chief justice of the Pennsylvania Supreme Court. The prisoners were to meet with Chief Justice Thomas McKean at East Fallowfield, where he would review their case. Finally, it seemed, a hearing—and liberation—was imminent: except that the guards, who had secret orders from the Supreme Executive Council, ignored the writs. Early the next morning they pushed on with their prisoners to Reading, where the rest of the party applied for writs of habeas corpus, and then to Lancaster. On September 16, back in Philadelphia, the ticklish matter of habeas corpus was taken care of by the Pennsylvania Assembly. A special act was passed suspending habeas corpus for just these twenty people in this one instance. The Assembly thereby relieved the guards and everybody else involved in the affair of legal liability for refusing a habeas corpus writ, and in the process further violated the Pennsylvania Constitution with an ex post facto law.[11]

On September 28, the procession crossed beyond the Pennsylvania border, through Maryland and into Virginia, and thereupon the plight of the exiles grew even murkier. Which authority were they *now* properly under? Who was responsible for protecting them, and perhaps more to the point, who was responsible for releasing them? Congress had initially "recommended" the arrests, but thereafter it had officially deemed the prisoners a Pennsylvania state concern. The Supreme Executive Council, whose president had ordered the arrests and banishment under its authority, unofficially deemed Congress the true authority in this affair. Indeed, without the aegis of Congress's recommendation and authority, the Council would not have carried out the arrests. And now the prisoners were in Virginia. Before leaving Philadelphia, they had asked the Council to clarify just this scenario. If taken into Virginia, they wanted to know, "To whose custody are we to be committed when there?" The answer had come back: "The Governor of Virginia, who will have some Instructions from the Congress about you." In this regard, the prisoners would have been far from heartened if they had gotten a glimpse of those "instructions," which included this piece of advice to Governor Patrick Henry of Virginia: "There is no doubt but that they [the Quaker exiles] will endeavor by means of the 'Friends' in Virginia to make disturbance and raise discontent there, but this may serve to put you on your guard."[12]

The party reached Winchester, Virginia, on September 29, and was greeted by "a number of men under arms"—"very clamorous," "the lower class of the people"—who demanded that the traitors vacate the town immediately and hasten on to Staunton. It took several hours for one of the conducting guards, a Lieutenant White, to defuse this potentially dangerous situation through an agreement with the local militia. The prisoners would be permitted to remain within a house in the town, under strict guard and forbidden communication with area Friends, until "more particular directions" were received "from the Congress and the Governor of Virginia." When those orders arrived—from Congress, and signed "John Adams"— they permitted the exiles to settle where they were. For the foreseeable future, at least, Winchester was deemed banishment enough for them. Winchesterites greeted this Congressional decree with an entrepreneurial change of humor. If they had to suffer the presence of city traitors, they might as well gouge them.[13]

And so the twenty Philadelphians had arrived at their place of exile. Their ordeal in Winchester would include exorbitant charges for room and board (which they, and not Congress or the state of Pennsylvania, had to pay for in cash), and a winter of rampant illness. Before it was over, two of them, both Tories, would run off and two, both Quakers, would die of disease. Meanwhile, every opportunity would be grasped, by the exiles themselves and their friends and family, to appeal to the proper authorities for a hearing, exoneration, and freedom. But, again, who was the controlling power? Letters and appeals went off to the Supreme Executive Council of Pennsylvania, to the Assembly of Pennsylvania, to the governor of Virginia. None, in truth, thought the exiles properly their concern; none, in truth, cared. And so the exiles languished, until April 1778, when the accumulated weight of reports about their illnesses and then two actual deaths, along with petitions and letters from their supporters and wives and then a pending visit from four of the wives to Lancaster, led the Council sitting in Lancaster finally to act. (So the Council was the true authority in this affair? But it was responding to a Congressional "resolve" and a "recommendation" by the Pennsylvania Assembly. It added up, wrote one of the exiles, to "a Juggle amongst them.") The Council had the prisoners brought to Lancaster, where, without a hearing and without full explanation, it told the exiles they were free to go home. And so on April 29 and 30, 1778, the sixteen surviving exiles—one "exceedingly broken and look[ing] like an old man," another "speechless," having apparently suffered a small stroke— returned to their families in Philadelphia.[14]

And what of those families?

Twenty-six-year-old Sarah Logan Fisher had been in love with Thomas Fisher for seven and a half years and married to him for five. They had two children and a third on the way. On September 2, as she recorded in her diary, three men came to their home and offered "my dear Husband" the chance to give his parole "to confine himself prisoner to his own House." When her husband refused, the three men gave him the choice of going with them or waiting for the arrival of an armed guard, which would forcibly take him into custody. What did he do? "My Tommy thought it best to go quietly with them."[15]

Two days later, with her husband still in jail and the inconceivable seriousness of the situation beginning to dawn on her, Sarah Fisher noted in her diary: "severe triall & difficulty, when my Husband in whom is center'd too much of my earthly comfort, is likely to be torn from me, by the hands of violence & cruelty, & I left within a few Weeks of Lying in, unprotected and alone." A week later, September 11—the day of expulsion—Sarah Fisher makes no diary entry. Neither does she the next day. She finally records the event of her husband's disappearance, in fractured diction that no doubt conveyed her state of mind, on September 13: "words can but faintly express the distress & anxiety of my since the Day before Yesterday when was tore from me by the hands of violent cruel men, my dearly beloved Husband. . . . they were dragged into the waggons, by force by Soldiers employed for that purpose, & drove off surrounded by guards & a mob."[16]

Thomas Fisher went meekly. The more rambunctious Pemberton brothers resisted. Israel Pemberton in particular exacted his pound of flesh. When the ubiquitous "three men" came to arrest him, the sixty-two-year-old so-called "King of the Quakers" refused to take any notice of them as "they were not Public officers." When they persisted in their efforts, he told them he could not possibly recognize them as officers until he had seen the actual arrest warrant with their names on it—which they didn't have. So they went away to find the warrant. Upon their return, Pemberton "invited them into a parlour," where he read the part of the warrant they would let him see—not failing at the same time to tell the three men that "he thought they had by undertaking the odious office . . . to deprive their fellow citizens of liberty . . . manifested a fondness for the exercising & supporting arbitrary power." Then, noticing that one of the men's names was not on the warrant, he made a special point of reproving *him* for "ye fondness" for tyranny. In the end he told the three he would not consent to become a prisoner and that they should go away, being sure to leave a copy of the warrant behind. Beyond that, if they wanted to discuss the matter further, they could come back later: but not too late—"we would have no night work." The three cowed men then did go away, and three hours later a militia colonel with an armed escort arrived, pushed his way into Israel Pemberton's house, and arrested him.[17]

No matter how the arrest scenes played out—with quiet resignation, with resistance and hysteria and actual physical violence, or with repartee and moral rebuke—for the families of the men arrested the emotional consequences were similar. The daughter of James Pemberton wrote to her grandmother on September 8: "An universal gloom seems to overspread every prospect. . . . each day unfolds tales of wretchedness and distress, and the mind ruminating on approaching horrors becomes a prey to the most melancholy and gloomy reflections. It is lonesome here, and rendered more so, by being depriv'd, cruelly depriv'd of our dear Parent's company, by a set of men who [seem] lost to all those fine feelings which form the humane and benevolent heart." Phineas Pemberton, the sickly twenty-three-year-old son of James Pemberton, wrote to his father on September 10: "Dear & honoured Father, Thy kind effect^g Letter I have just rec^d . . . & the melancholy consideration of being separated perhaps for ever from the tenderest of Parents has affected my Mind beyond the Power of Expression." Three and a half months later, Phineas's grandmother wrote of this "poor afflicted Phinny": "Poor Phinny mourns the absense of his dear Parent."[18]

Three men visited Elizabeth Drinker and her husband on September 2. When Henry Drinker refused his "parole," they told him to stay home and they would come back for him the next day—thereby leaving Elizabeth, Henry, and their five children to agonize the rest of the day and night in anticipation. The next morning, the men dutifully reappeared and Henry Drinker was arrested. Later that day, Elizabeth visited her husband at the Mason's Lodge, where she "mett with the Wives & Children of our dear Friends and other visitors in great numbers." Afterward, back home, she worried about her seven-year-old son, "my little Henry," who was "very low and Feverish."[19]

For Elizabeth Drinker, the deus ex machina of banishment played itself out the following week. There were many visits to her husband at the lodge, as well as a constant stream of visitors to receive at home. On September 9, while visiting her husband with her six-year-old daughter Molly and sixteen-year-old daughter Sally, she learned of the Council's order of banishment, to be carried out in two days time, and so "came home in great distress, and after doing the necessary for the Child went back near 10 at Night, found the Prisoners finishing a Protest against the Tyrannical conduct of the Present wicked rulers." As she wrote these words—which register this peaceful person's rising anger—she heard a cannon discharge out in the night. The next evening, September 10, her husband was permitted by the Council to eat and sleep at home: in preparation for his banishment the following morning.[20]

September 11 was a day of total confusion. The prisoners were scheduled to leave the city at nine in the morning, but the inability of officials to coordinate the necessary wagons and guards meant that nobody knew when they actually would leave. And then on top of everything else, for a good part of the day there was "a great fireing heard below" the town. Elizabeth Drinker noted this, along with the explanation: "It is suppos'd the Armies are Engag'd." At the Drinker house, the dreaded moment came after dinner, when a servant rushed in with news that "the waggons were waiting at the Lodge to take our dear Friends away." Elizabeth now "quickly went there; and as quickly came away finding a great number of People there but few women, bid my dearest Husband farewell, and went in great distress to James Pembertons . . . I came home at Dusk."[21]

The next morning, September 12, Elizabeth Drinker learned that the "fireing" had been the Battle of Brandywine, where General Howe had routed "part" of Washington's army and thereby cleared the way for the occupation of Philadelphia by the British army. And life went on. In the afternoon she heard "a Drum stop at our Door and a hard knocking succeed." The noise "a little fluttred" her. It proved to be—ludicrously—men with orders for her husband to appear for Revolutionary military service or supply a substitute in his stead. They were approximately twenty hours too late.[22]

With the physical departure of the exiles from the city came, for their families, the anxiety of *not knowing* where or how they were. One immediate fear was highlighted by the exiles themselves in one of their "Remonstrances" sent to the Supreme Executive Council: namely, that "the Indians have already commenced hostilities upon the frontiers of *Virginia*, not very far from the place of our intended banishment." This was a military situation ominously noted in the Revolutionaries' own journals, and nervously touched upon by one Quaker son in a letter to his exiled father: "the thought of the Indians committing Hostilities not far from [you] . . . has much afflicted my Mind." This particular affliction, moreover, could only have been worsened by the knowledge that: (1) the exiled Quakers were pacifists; (2) they, if anything, sympathized with *the native Indian* cause; and (3) in the case of an actual Indian attack, the Indians might associate the Quaker exiles with—of all people—the aggressive and expansionist Revolutionaries and treat them accordingly.[23]

Communications between the now distant exiles and their families were infrequent and restricted. All personal letters had to pass unsealed so they could be read by Revolutionary authorities. They could therefore not include too much information, for that might invite charges of espionage; nor, in reality, could they carry the deepest expressions of feeling, for what wife or husband would allow filthy prying Revolutionary eyes to invade *that* domain? Word-of-mouth news, as visitors to Winchester told friends who told acquaintances about what they had heard and seen there, served as a second source of information and a breeding ground for rumors. One such rumor, arriving in December via "an Ezekiel Edwards account of our dear Banished Frd^s," had the exiles being moved down and over the Shenandoah Mountains to Staunton—and thereby closer to Indian raiding parties. The prospect made at least one wife feel "miserable beyond expression." Yet the exiles were not moved; they stayed at Winchester. In early January a countervailing rumor reached Philadelphia: Congress had freed the prisoners. Responded one wife: "Oh my Heart, may thou be gratefull for this wonderfull favor, how shall I bear my own joy and extacy." A week later an amended rumor reached Philadelphia: Congress had been debating whether to release the exiles. *Had been.* Perhaps this meant, reasoned this same wife, that now the deed was done and the next knock on her door would bring her husband. "Oh what a painfull state of suspence am I now

in." An absolutely awful rumor hit Philadelphia on January 19, 1778: John
Pemberton was dead. Family and friends hesitated about telling his wife
Hannah. Happily the report proved false. Still, the rumor had worked its
damage. A young niece of John Pemberton's wrote to her father: "We heard
Uncle Johnny was dead it distressed us very much."[24]

It was of course illness and death that the families feared most, and these
fears took on the character of "gloomy Apprehensions" in March and April
when reports reached Philadelphia that "most" of the exiles were ill. Simultaneously, rumors circulated about the deaths of two of the exiles, Thomas
Gilpin and John Hunt. Then came solid confirmation. Gilpin and Hunt
had in fact died.[25]

With panic now gripping the families, the wives decided to try to inter-
cede with the Revolutionaries directly. Four of the women were delegated
to carry out the mission. They wrote to and then visited General Washington at Valley Forge, asking his permission for them to travel to Winchester,
which he gave. They then set off for Lancaster to appeal to government
authorities. Their husbands, they argued, needed to be released on human-
itarian grounds. One of these wives, Elizabeth Drinker, after a day spent
pleading with Revolutionaries, penned the immortal line: "we discourc'd
with 'em for some time, they appeard kind, but I fear tis from teeth out-
wards." Within the week their husbands and the rest of the exiles were brought
to Lancaster and then freed. This was not, though, because of the wives'
appeal per se, but because state and Continental authorities had already
decided the whole affair was an embarrassment and needed to be ended.[26]

Framing this *internal* experience of the families were the actual comings
and goings of various armies. Philadelphians got their first good look at
Washington's 9,000-man army on August 24, 1777, as it entered the city
from the north at seven in the morning, marched along Front Street,
turned right onto Chestnut, and headed out toward the Schuylkill River
and its rendezvous with General Howe's main force. Marching twelve deep,
the Continentals took three hours to clear the city. John Adams remarked
of the "show of Artillery, Waggons, Light Horse and Infantry" that it "will
make a good Impression upon the Minds of the timorous Whiggs for their
Confirmation, upon the cunning Quakers for their Restraint and upon the
rascally Tories for their Confusion." On September 26 Philadelphians got
their second good look at a grand army. This time it was the British army,
marching under Lord Cornwallis into the city along Second Street to take
up its occupation.[27]

In between these two dates was the night of September 19, when at about
two in the morning "the City was alarmed . . . with a great knocking at
peoples Doors & desiring them to get up, that the English had crossed the
Swedes ford at 11 oClock & would presently be in the City." The scene was
utter chaos, with "Waggons rattling, Horses Galoping, Women running,
Children Crying, Delagates flying, & all together the greatest consternation

fright & terror that can be imagined." But the alarm was premature. The Redcoats had not yet crossed the Schuylkill, nor would they for another week. This gave Revolutionaries like "Capt. Drury and Tom Bradford" a few extra days to harass Quakers, search their houses, and confiscate their goods. And then there was the night of September 25, when the last Revolutionaries slipped out of the city and during which citizens stayed up "to watch," fearful the Whigs' parting gesture would be to set the city ablaze.[28]

With the British occupiers came an instantaneous peace and tranquillity for the families of the exiles. While the percussive sounds of warfare could still be heard, they no longer emanated from within the city. Nor were roving Whig mobs to be feared anymore. Of course inconveniences and annoyances remained. For one, news from the families' loved ones now had to pass through two armies. And where the Revolutionaries had quartered on them the "intolerably Dirty" riflemen from places like Virginia, now the families were obligated to take English officers into their houses. This was especially unsettling because their husbands and fathers were in Winchester and these were strange men. Much more upsetting, though, was the generally topsy-turvy civil order. With all the strange soldiers wandering around, people feared prowlers and robbers. In this setting some wives came to appreciate the presence in their homes of officers who could provide protection in the middle of the night. Yet not all officers were so trustworthy. By the end of the winter there were "very bad accounts of the licentiousness of the English Officers in deluding young Girls."[29]

Still, the overwhelming fact of life, before as since September 26, was the absence of the loved ones. This ended April 29 and 30 with their return. A time of at least domestic joy seemed promised. Less than a month later, though, the British announced that they would soon evacuate the city. One exile's worried wife wrote of the confusing situation: "we may expect some great suffering when the ~~Englis~~ Americans again get possession." A few days later she characterized "the prospect of the English leaving us" as "more and more distressing." On June 3, a just-returned exile wrote: "the English Army appear to be on the point of leaving us, that we seem to be near ano[r] revolution."[30]

June 18, 1778, like September 26, 1777, was a changeover day: but in reverse. Out went Redcoats; in came Revolutionaries. Confided one Quaker to her diary: "Judge O any impartial person, what were my feelings." Wrote another, perfectly summing up the Quaker dilemma: "The English have in reality left us—and the other party took possesion." And that other party, true to form, immediately recommenced harassing Quakers.[31]

On July 2, the Continental Congress formally returned to the city. *The Revolution* was back in Philadelphia in its full panoply and glory, and two days later all could exult in the commencement of America's third year of freedom. Or almost all. As the wife of one of the Quaker exiles noted in her diary: "the anniversary of Independence, wich was celebrated with great Joy by some, the Congress had an entertainment prepared for them at the City

Tavern & a very great & repeated discharge of Cannon most of the Afternoon, which noise greatly affected Sister Fisher & made her much worse[.] in the evening an exhibition of Fire works at the City Tavern."[32]

For this particular group of Quakers, then, the Revolutionary experience had its own unique character which coalesced between the summers of 1777 and 1778. These Philadelphians, these Americans, read and heard the same rhetoric, heard the same noises, sighted the same nighttime illuminations as did their Whig neighbors, but to different effect. Those drumbeats that caused in Elizabeth Drinker a "fluttring": Here is a glimpse into a quality and intensity of experience that was this special group's alone. Take Drinker, for example. She still had thirty years to live. During that time, it's a safe assumption, she never again heard the sound of a drum without experiencing a "flutter"—as well as a stab and sometimes a rush of memories and emotions. For these Quakers, that is to say, the "Horrors of the night," as a Friend described the July Fourth 1777 Whig celebrations, would have an afterlife.[33]

And how were they to respond? What were they supposed, *what were they bred*, to think, feel, imagine?

A female Quaker minister wrote to one of the exiles with her advice. "Having felt a Near Simpathy in my mind with you," she began,

& fellow feeling also with and towards divers of you who are in Confinement with Desires that Greenness may not be lost but that by a close attention to the Gentle Voice of the true Shepherd all that are Really his Sheep, wherever Scatter'd may be preserved safe in the Knowledge of his Voice and not be carried from their strict attention by any Noise, or the subtil Voice of the Stranger in any transformation whatsoever, the world is now full of Noises, and the Strangers Voice hath been suffer'd to prevail with many, a text hath been brought to my memory at this time a short Exhortation by the mouth of a prophet. . . . Come, my people, Enter thou into thy Chambers, and shut thy doors about thee: hide thy self as it were for a little moment, until the indignation be overpast. For behold, the Lord cometh out of his place to punish the inhabitants of the Earth for their iniquity: o that you may be enabled to stand all storms or assaults.[34]

An exile's wife sought comfort in William Penn's *Epistle to the Children of Light*, and "particularly one passage," where the colony's founder

says speaking of those that trusted in the Lord, that when sufferings come: He will make you to lie down safely, even then when Darkness & confusion shall be th[ere] about you; yea ye shall live in the Fire, that will consume the stubble of the World, & your Garments shall not be so much as singed, for the Son of God, whom the Flames, as well as the Winds and Seas obey, will be in the midst of you![35]

For these Quakers, then, the drumbeats and cannon discharges of 1777–78, the rocks pelting their houses and shattering their windows, the violent men searching their homes and breaking their furniture and stealing their property and taking their husbands and fathers, the nighttime explosions and illuminations, were a vast challenge. It all called forth a special effort by a peaceful people, living in the town *they* had settled, not to grow angry. Yet in the face of this, who could avoid the thoughts of an exile's teenage stepson who confided to his diary that "the day must come when the Avenger's hand shall make thee suffer for thy guilt, and thy Rulers shall deplore thy Fate." Who could not feel hate? Who could not crave vengeance?[36]

*   *   *

And what did this experience impart to the exiles' children who remained in William Penn's geometrical City of Brotherly Love throughout the ordeal?

Rachel Parke had a dream during this year: "The City of Philadelphia appeared in the utmost Confusion & disorder, occasioned by the Invasion of an Enemy, amid the noise & tumult of the Multitude, the Cry of 'to Arms to Arms' was distinctly heard—during this period of Time, I thought our Saviour was upon Earth, and resided at my Fathers (who was one of his followers) which being observed by the people, the general Cry, was fire upon all that follow Jesus."[37]

Seven-year-old "Molle" Pemberton wrote her first letters during this year. Among these:

last six day morning I was so frighted with the roaring of cannon I did not know what to do Mamme told me not to be frighted but to lay in bed, mama calld Nanne up about 4 o Clock in the morning and sent her a top of the house to see where the fireing was for momme thought it must be very near when Nanne came down she told Momme that the fireing was above the town but sutch alight down the river that she thought there must be agrate many houses afire Mamme sent her up again then she counted nine ships all a fire down by glouster point if dady had been at home mebey mamme and sisters would not a been so frighted.[38]

Both girls lived in the old part of the city, with Rachel residing on Fourth Street near the Indian Queen Tavern and Molly on Second Street near Lodge Alley. Elizabeth Drinker and her children lived in the old quarter too, on North Front Street. At ten o'clock on the evening of October 11—the one-month anniversary of their father's exile—they were "frighted" by a "terrable cry of Murder." It turned out to be, according to Elizabeth, "the Bakers William, who I suppose was in Licquor." Several weeks later Elizabeth noted of her three-year-old daughter and eight-year-old son: "the long absence of their Father, appears strange to our two little ones, who cannot account, why their dear Daddy should be taken forcibly from them."[39]

At 117 South Second Street, four blocks from the Drinkers and a block from Molly Pemberton, lived another Quaker, a boy who was six when his father, Elijah Brown, disappeared and seven when his father reappeared eight months later, a boy who would grow up to do a curious thing in the young American republic. During the presidential administration of John Adams, Charles Brockden Brown would write novels. Gothic ones.

Part I
Facts and Fictions,
1650–1798

Nottingham Meetinghouse

Chapter 1

Children of the Light, 1650s–1777

In Brown family lore, their founding Quaker was "a seeking, religious man whose mind was drawn into careful endeavours after the Purity of Life." During the mid-seventeenth-century interregnum between Charles I and Charles II, this William Brown, a farmer in Northamptonshire, England, passed for a time in the communion of Baptists before covenanting with Puritans. But it was a chance meeting with an itinerant Quaker minister—whose goading testimony began with the words "O Earth! Earth! hear the word of the Lord"—that settled the fate of William Brown and five generations of Browns after him. "Convinced" by the itinerant's testimony, William took the stranger home with him, only to be greeted by his wife's "wherefore he brought that madman to their house." "Why woman," William replied, "he hath brought the Eternal Truth of God to us." Soon William's wife too was "convinced."

The Browns' convincements carried profound consequences for their children. Because they were Quakers, William Brown and his wife (she is unnamed in the memoir) were persecuted and "much stripped of their property for fines &c.," and their children had to grow up amid the abuse. For their eldest son—also named William—this brought on a spiritual "trial." When he was seven, William, Jr., being "thoughtful of the cause of these things," fell prey to the notion that "such a religion was not right that occasioned people to be brought under so great difficulty on account of it." These "insinuations," furthermore, pressed on his mind, until

one night after he went to bed, he was sorely tempted to curse the Almighty; under which trial a great terror came over him;—he was afraid to do so, and thereupon roared out aloud, which affrighted his mother that she came to his bedside to see what ailed him; but being favoured to resist the tempter, he was quickly helped so far over the temptation as to stop crying out. . . . He kept his condition to himself and did not discover it to any one at that time, and being thus preserved, he was not tried with the like again. It had a tendency to open his understanding and to convince him fully that his parents were right and that the religion they suffered for, was the truth itself, which in the end maketh men free indeed, and enables them to wish well and to seek the good of all men, even those who hate and persecute them.

It was some years later when William Penn received a charter grant from King Charles II for the province of Pennsylvania, and sometime after that when William Dewsbury, the "eminent minister of the Gospel" who had first "convinced" the elder William Brown, returned to the region of Northamptonshire to promote Quaker removal to America. The memoir records Dewsbury's testimony "to this effect": "'The Lord is about to plant the wilderness of America with a choice vine or noble seed which shall grow and flourish'; and in the language of a prophet divinely inspired, [Dewsbury] added nearly thus: 'I see them. I see them under his blessing arising into a state of prosperity.'"

William Brown, Jr., and his brother James embraced the vision and set their designs on America. The unmarried James sailed first and settled near Markus Hook in Chester County, Pennsylvania; while William, Jr., held by a wife who didn't want to leave, lingered in England. Happily, though—the memoir records—"the Lord wonderfully made way for and assisted him, insomuch that all difficulties relative to his removal disappeared," and "about the year 1696" William, Jr. sailed to New York. ("His wife died at sea.") Soon after, William "apprehended it his duty to remove further westward," and accordingly in 1702, with a new wife and family in tow, he traveled forty miles "far back in the wilderness" to settle at Nottingham on the Pennsylvania-Maryland border. His brother James, with his wife and children, followed. And thereafter in Nottingham the Brown family proliferated.[1]

The family history was incorrect in several details. First, while there was a William Browne of Northamptonshire who died around the year 1664, *he* wasn't the progenitor of the Nottingham, Pennsylvania, Browns. His brother Richard was. This Richard and his wife Mary had been Baptists and then Puritans before being "convinced" by William Dewsbury. So Richard Browne of Northamptonshire, a minister who died in 1662, was the family's founding Quaker. Second, *his* son James Browne came to Burlington, New Jersey, in 1677—four years *before* William Penn received his charter. So the scene at Northamptonshire with minister-promoter Dewsbury could not have happened quite the way it was described. James's brother William Browne could have been there, though, for he migrated to America sometime between 1682 and 1684. On the other hand, the chronology of the historic forty-mile trek into the wilderness of Nottingham was accurate. James and William Browne did move there in 1702, where they reserved five of the original thirty-seven township lots for themselves. Also accurate is the account of the Browns as religious seekers. In both Old and New Worlds, they were distinguished as what the anticlerical Quakers colloquially called "ministers." This meant they were attuned to the "Light of Truth" within; and they possessed the gift to "testify" about it to others.[2]

William Brown of the third generation of Pennsylvania Browns—and the source of this memoir—was a case in point. Born in Nottingham in 1705 (the James Browne above was his grandfather), he had heard the stories of the family's Quaker origins—of the first William Browne's "convincement," of the persecutions in Restoration England, of the second William Browne's "great terror" and subsequent emigration to America and settlement at Nottingham—from that second William Browne himself. And when he had come of age, he had become a minister. He also married into Nottingham's other noted ministerial family, the Churchmans, as did his sister and brother. The Brown-Churchmans, accordingly, were a village clan truly immersed in *the light,* and in the 1750s, when Pennsylvania Quakerism entered its crisis phase amid the challenges of the French and Indian War, Browns and Churchmans were at the forefront of Quaker reformers. Where other Quaker leaders sought compromise and accommodation, *they* held out for "the Purity of Life." In the mid-1780s, as a result, when William Brown's memories of the *ur*-family saga were recorded in a "memorandum," he could well feel that William Dewsbury's prophecy of the early 1680s had come true. In Pennsylvania, the descendants of William (really Richard) Browne of Northamptonshire had indeed met with spiritual "prosperity."[3]

Or had they? In the 1790s another descendant of Richard Browne of Northamptonshire would take up the subject of Brown family—and Pennsylvania Quaker—history, but to strikingly different effect. He would deal most directly with the theme in three novels, *Wieland, Arthur Mervyn,* and *Edgar Huntly,* but most of his fictional writings would pivot about the subject. This direct descendant, Charles Brockden Brown, as it happens, never lived in Nottingham. Yet it is a crucial determinant of his imagination, and therefore of his literary art, that his father, Elijah, had.

Elijah Brown was of the fourth generation of Pennsylvania Browns, and the great-grandson of the James Browne who had supposedly heard William Dewsbury's prophecy. Born in Nottingham in 1740, Elijah began to prepare to leave the village in the mid-1750s by attending school when he could in Philadelphia. There is no record where he boarded in the city, but the likely place would be his Uncle William Brown's house. (*That* William Brown, whose wife, incidentally, was John Churchman's sister.) In 1757 Elijah permanently settled in Philadelphia and commenced a career in commerce. Thereafter he found himself at the center of "history" as it pressed down most fatefully on William Penn's "holy experiment." For Elijah Brown personally, the consequence would be a life of striving and defeat and humble acceptance, of career twists and turns wherein the expected could give way, on occasion, to the unbelievable. For Elijah Brown's wife and children, the consequence would be emotional turmoil and insecurity. For them, mid- to late eighteenth-century Philadelphia would be a kaleidoscopic place where the familiar turned strange and the strange echoed with strains of the familiar. One experience alone they could count on not having: Prosperity, in any shape or form.[4]

*   *   *

The great Quaker John Woolman in his *Journal* described settlements like Nottingham this way: "It is the poorer sort of people that commonly begin to improve remote deserts: with a small stock they have houses to build, lands to clear and fence, corn to raise, cloaths to provide, and children to educate; . . . Friends, who visit such, may well sympathize with them in their hardships in the wilderness; and though the best entertainment such can give, may seem coarse to some who are used to cities, or old settled places, it becomes the disciples of Christ to be content with it."[5]

In the actual case of Nottingham, settlement began with a group of twenty Quaker families who petitioned William Penn in 1701 for a grant of 20,000 acres in what they hoped was southwestern Chester County. (The Maryland proprietor, the Calvert family, deemed it part of Cecil County, Maryland.) The following year Penn's agents authorized the surveying and settlement of an 18,000-acre tract, of which 15,000 acres were sold to the petitioners and 3,000 Penn reserved for himself. For William Penn, the township strengthened his charter claims vis-à-vis those of the Calverts, and it initiated the expansion of his colony west into the Susquehanna River Valley. For the twenty settler families who immediately took up residence and began cultivation of the area, the "Nottingham Lotts" promised farmland in abundance for themselves and their heirs. The families of William and James Browne acquired 2,500 acres between them.[6]

The soil was rich and ideal for wheat, and by the 1750s Nottingham—now divided into an East and West section—numbered the most flour mills in Chester County. Yet the township's property values stood the lowest in the county. The reason was Nottingham's relative isolation, its distance from markets. With Philadelphia fifty miles away and Wilmington thirty, transportation costs inhibited the marketing of Nottingham grain. Consequently, in Nottingham, where in the 1720s typical farms ranged in size from 245 to 400 acres and in the 1750s from 107 to 124 acres, there was plentiful economic "competence," but hard work could not and did not translate into new forms of wealth.[7]

Which, to John Woolman, was precisely the virtue of such a settlement. If not exactly a "desert"—average annual yields per taxpayer amounted to some five hundred bushels of grain, fifteen tons of hay, and the milk and cheese and butter and meat from six cows—Nottingham was in its inhabitants' minds a type of "wilderness," and the pious at least took pride in the thought. For this was a community that nurtured by force of circumstance a special intensity of religion. Here the faith of the fathers, the "light" that had exploded in George Fox "like a fire" in 1650s England and that had scorched William Penn in the 1660s, could burn on to illumine eighteenth-century America.[8]

Quakerism's founder, George Fox, experienced the essential revelation "that all people must come to the Spirit of God in themselves in order to know God and Christ." In William Penn's words, Quakers believed that "God, through Christ, hath placed a principle in every man, to inform him

of his duty, and to enable him to do it; . . . those that live up to this principle are the people of God, and those that live in disobedience to it, are not
God's people, whatever name they may bear, or profession they may make
of religion." In practical terms, this "main fundamental" of Quakerism dictated that the task of every true Christian was to attend to the presence of
the Spirit of God, of the "light," of the "voice," within himself or herself.
Revelation, for Quakers, that is to say, had not ended with the prophets. It
was ongoing. The same "voice" that spoke to Abraham, to Moses, to Jer-
emiah, and that spoke through Jesus, still spoke to men and women. The
problem was to *hear* it.[9]

Quakerism's "theologian," Robert Barclay, inevitably resorted to meta-
phor in his effort to define the special, mysterious nature of the Light. In his
Apology for the True Christian Divinity, he writes: "as the description of the
Light of the Sun, or of curious colours to a blind man; who, though of the
largest capacity, can not so wel understand it, by the most acute and lively
description, as a child can by seeing them. So neither can the natural man
of the largest capacity, by the best words, even Scriptur words, so wel understand the mysterys of God's Kingdom, as the least and weakest child, who
tasteth them, by having them revealed inwardly and objectively, by the
Spirit." The *inward objective manifestation in the heart.* Here was the gist of the
matter in the technical language of the sect. Quakers believed that personal or "inward" revelation—what others might term "subjective" revelation—
could be "objective," that revelation, in the words of historian J. William Frost,
"could be infallibly known because God spoke to the spiritual senses, and
one could determine the origin of the clear and distinct ideas that resulted."[10]

George Fox, amid the disruptions and persecutions of mid-seventeenth-
century England, was confident in his own "testimony." Similarly, people
like William Penn and William Dewsbury, who benefited from the charismatic and guiding presence of Fox, could be confident in the "objective"
nature of their revelations. But what about others? In mid-seventeenth-
century England sects and prophets—from Familists to Seekers to Ranters
and beyond—were as locusts. How was Quakerism both to promote and to
safeguard the authenticity of Friends' "inward" testimonies? Strict biblical-
ism was no answer, for Quaker doctrine held that personal revelation could
involve "knowledge" not available in Scripture, meaning that *authentic* revelation superseded biblical injunction. Sacerdotalism was no solution either,
for Quakers, believing everybody equal in their access to *the spirit,* repu-
diated all "hireling clergy," along with churches, sacraments, ceremonies,
ordinations, and tithes. (What they recognized were especially spiritual
individuals who served as lay missionaries and exhorters, and who were
sometimes called "ministers.") Nor could "reason" serve as an orienting
guide, for it was "natural," corruptible, and by definition inferior to *super-*
natural. Some other conserving and consolidating gauge, some other principle of order, therefore, had to be found.[11]

The solution devised by Fox and his followers was the expansive and hierarchical "meeting" structure that literally constituted the Society of Friends.
The root idea was that authentic personal revelation could be nurtured and
monitored and corrected within the context of a proper, all-embracing spiritual communion. The goal thereby was the promotion of "holy conversation"—and the simultaneous discouragement of unholy conversation and
disciplining of wayward behavior—all within a framework where the individual conscience remained, supposedly, uncoerced. This framework, this
special kind of social setting, Quakerism's leaders created through the hierarchical institutional structure of "the Meeting." At the base were the daily
and weekly meetings where local Quaker families congregated to share
private "testimonies." Then came the monthly meeting, where formal membership matters were decided and "ministers" were recognized and certi-
fied. Here applications for membership were received, births and deaths
recorded, certificates of marriage and removal issued. The monthly meeting also concerned itself with "the discipline." It counseled Friends who
transgressed against proper Quaker behavior, as set out in the *Book of Discipline*, and disowned those who refused to repent. Above the monthly meeting sat the quarterly meeting, which comprised several adjacent monthly
meetings and concerned itself with the business aspects of those monthly
meetings. It heard appeals from decisions reached in the monthly meetings. Finally, at the apex of the structure was the yearly meeting, which comprised representatives from the quarterly meetings within a large area. This
was the forum of ultimate appeal on matters from the quarterly and
monthly meetings, and where general policy "advices" and directives were
determined. Throughout the whole institutional apparatus—whose hierarchical force was softened by the existence of parallel gatherings like the
meeting on sufferings and the women's meeting—special emphasis was
placed, on the one hand, on families, and on the other, on the influence of
individuals "gifted by God." Ideally in meeting, extended families were nurtured in the true "light" by specially inspired ministers who weren't "ministers" in the formal sense of other denominations. They were plain, simple
individuals remarkable in their sense of Christ's *spirit*, and in *its* various
injunctions against tithes, swearing, war among Christians, mixed marriages, earthly pride, and so on.[12]

It was this understanding and culture that William Penn and his Quaker
cohorts, James and William Browne among them, brought to the Delaware
Valley. In Pennsylvania, these immigrants would conduct a "holy experiment" where Quaker principles and institutions were not the odd excep-
tion but the norm. Accordingly, when James and William Brown migrated
into the "wilderness" of Nottingham, they were securing a place where
"holy conversation" could prosper in their lifetime and beyond.

Within the overall Quaker saga, places like Nottingham were ideal havens
of "holy conversation." Within the Quaker saga as actually played out in

eighteenth-century Pennsylvania, though, not places *like* Nottingham but *Nottingham itself* performed a powerful function. Delaware Valley Quakerism discovered this in the mid-1760s when reforming purists, led by a Nottingham minister, took control of the central Quaker institution, the Philadelphia Yearly Meeting, an event that prompted one worldly Philadelphia Quaker merchant to note: "The Nottinghamites are all in their glory."[13]

In Nottingham by this time, six Browns were active as ministers, with William Brown of the third generation being the most prominent. The most influential minister of all, though, and father of the Nottinghamite elected clerk of the Philadelphia Yearly Meeting in 1767, was William Brown's brother-in-law, John Churchman. Churchman in this mid-eighteenth-century setting was a classic embodiment of Quakerism's religious idealism, an overpowering presence—"a seer." "I perceive thou art born for a warrior," a Friend had told him, and it was this crusading prophet that everybody growing up in mid-eighteenth-century Nottingham had to confront and come to terms with.[14]

"I was born in a wilderness place, where a few families had settled many miles remote from other inhabitants," Churchman wrote in his spiritual autobiography, recalling early eighteenth-century Nottingham. According to Churchman, when he was eight and attending "a small meeting," "the Lord" "by his glorious light discovered to me the knowledge of himself." Still "much given to play," in subsequent years Churchman "endeavoured through fear to fly from the voice of the holy spirit in my own heart." Taught to read by a local weaver, Churchman took great delight in the accomplishment, and thereby was led farther from the true path. Yet fortunately for his soul, the Lord afflicted him with recurrent cases of pleurisy between his ninth and eleventh years, and the experience "caused me to renew my covenant with him." Remembering these days, the adult Churchman drew the moral:

I leave it as a caution to parents, to beware of indulging their dear children in any thing, which may impress their tender minds with a desire after music, or such diversion when they grow in years; but that instead thereof, by living in the pure fear of the Lord, and near the spirit of truth in their own hearts, they may be furnished with example, and precept to direct the minds of their offspring, to attend to the voice of him who called to Samuel in days of old, and remains to be the same teacher to his people in this age.

After his father's death in 1724, Churchman underwent his true convincement, as "my old will in the fallen nature gave up it's life . . . my heart was made exceedingly tender, [and] I wept much." Soon after he realized—he was about twenty years old—that "if in patience I stood faithful, I should be called to the work of the ministry." His special passion in this area was for "the discipline." That is, he loved maintaining in his own and others' actions the purity of the faith. In 1735–36 his spiritual presentiment came

true. Along with William Brown and Dinah Brown—yet another Churchman who had married a Brown—he was recommended as a minister to the
Meeting of Ministers and Elders.[15]

John Churchman possessed a burning spirituality that threatened, upon
occasion, to run to extremes. For instance, once when he was riding his
horse, his craving for absolute purity kindled to the point where "it began
to look pleasant to me, to go into some remote place where I should not be
known." Churchman, fortunately, "When reflecting thus—what! abandon
mine acquaintance! violate my marriage covenant, and leave my nearest
connections! . . . suddenly knew this prospect of pleasure was from the evil
one"—and successfully beat back the temptation. It was this same yearning
that drove him, in the company of his brother-in-law William Brown and a
spiritual disciple, John Pemberton, to visit England, Wales, Ireland, and
Holland in the early 1750s on a religious mission. He labored for four
years, traveling over 9,000 miles, visiting perhaps 1,000 meetings and
countless families, averaging five meetings a week. In the process, while he
was often held at a distance by sophisticated and wealthy Quaker leaders,
he helped plant the seed of a reformation in English Quakerism as a whole.
And that seed, which had first germinated in the soil of 1740s Nottingham,
he brought back to Nottingham—and Pennsylvania proper—in 1754.[16]

John Churchman, in sum, was not a mere local or even trans-Atlantic
spiritual presence. He was perforce a powerful cultural and indeed *political* presence, and through him—as through his friends John Woolman,
Anthony Benezet, William Brown, his son George Churchman, and others—the evolving political culture of mid-century Pennsylvania came
under challenge. Again, the origins of this pressure for reform existed in
the personal spiritual cravings of humble individuals such as Churchman.
Yet historical circumstances soon accorded those cravings a broader outlet
and significance.[17]

Churchman himself highlights the key date as 1748, when the governor
of Pennsylvania called the colonial Assembly into session to grant money
to station a warship off the Delaware coast for the purpose of protecting British shipping from attacks by French and Spanish corsairs. Churchman happened to be in Philadelphia at the time. In his autobiography he
described the episode:

one night as I lay in my bed, it came very weightily upon me to go to the house of
assembly, and lay before the members thereof the danger of departing from trusting in that divine arm of power which had hitherto protected the Inhabitants of our
land in peace and safety. . . . [The next day] I requested the speaker that he would
go in and inform the members, that a country man was in waiting who had a desire
to be admitted, having something to communicate to them, and if they refused he
would be clear; he readily and affectionately answered he would, and soon brought
me word that they were willing.

Thereby Churchman raised the central issue that would roil Delaware Valley Quakerism—and Pennsylvania and indeed imperial politics—for the next thirty-five years. In no other British-American colony, it should be said, could such a confrontation have taken place. Nowhere else could a truly humble "country man" request a special audience with the ruling authorities and receive a serious and thoughtful hearing. The reason John Churchman was so received was because he lived in the Quaker colony, where he carried an impeccable reputation as an inspired man of the spirit. Leading citizens— and all Quakers—were just about obligated to listen to him.[18]

Thus Churchman was permitted to address the Assembly, and what he said out of his "private testimony" would attain its full relevance a decade later during the French and Indian War. "Tho' you now represent, and act for a mixed people of various denominations as to Religion," he told the colony's legislators, "yet remember the Charter is the same as at first; beware therefore of acting to oppress tender Consciences, for there are many of the Inhabitants whom you now represent, that still hold forth the same religious principles with their predecessors, who were some of the first adventurers into this, at that time wilderness land." As to the prospects of "warlike preparations" and the materialistic-martial value systems that promoted them, Churchman laid down a broad critique—the underlying principles which would become the program of "Quaker reform"—of what was about to engulf William Penn's "holy experiment."[19]

It was this powerful personality that the citizens of Nottingham met daily and weekly in and about the East Nottingham meetinghouse. They faced him, just back from his illustrious ministry in England, in 1754, when, "with a sorrow of heart," Churchman "beheld many of the youth in our society taking their flight as into the air, where the snares of the prince of the power thereof are laid to catch them." Of such youths as the fifteen-year-old Elijah Brown, Churchman "knew them not otherwise than by their natural features and a family resemblance, their demeanour and habit being so exceedingly altered in a little over four years." And Nottinghamites faced him at meeting on the morning of December 19, 1756, after which Churchman noted his sense of this isolated Quaker farming community:

I thought I felt a strong power of darkness and stupid ignorance, seemingly combined to make war against this solemn attention of mind; yet after patiently waiting some time, to my comfort I felt a secret victory, and the darkness vanished: Then, a voice was uttered in me attended (I thought) with Divine authority thus, *I will bow the inhabitants of the earth, and particularly of this land, and I will make them fear and reverence me, either in mercy or in judgment.*[20]

This was the village world Elijah Brown grew up in and which, two months later, in February 1757, he left for good. His departure was accomplished within the rules of the Meeting, for on February 19, 1757, the Nottingham Monthly Meeting issued the seventeen-year-old a certificate of removal, allowing him to transfer his membership to the Philadelphia Monthly Meeting. What is not clear about the move—but heavily suggested by circumstances—is the undercurrent of Brown family feeling associated with it. To explain this, one final litany of Brown family genealogy is required.[21]

Elijah's father, James, had married Miriam Churchman in 1734. She, like William Brown's wife, was the sister of John Churchman. (So John Churchman's father was Elijah's grandfather.) James and Miriam Brown had had a son in 1735, named Edward, a daughter in 1737, and Elijah in 1740. In 1750 Elijah's mother died, and soon after his father remarried. His father and new stepmother, named Elizabeth, proceeded to have a son in 1754 and another son in 1755. Now to the gist of the matter. Early in 1757 Elijah Brown left the Nottingham Meeting; nine months later his father and stepmother had another son; and at this point they did a most peculiar thing. They named their new son *Elijah*—as if the other Elijah, a healthy seventeen-year-old beginning his mercantile training in Philadelphia, were dead.[22]

One other curious thing occurred the year of Elijah Brown's departure from Nottingham. His cousin Esther was struck and killed by lightning.[23]

*   *   *

Elijah Brown settled into British North America's largest and wealthiest metropolis. Just a few years earlier Boston had held that distinction, leading the continent in such indices as population, export ship tonnage, and shipbuilding. But in the mid- to late 1750s Philadelphia bypassed Boston in all these categories. The Quaker City accordingly entered the Revolutionary era poised for expansion. Particularly conspicuous in the Philadelphia of 1757 were thousands of new Scots-Irish and German immigrants and the massive construction boom set off by the need to house them. As the city's population, which had numbered around 13,000 inhabitants in 1750, crested toward 20,000, some eighty new houses a year were being built, and between 1753 and 1760 the number of structures in the town increased by 29 percent. In the process, the town stretched physically from north to south along the Delaware River to an expanse of about two miles, while in its oldest section, bordered by Front and Third, Mulberry and Walnut streets, it assumed features of urban congestion. An English visitor around this time noted the streets "crowded with people, and the river with vessels." But what really astounded the Englishman was the price of housing: £100 currency per annum for rent of a comfortable house. Humbler dwellings could of course be let for considerably less, but the generally high real estate values were one of the consequences of a boisterous commercial economy.[24]

Politically in 1757, Philadelphia was in the midst of its gravest crisis ever, provoked by the exigencies of the French and Indian War. King George's

War in the 1740s—which had occasioned John Churchman's "address" to the Assembly—had framed the issue of how a colony led by a legislature devoted to pacifist principles could function within the eighteenth-century British Empire. At the outbreak of that imperial contest, Pennsylvania's governor, who represented the proprietary interests of the Penn family, had tried to get the Assembly to create a militia and undertake other defense measures. The Assembly, dominated by Quaker merchants and landowners, righteously refused to do so, and went on to call for the taxation of hitherto untaxed Penn family land holdings. This contest eventually gave way to the compromise of a volunteer militia and a voluntary Penn family contribution to the war effort. It yielded as well the clear definition of mid-eighteenth-century Pennsylvania's two key political entities. One was the Assembly, controlled by the "Quaker Party," a coalition of Quakers and other groups (like Germans) dedicated to the preservation of the colony's traditional political and religious liberties and values. The other was the Proprietary Party, centered in the Penn family back in England—who had long since fallen away from the Quaker ideals of their father—and their assorted colonial retainers.[25]

Fortunately for peace-loving Quakers and the Assembly, King George's War did not bring enemy troops and tribes to the province. The Assembly, therefore, could contribute its mite of funds "for the king's use" and still think of itself as upholding the cherished peace testimony. Between 1755 and 1757, however, as the French and Indian War broke out on its borders, the situation changed fundamentally. In March 1755, General Edward Braddock arrived as British commander in chief and demanded from the Assembly defense funds and troops. As in the past, squabbles ensued and compromises were worked out, and Braddock was eventually outfitted for his campaign. But then came disaster, as the general and his troops were wiped out along the Monongahela. Now the Quaker colony was exposed to the unprecedented. For the first time in its history, native Indians, provisioned and sometimes led by Frenchmen, attacked and killed Pennsylvanians. In the event, petitions from frontier settlers flooded the Assembly demanding defense measures, and a mob of frontiersmen—conspicuously of Scots-Irish extraction—arrived in the capital to press the case. Simultaneously, Quaker inquiries into the circumstances of the western hostilities came to focus not on British-French imperial issues but on the prior land policies of the Penn family proprietors, which western Scots-Irish settlers had particularly benefited from. The inquiries, moreover, yielded a provocative charge: the sons of William Penn had cheated the Delaware Indians, and the current warfare was the result. Also simultaneously, reports arrived from London that if the governing Quakers did not take war measures against the French and Indians, Quaker pacifists would be disenfranchised by royal decree, and the colony would pass into the control of others.[26]

The French and Indian War crisis almost inevitably, then, forced a re-configuration of Pennsylvania politics, and with that came the ascendance of new political leaders in the Quaker colony. This process involved, first, conscience-bound Quaker pacifists being persuaded by family and friends to resign their political posts for the duration of the war. Their offices were then taken up by other Quakers and non-Quaker allies not averse to defensive war. The resulting *new* "Quaker Party," in control of the Assembly, then proceeded to raise a militia and vote through other defense policies. Its leader, the Boston-born Benjamin Franklin, had hitherto been known for his business, philanthropic, and scientific endeavors and a general adherence to the country Whig principles of the Quaker party. (Which is not to say he didn't also get along well with key figures in the opposing Proprietary camp.) Franklin now emerged as champion of both traditional Quaker liberty principles and responsible defense policies.

Another ascendant leader in this mid-1750s context was Israel Pemberton. Third-generation heir of one of the colony's founding Quaker families, Pemberton was one of the richest merchants in the colony and the richest Quaker. Clerk of the Yearly Meeting, Pemberton had served the old Quaker Party as Assemblyman back in the early 1750s. In 1755–57, he emerged as the leader of a new force in Pennsylvania. A strict pacifist, he was at the same time a savvy and aggressive politician. And he possessed a vision. He sought to use pacifism in a militant way to return the colony to the founding ideals of William Penn. In his ends, then, he diverged fundamentally from Franklin. But in *means*—in his understanding and enjoyment of power and in his practical ability to manipulate the sources of power in Pennsylvania—he was Franklin's peer. He shared with Franklin too a bête noire: the Penns. Franklin hated them or, rather, absolutely detested their second-generation leader Thomas Penn, because *he* was narrow-minded, selfish, greedy, and condescending, or in a Whig word, "corrupt." Pemberton disdained the second-generation Penns because in cheating the Indians they had undermined the peaceable, and with that the spiritual, basis of the "holy experiment." In Quaker terms, these Penns were not "in the truth." Franklin and Pemberton shared one other attribute. In post-1755 Pennsylvania, both were prepared to go to considerable extremes to accomplish their ends.[27]

Philadelphia's commercial activity in the 1750s boded well for Elijah Brown's mercantile ambitions. But how was he to succeed materially *and* still remain a good Quaker? And what, in this time of general *reformation*, was a good Quaker? An added complication for Elijah here was the advent in precisely this period of the reform movement within Pennsylvania Quakerism led in part by his Nottingham relatives John and George Churchman and William Brown. Israel Pemberton sympathized with these men and was indeed their friend and ally, but he was a worldly, practical man and they were quietistic purists. They opposed the political adjustments and compromises spawned by the French and Indian War, the growing material wealth and values of Philadelphia, and the general "disunity"—or growing diversity—of Quakers. If Franklin and his Quaker Party allies represented one portentous force for principled change, so did the Quaker reformers. Most particularly, they insisted on a rededication to "the Discipline." They worried and thought and spoke much about this in the mid- to late 1750s, and the striving brought on Quaker "visions." John Woolman, for example, awoke in the darkness of an early February 1757 morning and

saw a light in my chamber at the apparent distance of five feet, about nine inches diameter, of a clear easy brightness; and near its center the most radiant; as I lay still without any surprise looking upon it, words were spoken to my inward ear, which filled my whole inward man: they were not the effect of thought, nor any conclusion in relation to the appearance, but as the language of the Holy One spoken in my mind; the words were, CERTAIN EVIDENCE OF DIVINE TRUTH; and were again repeated in the same manner; whereupon the light disappeared.[28]

John Churchman, as he prepared in the summer of 1756 to ride to Easton to attend a treaty conference with the Delaware Indians, dreamed

I was riding Eastward in the twilight, and saw a light before me towards sun-rising, which did not appear to be a common light, but soon observed the appearance of something therein, whereat the beast that I rode was much affrighted and would have run from it, which I knew would be vain; for I took it to be an Angel, whose motion was as swift as thought. . . . it was encompassed with a brightness like a rainbow.[29]

The common theme here was for true Quakers, amid the exploding historical complexities of the period, to hearken to and rely completely on *the voice.*

So with what, and with whom, would Elijah Brown identify? In leaving his village, did he also seek to leave the culture and values of Nottingham? Did he wish to distance himself from the connotations of another Churchman "vision," this one involving the appearance of "a large Company of Children moving or coming forward with even Steps, in a beautiful way, in similar Apparel; . . . all in a clean decent dress of a dove-like colour," which his cousin George Churchman interpreted "as appertaining to the future State of the Church, or her redeemed Members, after a time of purification now approaching"? Surely he did want to escape this lockstep monotony, as his move to Philadelphia testified. But how far was he willing to go? The country boy whose society and experience was bound up within the Nottingham and Philadelphia Monthly Meetings: was he prepared to go to the edge of Quakerism, or even beyond the fold? (His elder brother had been disowned by the Nottingham Meeting in 1756 for "fornication": for "keeping company" with one Sarah Oldham and getting her "with child," which pregnancy "occasioned their marriage by a Justice.") And if he stayed within the Society, what degree of compromise on basic principles was he prepared to accept? Did he want first and foremost the prosperity of material wealth? The record suggests he did, and for a while at least, he seemed to be on track to achieve it.[30]

Elijah Brown's commercial career can be traced in its basics. He began as an apprentice in the office of a Quaker merchant, but his first important career advancement came through marriage to Mary Armitt in 1761. She was a fellow member of his Philadelphia Monthly Meeting, and the daughter of Joseph Armitt, a well-to-do joiner, and Elizabeth Lisle Armitt. Joseph Armitt had died in 1747, leaving a considerable estate that included slaves, a three-story brick house and lot on Second Street, and assorted other properties. For Elijah Brown, Mary Armitt—in mercantile city terms—was an upwardly mobile match. Yet her true *commercial* benefit was not her dowry but the person of her brother-in-law. For Mary Armitt's older sister, Elizabeth, was married to Richard Waln, a prominent Philadelphia import-export merchant, whose grandfather had come to the colony with William Penn on the *Welcome*, and almost immediately after his marriage, Elijah Brown began tapping the resources of his new in-law. Thus in 1762 Elijah received from Richard Waln sugar, rum, molasses, and "sundries" worth some £120, which within a few months he dutifully repaid by cash, bills of credit, and occasional amounts of tea, molasses, and "sundries." Other business deals followed. Presumably, Elijah Brown was now a dry goods shopkeeper, who, through Richard Waln, was beginning to make trading contacts abroad.[31]

When he arrived in Philadelphia in the late 1750s, there were around 250 full-scale merchants—that is, wholesalers who traded in foreign markets. This is what Elijah Brown aspired to become. His chances for success in this context, as recently calculated by an economic historian, were about one in twenty-two. He, though, had the advantage of his brother-in-law, and by 1765 Elijah Brown could proudly sign his name as "merchant" on a protest declaration by Philadelphia's mercantile community against the Stamp Act. Though still without significant capital, he was to a small degree a wholesaler, and the future no doubt looked bright. But then came the disruptions of imperial politics, of local Philadelphia politics, and of the Revolution itself. For Elijah Brown, it all boded disaster.[32]

When the Townsend duties were passed in 1767, and in the aftermath Philadelphia's merchant community was pressured into joining the colonial nonimportation movement, only well-established merchants and/or those with built-up stocks of goods could prosper or at least hold their own. Richard Waln was one of these; Elijah Brown was not, and by 1768 Elijah's world was collapsing—for the first of many times. In January 1768 the Philadelphia Monthly Meeting singled out "Elijah Brown [for] having failed on the payment of his just debts, & it is apprehended thro' great Misconduct, & concealing his Circumstances from his Creditors." The

Meeting named a committee to examine him and report back to it. Elijah, in the aftermath, failed to give satisfaction, and so two months later the Monthly Meeting prepared a "Testimony against Elijah Brown," approved by Israel Pemberton, which read:

Whereas, Elijah Brown of this City, was educated & made profession with us the People called Quakers, for want of adhering to the Principle of Truth, neglected to fulfill his engagements, misrepresented the state of his affairs, declined taking the advice of his Friends in proper season, & by launching into greater extent of Trade and business than he had stock & ability to manage, became much more indebted than he hath effects to pay, b[r]ought a reproach on our Religious profession, & involved himself & family into great difficulties. We therefore cannot esteem said Elijah Brown a Member in Religious Fellowship, until he reforms his conduct, uses his best endeavors to satisfy his Creditors & seeks to be [reconsidered?] to their Meeting which is our desire for him.

Under this dispensation Elijah Brown could still attend weekly services—and his wife and children remained members of the Meeting in good standing—but until he changed his ways and admitted his culpability, he was formally "disowned."[33]

The imperial conflict and resulting revolutionary turmoil, accordingly, turned Elijah Brown into something of a desperate man and left him little room for the pursuit of "Eternal Truth." What he faced instead was one last speculative scramble in which his brother-in-law would advance him £460 for the purchase of a cargo to be sold in the West Indies. These goods were to be shipped from Philadelphia to the Caribbean on one of Richard Waln's vessels, which Elijah was to accompany as "supercargo" or commercial agent. This venture departed Philadelphia in late spring 1770, with Elijah instructed by his brother-in-law to take advantage, where possible, of the nonimportation agreement. If, Richard told Elijah, once in the West Indies, he hears "certain [definite] Accounts" that the duty on tea still applies, "lay out my Money in that Article, procure Dutch Papers for the Sloop, go to great [Eg]g Harbour & apply to Richd Sommers who will take charge of the Tea." Richard Waln signed his note: "I wish thee Success in this first Tryal and am affectionately thine."[34]

Elijah Brown's "adventure" met with at least moderate success, for he was able to pay back his brother-in-law's loan later in the year. Yet this was the practical end of his career as a "merchant." Never again would he engage with Richard Waln in such a business venture, and indeed, Waln's account books would henceforth indicate a depressing one-way relationship, with Elijah (and sometimes his wife Mary) borrowing money and never paying it back. This smuggling adventure to the West Indies also signified another type of denouement. Whatever Brown's political opinions on the widening and ever more complex imperial conflict, his devious deliveries to one "Richd Somers" at an out-of-the-way harbor in New Jersey would seem a long, long way from the Quaker principles of John Churchman and

Nottingham. By 1771, Elijah Brown, now reduced by business reverses to the identity of a mere "clerk," had much to feel anxious about. And things were about to get worse.[35]

*   *   *

Elijah and Mary Brown's fourth child came into a world inhabited by hovering forces that were about to come crashing down. As a birthright Quaker, Charles Brockden Brown—named after a wealthy merchant-lawyer on the Armitt side of the family whose own son Charles had recently died—would learn as a matter of course about the seventeenth-century persecutions that had made and defined his people. And as a Philadelphia Quaker, he would commence his childhood amid persecuting forces directed at . . . at *him*.[36]

Born in January 1771, Charles missed the onset of this fierce campaign against his people. At first it had been merely verbal, as in William Smith's 1755 *A Brief State of the Province of Pennsylvania*, which condemned Quakers for being a little too understanding of and accommodating to native Indians and German settlers. In this anonymous pamphlet by "a Gentleman who has resided many years in Pennsylvania," Smith, a close associate of the Penn family, called for all Quakers to take an oath of allegiance to the king, and a "test" or "declaration" that they would defend the colony against the Crown's enemies. This was to advocate a return to the circumstances of the English mid-seventeenth century, when the family of Richard Browne of Northamptonshire, among others, had suffered a constant stream of verbal abuse, fines, distraining of property, and the prospect of jail. The first threats of actual physical violence against Pennsylvania Quakers came in late 1763, when a group of mostly Scots-Irish frontiersmen took it upon themselves to murder in cold blood six Christianized Indians living in Conestoga and fourteen more being held in protective custody at the workhouse in Lancaster. The so-called Paxton Boys subsequently marched toward Philadelphia, avowing their intent to kill more Indians and any Quakers that got in the way. They in particular said they would catch and hang Israel Pemberton. It took the efforts of Benjamin Franklin, backed by a city militia, to halt the frontiersmen on the outskirts of Philadelphia and convince them to return to their homes in Lancaster County. The city's Quaker leaders, for their part, responded to these "cruel Unmerciful men," this "Company of Rioters . . . principally of Irish Extraction" with an *Address* that identified the Paxton Boys and their supporters with the "ambitious Men thirsting for Power" that Quakers had known, and been persecuted by, back in England. They meant "the Presbyterians."[37]

In the wake of the Paxton affair and with the French and Indian War over, the direct threat of murderous violence against Quakers subsided. Yet the din of anti-Quaker invective intensified, and in a few years the onset of another war would bring actual physical violence. Indeed, of the five

Quakers who signed the *Address* in 1764, three would be arrested in 1777 as "traitors" and escorted—by two Scots-Irish Presbyterian guards, it would turn out—to exile in Virginia. Fourteen other Philadelphia Quakers would suffer the same fate, Charles Brown's father among them.[38]

Charles Brown was born, then, into what might be termed a historically marked clan. He lived on Second Street in the dense hub of the city, in his Armitt grandmother's house. His immediate family counted his three older brothers, his grandmother, and his parents. (In 1773 a new baby brother, William, would die, and in 1774 another new baby brother, Elijah, would die.) For more extended family he had his uncle and aunt, Richard and Elizabeth Waln, and the Lisles. Beyond them there was the social hub of the Philadelphia Meeting, frequented by such Nottingham relatives as William Brown—now a resident of Philadelphia—and John and George Churchman. Here too was centered the activity of his clan's leadership group, which included the three Pemberton brothers and their wives, his uncle's brother, the minister Nicholas Waln, and such Quaker merchant families as the Henry Drinkers, the Thomas Whartons, and the Joseph Bringhursts.[39]

The most famous Philadelphian, of course, was Benjamin Franklin, but the most prominent public figure in Charles's own world was Israel Pemberton. Now in his late fifties, the "King of the Quakers," as the owner of seventy-one properties, held the distinction of paying the highest tax in the city. A former close political ally of Franklin, in the mid-1760s Pemberton had broken with Franklin over the latter's campaign to get the Crown to revoke Pennsylvania's charter and royalize the colony. For Pemberton, whatever the delinquencies of the second-generation Penns, William Penn's charter was the anchor and essence of what made Pennsylvania special. In the mid-1770s Pemberton came to oppose Franklin again when the latter turned against the Crown and threw in his lot with the Revolutionary groups in the colony. These people Pemberton himself could never join, not least because he had been battling—once with Franklin as an ally—their cultural impact and values for two decades. In 1756, for example, he had fought the tendency in the colony to turn the imperial conflict against the French and their Indian allies into a crusade to exterminate the Delaware Indians and thereby free up their lands. He had opposed such wartime measures as the bounty on Indian scalps, fearing it would "encourage the bloodthirsty Presbyterians to murder our friendly Indians to lay a foundation for a general war." He had put his money into this battle, too, founding the Friendly Association for Regaining and Preserving Peace with the Indians by Pacific Measures. Through peace conferences and a steady stream of gifts or tributes, the Friendly Association tried to counter the divisive effects of hostile and devious government policy on white-red relations. For his part in the creation of this organization—which was devious in its own inimitable way—the Paxton Boys wanted "to kill" Pemberton.[40]

Israel Pemberton did not forget this broader historical context amid the imperial issues of the 1770s. Accordingly, when the Massachusetts Revolutionary delegates came to Philadelphia in 1774 with their particular concerns, Pemberton peered at these men, as it were, *through* their "liberty" rhetoric. In one direct confrontation, he reminded them of their forebears' persecuting tendencies. He then listened to John Adams's reply in defense of New England and its glorious tradition of "liberty," before pronouncing: "Oh! sir, pray don't urge liberty of conscience in favor of such laws!" Pemberton was, in short, the standard bearer of another British libertarian tradition, and in the Philadelphia of Charles Brown's infancy he struggled—along with his brothers John and James and others—to defend and salvage it. Resistant to the Revolutionaries' pleas and no friend to the opposing side of would-be royalist grandees (though grateful to the Crown itself as the bestower and guarantor of the charter that had made William Penn's "holy experiment" possible), he worked hard within the Quaker community, and in particular through the Philadelphia Meeting, to remind Friends of their century-long heritage and spiritual mission. His perspective—which was likewise the perspective of his brothers and of Quaker reformers like William Brown, George Churchman, Anthony Benezet, and which was indeed the official policy of the Philadelphia Meeting—was unique in the Revolutionary context. It wasn't about "sides." It was about a special historical *context* that was the Quaker experience. Thus John Adams could both ally with Pennsylvania's Revolutionaries *and* hold himself above what he deemed their cruder non-New Englandish political notions. In the eyes of Israel Pemberton, though, these Revolutionaries—John Adams included—were "Presbyterians" all. And perhaps Adams proved Pemberton's point when he placed Pemberton on the infamous list of those Philadelphians to be arrested and exiled because they were "dangerous" to the Revolutionary cause. Pemberton *was* dangerous to that cause—but not because he was on the other "side."[41]

*   *   *

Charles Brown was three and a half when the Continental Congress convened in Philadelphia (the delegates first gathered informally at a tavern just down the street from him), four and a half when actual warfare broke out at Lexington and Concord, and five and a half when independence was declared. He would have been oblivious of these events, though he certainly heard the celebrations surrounding the Declaration of Independence. Instead, what he specifically experienced was the *Pennsylvania* Revolution taking place around and behind the American Revolution. This local event—with its historical links to, among other incidents in the past, the Paxton Boys affair—took loose shape throughout 1775, as extralegal "committees" formed in Philadelphia to promote political change and organize a militia system. By early 1776 the most radical of these commit-tees was pushing for militia rules that would heavily penalize those refus-ing to pick up arms. In July 1776 this Revolution found its constitutional expression through a convention that, in addition to writing and imple-menting a new radical state constitution, set a fine for all males between the ages of sixteen and fifty who didn't "associate" with—that is, join—the mili-tia and a special annual tax on every "non-associator" over the age of twenty-one. It also, in June 1777, prescribed an oath of allegiance to itself. The Philadelphia Meeting, for its part, forbade militia service, payment of fines and war taxes, and taking the oath. In the face of these Quaker principles, Revolutionary "committeemen" forcibly entered the houses of noncomplying Friends and distrained property. (On one recorded occa-sion, a "Capt. Hamilton"—or more acccurately, Lieutenant Colonel Alex-ander Hamilton—"came . . . with armed men & forcibly broke open the store door & took away a large quantity of goods.") Anti-Quaker riots broke out too. It was just as it had been in the time of George Fox and William Penn and Richard Browne of Northamptonshire. For Charles Brown, this Revolution veritably exploded on September 5, 1777, when "violent" men came to his door and took away his father.[42]

A key question bearing on the nature of Charles Brown's mature imagi-nation is *why* his father was arrested.

Technically, by their laws the Revolutionaries could have arrested any-body in Philadelphia who refused to take the prescribed oath of allegiance. Most such "nonjurors," though, they left alone, or punished through the confiscation of personal property. So the seventeen Quakers who were arrested in early September 1777 and marked for exile all had something *special* about them. Some, clearly, were targets because of their powerful leadership roles in the Quaker community and in particular their ongoing efforts to keep Friends, especially young, potentially arms-carrying Friends, neutral. Paramount among these were the Pemberton brothers. Other prominent Friends, like Henry Drinker and Thomas Fisher and Thomas Wharton, carried the tarnish of past quasi-Tory activities. These men—who for all intents and purposes were "Tories" in their opinions and lifestyles—had been variously implicated with obnoxious imperial policies, like the Tea Act, and/or had refused, on Quaker principle, to accept the currency script issued by the "war-making" Revolutionary government. It seems likely that this latter insult was the reason for the arrest of the two relatively hum-ble artisans, the joiner Thomas Affleck and the hatter Charles Jervis. And then there was Elijah Brown, who fit none of these categories. He wasn't influential; nor was he a Tory, for when Parliament passed the "Coercive Acts" in 1774 and prepared to close down the port of Boston in retaliation for the Tea Party, his spirited response was that "unless the people of England shortly rise in our favor both countries must be ruined." Instead he was guilty of something else.[43]

"These are the times that try men's souls." Thomas Paine had begun *The American Crisis* series in December 1776 to rally Revolutionary morale in the face of a critical military situation, and in early 1777 the Revolution in Philadelphia was picking up in intensity. By March and April 1777, as Howe's army maneuvered toward the city, forced confiscations of necessary military items increased and militiamen invaded more and more households in search of such articles as blankets. General panic on all sides spread. On April 19, 1777, Paine published the third installment of *American Crisis*, and here he included a savage attack on Philadelphia's Quakers. Invoking the principle that "When one villain is suffered to escape, it encourages another to proceed, either from a hope of escaping likewise, or an apprehension that we dare not punish," Paine called on the Revolutionary Council of Safety (formerly the Committee of Safety) to gouge and otherwise threaten nonjuring, nonassociating Quakers, whom he described as "like antiquated virgins" who "see not the havoc deformity has made upon them, but pleasantly mistaking wrinkles for dimples, conceive themselves yet lovely and wonder at the stupid world for not admiring them." And as for the principles of the Philadelphia Meeting and its leaders, they were "perverted." "O! ye fallen, cringing, priest-and-Pemberton-ridden people! What more can we say of ye than that a religious Quaker is a valuable character, and a political Quaker a real Jesuit." The necessity, as Paine saw it, was clear. "In the present crisis we ought to know, square by square and house by house, who are in real allegiance with the United Independent States, and who are not."[44]

A few days later, Revolutionary committeemen visited Elijah Brown and "warn'd [him] from selling any more [flour]." What this meant was that he was selling *on the open market* an item either already requisitioned for army use or reserved, at a "controlled" price, for the populace. Why Elijah Brown was doing this in the face of the Associators' regulations can be deduced. That there was recalcitrance on Brown's part seems evident—and indeed he must have continued to "sell" in the wake of this threat, because he *was* ultimately arrested. Recalcitrance, moreover, was part and parcel of his personality. He had perhaps shown this when he left Nottingham, and he definitely showed it when, on pain of disownment from the Philadelphia Meeting, he refused to take the necessary remedial steps to admit wrong and formally rejoin the Meeting. In addition to *attitude*, however, perhaps most directly relevant to Elijah Brown's 1777 choices was the fact that he had many debts and no money. And under the Revolutionary dispensation he had no prospect of making any money. He plainly needed to "sell," and as a consequence he was arrested.[45]

So Elijah Brown was arrested not because he was principled and courageous like the Pembertons; nor was he arrested because of his significance within his community. And he wasn't arrested because of his political opinions per se. The last of the group taken into custody—almost, it seems, as an afterthought—he was clearly different from the other exiles. They, for instance, had money to support themselves; he was absolutely broke, and his wife had to borrow from her brother-in-law to support him and the family over the course of 1777–78. (The loans were never repaid.) And then there was the most telling fact of all: Elijah Brown was the only Quaker in the group not offered the option, *as a "man of reputation,"* of giving his "parole" that he would "refrain from doing anything inimical to the United States of North America," in exchange for which he would be left at liberty. Evidently Elijah Brown, the "merchant" of the 1765 Stamp Act protest, was not deemed a "man of reputation" in 1777 Philadelphia. In exile too, Elijah Brown's troubled status was underscored by the fact that, in Winchester, Virginia, he lived apart from the main group of exiles. In truth, it was ironic that he was even there—a fellow Quaker "martyr" along with the likes of Israel and John and James Pemberton, the very men who had judged him and cast him out of the Meeting as unworthy in 1768.[46]

Arrest and exile could have been a good career move for Elijah Brown. After all, for a down-on-his-luck commercial man, an intimate, soulful experience with some of Philadelphia's wealthiest and best-connected merchants could have been just the ticket. Yet it wasn't to be. Prosperity was just not for him.

Chapter 2
From Terror to Terror to Terror, 1777–1793

I was at this time a child of six years of age. The impressions that were then made upon me, can never be effaced. I was ill qualified to judge respecting what was then passing; but as I advanced in age, and became more fully acquainted with these facts, they oftener became the subject of my thoughts. The words are Clara's and she is referring to a pivotal event in her life: "the end of my father." About *his* uncanny demise—which is tied up with a radiant burst of "light," a sharp sound "like the explosion of a mine," and a final lingering cloud "impregnated with light"—she muses: "When we recollect his gloomy anticipations and unconquerable anxiety; the security from human malice which his character, the place, and the condition of the times, might be supposed to confer . . . what are the conclusions that we must form?"[1]

Clara Wieland is a fictional character, created by Charles Brockden Brown in 1798. Her story, which concerns the psychological consequences for a family of their father's "mysterious" death, will be Brown's first published novel and will make him, the great-great-great-grandson of Richard Browne of Northamptonshire, the originator of the American Gothic genre.

*   *   *

Charles Brown was six years eight months old when his father disappeared in September 1777. Two weeks later the angry people responsible for his father's disappearance themselves disappeared and a new group of people, dressed in red coats, entered the city and settled in. Then seven months later, his father reappeared. Seven weeks after that the Redcoats disappeared, and soon after the angry people, looking dirty and fatigued, returned. On July 4, 1778, those people held a day-long celebration with gun and cannon discharges and evening fireworks at the City Tavern, which was located less than a block away from where Charles Brown, now seven years old, lived.[2]

This crucible of turmoil, crisis, inexplicable loss, and surprise recovery—underscored by explosions and light shows—was Charles Brown's childhood. The verbal attacks, the confiscations, the rocks through windows, the unwanted soldiers foisted on households, it could be said, were all part of the historical continuum for "the people called Quakers." As were "unjust"

Harriet Chew

imprisonments. In England such persecutions set the backdrop for the founding narratives of George Fox and William Penn; in Philadelphia, beginning in 1775, they were what a true Friend could and should expect.

The arrest and exile of Elijah Brown turned the Brown family into local Quaker celebrities. For material subsistence they could draw upon the resources of brother-in-law Richard Waln, who provided them with some £70 worth of "sundries" to tide them through the winter. Waln's personal solicitations, however, necessarily ended in late October when *he* was taken up by the Revolutionaries for "being a Tory"—which he certainly was—and given the choice of jail, declaring his allegiance to the Revolution, or removing to British-held New York. (Waln, not surprisingly, chose New York.) This left grandmother Elizabeth Armitt and the Quaker community as a whole to look after the Browns. Accordingly, 117 South Second Street received visits from concerned Friends. Some of these people, like the blue bloods Elizabeth Drinker and Sarah Logan Fisher, probably didn't make a practice of visiting the discredited Elijah Brown household before September 1777; but during this historic crisis they did. Thus there is a record of Elizabeth Drinker along with the Philadelphia Meeting minister Nicholas Waln—who was Richard Waln's brother—dropping in to see "Polly" Brown, and of Sarah Logan Fisher, in December, finding Mary Brown "very low, yet hoping her Husband would sooner be released than she expected." And on numerous other occasions the Women's Meeting, the Monthly Meeting, the Yearly Meeting, the Meeting on Sufferings took up the plight and concerns of the exiles and their families. From time to time, too, the exiles' wives gathered among themselves to plan strategy and sign petitions for their husbands' release.[3]

So while the disowned Elijah languished in Virginia, the Philadelphia Meeting enveloped the families of the exiles through the winter of 1777–78, with special spiritual counsel coming from the two prominent ministers (and Brown family relations), Nicholas Waln and William Brown. These ministrations, and no doubt the traumatic communal situation as a whole, eventually worked their effect on Elijah himself, for in February 1779—ten months after his return—he showed up at the Monthly Meeting "and presented a paper condemning certain parts of his Conduct some years ago, which then induced Friends to bear Testimony against him." The Meeting, in response, appointed two men, one of them his fellow exile James Pemberton, to examine the matter and in particular to hear Elijah "on the Motives of his present offering." The case of Elijah Brown, though, was a complicated one, and the examining committee reported that it needed "further Time." (To anticipate: In the end, Elijah would never formally rejoin the Meeting. On the other hand, it seems he still attended.)[4]

Charles Brown's childhood also had its elements of stunning ambiguity. How, for instance, to comprehend the events of October 4, 1779.

There had been rumors for a week "that the Militia were about to take up all the Tories & Quakers & would certainly create a most dreadful scene in the City." Quakers had to feel anxious, accordingly, when they awoke on Monday morning, October 4, to discover handbills posted about town urging militiamen to gather to "drive off from the city all disaffected persons and those who supported them." And that anxiety could only have deepened when at twelve noon a group of militiamen—some probably inebriated—showed up at the Pine Street meetinghouse just as the Yearly Meeting was letting out. For the time being at least, these militiamen interested themselves in a single individual, one Joseph Drinker, whom they arrested for doing in effect what Elijah Brown had been doing back in 1777: selling goods at market prices. But this wasn't the end of it. A Revolutionary Whig spectacle was in progress. Some 150 to 200 militiamen took Drinker, along with three other merchants, and marched them through the streets of Philadelphia "with the Drum after 'em beating the Rogues March." The route, for Quakers, was a threatening one. Beginning unsoberly at Burn's Tavern in the northwestern part of the city, it slowly wended its way toward the Delaware River and the old part of the town. Sometime after three in the afternoon the "mob"—as Quakers termed it—approached the Browns' neighborhood.[5]

To this point the procession was but another installment of the now familiar Whig street genre which traced back to the fast day of July 20, 1775, when Whig mobs first threw stones through Quaker windows. Yet this time something startlingly new was in the offing. At the Browns' block the mob turned right onto Walnut Street and at the next corner, on the left, it halted: in front of the home of James Wilson, a leading Revolutionary and signer of the Declaration of Independence. Along with Wilson inside this house was a contingent of other prominent Revolutionaries, like Sharp Delany—who in 1777 had helped make up the infamous list of soon-to-be exiled Quakers—and the Continental Army's quartermaster general, Thomas Mifflin. Now shots rang out as, incredibly, the two different groups of Revolutionaries set upon *each other*. It was all "terrible to hear," according to one of the Browns' Quaker neighbors. By the time yet *another* group of Revolutionaries appeared on the scene—this one a cavalry contingent led by Joseph Reed, president of the Supreme Executive Council—six or seven men were dead and some seventeen to nineteen lay seriously wounded. In the aftermath of the "Fort Wilson affair," twenty-nine militiamen were arrested by the cavalrymen and confined in the city jail, in a room below that occupied by the former Quaker exile Samuel Rowland Fisher. Fisher was under arrest again, this time for supposed "inimical correspondence" with enemies of independence, and his diary entry for this night runs: "The 27 Militia Men, so called . . . very noisy & turbulent, so that we were not fond of going much out of our Room. . . . [They] continued very noisy all night." The next day the militiamen were released by order of the Revolutionary leader who had had them arrested, Joseph

Reed, who now needed to worry about *his own* safety, "for many [Revolutionaries] in the City spoke very free against him & 'twas said threatened to shoot him."[6]

Less ambiguous for Quakers like Charles Brown were the Whig mobs of October 24, 1781, who celebrated news of Cornwallis's defeat to General Washington at Yorktown. It was the standard Revolutionary fare: Huzzahs and rifle shots and cannon explosions, followed, eventually, by insults against and attacks on "Tories" and Quakers. This celebration, though, turned out to be especially memorable, for the anti-Quaker riots came in waves and lasted from seven until ten that night. Recorded one Quaker of her home: "the Door crack'd and Violently burst open, when they threw Stones into the House for some time." She noted of other Quaker houses in the neighborhood: "after braking the door they enterd, and distroy'd the furniture &c—many women and Children were frightned into fitts." Noted another Quaker: "For two hours we had the disagreeable noise of stones banging about, glass crashing, and the tumultuous voices of a large body of men, as they were a long time at the different houses in the neighborhood." This was the treatment accorded just about all "unilluminated" Quaker homes, as well as many that tried to save themselves with the proper Whig candle displays. Anna Rawle summed up the day: "It seems universally agreed that Philadelphia will no longer be that happy asylum for the Quakers that it once was."[7]

It certainly wasn't to be for Charles Brown's family. Even with the war over, many of the Revolutionaries' wartime laws remained in place—like the loyalty oaths, the punitive taxations against nonjurors and consequent distrainments, the truncated civil rights. Part of what was going on was an intra-Revolutionary struggle for control of post-war Pennsylvania. This is what lay behind the October 1779 attack on James Wilson's house. One group of Revolutionaries, who came to be called "Constitutionalists," had been responsible for the radical "democratic" features (and, let it be said, the quick and distinctly undemocratic adoption) of the 1776 Pennsylvania Constitution, which included, along with a unicameral legislature, prescribed loyalty oaths to the new regime. The Constitutionalists, in subsequent control of the state legislature, had then prescribed additional loyalty oaths that in effect disenfranchised the constituencies that didn't agree with them. Meanwhile, another group, calling themselves "Republicans"—among whom was James Wilson—wanted to amend the 1776 Constitution. In particular they wanted a mixed, bicameral legislature, and they wanted an end to the exclusionary test oaths. All in all, the former group of Revolutionaries desired what historians term a "radical" Pennsylvania committed to economic "justice" (meaning: there would be a market regulated by price controls) and political "democracy" (meaning: the political process would be open to all adult white male taxpayers who agreed with the Constitutionalists on ideological essentials). By contrast, the latter group of Revolutionaries desired a Pennsylvania with an unfettered market and a franchise restricted by property requirements but not by political opinion. In such a "liberal" Pennsylvania, the Republicans were confident that educated and propertied men like themselves would be chosen to lead.[8]

For businessmen like Elijah Brown, the economic environment of post-war Philadelphia was impossible. He still had his prior debts and compromised reputation to worry about, and he now faced the added worry of a flood of new European competitors who were migrating into the city and its dry goods trade. Additionally, as a nonjuror, he had to do business within a political system that double taxed him and accorded him few civil rights. Indeed, by the terms of "Constitutionalist" Pennsylvania Elijah Brown was a noncitizen, and thus he could not legally buy or sell or transfer real estate, nor could he sue for debts. (Alas, he could still *be sued* by creditors.) Between 1783 and 1786, many dozens of the city's mercantile firms failed and some of its most prestigious citizens, like Abel James of redoubtable "James and Drinker," went bankrupt. In this setting it was probably a foregone conclusion that Elijah Brown's efforts to resurrect his business career would fail too; and they did. As a consequence, by mid-1784 Elijah Brown found himself, once again, in jail. This time his crime was the very opposite of "selling." If anything, he wasn't selling enough. As Richard Waln stated the case, "my poor unfortunate Brother in Law . . . has again involved himself in Debt. & is on that account in confinement in Philad[elphi]a." And the debt was of "conciderable amount."[9]

Some years later Charles Brown attempted to enlighten a friend about "my sad experience," and for the purpose he described a scene that must have been his own memory of visiting his father in Philadelphia's Walnut Street debtors' prison. "Imagine yourself," Charles prompts his correspondent,

in an apartment defended by an iron door and grated windows. A chearful fire blazing in the hearth surrounded by ten or twelve persons, the tenants of the same room. Among them there are scarcely two of the same nation or two that before their entrance into this mansion were not utter strangers to each other. Some of them are employed in conversation either mirthful or serious, either delicate and man[ner]ly or base and brutal. Another party is endeavouring to drown their sorrows in intoxicating spirits, another at the Card table practicing with amazing skill and eagerness all the wiles and artifices of Piquet and whist. What discord! What confusion!

As for the observer of this scene—"he that sits in the corner on a block sawn from the end of a hickory log fixed on the paper or the book before him in abstract attention"—Charles describes *him* this way: "He is akin to one of the unhappy prisoners[.] Filial affection has persuaded him to change the social circle and tranquility at home for noise and stench and interruption here."[10]

In such a room, in 1784, the ambitions, the dreams that had brought the great-great-grandson of Richard Browne of Northamptonshire to Philadelphia in 1757, collapsed forever. Henceforth Elijah Brown would scrape through life as a conveyancer, a real estate broker, a copyist, picking up small commissions here and there for renting or selling other people's property and for writing up other people's official documents.

Yet in his own inimitable way Elijah Brown remained undaunted, and in 1785 he wrote out a remarkable private document for his children in which he, Polonius-like, offered up his worldly wisdom. This parental "advice" he "most affectionately wishes—and prays" will be "often perused and most seriously observed" by his "beloved Offspring . . . in order that they may experience the real benefit and advantage gained by a due attention to the Important Truth which is found herein Recommended."[11]

It is an eccentric Quaker performance. About the earliest Hebrew precursors to the Quaker religion:

You need not be told, that they were very singular and different from others in their dress, and address; and, however light some may now esteem these things, they suffered greatly for the same.

About the admirable Quakers themselves:

There is such a dignity in the Truth, and such a nobility in appearing like Friends agreable to our known principles, that keeps even transgressors in awe, and Libertines at a distance.
    A deviation, opens a door to every hurtful thing, and introduces a acquaintance, that oftentimes leads to ruin in this World, and which is much worse, (though far be it from me to limit the Mercies of God) unfits us I fear for Happiness in the World to come. . . . A Cocked up hat, fashionable Cloaths, or using the plural number instead of the singular, may be call'd by you indifferent things; you may say, that speach is to convey Ideas, and what Religion can there be in having a Hat a little lower or higher? and in the same manner plead for every other liberty. . . . Our Predesessors in the Truth, we know from well grounded objections, laid aside greatly the exteriours Men had added to Religion, and recommended to us an inward Purity of Heart and Soul.

On attending Quaker services:

The frequent opportunities afforced us to meet together, are also great advantages; *I do entreat you, by no means neglect them.*—It is great encouragement to see a Meeting well and timely filled. I remember to have heard a friend once say in Testimony "That such as were indifferent about coming to meetings, were most indifferent when there." This is a truth to which I believe our experience will readily assent. Let us therefore in an especial manner guard against this indifferance; and tho' we may have attended many Meetings . . . yet if we miss but one, that one might have been to us, as the appearance of Jesus was to the Disciples when they were very low in their minds.

On social (and business?) relations:

Be exceeding[ly] choice of your company; for true it is, that evil communications corrupt good manners.

On reading habits:

Be as careful what Books you read; and avoid those tending to libertinism, and deism, *as you would an infectious Distemper.*

And finally, on assorted other practical matters:

I am not insensible . . . that great hurt hath been occasioned by the falling away of some men, from whom better things might have been expected, and that by their fall many have been wounded. . . . I have seen so much hurt sustained by some who have begun Right, by not keeping to the Simplicity and innocency they once knew, and began in, that I cannot but greatly desire our preservation and perseverance. . . . Imitate not those in a higher sphere of Life. Endeavour to live rather below than above your situation.—I have often seen exceeding hurt to individuals in this particular, who might have been comfortable, had they confined their way of Life to their situation in it; but by looking and aiming at a higher, have to support it, gone into hazardous undertakings, brought very great inconveniency on themselves.[12]

Here, then, in 1785 Philadelphia, is the Brown family: five sons (the eldest in his early twenties), two young daughters, and the two parents. Having moved out of grandmother Elizabeth Armitt's comfortable town house at 117 South Second, they rented an alleyway house nearby, between Third and Dock Streets. Mary Brown—by the scant evidence—was a devout, humble woman who stayed within the Meeting and kept her children in the Meeting. As a wife, it can be suspected, Mary would not always have been at peace with the choices her husband made: like when he ran himself into unmanageable debt in the late 1760s and got himself read out of the Meeting; like when he exposed himself to arrest and exile in 1777; like when he failed in the late 1770s and early 1780s to take the necessary steps to get back into the good graces of the Meeting and its potentially helpful merchant leaders; like when he exposed himself to arrest again in 1784, this time for "conciderable" debts that came to the attention of the non-Quaker civil courts of Pennsylvania; like when he moved the family out of her mother's house. Mary Brown, in this household, was forced to be necessarily practical. Whereas her sister was the wealthy mistress of Walnford, Mary had to guard over pennies, and her children intuited her displeasure when they splurged on such luxuries as books.[13]

Elijah Brown, the father, was something else again. Most damningly perhaps, he was a failed—and, in the minds of some, morally discredited —businessman in North America's greatest emporium. In 1785 he listed his occupation as "conveyancer." But in truth this was his least original quality. As for the rest: A profound and proud Quaker after his own lights whose thoroughgoing pacifism extended to the insect kingdom, he had been disowned by the Meeting in 1768 and was never formally to rejoin it (his brief effort in 1779 notwithstanding). Yet he counseled his children not to miss a single service, and pleaded with them not to marry outside the Meeting. (All the same, at least four of his children, Charles included, would marry non-Quakers.) A reader of Quaker devotionals who advised his children to stay away from "libertine" and deistic texts, he himself read the deist Mary Wollstonecraft and the atheist William Godwin and abstracted their works in a commonplace book, and he gave Wollstonecraft's *Historical and Moral View of the French Revolution* as a gift to his son Elijah, Jr. Indeed, his surviving notebooks reveal an earnest, moralistic Friend with an entertaining, humorous, and even silly side seldom seen in Quaker journals and letters of the period. Within his family, clearly, he was *a force*—though it's hard to say toward what exact effect. In the words of one of his children, "father" inspired "with Homers fame / And taught the high, heroic theme / That nightly flash'd upon my dream." And suggestively, Charles's epistolary persona "H.D." would write in a letter datelined "Philad. May 10, 1794": "My father's house was . . . governed on peculiar principles. How little would a curious stranger have been enabled to judge of the domestic maxims established in this city, by what he should gather from residence in our family."[14]

   Which is to say, Charles Brown had a quirky father with an incredible story behind him—a story that was in its historical essence *the story* of Pennsylvania Quakerism. And as Elijah's son—bone of his bone—that story was in Charles too. It was a matter of *if*, and after that, *when* and *how*, he would choose to tell it.

*   *   *

Chronology and fate dictated that the three eldest Brown sons learn how to make a living as soon as possible. While they probably attended the city's Quaker elementary schools (until those schools were shut down by the Constitutionalists' test laws), they all began commercial careers as soon as possible. Charles, on the other hand, entered the acme of the Quaker school system, the Friends' Latin School, in June 1781. Here he studied the Quaker classics, read the Bible, and attended meeting twice a week, in conjunction with lessons in Latin and Greek, mathematics, English literature, and geography. Who paid his tuition cannot be determined, but somebody did, as he was not carried on the school's rolls as a charity case. And so from 1781 to 1786 Charles mixed with Norrises, Whartons, Drinkers, Fishers, and Pembertons, as well as with the two boys who became his best friends, Joseph Bringhurst and John Davidson.[15]

   His teacher at Friends' Latin was a devout, well-educated Yorkshire-born

Quaker who had tried and failed to find a career in London. Robert Proud had then, at the age of thirty, migrated to Philadelphia in search of a better life. The quest began in 1759 in the home of William and Susanna Brown—Charles's great-uncle and aunt—where Proud set up as a tutor. (It's possible that a fellow boarder in the house at this time was Elijah Brown.) Proud's pupils soon included two sons of Israel Pemberton; and soon Proud was living in the home of Israel's brother James Pemberton, down the street from the Armitts. Soon, too, when the current master of the Friends' Latin School quit to take up a career in commerce, Proud—who possessed the somewhat rare combination of Quaker piety and sound classical training—was signed on as the school's new master of classics. (The erstwhile master, Charles Thomson, was destined to become a successful merchant and a leading Revolutionary, indeed "the Sam Adams of Philadelphia.") Proud labored at Friends' Latin for ten years before quitting to have his own go at commerce. In this, though, he failed, and in 1780 he returned to Friends' Latin.[16]

Charles Brown's schoolmaster was both an effective teacher and, during the years of Charles's attendance, a bitter, self-pitying man. Beyond this, he was an arrogant Tory who referred to American Whigs as "*upstarts*," "*Servile Sway*" who "by *violence* . . . usurp the power over their former masters and rulers." Back in 1777 Proud had expected to be arrested for his opinions. When his friends the Pembertons, the Fishers, Drinker, and the others were arrested and exiled to Virginia, Proud was surprised to be left alone by "the rebels," for, to his mind, he had been more "obnoxious" than the actual exiles. (Why he wasn't arrested is probably indicated by a letter he wrote to those exiles. Proud wrote from the Philadelphia area of the "Devastation of Armies around us" and of "the People, in divers Places, without Distinction of Age or Sex, Condition or Party, being plundered & ravaged of nearly all they had," and he noted his desire to visit Winchester. Yet he never did attempt the trip, nor did he even send this letter. He was, it seems, a man of deep intentions and peeves, but not action or influence; and the Revolutionaries treated him accordingly.) By 1779 Proud was describing America as "this accursed place" and contemplating a return to England. Yet he stayed where he was, and from 1780 to 1790 Proud ran the Latin School, mixing an obvious commitment to pedagogy with constant carping about his meager salary and his equally meager social status within the Philadelphia Quaker community.[17]

Charles Brown's five teenage years at Friends' Latin, then, for all their educational and perhaps social richness, were not a reprieve from the sorrowful childhood context of the late 1770s. The school's trustees were former exiles, his classmates included the exiles' children, and his teacher was a man who complained about living in a place "compass'd round by rebel foes," and who, the evidence clearly indicates, was actually bitter about *not* having been arrested and exiled himself. (That, it seems, would have been a distinction.) On the other hand, Master Proud was, for Quaker Philadelphia, an erudite man, and he did prompt the precocious Charles Brown on his intellectual way. It wouldn't be long before Charles was impressing others with his own brand of erudition. Perhaps also prompted in Brown by Proud was a strain of arrogance, along with the streaks of pedantry that would flash on occasion in Brown's literary criticism. In that criticism, let it be noted, Charles, as editor of the *Monthly Magazine* in 1799, would greet Robert Proud's one true accomplishment, the publication of his life's masterwork, *The History of Pennsylvania*, with the harsh—if accurate—characterization: the "uncouth narratives of an old man."[18]

But what was going on in Brown's imagination during this decade when the Pennsylvania Revolution was working itself out, when his father spent time in debtors' prison, when his mother had to worry about meeting the most basic household expenses, and when fifty-five delegates met at Independence Hall to create a new national government?

Charles later claimed that "since thirteen years of age, I have enjoyed a state of perfect liberty." This dates to 1784, the year of his father's imprisonment for debt, and would seem to indicate the disintegration of his father's active authority over him. Yet by no means was Charles at "perfect liberty" in 1784, at least in the sense of being free of the culture and institutions and authority figures of the Philadelphia Meeting, whose first and fifth day services he was required to attend by the rules of the Friends' Latin School.[19]

With this said, though, around this time Charles's ambitions did begin to declare themselves, and by the standards of the Meeting they were peculiar. Certainly orthodox—and just as certainly precocious—was an essay Charles wrote in 1783 on "Liberty of Conscience," in which he contemplated the "Hecatombs of Victims offer'd upon the gloomy altar [of the] Scotch League and Covenant." With David Hume's *History of England* as his source, twelve-year-old Charles noted the sorry and ironic spectacle of certain European Protestants who were "ready [to] burn in the same flames from which they themselves [had] so narrowly escaped, everyone that had the assurance to oppose them." Less *Quaker* were the literary ambitions that Brown exhibited toward the end of his tenure at Friends' Latin. These included plans and preliminary attempts to write epic poems about Columbus's discovery of America, Pizarro's expedition against Peru, and Cortés's American sojourn. By 1786–87, in fact, Charles Brown, in Quaker Philadelphia, aspired to be some kind of a poet. In his own terminology, which was the religious language of his tribe, he wanted to be a "Visionary."[20]

His first actual break from the institutional setting of the Philadelphia Meeting came in 1787, when he entered as an apprentice into the law office of a non-Quaker, Alexander Wilcocks. Two "cultural" issues were involved here. First was Wilcocks's status as a member of the city's Anglican elite. While this didn't bother Charles, and indeed to be accepted into Wilcocks's distinguished office was quite a testament to the sixteen-year-old Brown's intellectual abilities and reputation, it would have concerned the Meeting. Second there was the practice of law itself, which Quakerism deemed highly dubious, and which Charles himself considered morally questionable.[21]

A family reference point also existed. Brown's uncle, Nicholas Waln, had once stood among Pennsylvania's premier lawyers, and Waln's fine town house just down the block from the Armitt-Brown residence was a reminder of his former place at the head of the Philadelphia bar. But in the early 1770s Nicholas Waln had undergone a spiritual awakening. After winning a case ("I did the best I could for my client, gained the cause for him, and thereby defrauded an honest man out of his just due"), Waln decided to give up the unseemly practice of law to dedicate himself to religion. Once one of Philadelphia's leading attorneys, he metamorphosed into one of its most prominent Quaker ministers, which is what he was in the year Charles chose to move, as it were, in the other direction. Except, as the next few years would show, Charles *couldn't* go in that direction. In this he was too much like his uncle's brother, his great-uncle William Brown, and all the other ministerial Browns and Churchmans in the family heritage. Yet he was also different from them in one fundamental particular. Having lived his childhood in Revolutionary Philadelphia, Charles Brown did not feel and think like an orthodox Quaker. In fact, as the future would reveal, he didn't feel and think like anyone else, period. His imagination was unique.[22]

Brown worked in Wilcocks's office for six years. During this time he registered his desire for intellectual fellowship by joining a law club, whose members debated and analyzed and issued legal decisions on hypothetical cases. Meanwhile he registered his doubts about the law profession in letters to friends. His true passion he recorded in a journal fragment, dated, in the Quaker fashion, "6 mo 13. 1788": "Wilcocks being out of Town I have been at liberty to indulge myself" in writing poetry.[23]

The passion gained an outlet in the Belles Lettres Club, which Brown joined in 1786 or 1787. This group's mission, in his words, was "literary improvement" and "to enlarge the circle of . . . faculties, of which the human mind is capable." The members debated such topics as the virtuous or ill effects of novels, the nature of "compassion," the ethics of trading and commerce. They presented essays and original poems and bits of fiction. The Belles Lettres' membership included Brown's Latin School friends John Davidson and Joseph Bringhurst, other Quakers, and non-Quakers too. What the members had in common was youth, moral earnestness, and professional ambition. The club, which it seems evolved in the early 1790s into the Society for the Attainment of Useful Knowledge, was intended to promote the reasoning skills and literary style conducive to advancement and success in the professions. In Brown's words from the inaugural meeting, "It behooves us to make preparation for that awful crisis in choosing our future parts." Most of its members were in fact destined for successful careers in law, business, medicine, or religion, but not Brown.[24]

One curious poem Brown wrote during this Belles Lettres Club period reveals the nature of his difference from his Philadelphia peers. The poem, which appeared in the *State Gazette of North Carolina* in 1789, was supposed to be a tribute to the dying Benjamin Franklin, but the newspaper's editor took it upon himself to substitute the name "Washington" for "Franklin." As a result, what was really meant to be a celebratory "Inscription for Franklin's Tomb Stone" was published as the celebratory "An Inscription for General Washington's Tomb Stone." Brown later complained about this editorial translation, which turned a eulogy on a philosopher into "a slander" on a general and president who, according to the verse, "never participated" in battle. What Brown never mentioned, however, was the sly game he was playing with the original poem. For his Franklin eulogy had its experiential root in the anti-Franklin Quaker and Tory community of Brown's own Revolutionary childhood. It had, that is, its own secret Brown family context.[25]

Brown's poem is a reworking of another poem that had been written as an *attack* on the Revolutionary Benjamin Franklin. The original 1770s text had read:

But to covet political fame
Was in him a degrading ambition;
The spark that from Lucifer came,
Enkindled the blaze of sedition.

The author of these words is unknown, though in the Philadelphia Quaker community they were attributed variously to the Quakers Hannah Griffitts or Deborah Norris. Whoever the author, the poem is in the 1770s genre of Griffitts's "Horrors of the Night," that sardonic commemoration of "the glorious" anti-Tory, anti-Quaker riots of July 4, 1777.[26]

So the aspiring "visionary" Charles Brown, writing a poem in 1788–89 Philadelphia *in honor* of Franklin, chose for his model a poem written in 1776–77 in condemnation of Franklin, a poem moreover written out of the horrific Revolutionary experience that was the Brown family's burden. Brown then transposed the wording of the poem to yield a panegyric upon Franklin. But as the poem passed beyond Brown's control, a newspaper editor chose to print it with Washington's name in place of Franklin's, so that the published poem, as Brown described it, consequently "turns with horror and disgust from those who have won the laurel of victory in the field of battle" to General Washington! Farce aside, the key biographical fact here is that Brown began his literary career, wittingly or unwittingly— and Brown was far too clever for the irony of his borrowing to have been unwitting—with a work apparently about one thing that was in its essence really about something else. And that something else was the Pennsylvania Revolution: *his* Pennsylvania Revolution.[27]

That Revolution, too, was vibrantly alive in the law office of Alexander Wilcocks, for Wilcocks had a partner, Benjamin Chew, a birthright Quaker turned Anglican who lived in an elegant town house on Third Street. Chew was the most distinguished lawyer in Philadelphia and Wilcocks's father-in-law. He had been chief justice of the Pennsylvania Supreme Court before the Revolution as well as the colony's attorney general, a councillor, and the Penn family's lawyer. In 1777, because of the powerful offices he had held under the previous regime, Chew was exiled by the Revolutionaries to New Jersey for nine months. After the Revolution, however, Chew resumed his private practice in the city in partnership with his son Benjamin, Jr., and son-in-law Alexander Wilcocks; and in 1791 he regained his pre-Revolutionary place as Pennsylvania's top judicial officer when Governor Thomas Mifflin appointed him president of the newly constituted High Court of Errors and Appeals.[28]

Yet Benjamin Chew's significance for Brown lies elsewhere. He had a daughter who was twenty years old when Charles entered the Wilcocks-Chew law office. Her name was Henrietta, and Charles Brown's training as a novelist began with her.

*   *   *

Scholars have disagreed over the true character of Brown's so-called Henrietta Letters. Their editor published them as a genuine correspondence between a perhaps pseudonymous "Henrietta G." and Charles Brockden Brown. A subsequent literary critic ridiculed this notion, viewing them as obvious "fictional letters." This critic also pointed out the "indisputable fact" that if the letters were real, the opening heading of "Tuesday, morn, August 7" dated them to 1787, 1792, or 1798, and then ruled out the 1787 date because Brown was only sixteen. Yet that *was* Brown's age in 1787 when he entered the law office of Alexander Wilcocks and when he would have come into contact with Benjamin Chew's daughter Henrietta. And Brown explicitly says in a 1792 letter that "It was in the Summer of the year 1788, during my connection with the excellent and amiable Henrietta G.— that I first read the Eloisa of Rousseau" and wrote and "finished a Romance, in the epistolary form and after the manner of Rousseau." (Jean-Jacques Rousseau's *Julie, ou La Nouvelle Héloïse* was translated into English as *The New Eloisa.*) Other clues from the Henrietta Letters themselves point to Henrietta Chew as *the* Henrietta in the text. "Henrietta," writes their author, "is no more than three years older than himself." Henrietta Chew was born in August 1767, which made her three years five months older than Brown. The text implies a social and religious chasm between "Henrietta" and

"C.B.B"; Henrietta Chew, a member of one of Pennsylvania's most prominent families, was baptized as an Anglican in Philadelphia's Christ Church.
"Henrietta"'s letters are delivered by "Rachel"; Henrietta Chew's family
owned four slaves, one of whom was named Rachel. The Henrietta Letters,
the evidence indicates, seem to be a production of 1788.[29]

Yet the Henrietta Letters are not, for the most part, "real" letters.
Occasioned by a real person and a real relationship—though, given the
social and religious divide, probably not a close, intimate relationship—
they effloresce into a world of their own. They are a fiction, too. In 1788,
the moralistic and self-consciously proper Brown would never have written
to Henrietta Chew about "that bosom which is criminal to name," baiting
her: "thinkest thou that I shall not be irresistibly tempted to touch [it], to
gaze with too much greediness at its enchanting undulations?" Nor would
he have brought up for discussion "the frightful precipice," by which is
meant sexual consummation between the two of them. Such passages in the
Henrietta Letters are the obvious products of Brown's imagination. On the
other hand, in reading to each other the first two parts of *Eloisa*, as Brown
reports he and Henrietta did in 1788, the two would have shared the titillating experience of these words of Rousseau: "the parts of your scattered
dress present to my ardent imagination those of your body that they conceal. . . . this corset so slender which touches and embraces . . . what an
enchanting form . . . in front two gentle curves . . . oh voluptuous sight . . .
the whalebone has yielded to the force of the impression . . . delicious
imprints, let me kiss you a thousand times! . . . Gods! Gods! What will it be
when. . . ." And Charles and Henrietta would have read together about
St. Preux's and Julie's sexual consummation, which is put into perspective
by this passage: "To pretend to be insensitive while in the grip of passion
. . . to speak always otherwise than we think, to disguise all we feel, to be
deceitful through obligation and to speak untruths through modesty—that
is the usual position of all girls my age. Thus we spend the prime of our
youth under the tyranny of propriety, which at length is augmented by that
of our parents who force us into an unsuitable marriage. But in vain are
our inclinations restrained; the heart gives laws only to itself."[30]

A curiosity in Brown's text is its heroine's two names. Sometimes she is
Henrietta, sometimes Harriet. Why *these* two names? The latter is not nor-
mally a diminutive of the former. Brown's "relationship" in 1787–88, clearly
the main subject of the Henrietta Letters, was with a Henrietta. Why, then,
does his fiction, his imagination, keep switching to "Harriet"? The answer,
it seems, is that Henrietta Chew had a younger sister by that name who
was fourteen in 1788 and who was one of Philadelphia's great beauties.
Abigail Adams, for one, took notice of her in the early 1790s, and President
Washington, also in the 1790s, was said to be particularly fond of her.
(Indeed, in 1796 when Washington went to Gilbert Stuart's studio to have

the famous "Landsdowne" portrait done, he took Henrietta's younger sister with him, reportedly to make him smile.) In her beauty, her charm, her pedigree, her apparent *destiny*, Harriet Chew was clearly beyond a lowly legal apprentice's social reach, and she did in fact marry the son of one of the richest men in the United States, Charles Carroll of Carrollton. But she was not beyond his imagination's reach, as indicated by the text of Brown's first epistolary fiction.[31]

The Henrietta Letters are a milestone in Charles Brown's literary growth. They embody his first extended venture in the pleasures of what he calls the "unsanctified imagination," out of which he is beginning to make his fiction. Brown, moreover, knows what he is doing. He is purposefully cultivating a talent. A few years later, in a letter to his friend Joseph Bringhurst, Brown underscored the lesson learned. At the time Brown was writing a vignette, headed "Cuilli: Pays de Vaud," about "*Ma Petite Espouse*," Jacquilette—a fourteen-year-old—followed by this admission: "O my friend! How miserable should I be were I not rescued from the tedious or distasteful present, by the aid of an excursive imagination." In another letter to Bringhurst, headed "The Cocoa Tree. Pall Mall. London," Brown tells of his ventures in England, an upcoming trip to Switzerland, and his love for a "female" he hopes to marry. He says he writes "anonymous remarks for the London Chronicle." Then he shifts to the "Vine Street [Philadelphia] Sunday Morn" reality:

With what regret do I percieve that all this is the painting of my fancy only! And yet why may not imagination supply the place of reality? Why cannot the tongue and pen keep pace with the rapidity of thought! I laid aside the love-retracing pen last night at one oclock, and throwing myself on my bed spent an hour as delightfuly, in weaving the web of pleasing and fictitious narrative, as I remember to have spent any *unimpassioned* hour in my life.

What Brown is telling his friend here, what he is showing his friend, is that "reverie," allowing "ideas and incidents" to pass freely "in my mind," is at once emotionally consoling, fun, and the gist of literary art. It is also, as practiced in the Henrietta Letters, revelatory of Charles Brown, his imagination, and the tenor of one of his late 1780s Philadelphia relationships.[32]

Letter 1, dated "Tuesday, morn, August 7," reads like an actual letter from Henrietta Chew.

I am never so happy as when employed in writing to my friend; and I am willing to persuade myself that he receives no less pleasure from answering than I from the composition of my letters. . . . I know you value yourself extremely, and with justice, on the ease and vigor and correctness of your style. . . . How much more is my ear delighted in listening to thy amiable enthusiasm, to thy tender and pathetical effusions that bespeak the candor and sincerity of thy love than to all the volubilities and prettiness that compose a fashionable circle!

These sentences capture the way a twenty-year-old daughter of Benjamin Chew would write to the unusual and extremely literate sixteen-year-old student in her father's law office. And the closing "P.S. Rachel will put this into your hand" is how such a letter would get from the Third Street Chew household to Charles Brown. The only note that does not seem likely is the "thy"s, which the Anglican Henrietta would not use, unless she was entering into Brown's playacting spirit.

With letter 2, C.B.B.'s response, the fictionizing and fantasizing begin in earnest. Datelined, in the best concentrated tradition of Richardson and Rousseau, "Tuesday afternoon: Aug. 7," it lets the persona Brown will later dub the "Rhapsodist" loose. "I deliver the suggestions of my heart. I speak in my native character." Addressed to "Harriet," it runs on: "My imagination accompanied you to your chamber. She is alone (said I); her couch receives her; she sleeps. Why am I excluded? Would my presence profane the chamber? I yet feel the warmth of her embraces. They have made me miserable. To what a precipice have they conducted me? . . . Encircled by those arms and leaning on that bosom—felicity unspeakable! . . . Be my guide, my genius, my *spouse*."[33]

Subsequent letters seemingly seesaw between fact and fiction. In letter 8, for instance, Brown appears in character, writing to Henrietta Chew: "How charming are our interviews! How do I delight in recalling the circumstances of them to my memory! in community with you, in spending the night as I spent the evening, in thinking over all the thoughts that were in my mind and in repeating all the words that flowed from my lips while in company with you." Henrietta's response sounds like Henrietta Chew: "For how often have I told you that I feel a reciprocal affection for my youthful friend, and that I will not allow myself to be exceeded by him in the ardor and sincerity of my attachment." But that "Saturday Morn. 6 o'clock" signals the hyperagitated Rhapsodist again, and indeed there *he* is in "Henrietta"'s "Thou saucy and impetuous creature! Dost thou think thou has a property in my lips or that I will suffer such perplexing and incessant interruption from thy kisses? In good sooth I will act with more discretion for the future."[34]

In her next letter the very style of Henrietta/Harriet disappears; *she* is now using Charles Brown's distinctive diction. Words like "divination" and "Avaunt ye, horrid spectres" intrude, as does the passage "If you will continually disobey me, shall I not begin at length to question your fidelity, and in consequence renounce your allegiance. And this I suppose will be a terrible disaster, will convert the visionary into a maniac and crowd his fancy with horrid images of self-inflicted vengeance and destruction." Though delivered in a "Henrietta" letter, Brown is talking about himself.[35]

The actual person, the talking voice of Henrietta Chew, as it were, is perhaps discernible in the exchanges between the young urban woman craving cultivated conversation and knowledge and "my tutor." What she could have found in Charles Brown, her "youthful friend," is obvious. She was well read but informally educated; he was formally educated and could supply vital guidance. He was also very fluent in that lingua franca of their generation, the language of sensibility. And, perhaps not least, as an unsure sixteen-year-old Quaker, he could be counted on to be pliant. He was not an aggressive threat. What Brown found in Henrietta is equally obvious: the allure of sex and the opportunity to indulge his sentimental, Romantic side. As well, the two shared a profound Revolutionary experience, for they were both Philadelphia exiles' children. Thus, when "C.B.B" writes, "I have been a witness of various scenes and experienced many vicissitudes of fortune," Henrietta Chew was in a position to know that this was not just a literary conceit. And when C.B.B. deflects his correspondent's request for a detailed personal narrative with the line "no instructions could be derived from the melancholy tale equal to the severity of those wounds which your sensibility would inevitably suffer," Charles Brown was telling Henrietta Chew a literal truth. For in her mind, without doubt, the year 1777–78 was best forgotten. [36]

As for Henrietta's alter ego, "Harriet," *her* function in the text becomes clear in letter 11, when, like Rousseau's St. Preux, the hero gets to indulge "fatal reveries." *In imagination,* C.B.B. is hidden in her closet, and she is in her bedroom, and . . . she opens the closet door and exposes herself, in her "night dress."

How suitably adapted to the purpose of love! to shroud without obscuring your resplendent beauties, to shade without concealing that angelic [?] bosom. Could my eyes be otherwise than intoxicated by the sight. . . . What effect, my Harriet! must all these circumstances have unavoidably produced on a rambling and unsanctified imagination like mine? Was it possible for my glance to have been less passionate and eager.[37]

Charles Brown is enjoying through "unsanctified imagination"—six years before Monk Lewis would enjoy the "heavenly" Antonio through Ambrosia's magic mirror—the erotic spectacle of the future belle of Philadelphia in a state of undress, thinking of himself and her on the "verge of the precipice," and imagining their going off to get married. As Brown exclaimed to Bringhurst after another bit of fiction-making: "Hah! Hah! Hah! Bravissimo!" It was an indulgence of fantasy and an exercise of *un*sanctity that Brown would learn to push to extremes and nurture into his Gothic aesthetic.[38]

Eventually, though, in 1788 the fiction must end, and as the Henrietta Letters wind toward their close, they settle into some of the more prosaic truths of Brown's Philadelphia. These come in the final letters. "I saw myself obscure and mean," C.B.B. writes, "enrolled by adversity in the lowest ranks of mankind; distinguished from the rabble only by the love of literature. . . . I loved to indulge in visionary transports. . . . But the want of opportunities, of experience, and the consciousness of my obscurity and the meanness of my situation confined me to the region of fiction, and the only source of entertainment from my powers consisted in my own reflection." Then he had met Henrietta and "discovered with rapture and astonishment that those emotions which I had hitherto delighted to feign had suddenly become real, that I was actually enamored of an object that visibly and indisputably existed."[39]

*   *   *

Between 1787 and 1793 Brown worked at becoming a visionary writer. His main literary model was Rousseau. In the Henrietta Letters, Brown attempted a primitive version of Rousseau's *Eloisa*. In the 1789 "Rhapsodist," he can be observed cultivating the manner of Rousseau's *Reveries of a Solitary Walker*. In this work, Rousseau announces his literary design this way: "Having . . . formed the project of describing the habitual state of my soul . . . I saw no method of executing it, so simple, and so sure, as keeping a faithful record of my solitary walks and the meditations which accompanied them when I leave my mind free, and my ideas follow their propensity without resistance or constraint." What results from these walks and the associations and memories, the "reveries," they spawn, is a series of literary excursions on such topics as happiness/unhappiness, botanizing and the joys of nature, when to lie/when to tell the truth, the pleasures of imagination, and, most centrally, the ever-present persecution suffered by the egomaniac Jean-Jacques Rousseau. *Reveries* was first published in 1782, annexed to *The Confessions*, and was readily available in Philadelphia by the mid-1780s in both French and English versions. Brown probably read it, but no direct evidence exists to prove that he did. Yet perhaps Brown, who was self-absorbed and self-indulgently imaginative in precisely the way of Rousseau, which was the emerging "Romantic" way, concocted the "reverie" method out of his own resources and tendencies.[40]

Four installments of "The Rhapsodist" appeared in Philadelphia's *Universal Asylum and Columbian Magazine* between August and November 1789. In Rhapsodist 1, its author begins to define who he is. "A rhapsodist," he informs, "is one who delivers the sentiments suggested by the moment in artless and unpremeditated language. . . . He pours forth the effusions of a sprightly fancy, and describes the devious wanderings of a quick but thoughtful mind." Rhapsodist 2 fills out the portrait. A rhapsodist is fond of "solitude." He

loves to converse with beings of his own creation. . . . To his strong and vivid fancy, there is scarcely a piece of mere unanimated matter existing in the universe. His presence inspires . . . being, instinct, and reason into every object, real or imagined . . . . He turns from the feast of reason and ridicule with the same unsurmountable disgust, and waits impatiently for the hour of departure, when he shall be left to the enjoyment of himself, and to the freedom of his own thoughts. It is only when alone that he exerts his faculties with vigour, and exults in the consciousness of his own existence.[41]

Brown's Rhapsodist, in sum, for whom life "is literally a dream," is akin to Rousseau's daydreaming solitary walker, as he is a renamed version of Brown's own visionary self. More broadly, he is an expression of the radically individualist spirit then announcing itself throughout Germany, France, and England, and whose most famous early expressions were *La Nouvelle Héloïse* itself (1761) and Goethe's *The Sorrows of Young Werther* (1774). In the American setting, Brown was precocious in this strain, and his youth and limited experience show. Where the elderly Rousseau's reveries touch upon amazing plots and conspiracies, famous philosophes, Parisian adventures, and elegant communings with nature, the eighteen-year-old Brown's thoughts never really drift anywhere. There is no convincing experience behind them. The resulting text is juvenile and thin, as it had to be, and the teenage Brown is finally forced to admit in Rhapsodist 3: "I am indeed at present little more than a Rhapsodist in theory." Yet the performance does signify Brown's launching as a "visionary" on a literary quest that, in its own proper time, would generate its own powerful and authentic visions.[42]

Brown worked at developing this literary technique in the late 1780s and early 1790s, as his letters to his two closest friends from this period reveal. One friend, William Wood Wilkins, a year younger than Brown, was a Quaker from Woodbury, New Jersey, who had attended the Quaker Grammar School in Philadelphia and then began a law apprenticeship. Introduced to Brown in 1789 by mutual friends, in July 1789 he joined the Belles Lettres Club. Almost immediately, it seems, Brown and he struck up a special friendship, with Brown coming to deem Wilkins "my Other self." By the end of 1792, the two moved into an apartment together.[43]

Their relationship, like Brown's with his "Henrietta," could be termed Romantic. Literature was very important to them, and they strove to feel deeply the way Goethe's or Rousseau's characters feel. In Brown's ardent words, "the fictions of Romance must be realized." Accordingly, the two unveiled their souls to each other; they had spats; they abjectly and profusely apologized; and then they started all over again. They were self-consciously part of a most special group. While they socialized with the ten or so members of their literary society, only themselves and Joseph Bringhurst were truly "kindred spirits." Their concerns were friendship, love, sincerity, sensibility, true morality. In personality, Wilkins—"thou man of infinite jest"—was the lighter of the two. Sometimes he was too light. "I am conscious," he said to Brown, "that I often offend your Understandings and sometimes wound your Delicacy by unpardonable Levity and Carelessness."

Brown was the heavier. Oftentimes, he was too heavy. "Being!" he could write to Wilkins, "What is it but a burthen? Let me throw it from my shoulders. . . . To perish forever To sleep without Interruptions—How desirable and yet how dreadful." Their relationship was suffused with tension, but not, as in Brown's relationship with Henrietta/"Henrietta," overt sexuality. What instead charged them was the weight of the future. What would they make of themselves and their special talents?[44]

Wilkins, for all his literary pretensions, was set on a career in law. "I want to be *rich*, Charles," he asserted. He planned to be an "attorney at Law" in 1793 and to apply for a commission as "counsellor at law" in 1796. (What he didn't anticipate was his death in 1795.) Brown, just as resolutely, was set on a career in literature. This ambition exudes from the correspondence and it illuminates Brown's place in early 1790s Philadelphia. In this transition period to the Romantic age, many young men and women were devotees of "sentiment" and "belles lettres." Aside from the legal tomes of Blackstone and Viner and the texts of Aristotle, Plato, Milton, Locke, Hume, and others that were the prerequisites for professional careers, young Philadelphians relished the novels of Rousseau and Richardson and Goethe, among others. For them, matters of "virtue" and "vice" were cast in the domestic situations of Clarissa and Lovelace, Werther and Charlotte, St. Preux and Julie. Charles Brown was one of these youths. What was different, what was in fact truly special about him, was that in his widening circle of acquaintances, he alone wanted and tried to write his own fictions in the manner of Rousseau and Richardson.[45]

Thus in letters to Wilkins he drifted in and out of "reality." When drifting *out*, he was a self-professed visionary "not answerable for his sentiments or actions," and he turned Wilkins, in effect, into his "Julie." Wilkins served as his conduit into experience. "I will willingly become a pupil to you and be taught, by my amorous friend, the art and mystery of a Lover," he wrote. In the event, he recounted dreams. He spoke of "a prostitute." Aping the orthography of Rousseau and Richardson, he experimented with style: "I grow unsufferably weary. I must sleep— doze, I mean; pos-itively I-m-m-ust sl-sle-sleep—." Then, in a concentrated moment, he let himself become *Jean-Jacques Brown*, in a letter to Wilkins datelined "Cuilli Pays de Vaud. Wednesday morn":

I am now in the midst of a delightful country. . . . Here am I immured in pleasing and enchanting solitude, banqueting on classical literature, or conversing with rural simplicity. . . . I shall only mention that I live with an honest and thrifty husbandman, riot daily in the innocent and healthful luxury of wine, cheese, and butter, and am, (would you think it?) preceptor to my landlord's youngest daughter, who, possessing a fine understanding, a taste for reading, and a delicate constitution, her father is determined shall become a woman of importance. I am afraid, my friend, that my destiny is fixed, my matrimonial destiny, I mean, and that I shall live and die at the feet of Jacquelette. . . . *ma petite espouse*, for thus I always distinguish her from her equally beautiful but less accomplished sisters.[46]

Brown was imagining himself, à la Rousseau, as the Swiss St. Preux and Jacquelette was his "Julie." Only in this way could he write about exotic visits in the Franche-Comté and to Geneva. His felt bugbear, as a writer, was lack of experience. So, it would seem, in order to write like Rousseau, like Richardson, he had to make it all up. Except that Charles Brown didn't make it all up. Even here, the "honest and thrifty husbandman" is recognizably Wilkins himself, "the banks of the lake" he sits on are the Delaware's or Schuylkill's, and no doubt the pupil, "my landlord's youngest daughter," is an actual Philadelphian. Brown embellished, exaggerated, transposed, fantasized. But what he wrote was grounded in verifiable experience. And in memory.

*   *   *

Brown's people, the Quakers, were supposed to cultivate their visionary powers, and Brown's own family boasted some notable visionaries. But Quaker "visions" were most definitely *not* supposed to lead to novels or "fiction." In Charles Brown's case, though, they did, and this marks him as unique both in his own Quaker community and in 1790s America at large. Yet in the broader Atlantic literary world Brown was not entirely alone in his quest. Two contemporary visionaries, Wordsworth and Coleridge, were fellow travelers. Though different from Brown in nationality and denominational heritage, these two shared with him, along with family roots in rural seventeenth-century England, the encompassing Romantic frame of late eighteenth-century British-European-American culture. Like Brown, they were in search of "vision." Like them, Brown found great pleasure in the powers of youthful imagination. And for all three inchoate literary careers, the subject of "revolution" occupied a central place. In Brown's Philadelphia case, however, the experience of revolution was physical, brutal, and morally disorienting. It was this, in the end, that diverted his literary course into its peculiar channel, as a brief comparison of Brown with the young Wordsworth and Coleridge helps to show. English Romantics, so much like Brown in their "visionary" creative techniques, liked reading Gothic novels; Charles Brown, an idiosyncratic American case, went on to write and publish them.[47]

William Wordsworth was a year older than Brown. Born in 1770 and brought up in the Lake District of England, he lost his mother in 1778, and thereby the boy who loved to ramble amid woods and streams and crags lost his home. Along with his brothers, but separated from his sister, he moved to the village of Hawkshead, where he boarded with a stranger and attended the grammar school. A few years later his father died. In 1787 Wordsworth moved on to Cambridge University. In 1790, and again in 1791–92, Wordsworth traveled to revolutionary France in search of an animating idealism. What he found there, initially, was the feeling of "bliss . . .

to be alive," but as the Revolution soured, so did the feeling, and by the time he resettled in rural England in the mid-1790s, the Revolution was the great letdown of the age. Somehow, it was to be transcended through "vision." Accordingly, in 1795 to 1797, amid the natural splendors first of Dorset and then of the West Country, Wordsworth sought to cultivate his "visionary power" in earnest and with discipline. Out of this effort came "Tintern Abbey" and his other contributions to *Lyrical Ballads* (1798). Then, with the early draft of "The Prelude" in 1799 and its development in 1803 to 1805, Wordsworth's visionary power proliferated.[48]

Prelude was Wordsworth's self-conscious quest into his experience and imagination. What Wordsworth discovered, amid "unmanageable thoughts" and "a voice / That flowed along my dreams," was a fundamentally whole-some and recuperative force.

What beauteous pictures now
Rose in harmonious imagery! They rose
As from some distant region of my soul
And came along like dreams.

Wordsworth was especially interested in the precincts of his childhood, which he deemed "the hiding-places of my power." Searching these "days gone by / Come back upon me from the dawn almost / of Life," he found "A Child" who "held unconscious intercourse with the eternal beauty." He found

the charm
Of visionary things, and lovely forms
And sweet sensations, that throw back our life
And make our infancy a visible scene
On which the sun is shining.

And he found, at the heart of himself and his imagination, a blessedly "cheerful confidence in things to come." His literary "reverie," that is, ulti-mately led him to the happy and benign "consecrating" power that his "Imagination" and external "Nature" shared in common. From this source he would generate his mature poetry.[49]

Samuel Taylor Coleridge was a year younger than Brown. He was born in 1772 in the West Country town of Ottery St. Mary, Devon, where his father was the vicar. Though he did his share of exploring the surrounding fields and the course of the River Otter, Coleridge's early existence was more town-centered than Wordsworth's. (In a later poem, when the adult Coleridge dreams of "my sweet birth-place," he sees "the old church-tower / Whose bells, the poor man's only music, rang / From morn to evening, all the hot Fair-day.") The youngest child in a large family, Coleridge's ener-gies and truly exceptional talents were dedicated to discovering ways to draw attention to himself.[50]

The year 1779 was a watershed for Coleridge's imagination. First he fell victim to an epidemic of the deadly "putrid fever," and while lying ill he had the first of what would prove a lifetime of riveting and profoundly unsettling nightmares. The same year he underwent what he later deemed the pivotal emotional experience of his life. In the midst of a vicious fight with a brother (according to Coleridge, his brother gave him a "severe blow" in the face, after which Coleridge ran at his brother with a knife), his mother came in and grabbed Coleridge by the arm. Expecting a flogging, Coleridge broke away from her and ran off into the fields and woods, finally hiding himself under a bridge, where he fell asleep. That night half the town turned out in search of the missing Samuel. When he awoke the next morning, he could see off in the distance "the Shepherds and Workmen" looking for him, but he was frozen and too weak to move and had no voice to call out. He thought he was going to die. A fox-hunting squire found him and brought him home, where his mother greeted him not with a cudgel but with joy.[51]

Coleridge's childhood world ended abruptly in 1781 with the death of his father. All at once, the family's material and social circumstances collapsed, and Coleridge was shipped off to London's Christ's Hospital, the "blue-coat charity school," where he now spent almost a decade "'mid cloisters dim" where he "saw nought lovely but the sky and stars." A brilliant student, Coleridge moved on to Cambridge University in 1791. Here, like Wordsworth two years earlier, he sought idealistic meaning in the struggles of the French Revolution. Eventually, radical politics, Unitarian theology, and a passion for poetry, science, and nature drew him into a scheme to establish a radical commune in, of all places, Pennsylvania. Inspired by Rousseau and William Godwin, among others, Coleridge and "a small Company of chosen Individuals" formed the plan "of trying the experiment of human Perfectibility" on the banks of the Susquehanna River. He hoped to have this "Pantisocracy" or "all-governing-society" in place by September 1795, but the plan never amounted to anything. Coleridge left Cambridge in late 1794 and traveled; in 1795 he married and moved to Bristol. He made his living as a freelance writer and lecturer on politics and religion. In late 1796, in search of a creative base "to muse on fundamental & general causes," he moved back to his native West Country. There his friendship with Wordsworth and his visionary power blossomed.[52]

Coleridge composed "Kubla Khan" (he later said) "in a sort of Reverie brought on by two grains of Opium . . . in the fall of the year, 1797." In this poem his imagination discovered a "deep romantic chasm which slanted / Down the green hill athwart a cedarn cover! / A savage place!" where, "'mid this tumult Kubla heard from far / Ancestral voices prophesying war!" The next year, in the alternately sublime and nightmarish landscapes of "The Rime of the Ancient Mariner," and in the central drama of the poem, which involves a terrible sin, a rejected man who suffers exile, a craving for "home," and a return home, but under transformed and unsatisfying circumstances, he tapped the archetypal vein of his experience.[53]

Charles Brown's "rhapsodizing" needs to be viewed in this broader Romantic-era context. For like Wordsworth and Coleridge, Brown was committed to achieving "the consciousness of his own existence," to seeking out his "visionary" self. By his Quaker upbringing too, he was charged to find, in Wordsworth's phrase, "the mind's Internal echo." And as with them, historical *revolution* was to play a key part in the process.[54]

To Coleridge and Wordsworth, "revolution" meant the French Revolution and its shock waves. For a period, Coleridge indulged in Jacobin-edged radical politics in England and was at one point under surveillance by agents of William Pitt's Tory ministry. Yet he was always too mysterious, too incomprehensible, too unconventional in every way ever to be in any real danger for his views or actions. Besides, he abhorred the atheistic simplifications of the Revolution as much as Edmund Burke did. Wordsworth was the more polemically radical of the two, and he nursed a real sympathy with the efforts of the French Jacobins. If, as well, he had published some of the things he wrote in the early to mid-1790s, he would have been in trouble with the English authorities and likely would have faced the rigors of the treason acts. Yet, always, Wordsworth held back. Ultimately the Revolution was an abstraction for him. He makes this point in *Prelude*, where he says of his pilgrimage to revolutionary France: "I looked for something which I could not find, / Affecting more emotion than I felt." Consider too his poetic relation and experience of the 1792 September Massacres, when over a five-day period Parisian mobs murdered some one thousand prisoners. Wordsworth was in France at the time, staying in either Blois or Orléans. A month later he traveled to Paris and visited the place where the dead and dying had been "upheap'd." That night, he writes in *Prelude*, he didn't sleep.

The fear gone by
Pressed on me almost like a fear to come.
I thought of those September massacres,
Divided from me by a little month,
And felt and touched them, a substantial dread.

And yet now, in October, the square was quiet and peaceful, as those five days in September had been for Wordsworth.[55]

For Charles Brown and *his* visionary quest, on the other hand, there could never be anything abstract in "revolution"; nor could he ever feel "divided" from its force. His revolution was longer-running than Wordsworth's and Coleridge's. Starting with the anti-Quaker riots of post-1775 Philadelphia and exploding with the Revolutionaries' arrest and exile of his father in 1777–78, it bled into "theirs" in the 1790s as French revolutionary politics penetrated America. But the visions the American Revolution generated in Brown were unlike those of his two English contemporaries.

Wordsworth's visions tended toward the pastoral and Coleridge's toward the exotic and sublime. Brown's, spawned in the soil of Quaker Philadelphia, materialized in dark Gothic forms.

*   *   *

In writing the Henrietta Letters, Brown had begun to cultivate his visionary powers, but in a blatantly derivative manner. He was trying to match his limited experience to the format of Rousseau's *Eloisa.* His correspondence with Wilkins continued this vein. By the early 1790s, though, Brown began to experiment in a new direction, as he started to let his "reveries" move away from European models and into the precincts of his own most profound experience. His first forays were in letters to the dear friend who "knowest more than any other."[56]

Joseph Bringhurst, a hardware merchant, was four years older than Brown. His family were prominent members of the Philadelphia Meeting. In September 1777 both Joseph's father and uncle had signed a remonstrance, sent by the city's Quaker community to the Revolutionary Supreme Executive Council of Pennsylvania, protesting the arrest of Charles Brown's father and the other Quaker exiles-to-be. Presumably, too, the Bringhursts had been in Philadelphia during the subsequent anti-Tory and anti-Quaker riots, like that of October 1781. Brown's friend Bringhurst, therefore, who was age ten in 1777 and fourteen in 1781, was in a position to suspect what Brown was alluding to in mid-1792 when Brown wrote the following:

Suppose . . . I should tell you, that when eleven or twelve years of age I spent twelve hours in each day, that is, that I passed the night, for 8 months together in a *Jail.* In an apartment in which my chambers were hourly woken by the clanking of chains and bolts & iron doors. Where my ears were continually assailed by blasphemies or obscenities. Where there was a continual Suspicion of Inhabitants, of various and opposite characters, associated by Calamity. Wouldst thou place any credit in the narrative? I assure thee, my friend it is literally true.[57]

Was Brown being serious, or playfully literary? *My chambers hourly woken by the clanking of chains and bolts & iron doors. Assailed by blasphemies or obscenities.* This sounds like Ann Radcliffe and Monk Lewis. But it would have to be early Radcliffe—*The Castles of Athlin and Dunbayne* (1789)? *A Sicilian Romance* (1790)? —because *The Mysteries of Udolpho* had not yet been written. And it couldn't be Lewis, for he had not yet graduated from Cambridge. If inspired by a text, a good candidate might be Edmund Burke's 1790 *Reflections on the Revolution in France,* with its sensationalized description of Marie Antoinette's plight, wherein a "band of cruel ruffians and assassins, reeking with . . . blood, rushed into the chamber of the queen, and pierced with an hundred strokes of bayonets and poniards the bed, from whence this persecuted woman had but just time to fly almost naked."[58]

Or could it actually be *literally true?* The "eleven or twelve years of age" suggests the October 1781 Yorktown riot, when Brown was ten years nine months old. The "8 months together in a *Jail*" suggests the eight months of his father's exile in Virginia, when Elijah Brown was in a jail and the Brown family no doubt felt like they were in one. And as for the "clanking of chains and bolts & iron doors," the "blasphemies," "obscenities," the "Suspicion of Inhabitants . . . associated by Calamity": this evokes nothing so much as the searing and unforgettable Philadelphia experience of Charles Brown from his sixth year into his early teens.[59]

By 1792–93, it would seem, Brown had come to realize that he possessed a meaningful past. He further recognized that his experience could compel his art. His letter to Bringhurst continues:

Suffer your imagination to connect with this incident all the Circumstances by which it is accompanied. I will not enumerate them. I cannot bear the repetition. And then thou child of Sencibility! . . . tell me how thou wouldst have acted in similar circumstances or what emotions would the recollection produce. What Scenes could I describe!—and in what colours!—In every character of Son and Brother and man my sad experience has been too extensive.[60]

To his friends, to "Henrietta," Brown was always making veiled reference to my "sad," "mournful" experiences, and they always responded to him in the scripted Romantic way ("Oh Poor Charles"), or else they scolded him for his "delight in Mystery," lecturing him that "The man of Truth, Charles! the pupil of Reason, has no mysteries." What he was doing in these letters to Bringhurst, though, was exhibiting an excitement, a power, in his possession of this "experience." He reveals how he, as a writer, could draw on his memories and his emotions and transpose them into new concoctions. The exercise was painful, but it was creative too, maybe even powerfully so. Not the clichéd heartsickness of Rousseauean St. Preux-like characters, then, but the hydra head of *revolution* was to become Brown's special subject.[61]

*   *   *

And with news of the September Massacres in Paris reaching American shores in late 1792, the nation's capital was about to become the epicenter of the next "Jacobin" phase of the American Revolution.

In March 1793, word came to Philadelphia of Louis XVI's execution. (The American minister in Paris, Gouverneur Morris, wrote home to his government: "The late King of this Country has been publickly executed. He died in a Manner becoming his Dignity . . . On the Scaffold he attempted to speak but the commanding Officer . . . ordered the drums to be beat . . . The Executioners threw him down and were in such Haste as to let fall the Axe before his Neck was properly placed so that he was mangled.") In April President Washington issued his "Proclamation of Neutrality," with its call for American impartiality toward the "belligerent Powers" of Europe. In May arrived the new French republic's ambassador, "Citizen" Genet, carrying instructions from his government to draw the United States into cooperation with the French imperial struggle against England. Secretary of State Thomas Jefferson, for one, was delighted by Genet and the fillip the diplomat would give to American "liberty," and he was encouraged by the "thousands and thousands of the *yeomanry* of the city" that "crowded and covered" the wharves to greet Genet's frigate, the *Embuscade*. By late June and early July, though, Genet's antics—which included disobeying an explicit presidential order not to let sail a French privateer fitted out in Philadelphia in violation of the Neutrality Proclamation—disenchanted Jefferson to the point where he wrote to his friend and fellow pro-French partisan James Madison that "Never, in my opinion, was so calamitous an appointment made." At the same time the secretary of state urged Madison, "for god's sake," to "take up your pen" and "cut" the secretary of the treasury, Alexander Hamilton, "to peices in the face of the public."[62]

In Paris, in late July, the Jacobin Robespierre was named to the Committee of Public Safety, and in early September his fellow Jacobin Danton declared that "terror is the order of the day." Meanwhile in Philadelphia the political split within the ranks of the victorious American Revolutionaries, defined on one side by Hamilton's Whig fiscal policies and on the other by Jefferson's Whig agrarian dreams, grew wider and fiercer. Popular citizens' clubs, the Democratic-Republican societies, formed to promote French revolutionary ideals and police Washington administration policies. Only the outbreak of another sort of terror—a yellow fever epidemic—momentarily quieted the rising political violence. This contagion too had its "revolutionary" aspect, for it almost certainly arrived with a French émigré fleet in late July, early August. This veritable armada carried to Philadelphia thousands of white refugees, along with black slaves and free mulattos, who had survived the bloody events of the black slave rebellion on the island of Saint-Domingue. It also transported infected *Aedes aegypti* mosquitoes from the Caribbean, and between late August and October a viral terror, making absolutely no distinctions as to party or belief or ethnic tribe or race, killed almost one-tenth of the city's population.[63]

Chapter 3

Revolutionary Reverberations, 1793–1798

In October 1795, Charles Brown proclaimed himself a Godwinian, or at least he referred to the English atheist William Godwin's *Enquiry Concerning Political Justice* as "my Oracle." This is not surprising, for many young proto-Romantic writers and visionaries in the mid-1790s, Wordsworth and Coleridge among them, found in Godwin a guru of sorts. What does seem surprising, however, is that Brown's fifty-five-year-old father also busied himself with Godwin.[1]

There is in one of Elijah Brown's notebooks a long transcription from *Political Justice* that dates from before mid-1795. This follows a similarly long transcription from the feminist Mary Wollstonecraft's *An Historical and Moral View of the French Revolution*. Subsequent entries in the notebook, made between late 1795 and the end of 1796, include transcriptions from "A Confession of Faith—Containing 23 Articles—of the People Called Quakers" and assorted other English Quaker testimonies. These intellectual juxtapositions—atheistic rationalism, deistic feminism, "orthodox" Quakerism—seem bizarre, except that they perfectly express the devout and eccentric Quaker seeker that Elijah Brown was. And they do make logical sense, for in the 1790s there was no writer more relevant to Elijah Brown's experience and concerns than William Godwin. This makes Godwin absolutely essential to Charles Brown's experience and concerns, too.[2]

William Godwin, born in 1756 in Cambridgeshire Fens (about sixty miles from the ancestral Northamptonshire home of the Browns), dedicated himself as a youth to a simple enough proposition: "I will follow truth wherever she leads." The life that resulted led him first out of the Calvinist Dissenter faith of his minister father and grandfather, then out of Christianity altogether, and finally to renown as a philosopher and novelist in 1790s London. On the night of August 21, 1796, it led to sex with Mary Wollstonecraft—the man of truth was meticulous about these details in his diary—and thereafter to a short reign, with Wollstonecraft, as the British king and queen of what detractors came to call the Modern Philosophy. In a rare act of outright hypocrisy—hypocrisy because he deemed marriage, like the social practice of "gratitude," irrational and destructive in its tendency—Godwin married Wollstonecraft in a church ceremony in March

Mid-1790s New York: Federal Hall and Broad Street

1797, owing to the fact that she was pregnant and did not want to give birth to another illegitimate child. (She already had one.) He then compounded the lapse from truth by keeping the marriage secret for several weeks, until he returned to his Godwinian senses. The great intellectual partnership of the age ended tragically, though, for in September 1797 Mary Wollstonecraft Godwin died after giving birth to a daughter. When news of the sad event reached New York, an ardent young American Godwinian, Elihu Hubbard Smith, wrote in his diary: "The loss of 50,000 french & as many Austrians, on the Rhine or in Italy, would have affected me less."[3]

In the United States, Godwin was a relative unknown, a cult figure to bookish, iconoclastic young men like Smith (and Charles Brown), until he achieved overnight notoriety in 1799 with the American reprinting of his *Memoirs of the Author of a "Vindication of the Rights of Woman"*. American readers had generally been admirers of Mary Wollstonecraft and her pioneering *Rights of Woman* (1792), but her husband's unprecedented exercise in biographical truth-telling changed all that, as his portrait of his wife included her suicide attempts, graphically detailed ("The rain suggested to her the idea of walking up and down the bridge, till her clothes were thoroughly drenched and heavy with the wet. . . . She then leaped from the top of the bridge, but still seemed to find a difficulty in sinking"), her adulterous designs on the painter Henry Fuseli ("Mr. Fuseli was a married man, and his wife the acquaintance of Mary"), her "affair of the heart" relationship with the rakish American father of her first daughter, and the physical embarkation of their own relationship ("Mary rested her head upon the shoulder of her lover"—himself—"I had never loved till now. . . . We did not marry"). Godwin's *Memoirs* was as original and shocking as *Clarissa* and *The Monk*, and it set the cause of American feminism back decades. After 1799, to be a "Godwinian" in America was to carry the odor of atheism and sexual libertinism.[4]

Godwin wrote his masterwork, *Political Justice*, with the intention of transcending the partisanship and violence of French Revolutionary Europe. In England the initial enthusiasm which had greeted the fall of the Bastille in 1789 and the apparent French turn toward a constitutional monarchy had been challenged in 1790 by Edmund Burke's *Reflections on the Revolution in France*, a work which boldly predicted the bloody horrors that must follow in France from a revolution justified in terms of abstract principles about "natural rights." Burke's polemic in favor of British custom and tradition, of king and church and aristocratic privilege, provoked dozens of pro-Revolutionary responses, including Mary Wollstonecraft's own *Vindication of the Rights of Men*. But the most significant was Thomas Paine's two-part *Rights of Man* (1791, 1792), which ridiculed Burke's preference "for the authority of the dead over the rights and freedom of the living" and extolled the French revolutionaries for bringing more liberty and rights to France than England had ever enjoyed.[5]

Revolutionary violence came to England on July 14, 1791—Bastille Day—when a Tory mob in Birmingham chanting "Church and King" attacked and burned down two Dissenter meeting houses and the home, library, and laboratory of the pro-Revolutionary Unitarian minister and scientist Joseph Priestley and then destroyed the houses of other prosperous Dissenters, Quakers included. Similar "Church and King" riots subsequently broke out in Manchester and Nottingham. In response a pro-Revolutionary reform movement sprung up across Britain in 1792, taking the form of small-scale political clubs for which Paine's *Rights of Man* served as bible. (Analogous clubs, the Democratic-Republican societies, would emerge in the United States in 1793–94.) The Tory government of William Pitt countered by banning *Rights of Man* and issuing a proclamation against seditious writings in general. In December 1792 Thomas Paine was put on trial and convicted in absentia (he was in Paris) for seditious libel. Seven weeks later, and three weeks following the execution of Louis XVI in Paris, Godwin's *Enquiry Concerning Political Justice, and Its Influence on Modern Morals and Happiness* appeared.[6]

The book Charles Brown called his "Oracle" offers neither pro- nor anti-French revolutionary arguments, neither British Whig nor Tory polemics, but instead a dispassionate philosophical critique of the mainstream British political tradition of Lockean Whig liberalism. Where Locke and his myriad disciples—including the entire group of Americans who had made a revolution in Philadelphia in 1776 and defined a new nation in Philadelphia in 1787—outlined a political world in terms of "contracts" and "natural rights," Godwin envisioned a society grounded in principles of what he called pure philosophy or "science."[7]

Its atheism aside, *Political Justice*, in its single-minded pursuit of "truth" and in its criticisms of particular aspects of the modern European political world, is a very Quaker-like performance. The work as a whole is a critique of the historical institutions of "coercion" designed by human beings for purposes of power and order. None of these institutions or practices, for Godwin, are ultimately justifiable in a philosophical sense (though they may be justifiable as *temporary* expedients), for they all infringe on that highest and most essential thing, the individual conscience. Godwin, that is to say, is an anarchist. He is hostile to "government" in general and to all structures set up by groups of people to coerce other groups of people in thought and action. He is most critical of the most oppressive instances of "government," of those cases where coercive regimes trample most abusively on individual conscience.[8]

To follow Godwin from his general pronouncements about "truth" and "justice," through his understanding of how man can only approach these ideals by way of the unfettered expression of "private judgement," down into his specific discussions of how these "philosophical" ends are undermined in history by the coercive activities of "elites" and "parties," is to take (from one angle) a very Quakerish journey, especially since some of the key examples Godwin uses to illustrate his point, like the religious establishment laws, test acts, and oaths of mid- to late seventeenth-century England, were the historic formative ground of Quakerism itself. And for Pennsylvania Quakers in the 1790s to read Godwin's discussions of the manipulations and abuses of "political associations," especially in times of revolution, was for them to contemplate the all-too-familiar spectacle of Lockean liberalism in action, or what in their experience had been American Revolutionary Whiggism.[9]

It is in this sense that Godwin's radical rationalism, his belief that "truth is omnipotent," has a Quaker ring to it. When he writes, for example, that "If there be any truth more unquestionable than the rest, it is, that every man is bound to the exertion of his faculties in the discovery of right, and to the carrying into effect all the right with which he is acquainted," he could be stating the Quaker imperative for the individual at all times to seek truth. And when Godwin explains "the genuine principles of human society," how "truth" spreads through unfettered communication between individuals speaking their consciences—"in a state where every individual within the society, and every neighbour without, was capable of listening with sobriety to the dictates of reason"—he could, if "inner light" is substituted for "reason," be describing a Quaker meeting writ large. And William Penn himself could hardly improve on Godwin's general description of a righteous political order: "It were earnestly to be desired that each man was wise enough to govern himself without the intervention of any compulsory restraint; and, since government even in its best state is an evil the object principally to be aimed at is, that we should have as little of it as the general peace of human society will permit."[10]

Beneath the guiding ideals, too, when *Political Justice* gets down to the specifics of practical and revolutionary politics, it describes situations only too well known by Quakers—and little thought of by American Whigs like John Adams, Thomas Jefferson, and Alexander Hamilton, much less the Girondins and Jacobins bloodily fighting for control of France. The general problem with political associations, according to Godwin, is that in them "the object of each man is to identify his creed with that of his neighbour . . . [and to] learn the Shibboleth of a party." Such groups exist to "terrify the rest of the community from boldness of opinion, and chain them down to their prejudices, by the alarm which is excited by their turbulence of character." Yet "Truth can scarcely be acquired in crowded halls and amidst noisy debates." Godwin sees the cause of truth as especially hampered in times of revolution. In his words, "An attempt to scrutinise men's thoughts and punish their opinions is of all kinds of despotism the most odious; yet this attempt is peculiarly characteristic of a period of revolution." Nor does Godwin avoid the central irony and crux here: "Revolution is instigated by a horror against tyranny, yet its own tyranny is not without peculiar aggravations."[11]

In all, then, Godwin's *Political Justice* offers a rigorous critique of the central principles of Lockean liberalism and the Whiggism of the American Revolution, and this critique was in profound accord with the historical experiences, and cultural values, of Pennsylvania's Quakers. The Whigs' concepts of "rights" and "contracts" and "majorities," according to Godwin, are not the ultimate means to a righteous, "just" society. He makes the point in words that John Woolman or Anthony Benezet or John Churchman could have used: "There cannot be a more absurd proposition than that which affirms the right of doing wrong. . . . It cannot be too strongly inculcated, that societies and communities of men are in no case empowered to establish absurdity and injustice; that the voice of the people is not, as has sometimes been ridiculously asserted, 'the voice of truth and of God'; and that universal consent cannot convert wrong into right."[12]

It was certainly a message Elijah Brown, a born, bred, and duly persecuted Quaker, did not have to learn in the 1790s. Charles Brown too had been born into and weaned on this message as a Quaker son in Revolutionary Philadelphia. Accordingly, for him to proclaim himself a Godwinian in 1790s America was for him to assume a "political" stance perhaps only non-Whigs could comprehend. It was to take a perspective *outside* American Whiggism and therefore outside the first party struggle between Republicans and Federalists. A true Godwinian, as a true Quaker, could be neither of these. Instead he (or she) was that special person singled out in *Political Justice*:

The most insignificant individual ought to hold himself free to animadvert upon the decisions of the most august assembly; and other men are bound in justice to listen to him, in proportion to the soundness of his reasons, and the strength of his remarks, and not for any accessory advantages he may derive from rank or exterior importance.

Godwin, writing in mid-1790s England, was here expressing an ideal. The words, though, evoke a Pennsylvania historical reality. Charles Brown, for instance, only had to think of his great-uncle, John Churchman, to conjure up the local type of this "insignificant individual": the humble Nottingham farmer who, disturbed in 1748 by the Pennsylvania Assembly's decision to equip a warship, "requested the speaker [of the Assembly] that he would go in and inform the members, that a country man was in waiting who had a desire to be admitted, having something to communicate to them." This was the deepest ethos of Charles Brown's tribe.[13]

Only Charles Brown was a strange type of Quaker. The dislocations and transvaluations of the Revolution had seen to that. Nor could he be a good Godwinian. The Revolution had seen to that too. A good Godwinian, after all, was above everything "sincere," meaning clear, direct, "transparent" in thought, views, and speech. William Godwin himself was famously *sincere*, to the extent that when unwanted friends or visitors came to call at his house, he insisted on sending them away not with a polite servant-delivered "Mr. Godwin's not in" but with "Mr. Godwin doesn't feel like seeing you now." Charles Brown, on the other hand, was in his personality the obverse of sincere. He was, as his friends described him, in "disguise," "obscure & unintelligible," "mysterious." And he never *sincerely* told the truth about his own deepest experiences, except in his own way—through his fiction.[14]

*   *   *

While he continued for several more years to dangle before his family the hopeful prospect of a career in law, Brown in fact gave up the profession for good in the summer of 1793 when he left Alexander Wilcocks's law office and headed off to Connecticut to visit a new friend, the future Godwinian Elihu Hubbard Smith.

Brown was twenty-two years old, and on the eve of this, his first extended trip beyond the Delaware Valley Quaker pale, he had an anxious dream about himself and Joseph Bringhurst, which he related to his friend:

thou and I were wandering in the region of Romance: In Spensers fairy land . . . we were Pilgrims . . . going to perform our devotions: at the temple of some divinity: [whom] I know not but methought it was of great importance and that all our happiness depended on the success of our journey. Methought our way lay th[r]ough many wild, unknown and dangerous regions, but that perseverance at length placed us within sight of the temple, but, methought, between us and it flowed a streem, on the opposite bank of which the temple was erected, and that we could reach it, no otherwise than by passing through the river. This after many doubts and delays . . . we resolved to attempt and accordingly methought you lifted me in your arms and walked through the streem . . . but as soon as we had gained the opposite bank and were congratulating ourselves on the happy terminations of all our labours, a gigantic knight, arrayed in black armor and of fierce and terrible mein . . . rushed suddenly out of the neighbouring forest and seizing me who was speechless with afright placed me before him on a steed, who like himself was coal black, and inspite of all my cries and struggles, road furiously away with me into the wood. On looking back I thought I saw you still standing on the brink, but exhibiting marks of the utmost horror and despair. At length on the observing that you had irretreavably lost me, I thought you attempted to throw yourself in the Streem, but suddenly a woman, who methought was your mother, appeared behind you, and pulled you back.

The nightmare ended here with Brown awaking "in much distress and horror."[15]

Brown's first "exile amongst Aliens and Strangers" began in the Litchfield, Connecticut, home of Smith, whom Brown had met back in 1790–91 when Smith had attended medical lectures given by Benjamin Rush at the College of Philadelphia-University of Pennsylvania. Smith was the same age as Brown, and like Brown he was a self-conscious truth-seeker. Only where Brown carried a five-generation Quaker heritage, Smith trailed five generations of New England Puritanism behind him. Educated primarily by Congregational clergymen, Smith was already busy at the age of five, as he later wrote, "committing to memory & repeating every Sunday at home, & every Saturday at School, the Catechism of the Assembly of Divines at Westminster; besides the Lord's Prayer, night and morng., & a variety of other pious lullabies in rhyme." Sent to Yale in 1782, the preteen Smith mixed in (he later said) with sarcastic, dissipated, impious older youths, and in the exchange lost not only his Calvinist inheritance but his Christian faith altogether. After graduation, Smith was sent to Timothy Dwight's Greenfield Academy, where, under Dwight's intellectual prodding, he gained back his faith. But after a year in Greenfield, Smith returned home to Litchfield, and now his "doubts and difficulties" about the morality of Christian doctrine began "fast-growing." So when Brown met him in 1790– 91 Philadelphia, Elihu Smith, an aspiring doctor and poet, was a young man in the final phase of sloughing off once and for all the Christian doctrines of his heritage and upbringing—and worrying about how he was going to tell his pious parents, whom he knew would be devastated by the news.[16]

Brown's new friend was a young man of impressive social connections. The world Smith introduced Brown into included among its regulars: Theodore Dwight, a lawyer and the future secretary of the Hartford Convention (which in 1814–15 would seek New England's secession from the United States and its Virginian dynasty of presidents); Timothy Dwight, future president of Yale and future "pope" of Connecticut Congregationalism; Noah Webster, the future lexicographer, who had been Smith's music teacher; Oliver Wolcott, future secretary of the treasury; and Uriah Tracy, current Federalist congressman, future senator and staunch advocate of the Alien and Sedition Acts, and eventually, like Theodore Dwight, a leader in the secessionist Hartford Convention. These were the very people in the decades ahead who would lead the last Puritan stronghold, Federalist Connecticut, and its established Congregational Church against the encroaching tide of "Infidelity" and Jeffersonian Republicanism. Elihu Smith himself, after moving to New York, could worry about "the probability, or possibility, of my being prosecuted, on the Statute against Blasphemy, should I once again reside in Connecticut." Still, Smith was of *this* tribe, and these were his friends, and during the summer of 1793 Charles Brown deemed these "first people of Connecticut" remarkably interesting and kind. Among them, he wrote to Joseph Bringhurst, he felt like Rousseau's St. Preux in the wonderful Wolmar household.[17]

Elihu Smith was Brown's first close friend who was not a Quaker; and Brown, along with Joseph Bringhurst, seems to have been Smith's first close Quaker friend. Radically dissimilar in personalities—Brown being flighty, moody, and intellectually playful; while Smith was solid, unwaveringly earnest, and an intellectual literalist (it is in itself comic that Smith once contemplated writing a comedy)—what they shared was their quest for "the temple of Truth" and a sense of themselves as special and courageous, as "stand[ing], as it were, isolated from the rest of mankind," as indeed members of a new intellectual and moral elite. They could (quite seriously) refer to themselves and their ilk as *little children of Truth*," "conductors of virtue" who, in the interest of "our Philosophy," "disarm the lightnings of superstitious fury."[18]

Smith moved from Connecticut to New York in September 1793 to commence a medical practice. Finding too few patients to practice on, he dedicated most of his time to moral and cultural self-improvement. For the purpose, besides joining the Manumission Society, Smith in late 1793 to early 1794 began a social group, the Friendly Club, that gathered on Saturday evenings to discuss books, politics, poetry, philosophy, and religion. This club was marked by an undoctrinaire federalism and a commitment to "free thought" that courted the edges of unbelief. Its membership included the theater impresario and playwright William Dunlap, the young merchants Horace and Seth Johnson, the law professor and struggling lawyer (and future renowned jurist) James Kent, as well as Charles Adams, the ne'er-do-well son of the nation's vice president. Under Smith's prodding, club discussions persistently and variously took up the radical French Enlightenment doctrine of "the *perfectibility of man*," that is, the issue of whether mankind, through applied reason, could and would inevitably continue materially, intellectually, and morally to "improve"; and just as persistently discussions subjected the doctrines and institutions of Christianity to critical review. In this context, Godwin's *Political Justice*, published in 1793 and revised in 1796, acted as a goad to ever more radical debates.[19]

In the fall of 1793, Brown, needing "Money! Money! . . . the want of which is the first of miseries," took a job in Philadelphia as "master" of the Friends Grammar School. He thereby, in the wake of his Connecticut sojourn with the emergent unbeliever Elihu Smith, found himself in a position of religious responsibility vis-à-vis the tender minds of young Quaker pupils. This meant that whatever was going on in his imagination at this point, *externally* he had to be the very picture of Quaker piety.[20]

About this year in Brown's life there is sparse information. In late July, writing from Hartford, Brown had professed himself "not happy" on account that "None of my hopes have been fulfilled." Those hopes integrally involved his literary ambitions, and indeed, while he had yet to write anything of value in his own eyes, he had been working on short stories and thinking about story ideas when he returned to Philadelphia the first week in August.[21]

This was the week when the first cases of a strangely malignant fever were breaking out at a waterfront lodging house on the northern edge of town, some four blocks from 159 Vine Street, where Elijah Brown had moved his family in 1790. During the next ten days other instances of this violent and deadly fever appeared in the Water Street area. Elihu Smith's mentor, Dr. Benjamin Rush, brought in to investigate by the city's health authorities, concluded on August 19 that the cases were related and signified an epidemic of the "bilious remitting yellow fever." On August 23, city officials confirmed what people feared, that Philadelphia faced a pestilence. Three days later doctors requested that bells no longer be rung for funerals, as the sound was too dispiriting. A Philadelphian fleeing the city in late August described what he left behind as "A large City with the Houses shut up and the Streets empty except for the french Sailors, People of St. Domingo [Haiti] of all Colours with their Heads tied[,] a few Citizens whom you do not know posting along with Sponges in their noses and the Herse Constantly passing." By early September most residents who could do so either had left or were preparing to leave—and they would stay away until the first frosts of late October and early November killed off the contagion.[22]

According to the later testimony of a friend, Brown and his family fled the city in time to avoid the "influence" of the yellow fever. If so, the logical asylum for them would have been Uncle Richard Waln's New Jersey estate, Walnford. Charles Brown was certainly in the city at the plague's outbreak, though, and for an aspiring writer the experience was not without its benefits. A week before his return to Philadelphia, Brown had declared "domestic history"—"*Life & Manners*"—"my favourite science," and specified his desire to study "the personal character of individuals, their visages, their dress, their accent their language their habits, manners and opinions; their *personal behaviour*." Back in Philadelphia Brown contemplated his own potential literary domain in relation to the awesome accomplishment of Richardson's *Pamela, Clarissa*, and *Sir Charles Grandison*. Writing to Bringhurst, Brown noted that many of Richardson's "facts do not fall within the sp[h]ere of our own immediate observation." Still, he added hopefully, "how pregnant of strange events is our own domestic experience." Brown claimed to "have already imagined the leading incidents and general outlines of a tale" of his own. But in his "present situation," he grumbled, "it is absolutely impossible to begin it." This was written on August 16—three days before Benjamin Rush's diagnosis and six days before Philadelphians' worst fears were publicly confirmed. In very short order, then, Brown would get the chance to observe the "personal characters" of his Philadelphia neighbors in the face of a historic scourge, and from these "facts" would derive, over the next five years, his novel *Arthur Mervyn; or, Memoirs of the Year 1793*.[23]

The "present circumstances" that so depressed Brown in mid- to late 1793—which he said deprived him of "tranquility of mind and disembarrassment of views"—involved his penurious Philadelphia existence. His parents' Vine Street address matched Elijah Brown's straitened career. This was where in 1777 a "rabble" of boys had thrown stones at Elijah and his fellow exiles as they were being carted away by Revolutionaries to Virginia.

The neighborhood bordered on the outer edge of "Helltown," where at night the city's apprentices, servants, slaves, and sailors congregated to drink, carouse, gamble on cards, dice, cockfights, bull-baiting, and boxing matches, and sought out opium, Spanish flies, and prostitutes.[24]

Of his three older merchant brothers, at least two, James and Joseph, lived on their own in the vicinity of Grandma Elizabeth's South Second Street house. Charles, though, remained with his parents, and along with his mother, his sister Elizabeth, and younger brother Elijah, he was still a member in good standing of the Northern District Monthly Meeting. As for his employment, it cannot be established whether he continued at the grammar school after the 1793–94 session. What can be deduced, though, is that Charles Brown was under pressure from his family *to do something* a bit more remunerative, and he was holding them off by saying he was studying informally for the bar. Thus when his friend William Wilkins died in early 1795, Brown wrote to his brother James that "Wilkins' life was, indeed, the pledge of my success in the legal profession[.] It was necessary also to my qualification as an atorney. The knowledge that was necessary, most necessary, practical skill, the result of experience, was only [divinable?] from him." Why this would be the case is unclear, for surely Brown could "divine" practical skill from any number of attorneys he knew. Nevertheless, Charles now told his older brother that Wilkins's death "hath prevented me from fulfilling your expectations and obliged me to defer my admission till the succeeding term."[25]

In 1794 Brown began courting Debby Ferris, the pious Quaker daughter of a very pious Wilmington Quaker watchmaker, and both Brown and his best friend Joseph Bringhurst desired her. Brown, for his part, accorded Ferris something of the "Henrietta" treatment, showering her with his special brand of "poetical epistles." Bringhurst, meanwhile, wooed her as "my Laura," telling her that he was "thine Petrarch" and she was "absolutely necessary to my happiness—that without her society the world would be a desert, life an [unenviable] burthen to me." In the contest Bringhurst won out, and in March 1795 he and Debby became informally engaged. Brown conceded the issue to his friend later in the year, writing to Bringhurst that "Whatever might have formerly been my hopes, and thou knowest that they were not a little presumptious . . . to be her friend is the utmost limit of my present wishes." It can be surmised here that Brown, in reality, stood little chance with Debby Ferris, for apart from all other personal considerations, at this point in his life he was not pious enough for her; and Joseph Bringhurst was. And in any case Brown's friendship with Bringhurst was patently more important to him than any woman in these years, especially in view of the fact that of his three dearest companions in the world—John Davidson, William Wilkins, and Joseph Bringhurst—only Joseph was still alive.[26]

It was in the midst of these activities that Brown removed to New York for the summer of 1795 and there joined the heterodox discussions of the Friendly Club. (This gesture alone was hardly calculated to quicken Debby Ferris's affections.) As part of his initiation into this new circle—he was its only Quaker—Brown gathered with Smith and William Dunlap in the New Jersey countryside and enacted a makeshift ritual. A "three-partile Tree" was made the "emblem of our friendship," with the apparent moral being that, as the tree's three limbs matured and grew together—Charles's was "the slenderest one . . . which grew in the middle"—so too would the Smith-Brown-Dunlap bond.[27]

*   *   *

The streets of New York were not as flat or regular as Philadelphia's, and according to one French visitor, their "varied direction . . . makes the topography of this town difficult to follow." Yet the city resembled Philadelphia in its ethnic and religious diversity. In 1795 twenty-two houses of worship stood amid its 45,000 residents, running the gamut from Episcopal, Presbyterian, Methodist, Baptist, and Quaker, to Dutch Reformed, German Lutheran, Moravian, and French Protestant, to Roman Catholic and Jewish; and soon to come would be a Universalist Church and a Deistical Society. Like Philadelphia, too, New York in 1795 was in the opening phase of an immigration deluge from France, the French West Indies, Scotland, England, and especially Ireland. From September 1794 to September 1795 alone, some 1,000 to 1,200 new houses—most of shoddy, wooden construction—were built to accommodate the new arrivals. Also reminiscent of Philadelphia were the yellow fever summers, which struck New York consecutively in 1791, 1792, 1793, 1794, and which would strike again, in the most virulent strain yet, in 1795. Distinctly unlike Philadelphia, though, was the role of Quakers in the city's history and politics. In New York's early history Quakers were denied the franchise and up until the 1730s Quaker votes could still be challenged in elections; not until the 1770s could Quakers legally give evidence in criminal trials or hold high public office. There was nothing in New York like the silent but palpable authority of the Philadelphia Meeting. In its stead was the ubiquitous "bustle of trade."[28]

New York City changed Brown. Hitherto, as demanded by his Philadelphia Quaker heritage and surroundings, there had always been the veneer of Christian piety about him. For instance, in the Belles Lettres Club and the Society for the Attainment of Useful Knowledge, there was clearly a religious boundary beyond which discussion—and Brown—could not go. Members could debate the provocative question of the moral or immoral nature of suicide, but the subject of Christianity itself was not on the table. In New York a different standard prevailed. Not only was Christianity itself up for debate; Elihu Smith actively proselytized for unbelief. He was working on James Kent and Kent's wife. He would try to "convert" the wife of Uriah Tracy. And in Brown he thought he had a most impressive catch. Brown, to be sure, encouraged Smith in this notion, writing to Smith in mid-1796 that "Joseph [Bringhurst] . . . contemns our Philosophy." By "our Philosophy" Brown meant Godwinian rationalism, and Joseph Bringhurst did condemn this non-Christian doctrine, just as Elihu Hubbard Smith certainly embraced it. And Brown, just as certainly, *said* he embraced it. On the other hand, what did *the saying* mean from a man who could acknowledge that he "thought [him]self at liberty to vary circumstances, in the narration?"[29]

Brown's new manner appears in his letters to Bringhurst in October 1795—letters written at the time when Brown was coming to concede the fact that Debby Ferris preferred Bringhurst to himself. In his "old" pre-Friendly Club manner, Brown tempered his Romantic philosophizing with pious glosses. To his speculations about "the summits of piety and virtue" accessible to the heroic few—like "Bringhurst and Brown"—he would append: "Shall I not say that the life only of one virtuous man has been recorded for the instruction of mankind? I can only mean that of the divine *Son of Mary* . . . That he actually lived there is no doubt." Whatever Brown really meant by this, his phrasing allowed Bringhurst—or anybody else—to parse a Christian position. After the summer of 1795, though, Brown drops the drapery (though not the circuitous Brownian style). "I listen with respect to your arguments on the subject of Christianity," he writes to Bringhurst in October 1795, "but, my friend, we are far from well understanding each other on this subject."

If the moral precepts of Christ's are good they are mine because they are true, if bad nothing can induce me to esteem them good, and there can be no question about the propriety of endeavouring to exterminate pernicious and erronious doctrines. . . . If Christ was no more than Pythagoras or Socrates, the acceptance of his doctrines, moral or metaphysical, must depend upon their intrinsic evidence. . . . And in attacking these tenets [of Christianity], in reducing Christ to the rank of the Grecian Sages, do I assail the bulwarks of Christianity, in your opinion? I suppose you will answer yes. If so I can make no scruple to answer all your questions in the affirmative[:] "I really think Christianity, that is the belief of the divinity of Christ and future retribution, have been pernicious to mankind? That it has and does destroy friendship and benevolence? That it has created war and engendered hatred, and Entailed inexpressible calamities on mankind. . . ." I answer that these effects have flowed from the belief of the divinity of Christ and a belief of future retribution.

Brown concludes his feline performance with the more direct: "I once thought, as possibly, you now think that religious belief were desirable, even if it were erronious. I am now of a different opinion, and believe that utility must always be coincident to truth." In his next letter Brown clarifies the thing unsaid and danced around in the former. "By my Oracle I thought you would discover without more ado Godwins Enquiry."[30]

So there, *seemingly*, it is. Brown had come around to Smith's way of think-ing and he now opposed Bringhurst's Quaker faith. Yet as always with Brown the situation was more complicated than it might appear. In this case the complication involves a cultural or tribal divide: the fact that Brown and Bringhurst spoke in a personal language and a cultural code, the nuances of which were unknown to the New Englander Smith. Thus Smith was bound to be confused and misapprehend some of the things Brown said. Meanwhile Brown, the emerging romancer, was positioned to sport, if he so chose, with Smith's credulity.

From his perspective, Smith viewed Brown and Bringhurst as a bit odd in their quaintness of speech and manner, though attractively so. Smith even took to emulating their "bald-face stile," as he termed their Quaker-ish unpretentiousness—to the annoyance of his more pretentious, formalis-tic Connecticut friends like Theodore Dwight. (Dwight clearly considered Smith's new informality a sign not of Quaker influence but of revolution-ary "French" contamination.) During a business trip to Philadelphia in January 1796, Smith got the chance to observe the extended Brown clan close up when he was invited to stay at 117 South Second Street, which the elder Elijah and Mary Brown had moved back into. Here he met Charles's parents, siblings, and friends. To a New York correspondent he described the clan as "cheerful, intelligent, polished & well-informed, how infinitely are they removed, from the cypress-visaged, & selfish *Quakers* of New York!" (One reason Smith did not meet Quakers like this at the Brown home was because the Elijah Brown family didn't socialize with *those* blue-blood Quakers in Philadelphia—and hadn't since Elijah's embarrassing debt problems and disownment in the late 1760s.)[31]

While in Philadelphia, Elihu Smith failed to detect a tribal drama that was roiling the world of his Quaker friends.

Joseph Bringhurst and Debby Ferris had become engaged in the spring of 1795, and in late October Brown wrote to his friend about "You and Laura . . . marching, [slowly] perhaps, but certainly to the fare of Matrimony." Something unpleasant, however, was hovering over the heads of the couple, and it struck them in April 1796 when the Southern District Monthly Meet-ing announced its decision on a pending matter concerning the groom-to-be. "Joseph Bringhurst Jun. of this city," the Meeting reported,

thro inattention to the monitors of the spirit of Truth in his own mind, which sets bounds and limits to worldly pursuits and would have preserved him in Safety and consistency of conduct, hath launched into Trade and business beyond his ability to manage, and neglecting to keep his accounts in such proper order as to ascertain a clear state of his affairs, his Circumstances became much embarrassed and he failed in making payment for Goods, which, to a large Amount he had been interested with, Complaints thereof being made he was tenderly treated with and it appearing that his Creditors were likely to sustain a great loss he was advised to resign all his property into their hands and lay before them a just statement of his Situation, which he declined, and disposed of a considerable part of the Goods without making an equal distribution among his Creditors; and being compelled by the Laws of the land to give up his remaining Effects, they were then assigned to persons in trust for the benefit of the sufferers, being very far short of a sufficiency to satisfy their Demands.[32]

By "declining" the counsel of the Meeting Bringhurst had exposed himself to censure, and on April 27, 1796, the Society of Friends officially disowned him, "until from a right sense of his transgression he is enabled to condemn the same to satisfaction, and manifests a real concern for the promotion of the cause of Righteousness and Justice, by using his utmost endeavours to discharge his Debts." Bringhurst had an additional problem too. As the Meeting hints, Bringhurst is charged not just with commercial malfeasance and spiritual recalcitrance; there is allusion here to serious moral impropriety in the way he chose selectively to pay off his creditors. This part of the indictment was apparently still alive in January 1797, when Debby Ferris's brother wrote her about "this dreadful story" he had heard about Bringhurst. Unfortunately the brother does not recite in his letter the particulars of the case, but whatever they were, if true, it is unlikely Joseph Bringhurst would have had a viable commercial future in the Delaware Valley or anywhere the "dreadful story" was known. In any case, in order to marry the pious Debby Ferris, Joseph Bringhurst had to both disprove the rumor and take the humbling actions insisted on by the Meeting. Only in that way could he rejoin the Meeting, and hence reacquire the right to wed his fiancée.[33]

That Charles Brown was powerfully affected by his best friend's personal crisis is indicated by two letters Brown wrote to Elihu Smith in the immediate wake of Bringhurst's disownment. Brown's letters no longer exist, but Smith's responses to them do, and the nature of Brown's missives can be inferred from these. What is entirely clear is, first, that Brown wrote to Smith in his melancholy, self-pitying, allusive style and, second, that Smith had never received such a performance from Brown before. Thus Brown tells Smith (who is quoting from Brown's letter) that "[I] have been the child of passion, & inconsistency; the slave of desires that can not be honorably gratified; The Slave of hopes no less criminal, than fantastic"—to which Smith, uncomprehending, responds: "What, my friend, is the meaning of all this? And what am I to learn from this? Or, rather, what are *we*— Dunlap & Smith—to learn from it? If you meant that we should understand you, why were you not explicit. If you had no such intention, where was the necessity of introducing such a passage?"[34]

Brown had written many letters like this to Bringhurst and Wilkins, especially in 1792–93, and they had received them in the spirit of the Belles Lettres Club and their friendship. It was a style, a literary manner, and it was an emotional side of Brown, the mood he fell into when making oblique reference to his past traumatic experiences, like his father's imprisonment for debt or the horrors of wartime Philadelphia. Elihu Smith, in May 1796, responded to *this* Brown with annoyance and a good Godwinian dousing. "Why do you so much delight in Mystery?" he asked.

Do you, of choice, give to the simplest circumstances the air of fiction? or have you been so long accustomed to deal in visionary scenes, to intertwine the real with the imaginary, & to enwrap yourself in the mantle of ambiguous seeming, that your pen, involuntarily borrows the phraseology of fancy, & by the spell of magic words, still diffuses round you the mist of obscuring uncertainty? The man of Truth, Charles! the pupil of Reason, has no mysteries. He knows that former errors, do not constitute him guilty now—& he has nothing to conceal. He seeks only to know his duty, & perform it, & he has no occasion for disguise.

Smith continues: "Why will you continue to remind" your friends that "there are secrets? that you have science [knowledge], which they must not have? Why will you allude to misfortunes of which they are ignorant, & from which therefore, they can not relieve you? . . . Are you, yourself, conscious how much this is a prevailing fault, both in your speech & writing?"[35]

One of the "obscurities" Smith complains of is Brown's report of the travails of Joseph Bringhurst. Again, Brown's actual letter no longer exists, but here is what Smith says of it: "The passage in regard to Bringhurst . . . was so obscure as to leave me in doubt. You talked of the terror he had conceived of imprisonment, the value he set upon unimpeached integrity, &c. from whence I concluded that he had been in Jail, & had been declared insolvent &c." What Smith has done here is translate Brown's words—and Brown obviously provided additional information in his letter—into terms he, Smith, understood: namely, what bankruptcy entailed and meant in a place like New York. But Bringhurst's situation was far more complicated than that. From an old Delaware Valley Quaker family, he was an insolvent pious Quaker who, in the Quaker City, not only potentially faced what all bankrupt Americans faced—a court proceeding and debtors' prison— but was also caught in the coils of a traumatic tribal ritual. Moreover, Bringhurst had been all set to marry his beloved when this debacle broke, and now circumstances dictated that he could not marry her until he satisfied the stringent moral requirements of his tribe. Smith complains here about the "obscure," allusive language that Brown employs to relate his friend's difficulty, but Bringhurst's dilemma was so complex and so foreign to Smith's world that some such "artistic" license, on Brown's part, was perhaps called for to convey the true "terror" of Bringhurst's plight. (Or at least Brown chose to evoke it in this manner.) Elihu Smith, in any event, gathered from Brown's rendition that Bringhurst was in prison, which in fact he was not. And yet from Brown's perspective—Brown, whose own father had been disowned for debt, and whose father had thereafter suffered a marginal economic and moral position within the Quaker community, eventually landing in debtors' prison—to write allusively of "fear" and "terror," to *sensationalize* was a way to approach nearer to "the facts" of Joseph Bringhurst's ordeal.[36]

Smith was clearly stimulated by his extended exchange with this "side" of Brown. True to his profession and Godwinian philosophy, he got to act "the Physician," trying to bring health and order to Brown's condition. Brown, too, savored the exchange. Indeed, he can be detected playfully—creatively—manipulating Smith's earnestness, caring, and literal-mindedness. This is revealed in a letter he wrote to Bringhurst immediately after receiving Smith's initial, sometimes scolding letter. "I have just received a most charming letter from Elihu," Brown writes to Bringhurst. "I assure thee he plays the philosopher with singular grace. It is full of censures, indeed, but these censures manifest a soul, glowing with benevolence and dignity. I cannot tell thee how much those proofs of moral improvement delighted me." In his own developing Brownian way, it could be said, Charles Brown had Elihu Smith on a string.[37]

Here, then, is the spectacle of an artist manipulating his "materials" for unforeseen imaginative ends. Brown's basic resources are his own experiences and memories and emotions, and his tribe's history. What is happening, in 1795 to 1797, is that Brown, in the alien context of Elihu Smith's New York, is being provoked into looking at, into *re*conceiving, into recasting those materials in new and highly original ways.

Consider as one element of this context Elihu Hubbard Smith's "courtship" of the wife of Connecticut congressman Uriah Tracy.

Susan Ball had been one of Smith's childhood teachers, and the adult Smith remembered how as a four-year-old he was "often admitted to sit on her lap, receive her caresses, and she uncommonly beautiful & engaging." During a trip home to Litchfield in late 1795, Smith renewed his acquaintance with Susan Ball—now Susan Ball Tracy—and clearly he was captivated. Immediately he lay siege: not to her body—she was, after all, respectably married—but to her soul. Thus, while the two enjoyed each other's company in the late fall of 1795, they discussed Mary Wollstonecraft's works, William Godwin's novel *Caleb Williams,* and his *Political Justice* ("This last is in Town; & Mrs. T will read it"). By the time he was ready to leave Litchfield, Smith noted in his diary: "I am tolerably sure that when she has attended somewhat to the subject [of 'the principles of morals']—read Godwin, & other authors, which I will lend her to read, we shall not widely differ."[38]

Smith's romantic crush on Susan Tracy, who was twelve years his senior, is evident in his first letter to her following this visit. Writing from New York, Smith expressed his frustration that in Litchfield he had been obligated to visit so many family members and friends. As a result, he told Susan Tracy, he had not been free to do what he really wanted, which, "unless it were possible, (which it is not)," was to "confine my visits to a single family, & almost *to a single individual.*" He means, of course, to Susan Tracy. The intimacy established, Smith—that Godwinian lothario—goes on to discuss the titillating topics of "truth, "Justice," "Duty." He writes in his "we special few" tone, contrasting the "few persons, fewer than, at first glance, you would imagine, [who] act from motives of duty" to those, "the greater part" who "continue, thro' life, the blind & passive machines of imitation or fear." Smith, in his letter, disarms Mrs. Tracy with such locutions as "I know you have confidence in my sincerity." On the subject of a possible relationship between them, of "whether it is right for us, situated as we are, to maintain an epistolary intercourse," Smith supplies the Godwinian answer: "For myself, I have no secrets—I have nothing of which to be ashamed." After, finally, his long attempt to lure Susan Tracy away from the doctrines of Christianity and in the direction of his rationalistic faith, he concludes, "Were I writing to any other than you, it might become me, perhaps, to demand forgiveness, once again, for troubling you so long on this topic: But I left you reading 'Political Justice'; & I should pay an ill compliment to the author, & your own understanding, were I ever after to speak to you in any language save that alone of 'truth & soberness.'"[39]

In subsequent letters Smith stepped up the campaign to initiate Susan Tracy into "the very temple of Truth." Assaulting her "System" with long arguments, Smith worked his way around to the coy appeal: "Do not reply to all this, that 'It is talking in the clouds' for, tho' I have been, as it were, seduced into this strain, & had no intention of straying into it, when I began to write, yet I am confident that you can not misapprehend me."[40]

Alas, the seduction failed. Smith did not get what he craved, and in June 1798 he had to concede defeat, noting in his diary (after receiving a letter from Mrs. Tracy) that "I am sorry to find her converted, by the French Revolution, to Christianity."[41]

Now the relevance of this exchange for the tale of Charles Brockden Brown involves not what he made of it, but what his imagination *might* have made of it. Elihu Smith, for sure, deemed this relationship with Mrs. Tracy impeccably moral. What was he after? Smith would say he was, laudably, only interested in bringing Mrs. Tracy to "truth." Perhaps bits of the correspondence—like where he actively tries to turn Mrs. Tracy against Christianity—Smith would prefer the orthodox Christian *Mr.* Tracy not to see. Still Uriah Tracy was Smith's friend too, as was Mrs. Tracy, and even while Smith was writing to *her*, he was uprightly socializing with *him* in Philadelphia. In his own sense of self, Smith had nothing to hide. He was, as his rhetoric consistently announced, the quintessential Godwinian "sincere" man.

But what might Charles Brown, in his "visionary" mode, have made of Smith's letters? *What if* he chose to view them not as the product of a "sincere" truth-seeker, but as the duplicitous missives of a seducer—and a most vile seducer at that, for Mrs. Tracy was happily married and the maternal core of a pious family. Now *that*, to such an imagination as Brown's, would be some "romance," and truly revelatory of what he termed the "moral life."

To hypothesize in this way is to begin to trace in some of the subtleties of the intensely provocative setting of mid-1790s New York. Brown would soon be writing stories, "Memoirs of Carwin, the Biloquist" and *Ormond* in particular, peopled with "Godwinian" characters. These characters, for the most part, Brown would portray in dark, cynical hues as his hero/villains. Brown's "sources" for these depictions would include the English "Jacobin" novels of Godwin and Thomas Holcroft and Robert Bage, French revolutionary memoirs, and the 1790s literature on the supposed rationalist conspiracy of the "Illuminati." But his sources would also be actual people he knew. In Philadelphia, it seems clear, Brown had no personal experience with people who justified everything in rationalist "Godwinian" terms. But in New York, through the Friendly Club, he did, and Brown would use this experience, indeed he would interrogate this experience, in his fiction.

An especially provocative presence for Brown in mid-1790s New York had to have been Charles Adams, son of the vice president. A very close friend of Elihu Smith's and an early member of the Friendly Club, Charles Adams stopped attending club meetings in late 1795. Why he did so is probably explained by simple context, for this was the period when John and Abigail Adams's youngest son moved beyond their pale: when he involved himself with shady characters and financial schemes, when he squandered $4,000 his brother John Quincy had given him to invest, and when he lapsed into the alcoholism that would in a few years kill him. In other words, embarrassment alone would seem to suffice as an explanation for the sudden absence of Charles Adams from the fellowship that demanded "sincerity" and steadfast dedication to "the truth."[42]

Yet while Charles Adams no longer attended club meetings, Smith continued to visit Adams, and on one such visit to his friend's apartment Smith ran into Charles Adams's father. The great John Adams, Smith recorded, somewhat surprised him, as "Mr. Adams's manners are more agreable than I supposed them to be. There is no affectation, or pride observable in him." For two hours—"& for at least an hour alone in his company"—Smith conversed with the vice president, who held forth on the compelling subject of the true "origin of the American Revolution." Of John Adams's more off-the-cuff remarks, Smith found one worthy of precise quotation: "In the course of some remarks on Pennsylvania, Mr. Adams said—that 'William Penn was the greatest land-jobber, that ever existed; & that his successors in the administration of that government, had continued the same policy.'"[43]

This unexpected interlude with the famous American Revolutionary occurred on November 30, 1796, and upon leaving Charles Adams's apartment

—and John Adams's presence—Smith returned home, where (his diary records) he "found Ch. B. Brown." Smith does not record what he and Brown talked about, but there's no way he didn't regale Brown with the vice president's dig at William Penn and the Pennsylvania Quakers, as well as relate John Adams's "interesting" comments on the Revolution.[44]

Revolutions, indeed, were a particular interest of the Friendly Club at this time. In August 1796, Smith, Dunlap, and Brown gathered for a holiday in Perth Amboy, New Jersey, and Helen Maria Williams's *Letters from France* was the book of the moment. Smith was even thinking about "a tale in Miss Williams's Letters, of an old gentleman, in the neighbourhood of Vaucluse, his niece & son—ruined by the horrible blood-hounds of Robespierre" as the basis for a good drama he would write. Also absorbing the friends was Honoré Riouffe's *Revolutionary Justice Displayed, or, An Inside View of the Various Prisons of Paris, under the Government of Robespierre and the Jacobins.* This was a work Smith had brought to Brown's attention months before, with the recommendation: "we [the Friendly Club] have been considerably amused & pleased by [it]."[45]

To contemplate Charles Brown in this setting is to glimpse the special status, the exquisite experiential tension and irony, that stood behind his art. In this regard, none of the Friendly Club members had a clue as to how fundamentally different in experience he was from them—his Quaker quaintness of speech apart. Charles Adams could not have known the part his father, John Adams, had played in the Brown family saga. Nor could the medical doctor Elihu Hubbard Smith have guessed the thoughts and emotions, the memories, his rehearsal of John Adams's comments on the Revolution would loose in Brown. Nor would he have understood the reference to the Penn family's "land-jobbing" (which Philadelphia Quakers knew all about—and which Brown would evoke in his last Gothic novel, *Edgar Huntly*). And then there were such passages as this in Riouffe's *Revolutionary Justice Displayed*:

[Luxembourg prison] was soon full of people. Every day legions of citizens were brought in, torn from their trades and families; after being paraded through the streets, and represented to the people, as the vilest of traitors; although they were mostly victims of private malice and design.

And this:

Forty persecuted fathers of families, farmers and mechanics, had been sent . . . to the prison of the *Conciergerie*; and in that miserable place most of them fell sick, in want of every thing; without resources, without acquaintance, and without help.

And especially this:

at 5 o'clock in the evening . . . a confused sound was heard of voices in the street, which announced the approach of some catastrophe. A large waggon, drawn by

four horses, soon made its appearance; preceded by four gendarmes, and a messenger of the revolutionary tribunal. . . . This ferocious being immediately gave
orders to the gaoler to ring the bell, and to collect all the prisoners in the court. . . .
The whole being met: the revolutionary messenger opened his list, holding in his
hand at the same time certain decrees of accusation; and every one listened in a
mournful silence, to hear what he had to say. The gaoler desired to have all the
names called, and had made a beginning to read them, when the messenger, taking
the list out of his hand, began to read it himself. . . . At length the fatal list was com-
pleated, and after the horror of an hour, during which every one deplored the fate
of those who were marked for destruction, and expected himself to make up a part
of the cargo, the messenger pronounced that the rest might return to their chambers. The butcher then ordering his victims to pass in review before him, counted
them several times; and when he was fully satisfied that he had the eleven prisoners
designated on his list, they were immediately hurried into the fatal waggon.

It is safe to say that Charles Brown would not have responded to such depictions, as did his New York friends, with "amusement" and "pleasure."[46]

*   *   *

On the other hand, the New York spectacle of one of the American republic's great men beginning to self-destruct amid the partisan turmoil of the
mid-1790s must have carried for Brown its entertainment value: considering that two decades earlier this man, as a lieutenant colonel in the Continental Army, had first come to the attention of Philadelphia Quakers when
he broke into their homes and forcibly "distrained" food and blankets.

Alexander Hamilton had traveled a long way since then. As secretary of
the treasury his financial program had set the agenda of Washington's
administration—to the horror of his rival, the secretary of state. Jefferson
feared that Hamilton, with his plans for a strong central government with
a national bank and a perpetually funded national debt, sought to recreate
in the United States a Britain-like polity, in which "paper aristocrats"—
mercantile capitalists—would hold the upper hand. In opposition Jefferson desired a more decentralized polity in which, presumably, "farmers"
like himself, and their agrarian values, could predominate. But from the
moment Revolutionary France declared war on Great Britain and Holland
in February 1793, Hamilton's political star was in the ascendant.

Thus, when news of the European war reached Philadelphia in April, the
Anglophile Hamilton, to the Francophile Jefferson's annoyance, had pushed
for an immediate presidential decree to keep the United States and its commerce neutral in the imperial struggle; and within the week Washington
had issued his Neutrality Proclamation. In May 1793 Hamilton had warned
Washington about Citizen Genet, while Jefferson first embraced the French
Girondin minister as a political godsend who would help to galvanize "the
people" against "our monocrats." Thereafter, in the wake of Genet's efforts
to rally the American populace behind French interests—and against

Washington's policies—the president had come to rely increasingly on Hamilton's advice in important political matters. In 1793–94 Hamilton had encouraged Washington in the belief that the pro-French Democratic-Republican societies which were popping up across the nation like mushrooms—and which the Virginians Jefferson and James Madison viewed as authentic expressions of grassroots democracy—amounted to "Jacobin" clubs. By October 1794 Washington more than agreed, fearing that "if these self-created societies cannot be discountenanced, they will destroy the government of this country." When farmers in the West resisted paying a tax on whiskey stills—as required by the Hamiltonian federal excise law of 1791—Hamilton had insisted that an army needed to be dispatched to teach the tax evaders, and others of like mind, a painful lesson. Washington first tried to settle the matter peacefully through suasion and threat. But when that approach failed, he took the Hamiltonian route and assembled a 15,000-man militia to suppress the Whiskey Rebels, and in October 1794 Alexander Hamilton himself rode out to western Pennsylvania in command of the force.[47]

Hamilton's final great contribution to the Washington administration had been the Jay Treaty. This had been necessitated in 1794–95 when British men-of-war—carrying out a new British government policy—began attacking American merchant ships which traded in the French West Indies. Jefferson and Madison wanted to retaliate through anti-British trade legislation, but Washington opted to send a special envoy to England to try to work out the range of grievances still existing between Great Britain and her former colonies. He thus sent to London the chief justice of the United States, John Jay, along with instructions written by Hamilton that were to guide Jay in the negotiations. The resulting treaty—brought back to Philadelphia in March 1795, debated and ratified by the Senate in June, and signed into law by the president in August—advanced Hamilton's vision of a prosperous Anglo-American trade, and in the process it inflamed and divided the republic as no event since the Revolutionary period.[48]

By this point in mid-1795, Thomas Jefferson had long since retired back to private life in Virginia. Having grown weary of political infighting and his own insignificance in Philadelphia, he had resigned from the cabinet in December 1793. Alexander Hamilton, for his part, never grew weary, of politics or anything else. His energy was preternatural. But after six years in public office his personal finances were in serious disarray, and so in early 1795 Hamilton too, a "colossus" at the peak of his influence and reputation, resigned from the cabinet and returned to his law practice in New York. Which is where Charles Brown was in July 1795, visiting Elihu Smith.[49]

Hamilton's stunning demise, which would conclude in 1804 at Weehawken, New Jersey, with Aaron Burr's bullet in his side, began at noon on July 18, 1795, in front of New York's Federal Hall, about three blocks from Smith's Cedar Street residence. For days the Democratic Society of New York had been distributing handbills and newspaper notices calling on "citizens" to gather "to deliberate upon the proper mode of communicating to the President, their disapprobation of the English treaty." At the appointed time and place more than 5,000 angry New Yorkers assembled, and at the stroke of twelve they were greeted with a surprise: the five-foot seven-inch Alexander Hamilton, surrounded by a phalanx of Federalist supporters, "was mounted upon a stoop," and he attempted to address the gathering. Hamilton's efforts were met with a chorus of "hissings, coughings, and hootings," and the Republican Brockholst Livingston shouted him down. Still he soldiered on. Hamilton introduced a resolution, which was read to the crowd from the balcony of Federal Hall. As the New York *Argus* reported the scene, "a momentary silence took place—but when the citizens found that the resolution *declared it unnecessary to give an opinion on the treaty*, they roared, as with one voice: *we'll hear no more of it; tear it up, &c.*" The situation eventually deteriorated to the point of violence. A Friendly Club member in attendance, Seth Johnson, later reported: "it is said in the heat of the business that Edward Livingston pointed to Mr. Hamilton and said 'Take care, or that man will ruin you' which in the temper of those around him, might have led to assassination." According to Brown's friend, "Stones were thrown at Hamilton one of which grazed his head." The former secretary of the treasury was forced to retreat from the scene.[50]

But there was more. As Hamilton marched away from the debacle, he came upon a loud public argument between the Republican James Nicholson and a Federalist. Fearing the two would incite a riot, he tried to quiet them, only to be denounced by Nicholson as an "Abettor of Tories." When he tried to get the two men to move their argument indoors, Nicholson told him he would not listen to Hamilton because Hamilton had "declined an interview"—that is, a duel—"upon a former occasion." "No man could affirm that with truth," Hamilton snapped, and promptly challenged Nicholson to a duel.[51]

And still there was more, for as Hamilton stalked away from *this* scene, he ran into another group of Republicans and, now quite out of control, he warned them that if his opponents "were to contend in a personal way" he was ready to fight. Then waving his fist in the air, he offered "to fight the Whole *'Detestable faction'* one by one." When yet another Livingston accepted the challenge and offered to fight with pistols "in half an hour where he pleased," Hamilton snarled that he already "had an affair on his Hands," but that he would duel with Livingston after his duel with Nicholson. (Friends later defused the situation and both "affairs" were forestalled.)[52]

Hamilton next conspicuously lost his head in public during the congressional elections of December 1796, and again Charles Brown was in town. The contest involved the Republican incumbent, Edward Livingston, and the Federalist challenger, James Watson. Livingston had been a vociferous opponent of the Jay Treaty in Congress, and Hamilton wanted him defeated.

To this end he frenetically patrolled the city on horseback, visiting every polling place during the several days of voting. For his efforts the former secretary of the treasury was again "horribly treated" by the populace. Worse still, it was to no avail. On the eve of the election Hamilton and his lieutenants realized that his local nemesis, Edward Livingston, was likely to win.

So they decided on a last-minute smear campaign. They distributed three thousand handbills charging that the Republican candidate—or more precisely "the Aristocratical, Democratical, Jacobinical Edward Livingston"—had compromised himself by association with a Republican merchant congressman from Philadelphia, one John Swanwick, who, the allegation ran, was guilty of serious financial improprieties in his extensive import-export business, who was, in effect, a swindler. The New York voters were not impressed, however, and they returned Livingston to Congress with a comfortable majority.[53]

This was precisely the sort of partisan politicking that the Friendly Club, in its higher mission, existed to abhor. Yet most of its members were Federalists and a few were acquaintances of Hamilton. Seth and Horace Johnson, for example, both Federalists, were storekeepers who went out of their way—and over their financial heads—to hire the former treasury secretary as their business attorney. The brilliant James Kent, a Federalist whose law career was just beginning to take off, quite naturally idolized Hamilton. Elihu Smith too was a Federalist, though of an insistently nonpartisan variety. He had met Hamilton twice, once back in late 1795, when the two had discussed the yellow fever and "Col. Hamilton" had "detailed the history of his own Case [of the fever], in Phila. 1793, & of the mode of treatment pursued." Smith afterward noted in his diary: "He speaks very correctly, & sensibly; but with more hesitation than I expected in a man, so accustomed to public speaking." The second time Smith was more impressed. This was in March 1796 at a Manumission Society gathering, where Hamilton formally defended the reputation of a society member who was under attack. Smith wrote in his diary: "This is the first opportunity I have had of hearing Mr. Hamilton speak; & I heard him with pleasure, tho' he opposed me. His method is clear, his style precise, his argumentation pointed & forcible, & his manner emphatic. This manner is calculated to have as much effect, as his argument."[54]

Smith learned more about Hamilton in the midst of the December 1796 congressional campaign. Dining one afternoon at Seth Johnson's, the conversation inevitably turned to politics, and a guest at the meal, Henry Remsen, told quite a story.

Remsen had been a clerk under Jefferson in the State Department, and he gave an account of "the licentious & indiscriminate indulgence of Mr. Hamilton . . . in the use of women: even those of the most common kind, & in the most common houses." Remsen then, according to Smith, related an anecdote of this same celebrated man, much less to his credit. When Mr. H. was Secretary, his office was opposite to the Bank of North America. On the day when the subscription was opened for the National Bank, people crowded to subscribe, in the morning. As they were rushing thither, Mr. H. came to the door of his office; &, pleased with the success of his project, which had been violently opposed, by his political antagonists, he stood there, *clapping his hands*, & shewing other marks of exultation for near fifteen minutes. This Mr. Remsen told me, expressly, that he himself saw.

Smith was disturbed by this report, but ever the Godwinian, he tried to draw a fair and useful moral. "In respect to Mr. H's amours, it does not appear that they influence, in the least, his political conduct. He gratifies his appetite, rather than his passions. He repairs to a brothel; but he has no mistresses on whom he lavishes his fortune, & to whom he surrenders his independence."[55]

Elihu Smith, it can be inferred, voted for the Hamiltonian candidate in this election, as did the Johnsons and Kent. Charles Brown did not vote Federalist, or Republican. As a Philadelphian in New York he was not permitted to vote at all. Yet the Hamiltonian spectacle of 1795–96 did meaningfully engage his imagination, for three years later, when he published his third novel, *Arthur Mervyn; or, Memoirs of the Year 1793*, the fictional hero/villain in the tale, Thomas Welbeck, would be patently modeled in part on the real-life figure of John Swanwick, and would carry accents of Alexander Hamilton too.[56]

Brown knew quite a lot, it turns out, about the bogeyman of Hamilton's smear campaign. He knew that—like his own future "Tom Welbeck"—John Swanwick was "foreign-born" in Liverpool. That as a boy in Philadelphia Swanwick suffered indignities during the Revolutionary War on account of his Tory father. That in 1777 he took the Revolutionary oath of allegiance and went to work as a clerk in Robert Morris's counting house. That Swanwick was brilliant at business and indeed became the mastermind behind Robert Morris's economic empire, a vast network that notoriously mixed private and public ventures. That in 1783 he was made a partner in the firm of Willing, Morris, and Swanwick, and thereafter sat on the boards of insurance companies and banks. And that then something shocking occurred. This foreign-born Liverpudlian, who had emerged in the late 1780s and early 1790s as one of Philadelphia's leading Federalists, in 1791–92 *switched sides*. He transfigured himself into a Republican leader of the "new Irish" community of recent immigrants. In 1794 he joined the Pennsylvania Democratic-Republican Society, and from then on Swanwick—described by one nonadmirer as "slippery as an Eel. . . . the greatest insurgent in the state . . . he is universally hated and despised," and by a fellow Republican as a "contemptible creature"—reigned as one of Jefferson's and Madison's lieutenants in the state. When he won election to Congress in 1794, he drew his support from the newer and poorer wards in the city, which six years later would help elect Jefferson president.

So much was common knowledge to any well-informed Philadelphia Quaker. What was not well known, what was in fact quite arcane knowledge, was the apparent reason for Swanwick's "miraculous" transformation in 1791–92. For—again like Charles Brown's future hero/villain "Tom Welbeck"—John Swanwick was "a forger," implicated in a criminal scheme that involved his circulation of $36,000 in fraudulent certificates. This transpired in early 1791, when he was still a solid Robert Morris/Alexander Hamilton-type Federalist. Whether Swanwick was an actual accomplice in the swindle or just an unknowing participant was never established. And the wealthy Swanwick somehow made the affair go away. (In 1796, when Federalist newspapers "overflowed with gross and furious calumny" against Swanwick, the "forgery" charge curiously never cropped up.) Yet a clerk in the Treasury Department, George Remsen, had a great deal of information about the scheme and *he* thought that Swanwick was indeed a counterfeiter. In any case, Swanwick personally benefited from the fraud and, "slippery as an Eel," was never brought under prosecution.

That Charles Brown knew all of this is virtually certain, for his brother Armitt worked as a clerk alongside George Remsen in the Treasury Department in the early 1790s. Furthermore, the Remsen family and the Walns were old business associates. Remsen and Co., a New York retail establishment, bought and sold the flour and wheat ground by Charles's rich Uncle Richard Waln at his Walnford, New Jersey, estate (where young Charles Brown spent time during the Revolution, and which would have been the likely refuge for the Brown family to ride out the yellow fever summer of 1793).[57]

It is characteristic that Brown did not divulge this priceless gossip to Elihu Smith in the midst of the New York congressional election in which "John Swanwick" was the mystery villain of the moment. (If he had told him, Smith, the man of truth, would inevitably have recorded the "useful" information in his diary.) Instead he put it to use in *Arthur Mervyn*. As, perhaps, he put "Alexander Hamilton" to use.

Charles Brown would have learned from Elihu Smith in 1796 New York that Secretary Hamilton, when infected with the yellow fever in Philadelphia in August 1793, was treated by Dr. Edward Stevens. This knowledge might or might not have influenced his decision to name the narrator of his *Memoir of the Year 1793* "Dr. Stevens." Certainly Dr. Stevens's patient in the novel, the eponymous Arthur Mervyn, has no similarity to the real-life Hamilton, as Arthur is a rube from Chester County. And the hero/villain of the tale, Thomas Welbeck, clearly wears the local attributes of the real-life John Swanwick, who, like Welbeck, was a "Proteus" whose own tragic and bitter end, with its acute financial embarrassment and bankruptcy in 1797 and death in July 1798 as a victim of the yellow fever, adumbrated the fictional end of Welbeck in 1793 Philadelphia.[58]

Yet in one key feature the fictional Thomas Welbeck departs from the example of John Swanwick. For in *Arthur Mervyn*, Welbeck, "the slave of depraved appetites," is a sexual libertine who "could not fail of being quickly satiated with innocence and beauty." On one occasion, though, *he* is ensnared, by the youngest daughter in a family who "found him a proper subject on which to exercise her artifices. It was to the frequent demands made upon his purse, by this woman, that part of the embarrassments in which Mervyn found him [Welbeck] involved, are to be ascribed."[59]

When Brown wrote these words—probably in early 1799—he could not but have a particular individual in mind: the celebrated man who Smith concluded "gratifies his appetite, rather than his passions," who "repairs to a brothel; but he has no mistresses on whom he lavishes his fortune, & to whom he surrenders his independence." Which, as far as Smith, and Brown, knew in December 1796, was true.

Only as they—and the American public—subsequently learned in August 1797, this was not true, for in that month Alexander Hamilton published an astonishing document. "Mr. Hamilton's Vindication &c," as Smith called it, or "The Reynolds Pamphlet" as it has become known, was designed to rebut charges that he had engaged in "improper pecuniary speculation" while treasury secretary. This he had never done, Hamilton averred. As a public servant his actions were always impeccably above reproach. However, while secretary, he confessed, he had been involved in a private "crime," which involved his sexual liaison with a Maria Reynolds in 1791–92 Philadelphia and the efforts of her husband—probably with her connivance—to blackmail him, the secretary of the treasury.[60]

"The Reynolds Pamphlet" offered a tale more compelling than any yet captured in American fiction. The opening sentence alone stands without peer in the early American seduction genre. *Some time in the summer of the year 1791, a woman called at my house in the city of Philadelphia and asked to speak with me in private.* That woman, with "a seeming air of affliction," informs Hamilton "that her husband, who for a long time had treated her very cruelly, had lately left her, to live with another woman," and that as a fellow New Yorker she "had taken the liberty to apply to my humanity for assistance."

I replied, that her situation was a very interesting one—that I was disposed to afford her assistance to convey her to her friends, but this at the moment not being convenient to me (which was the fact) I must request the place of her residence, to which I should bring or send a small supply of money. She told me the street and the number of the house where she lodged. In the evening I put a bank-bill in my pocket and went to the house. I enquired for Mrs. Reynolds and was shewn up the stairs, at the head of which she met me and conducted me into a bed room. I took the bill out of my pocket and gave it to her. Some conversation ensued from which it was quickly apparent that other than pecuniary consolation would be acceptable.

With the sex consummated, the tale deftly advances. Soon the cuckolded husband, Mr. James Reynolds, is standing in the office of the secretary of the treasury and asking for a job as a clerk. Hamilton refuses him, knowing what he knows (or thinks he knows) about James Reynolds's character. Alas, the hero/victim narrator reports:

The intercourse with Mrs. Reynolds, in the mean time, continued; and, though various reflections, (in which a further knowledge of Reynolds' character and the suspicion of some concert between the husband and wife bore a part) induced me to wish a cessation of it; yet her conduct, made it extremely difficult to disentangle myself.[61]

"The Reynolds Pamphlet" combines the lubricity of *The Monk* with the moral complexity of *Clarissa*, and it anticipates the genre of "truth biography" that William Godwin would pioneer in 1798 with his *Memoirs* of Mary Wollstonecraft. Hamilton even gives the work an epistolary turn, and depth of perspective, by appending actual letters as documentation. Those from the Reynoldses are irresistible.

Thus, some time after the commencement of the affair, Hamilton receives this from Maria:

Dear Sir:—I have not tim to tell you the cause of my present troubles only that Mr. has rote you this morning and I know not wether you have got the letter or not and he has swore that If you do not answer It or If he dose not se or hear from you to day he will write to Mrs. Hamilton he has just Gone oute and I am a Lone I think you had better come here one moment that you May know the Cause then you will the better know how to act

Next he receives a letter from Maria's husband:

SIR: I am very sorry to find out that I have been so Cruelly treated. . . . Sir you took the advantage a poor Broken harted woman. instead of being a Friend, you have acted the part of the most Cruelist man in existance. you have made a whole family miserable. She ses there is no other man that she Care for in this world. now Sir you have bin the Cause of Cooling her affections for me.

Two days later he receives from the husband another letter:

SIR, . . . *your being in the Station of life* you are. induses me to way every Surcomcance well Respecting the matter it will be impossible for me ever to think of liveing or Reconsiling myself to Stay with a woman that I no has plased her affections on you . . . I am that man that will always have Satisfaction by some means or other when treated ill.

Two days later:

SIR, . . . its true its in your power to do a great deal for me, but its out of your power to do any thing that will Restore to me my Happiness again for if you should give me all you possess would not do it. . . . now Sir I have Considered on the matter Seriously. I have this preposial to make to you. give me the Sum of thousand dollars and I will leve the town. . . .

Hamilton pays the thousand dollars, but still the letters, and requests for additional funds, keep coming. This from Maria, datelined "Sunday Night one O'Clock":

My dear friend[,] In a state of mind which know language can paint I take up the pen. . . . Is deaf to my anguish and has marked me out for the child of sorrow oh my dear friend wether shall I fly for consolation. . . . Comply with this Last Request Let me once more se you and unbosom Myself to you perhaps I shal be happier after It. . . . adieu my Ever dear Col hamilton you may form to yourself an Idea of my distress for I Cant desscribe It to you Pray for me and be kind to me Let me se you death now would be welcome Give.[62]

Charles Brockden Brown, author of the Henrietta Letters and "The Rhapsodist," had yet to devise anything this good. Yet "The Reynolds Pamphlet" had another point of significance for him: the blackmailers Maria and James Reynolds. He knew them! Back in 1791–92 Philadelphia, at 159 Vine Street, when he had been writing letters to his friends Wilkins and Bringhurst, bemoaning that there was nothing interesting to write about and imagining himself in Pays de Vaud and London, anywhere but Philadelphia, right next door at 161 Vine—*literally on the other side of the of the brick wall he was staring at*—James and Maria Reynolds were carrying out a sexual sting operation against the second most powerful man in the United States.[63]

Patently there were local things—subjects, characters, plots, events—a Philadelphia Quaker novelist could mine for his art, if he only he learned how imaginatively and emotionally to channel into them.

*   *   *

Brown stayed in New York through the fall and winter of 1796–97, and during this time he began writing a piece he would publish in 1798 as *Alcuin: A Dialogue*. A Friendly Club-type exercise which addresses "the rights of women," a suddenly controversial topic in the wake of Mary Wollstonecraft's *Vindication of the Rights of Woman* and Godwin's *Political Justice, Alcuin* exhibits the intellectual qualities that so impressed Brown's New York friends and that marked him as unique in the partisan ideological world of 1790s America.[64]

While Thomas Paine's *Rights of Man* pushed a century of Lockean *male* rights debate toward its logical end—and in the process helped to define the division in American politics between Republicans and Federalists—Wollstonecraft's *Vindication of the Rights of Woman*, by raising the issue of where the other sex stood in all this, initiated in America serious public discussion of women's rights. Brown, back in the Henrietta Letters, had exhibited a respect for female intellect and an advocacy of a fuller education for women. In the Friendly Club, under the prodding of Smith's

Godwinianism, these not uncommon sentiments came under further scrutiny and challenge. With *Alcuin: A Dialogue*, Brown entered explicitly into the 1790s women's rights debate.[65]

There is much of Charles Brown in the conversation between the widow Mrs. Carter and Alcuin. Alcuin, for one, is a lowly schoolteacher—a position Brown himself had recently occupied—who knew "the pride of poverty" and "the bashfulness of inexperience." His "slender experience" in particular chagrins Alcuin, as it did the Rhapsodist, for it restricted the range of his imaginings and marked "the beings" of his fancy as "too uniform, and somewhat grotesque." "No one can work without materials," Alcuin fears, and his problem—like Brown's—is that "My stock is slender."[66]

Alcuin shares too his creator's general views about education. When Mrs. Carter laments her lack of a formal education, Alcuin asks "Whether most knowledge be obtained by listening to hired professors, or by reading books." Alcuin clearly believes the latter, as surely did Brown, who, while the equal of any Friendly Club member in the breadth of his reading, was one of the few members without a college education. Alcuin further voices Brown's objection to the narrow and crass purpose of the formal, or "public," education system. "For my part," he states, "I entertain but little respect for what are called the liberal professions, and indeed, but little for any profession whatever. If their motive be gain, and that it is which constitutes them a profession, they seem to be, all of them, nearly on a level in point of dignity. The consideration of usefulness is of more value." This, for Brown, is to invoke an aspect of his Quaker heritage and to align it with Godwinian concerns. At one point earlier in the dialogue Brown has Alcuin invoke the Quakers specifically, in response to Mrs. Carter's lament that the pulpit, like medicine and law, was closed to women. As far as the experience of the Congregationalists, Presbyterians, and Episcopalians in the Friendly Club went, this was true. Yet Alcuin—like his Quaker creator—knew that "there are other sects which admit females into the class of preachers," and it is with this invocation of his Quaker perspective that Brown positions his "dialogue" for original twists.[67]

Alcuin is about politics, writ large. The discussion is kicked off with Alcuin's "Pray, Madam, are you a federalist?" It was the question everybody was asking in 1796 New York. But Mrs. Carter responds by shifting focus to the issue of her place, as a woman, within the American system, and as Alcuin answers her back, Brown sets in dialogue the two polar "women's rights" arguments of the 1790s: the sentimentalist position, with its stress on women's supposedly more spiritual nature and its patronizing conclusion that "women are superior"; and the Wollstonecraftian counterposition, with its view that whatever biologically separates men and women, intellectually and morally they are equal, and that therefore to render women virtuous and a force for social improvement, women needed an education equal to that accorded men.[68]

There is, however, a third dimension to *Alcuin,* for beneath the "dialogue," the ideological debate on women's rights, exists a structure and progression of political argument that reveals, for the first time in his career, Brown's capacity for intellectual and imaginative originality. That is to say, Brown uses the dialogue, first, to define the Whig system of politics embodied in the American constitutional system and, second, to critique that system from within Whiggism's own premises; and then the text vaults beyond American Whiggism proper into a Quakerly-Godwinian vision of a more rational, egalitarian, just society. *And then,* Brown finishes by setting up the basis for a critique of *that* "visionary" system.

The orthodox Whig case—"The maxims of constitution-makers"—is presented in bits through both Mrs. Carter and Alcuin. First the bedrock principles: "All power is derived from the people. Liberty is every one's birthright. Since all cannot govern or deliberate individually, it is just that they should elect their representatives. That every one should possess, indirectly, and through the medium of his representatives, a voice in the public councils, and should yield to no will but that of an actual or virtual majority." And then the standard Whig explanation for the apparent deviations from the stated ideal: "Shall the young, the poor, the stranger, and the females be admitted indiscriminately to political privileges? Shall we annex no condition to a voter but that he be a thing in human shape, not lunatic, and capable of loco-motion? and no qualifications to a candidate but the choice of a majority? Would any benefit result from the change? Will it augment the likelihood that the choice will fall upon the wisest? Will it endow the framers and interpreters of law with more sagacity and moderation than they at present possess?" This was the argument behind the suffrage restrictions of the federal constitution, accepted by (male) Republicans and Federalists alike.[69]

In *Alcuin,* though, Whig principles are employed to undermine existing Whig practices. Brown gives Mrs. Carter the honor of the assault. "Plausible and specious maxims! but fallacious," she opines.

What avails it to be told by any one that he is an advocate for liberty? We must first know what he means by the word. We shall generally find that he intends only freedom to himself, and subjection to all others. Suppose I place myself where I can conveniently mark the proceedings at a general election. "All," says the code, "are free. Liberty is the immediate gift of the Creator to all mankind, and is unalienable. Those who are subject to the laws should possess a share in their enaction. This privilege can be exercised, consistently with the maintenance of social order, in a large society, only in the choice of deputies." "Pray," says the officer, "are you twenty-one years of age?"—"No."—"Then I cannot receive your vote; you are no citizen". . . A second assumes his place. "How long," says the officer, "have you been an inhabitant of this State?" . . . A third approaches, who is rejected because his name is not found in the catalogue of taxables. At length room is made for a fourth person. "Man," cries the magistrate, "is your skin black or white?"

Now Mrs. Carter prepares her punch line. Surely, she assumes, since she is neither a minor nor without property nor an immigrant nor black skinned, the magistrate will allow her to vote. But no: "I am a woman."[70]

The result, Mrs. Carter summarizes, is that in "this happy climate all men are free: the people are the source of all authority; from them it flows, and to them, in due season, it returns," but nonetheless, "It has been sagely decreed, that none but freemen shall enjoy this privilege, and that all men are free but those that are slaves. When all these are sifted out, a majority of the remainder are entitled to elect our governor; provided . . . [But] I am tired of explaining this charming system of equality and independence. . . . I am a woman. As such, I cannot celebrate the equity of that scheme of government which classes me with dogs and swine."[71]

It is an argument that Alcuin, for all his forays into the sentimental glories of woman's "separate" sphere, cannot compellingly answer. Nor is the powerful logical and emotional evocation of this position in the text surprising, given the fact that Charles Brown's own father was similarly classified in 1780s Pennsylvania as among the "dogs and swine" by the ruling "Constitutionalists"—not because Elijah Brown was nonwhite or untaxed or female, but because he refused to sign an "oath of allegiance" to the people who had previously exiled him for treasonous acts he never, to his mind, committed. As a result, for the Elijah Brown family, the meaning of citizenship and the reasons for its truncation were not academic points.[72]

The first half of *Alcuin*—the part Brown apparently wrote in late 1796 to early 1797—ends here. With the second part of the dialogue, written between mid-1797 and early 1798, Brown moved beyond the conventional women's rights dialogue and indeed the Whig frame altogether, into a "visionary" realm that was his special domain.[73]

"Visionary" journeys, of course, were the marrow of Brown's people, dating back to the founding time of his great-great-great-grandfather and grandmother. Brown's own childhood and education had involved the witnessing of "visions" testified to in meeting and the reading of "visions" recorded in Quaker testimonies and autobiographies, like the one published by his grandmother's brother, John Churchman. And Brown's own dreams—like the one about his separation from Joseph Bringhurst—were (or could be) Quaker "visions" of a type too. When he called himself a "visionary" in 1787, then, he referred both forward to his ambitions as a poet and backward to his cultural heritage. This means that what Coleridge (whom the Friendly Club was reading in 1797–98) and Wordsworth were attempting to do in 1790s England out of their own idiosyncratic imaginative resources, Brown could claim in 1790s America by profound cultural warrant.[74]

Brown invokes the tribal rite in the second part of *Alcuin*, when he takes a journey beyond the Whig context of 1790s America and into a "visionary" world of Quakerly Godwinianism. He travels, or rather Alcuin travels, in imagination, to a society that answers all the arguments raised by Mrs. Carter in her critique of American Whig realities, a society that is called "a paradise of women."[75]

Alcuin comes upon and questions "a stranger" in this visionary place. "I have met," Alcuin says to him,

with those, whose faces and voices seemed to bespeak them women, though as far as I could discover they were distinguished by no peculiarities of manners or dress. In those assemblies to which you conducted me, I did not fail to observe that whatever was the business of the hour, both sexes seemed equally engaged in it. Was the spectacle theatrical? The stage was occupied sometimes by men, sometimes by women, and sometimes by a company of each. The tenor of the drama seemed to be followed as implicitly as if custom had enacted no laws on the subject.

Alcuin tells the stranger that "I find among you none of those exterior differences by which the sexes are distinguished by other nations," and when asked to specify, he mentions "dress." "The men and women of our country are more different from each other in this respect, than the natives of remotest countries." When Alcuin presses the stranger on his people's habits, the answers—while no doubt novel to Friendly Club members—would not have been alien to Philadelphia's Quakers. Thus the stranger explains the end for which "we dress":

Is it for the sake of ornament? Is it in compliance with our perceptions of the beautiful? . . . But ornament obtains no regard from us but in subservience to utility. We find it hard to distinguish between the useful and beautiful. When they appear to differ, we cannot hesitate to prefer the former. To us that instrument possesses an invincible superiority to every other which is best adapted to our purpose.

As Brown sketches more and more of this "visionary" world of true gender egalitarianism, it is clear—but probably not to his Friendly Club audience—that he is invoking not only William Godwin but also George Fox.[76]

In the New York setting of the mid-1790s, that is, Brown could appear the radical Godwinian merely by slightly recasting the principles and customs of Quakerism. Thus "the stranger":

We are born with faculties that enable us to impart and receive happiness. There is one species of discipline, better adapted than any other to open and improve those faculties. This mode is to be practiced. All are to be furnished with the means of instruction, whether these consist in the direct commerce of the senses with the material universe, or in intercourse with other intelligent beings. It is requisite to know the reasonings, actions and opinions of others, if we seek the improvement of our own understanding. For this end we must see them, and talk with them if present, or if distant or dead, we must consult these memorials which have been contrived by themselves or others. These are simple and intelligible maxims proper to regulate our treatment of rational beings. The only circumstance to which we are bound to attend is that the subjects of instruction be rational. If any one observe that the consideration of sex is of some moment, how must his remark be understood. Would he insinuate that because my sex is different from yours, one of us only can be treated as rational, or that though reason be a property of both, one of us possesses less of it than the other. *I am not born among a people who can countenance so monstrous a doctrine.*

Which is to say that Alcuin's journey is to the "vision" of a society grounded in reason and utility, equality and justice, where practice and principle are perfectly aligned, that is part Godwin, part Society of Friends.[77]

Brown doesn't stop here, though. Having exposed the logical absurdity of Whiggism's restrictive franchise (at least as it concerned adult, property-owning women), and then posited—à la Godwin—a more rational and just society, his intellectual rigor and playfulness are such that he must now critique *that creation*, which he does by bringing up the most controversial part of 1790s Godwinianism.

Marriage, for Godwin, was an irrational institution that too often binds unhappy and antagonistic persons in a relationship destructive to all concerned. "Reason" dictates that a man and a woman should live together when love and affinity and/or common interests unite them, and that they should separate when those forces fade. Certainly no legal marriage institution is necessary to the process and, indeed, that coercive institution only offends and perverts "reason."[78]

Brown, in the final section of *Alcuin*, ventures into this territory with great relish and wit. He has Mrs. Carter attack Godwinianism, and in the process—incidentally—set out the ground that he, Brown, will explore in his novels. "A class of reasoners has lately arisen," says Mrs. Carter, in referring to people like Elihu Hubbard Smith and, presumably, C. B. Brown,

who aim at the deepest foundation of civil society. Their addresses to the understanding have been urged with no despicable skill. But this was insufficient. It was necessary to subdue our incredulity, as to the effects of their new maxims, by exhibiting those effects in detail, and winning our assent to their truth by engrossing the fancy and charming the affections. The journey that you have lately made, I merely regard as an excursion into their visionary world.

In response, Alcuin (of all people!) invokes the Wollstonecraftian case about the potential cruelties and inequities of the marriage condition for women—which Mrs. Carter herself had used *against him* in part 1 of the dialogue. But now *she* goes on to contemplate the consequences of doing away with the admittedly imperfect institution, asking, "Perhaps if entire liberty in this respect were granted, the effects might constitute a scene unspeakably more disastrous than any thing hitherto conceived." After all, "That which is commonly called love is a vagrant and wayward principle."[79]

Alcuin: A Dialogue, having passed from the precincts of Whiggism to Godwinianism, ends in an imaginative realm that will be the frame of Brown's novels: the realm of *what if*. Brown even has Alcuin thinking this way by the final pages! Thus Alcuin asks Mrs. Carter: "But what effects . . . may be expected from the removal of this restraint, upon the morals of the people? It seems to open a door to licentiousness and profligacy. If marriages can be dissolved and contracted at pleasure, will not every one deliver himself up to the impulse of a lawless appetite? Would not changes be incessant. All chastity of mind perhaps, would perish. A general corruption of manners would ensue, and vice would pave the way for the admission of a thousand others, till the whole nation were sunk into a state of the lowest degeneracy." Here is the specific subject of the future *Ormond*, but more to the point, here is the *what if*, applied to the cultural-intellectual schemes of the 1790s, that will for the next few years guide the imaginative life, and the novels, of Brown.[80]

*   *   *

On Saturday evening, October 29, 1796, the Friendly Club gathered at Elihu Smith's house on Cedar Street, and William Johnson read to the membership, with Brown present, "the History of the interior state of France during the latter part of the reign of Robespierre, & for several months after his fall, written more than two thousand years ago, by Thucydides, but then predicated of Corcyra." A few days before Smith had finished reading the third part of Erasmus Darwin's *Zoonomia*; and a month later Smith would have his memorable interview with John Adams, who "exprest a fear" to Smith "lest there should never be any good history of the Revolution written." Meanwhile, back in Philadelphia, Brown's dearest friend, Joseph Bringhurst, was being hounded for debt.[81]

Brown stayed in New York through the winter, and then in March 1797, as John Adams assumed the presidency, he returned home to Philadelphia, where he began to write and publish his first "fiction" grounded in his family's extended experience.

"The Man at Home," thirteen semi-linked sketches, appeared in Philadelphia's *Weekly Magazine* in early 1798. The setting is "a chamber" in the suburbs of 1797 Philadelphia, and the narrator, the "man at home," is a sixty-year-old hiding out from his creditors. If they find him, his fate will be incarceration in Philadelphia's debtors' prison.[82]

The first installment relates how the narrator has come to this sorry pass. He is, or was, a merchant, who a while back had retired with a sufficient fortune to live "at my ease." Subsequently his former business partner had asked him to co-sign on a note, the sum of which "was little less than my whole fortune." The narrator signed this piece of paper, and because of that act—and his partner's ensuing financial collapse—a writ was issued for his arrest. It was "in order to elude this process," the narrator writes, that "I have changed my dwelling." He now finds himself holed up in his washerwoman's house, and with nothing else to do, he decides to amuse himself by "recording my thoughts." So he picks up his pen, and "The Man at Home" is the result.

From this starting point, the narrator lets his thoughts wander. He begins installment 2 with reflections on the nature of debt, before turning to the gist of his current plight, which is "Pay or go to prison." He sums up his moral position: "I will not pay. There I may be wrong. But I will not go to prison. There I may be right." From here he goes on to consider his hostess, an Irish washerwoman, and her life story. This introduces the historical theme of the Irish: their "rage of emigration"; their settlement in Philadelphia; their service in the Revolutionary army. For his washerwoman Kate, born "in a cottage on the banks of the Shannon," this saga had brought her to Philadelphia and a series of encounters and relationships, and finally, after the yellow fever devastations of 1793, to a humble dwelling on the outskirts of the city, where in 1797, alone and without family, she provides a room to her former benefactor, who is the narrator. He summarizes his relationship with Kate: "I gave her competence and comfort; she saves me from jail."

In subsequent installments the narrator's imagination continues to wander. In installments 3 and 4 it fastens on a potential mystery. There's a locked chest in his room: Did it contain silver or gold, English guineas or Mexican dollars? He asks Kate, but she doesn't know much. So he entertains thoughts of breaking it open. Meanwhile he lets his "train of reflections" ramble on. He contemplates his own life and its most edifying episodes. Two past adventures in particular stand out: One, when he endured six weeks in a Neapolitan lazaretto, or quarantine ward, where "I was immured in a dark and noisome apartment, and condemned for the most part to absolute solitude, and the prey of a lingering disease." In this place, he now reflects, "were founded and reared to maturity all the notions that I now hold most dear, respecting the rights and duties of men and the principles of social institution." The second adventure occurred when he was "a merchant, [and] my curiosity as well as interest, prompted me to act the supercargo with respect to my own property" and undertake an overseas trading venture. "This period was fertile of instruction, by affording me occasions and topics of meditation." The narrator concludes this reverie by noting his hope that perhaps some new lessons, new "truths," might "spring" from the mysterious chest.

To this end, the narrator goads Kate to go out and ask neighbors about the house and its prior occupants. Kate does this, and when she returns she (of course) has a story to tell: about a French family, the Demoivres, who had previously lived in this place and fallen victim to the yellow fever in 1793. And so a second historical theme is introduced: the French émigrés in early 1790s Philadelphia. Now, his curiosity piqued, the narrator can't help himself: He breaks open the chest. At first he finds nothing, but then—the introduction of a Gothic convention—he discovers a "A cavity concealed! A false bottom!" And here he comes across a most precious manuscript. It is a history of the American Revolution. The narrator reflects: "How worthy of the wise to investigate the causes that gave birth, and conducted, to a prosperous issue, that revolution! Hitherto, with regard to these particulars, mankind have been imperfectly enlightened."

We, the reader, are now into installment 8, and we learn that the author of this history had fallen victim to the yellow fever in Philadelphia during the summer of 1793. The narrator salutes this unknown historian, whose "heroism was of a species so new, and so singular. To serve the cause of his country and of liberty by such means!" And the narrator announces his intention to take up the dead historian's burden.

I bless my fate, that has made this chamber my prison. Thus have these inestimable records been preserved. I will make myself the benefactor of my country, and of mankind, by effecting their publication. . . . [The tale's] authenticity cannot well be denied. It unfolds the causes, and exhibits the true agents in a transaction of high importance in the American revolution. . . . With respect to the agents themselves, surely never was human nature depicted in lights equally grand and forcible.

But now the narrator does a strange thing. This historical tale, which we are told "has every claim to excite attention" and which "will merit being ranked among historical monuments," and which "has all the circumstantial and picturesque minuteness of a romance": *He doesn't tell it.* Instead he uses his last five installments to: (1) recount more fully the story of the Demoivres; (2) relate details from a book he's lately read on the history of one of the ancient colonies of Magna Graecia; (3) offer reflections provoked by another book, Erasmus Darwin's *Zoonomia*; and (4) conclude with a summary of his future prospects as a debtor.

Yet if the narrator in "The Man at Home" doesn't tell the "enlightening" story of the American Revolution, his creator, Charles Brown, does. For on closer inspection, installment 11, which tells "the history of intestine commotions" in Magna Graecia, looks suspiciously like the history of the American Revolution dangled in installment 8. It is patently based on the chapter from Thucydides' *History of the Peloponnesian War* read by the Friendly Club at its October 29, 1796, gathering. And it is clearly inspired by Williams's *Letters from France*, and especially Riouffe's *Revolutionary Justice Displayed*, which in places it echoes directly. But most fundamentally, this "history of intestine commotions," when checked against the relevant events and documents of late 1770s Philadelphia, turns out to be none other than the story of Brown's own Revolution.

"The nation," this history begins, "comprehended a commercial city, peopled by eighty thousand persons, with a small territory annexed. Two factions were for a long time contending for the sovereignty. On one occasion, the party that had been hitherto undermost, obtained the upper place. The maxims by which they intended to deport themselves were, for some time, unknown. That they would revenge themselves upon their adversaries, in any signal or atrocious way, was, by no means expected. Time, however, soon unfolded their characters and views."

What follows in the text is mostly a quite literal depiction of the Pennsylvania Revolution *as the Brown family knew it.* Charles Brown exaggerates parts of the story (late 1770s Philadelphia, for instance, had 25,000 inhabitants, not 80,000) and sensationalizes parts ("victims" weren't, as his text has it, "strangled"—except figuratively; they were intimidated, arrested, imprisoned, exiled). But in the main he offers up a precise rendering of the Revolutionary context of the late 1770s.

Here is Brown's description of the revolutionary party in power in "Magna Graecia," with the factual references to late 1770s Philadelphia— namely, to the activities of the Pennsylvania Revolutionaries, and in particular the Supreme Executive Council with its list of forty-one "inimical" citizens, the series of arrests carried out by Philadelphia militiamen between September 2 and September 5, 1777, and the experiences of the arrestees and their families—highlighted:

The ordinary course and instruments of judicature were esteemed inadequate to their purposes. These would not allow them to select their victims, in sufficient numbers, and with sufficient dispatch. *They therefore erected a* secret *tribunal, and formed a band of* three hundred *persons, who should execute, implicitly, the decrees of this tribunal. These judges were charged with the punishment of those who had been guilty of crimes against the* state. *They set themselves to the vigorous performance of their office.*[83]

On other occasions it has been usual to subject to some appearance of trial, the objects of persecution; to furnish them with an intelligible statement of their offences; to summon them to an audience of their judges; and to found their sentence on some evidence real or pretended . . . . *The members of this tribunal were convened,* daily, for no other purpose *than to form a catalogue of those who should be forthwith sacrificed.*

The avenues to the hall where they assembled were guarded by the troop before mentioned. Having executed the business of the day, the officers of this band of executioners were summoned, and the fatal list was put into their hands. The work of death began at night-fall. This season was adopted to render their proceedings more terrible. For this end, likewise, it was ordered that *no warning should be given to the men whose names were inscribed upon this roll, but by the arrival of the messengers at their door.*[84]

These, dressed in peculiar uniform, marched by night *to the sound of harsh and lamentable music, through the streets of the mute and affrighted city. They stopped at the appointed door, and admission being gained, peaceably or by violence, they proceeded, in silence, to the performance of their commission.* The bow-string was displayed; *the victim torn* from his bed, *from the arms of his wife, from the embraces of his children,* was strangled in an instant; and the breathless corpse, left upon the spot where it had fallen. *They retired,* without any interruption to the silence, *and ended not their circuit till the catalogue was finished.*

To inflict punishment was the intention to these judges; but they considered that our own death is not, in all instances, the greatest evil that we can suffer. . . . *The tribunal therefore conducted itself by a knowledge of the characters of those* whom its malice had *selected. Sometimes the criminal remained untouched, but was compelled to witness the destruction of some of his family.* Sometimes his wife, sometimes his children were strangled before his eyes. *Sometimes, after witnessing the agonies of all that he loved, the sentence was executed on himself.*

The nature of this calamity was adapted to inspire the utmost terror. *No one was apprized of his fate. The list was inscrutable to every eye but that of the tribunal. The adherents to the ruling faction composed about one third of the inhabitants. . . .*

The rage and despair which accompanied the midnight *progress of the executioners, scarcely excited their attention. Their revels and their mirth suffered no interruption or abatement.*

It was asked in vain, by the sufferers, when the power which thus scattered death and dismay was to end. No answer was returned. They were left to form their judgment on the events that arose.[85]

"The Man at Home," coming in late 1797, early 1798, marked out the thematic parameters and rhythms of Brown's maturing imagination, as it foreshadowed his characteristic literary strategy of disguise and concealment. There is here the associational method of the Rhapsodist, and the use of Gothic devices. There is a concern with the moral function of his writing which derives from his Quaker heritage and is recast now into Godwinian philosophical terms. There are the intermixed themes of the Irish, the French Revolution and its detritus, and the yellow fever. More covertly, there is a profound empathy with the life experience of his father. In this regard, beyond the central experience of "a debtor in Philadelphia"—which is, alas, what Elijah Brown was—the two key learning episodes the "man at home" dredges up on "tasking my memory"—the lazaretto and the business venture as a supercargo—were Elijah Brown's experiences too (the elder Brown's "lazaretto" being early 1778 Winchester, where most of the exiles got seriously ill and two died; and his business venture being his own voyage abroad, to the West Indies, on his brother-in-law's vessel in 1770). Finally, there is the all-encompassing historical experience of being a Quaker in Revolutionary Pennsylvania. Charles Brown would never again treat this topic as "factually" as he does in the eleventh installment of "The Man at Home," but he would seldom in his writing *not treat it.* The novels soon to come—four in the next two years—would simply transmute it into Gothic "fiction."

Interlude
Philadelphia, 1795–1799:
"renderings in the bowels of nations"

Revolutionary conditions returned to Philadelphia in the mid-1790s as the partisan passions ignited by Citizen Genet's arrival in May 1793 and dampened by the ensuing yellow fever epidemic rekindled in 1794 with news of the spreading French terror, a successful slave rebellion in Saint-Domingue, and British naval attacks on American shipping. Once again militant crowds roamed through neighborhoods, this time with men dressed *à la française,* sporting chopped hair, pantaloons, laced shoes, and liberty caps, and calling each other "citizen." When John Jay left for England on his diplomatic mission in May 1794, a "mob" met to hang, guillotine, *and* blow him up in effigy. In September, the Washington administration mobilized against the Whiskey Rebels who were defying federal tax collectors out in western Pennsylvania. This brought marching militias again to Philadelphia's streets. Oliver Wolcott, comptroller of the treasury, observed in October that the "fuel for an explosion is doubtless prepared; our public happiness must of necessity be exposed to the risque attending great revolutions of manners and opinions."[1]

The partisan passion and violence gained a focus in mid-1795 when the humiliating terms of the Jay Treaty were made public. In response demonstrations were organized, and pro- and anti-treaty "mobs" worked the streets. The new political alignments, with their new political rhetoric of abuse, had a test run in the local, state, and national elections of 1796. What followed then were the culminations of 1797–98 and beyond: beginning with the "XYZ" revelations about the French Directory's attempt to extort money from the American government, the American government's army and navy bills and general military preparations, French attacks on American merchant ships in the West Indies, and Congress's passage of the xenophobic Alien and Sedition Acts. Once again, it could be said, the United States was at war; as once again Americans were being sorted out into "patriots" and "traitors." And once again, in Philadelphia, mobs broke the windows of political opponents, and gunfire routinely accompanied election day contests and Independence Day celebrations. Even cannon sounds had returned.[2]

The Quaker Elizabeth Drinker, still living (as she had in the 1770s) on North Front Street, was clearly unsettled by these conditions, as evidenced by her obsession with fires. Not just the common and expected house or stable flare-ups in Philadelphia, but any news or rumors of fires breaking out in Boston or New York or Norfolk or Charleston, or Somerset County, New Jersey, commanded her attention. In her diary she doesn't specify the rationale for her nervous interest, but it is clearly bound up with her fear of the French Revolution and its potential agents.[3]

In these years Elizabeth Drinker spends more and more of her time reading. She takes up such recent works as Wollstonecraft's *Vindication of the Rights of Woman* and Riouffe's *Revolutionary Justice Displayed*, along with *Caleb Williams*, *The Mysteries of Udolpho*, and *The Monk*, but also—and not coincidentally—her thoughts drift back to the painful and, for her, analogous time of the late 1770s, when Revolutionary "mobs" had arrested and exiled her husband. In March 1795, for instance, the death of Thomas Affleck reminds her of the "22, who were sent into banishment with my Husband in Sepr. 1777," and the October 1795 funeral of Jane Roberts calls up her memory of the execution of Jane's husband, the Quaker John Roberts, along with Abraham Carlisle, "about 17. years ago." In March 1798, in the wake of a fistfight on the floor of Congress between the two New Englanders Matthew Lyon and Roger Griswold, and a "mob fashion" electioneering contest that was bringing Jeffersonian Republicans—or what she called

Frigate *United States*

"Jacobins"—to power in the state and city, and as war with France loomed, she reads "The Address to the Inhabitants of Pennsylvania by our Friends and others who were then prisoners in the Masons Lodge, 20 years ago." "It revived old feelings," she reports. In May 1798, with war fever rampant, and after the national Fast Day proclaimed by President Adams, during which all the shops in the city were shut up, "save Quakers and Democrates, which were keept open, from different principles," and with troops of light-horsemen patrolling the city, she travels even further back into the Pennsylvania Quaker past by reading "a pamphlet, entitled, A Narrative of the late Massacres in Lancaster county of a number of Indians, friends of this province, by persons unknown . . . dated 1764." Of this work she notes: "I read it at the time of publication, the Shocking Murders and the circumstances are fresh in my memory."[4]

Much had changed in Philadelphia since the days of the Paxton Boys and the Revolutionary War. Quakers, for one, had long since given up any semblance of clan political power in the city where their absolute numbers had peaked and their relative numbers were in sharp decline. Among Philadelphia's now 50,000-plus inhabitants there were over ten thousand Germans, several thousand recent French émigrés, and some three thousand African Americans. As for the two powerful political-ethnic-religious entities of the past, Quakers and Scots-Irish Presbyterians, the Quaker community numbered slightly over 5,000 in the 1790s and early 1800s. This means that in the early to mid-1790s Friends made up around 10 percent of the city's population, but that by 1800 their share had dropped to around 6 percent. Meanwhile, every year in the decade brought to the city some 3,000 new Irish refugees from the European revolutionary turmoil. (By 1800, it has been estimated, perhaps 12 percent of Philadelphia's population was made up of Irish immigrants who had migrated in the 1790s alone.) Elizabeth Drinker registers her sense of this latter development in a remark about "a mobb" "riseing" in the Northern Liberties— where recent Irish immigrants were concentrated—and in her anxiety over the possible political activities of the pro-French revolutionary United Irishmen. Indeed her obsession with fires is seemingly linked with her fear of the Irish "inserrection[ist]s."[5]

In this thought, *new* linked up with *old*, at least in a Philadelphia Quaker's imagination. The "riotous doings" of the July 4, 1795, celebrations to which Drinker referred were part and parcel of the anti-Jay Treaty campaign led by, among others, John Swanwick and Blair McClenachan. Swanwick had emerged in the early 1790s as a pioneer in the new partisan methods of campaigning and a leader of the "new Irish" community. A member of the pro-French Democratic Society of Pennsylvania, in 1794 he became the first of the new-style politicians in Philadelphia to win election to Congress. Blair McClenachan, in 1796, was the second. McClenachan, a native-born Irishman and president of the Democratic Society, represented the new

1790s Jeffersonian Republican Irish constituency in his politics; but he also symbolized *the old* cultural "Irish" element, for, having come to Pennsylvania in the early 1770s, he had been one of the "Presbyterians" in the 1770s pushing and exploiting the Pennsylvania Revolution. (For his efforts he had ended up as a successful merchant in 1780s, early 1790s Philadelphia, and the owner of Cliveden, the Germantown estate that Benjamin Chew—Henrietta's father—had had to sell because of the Revolution.) This nexus of new and old, this cultural feeling of déjà vu, was evoked by Elizabeth Drinker's husband, Henry, when in February 1798 he did, in the eyes of his wife at least, a surprising thing: for the first time since Pennsylvania Revolutionaries took his suffrage away in 1776–77, he voted in a civic election. (This election day entry in Elizabeth Drinker's diary reads like an entry from the 1770s: "Drum and Fife, a Croud with lighted Candles, a little mob fashion, went by this evening.") In this context it isn't that the Drinkers are thrilled when Federalist candidates prevail; it's just that it makes them somewhat less uneasy than when "Jacobins," and especially *Irish* "Jacobins," win out.[6]

The Philadelphia Quaker Meeting responded to the new conditions of the 1790s by strengthening the Discipline. In particular it addressed the crisis of "the rising generation." This involved the predilection of Quaker "children and youth" to join in the city's partisan political activities and their corresponding tendency to stay away from weekly meeting. The Meeting restated its basic principles in a 1799 Epistle:

We . . . cannot join with such as form combinations of a hostile nature against any; nor can we unite with, or encourage such as revile and asperse those who are placed in authority over us; for it is written, Acts xxiii v. "Thou shalt not speak evil of the ruler of thy people." We therefore intreat . . . "When you see divisions and parties, and renderings in the bowels of nations, and rumors and tempests in the minds of people, then take heed of being moved to this party or to that party, or giving your strength to this or that, or counselling this way or that; but stand single to the truth of God, in which neither war, rent nor division is."[7]

Elizabeth Drinker displayed her own proper Quakerism in her reaction to the swarms of citizens—she estimated 20,000—that in early May 1797 flocked to the docks to witness the launching of the frigate *United States*. Her comment: "The first vessel that ever was built here, and I wish I could say it was the last that ever would be." By "vessel" she didn't mean "vessel," for shipbuilding had long been a staple of Philadelphia's economy, not to say a vital component in the prosperity of Quaker merchants like her husband. She meant a *warship*.[8]

Charles Brown, who was still a member in good standing of the Northern District Monthly Meeting, went to check out the *United States* on May 4, 1797, in the company of Elihu Hubbard Smith and Uriah Tracy. Smith was in town attending a Manumission Society convention and, as always, in the midst of a social whirl. Part of his time Smith spent with his politico friends, like Federalist Representative Tracy and even President Adams, who invited Smith to dine with him at the presidential mansion. Smith also spent time with prominent local Republican citizens Benjamin Rush, Dr. Wistar, and Blair McClenachan. At other times he socialized with Charles Brown and *his* Quaker coterie, including Bringhurst, Thomas Cope, brother Armitt Brown, and Timothy Paxon. One day Smith, along with fellow Manumission Society colleagues William Dunlap and Samuel Mitchell, and Brown, visited the city's Walnut Street jail—which thirteen years before had held Brown's father—and "spent two hours [there], with great satisfaction."[9]

Smith, in his diary, does not record Brown's sense of the experience; nor, four days earlier, had he recorded Brown's feelings about the Quaker City's first warship. And as Smith left Philadelphia for New York early on the morning of May 10, he missed the thousands and thousands of citizens who passed by the Brown house on Second Street on their way to view the *United States* at the navy yard, and so he could not record Brown's comments about that spectacle. Nor, for that matter, did he mention in his diary the writings—"The Man at Home" and *Alcuin* among them—that Brown was at work on. All the same, in the midst of a city once again smoldering with revolutionary politics, Brown's imagination was at work.[10]

Part II
Fictions and Facts, 1798–1800

". . . on the top of a rock whose sides were steep, rugged, and encumbered with dwarf cedars and stony asperities, he built what to a common eye would have seemed a summer-house. The eastern verge of this precipice was sixty feet above the river which flowed at its foot. The view before it consisted of a transparent current, fluctuating and rippling in a rocky channel." *(Wieland; or, The Transformation, an American Tale)*

Chapter 4

Sins of Fathers

Wieland was inspired by an actual murder in upstate New York, an account of which Brown could have read in the *New York Weekly Magazine* in late July 1796. As the newspaper recalled the incident, one James Yates, bidden by a "spirit" to destroy all his idols, in succession "dashed out the brains" of his two sleeping sons, killed his baby daughter, and beat his wife to death with a "stake from the garden fence." Yates then destroyed his eldest daughter, after making her dance and sing beside her mother's corpse. He then assaulted his sister. She, however, got away. Captured by neighbors, Yates refused to repent for his acts. Instead he prostrated himself on the ground and exclaimed: "my father, thou knowest that it was in obedience to thy commands, and for thy glory, that I have done this deed." Taken to jail as a lunatic, Yates twice escaped, both times being recaptured.[1]

Sometime after reading the newspaper account, Brown set down his thoughts for a dramatic treatment in an "outline." He began seriously writing the novel in Philadelphia in the spring and early summer of 1798 and worked on it in New York through the rest of the summer. *Wieland; or The Transformation, an American Tale* was published, in New York, in September 1798.[2]

One indication that *Wieland* concerns aspects of Brown himself and his own life experience is in the names he initially accords his three protagonists. In the "outline" they are *Charles*, *Charl*otte, and *Caro*line. (In the actual novel these are changed to Theodore, Catharine, and Clara.) A second apparently calculated feature of the novel is the age given to its narrator, Clara, at the time of the mysterious "end" of her father. This is the key family experience around which everything else in the story revolves, and when it occurs, Clara is six: the precise age of Brockden Brown at the time of *his* father's mysterious "demise," that is, when Elijah Brown was arrested, imprisoned, and exiled by fellow Philadelphians. The fictional Wielands, like the historical Browns, are to be embroiled in the consequences of a disorienting family trauma.[3]

* * *

In its broadest aspect *Wieland* is grounded in the radical pietist origins of William Penn's colony, which context Brown invokes in various ways. For instance, when he gives his Wieland family a French Protestant "Camisard" past, he calls up the heritage of a Brown family friend and the most renowned mid- to late eighteenth-century Philadelphia Quaker of all, Anthony Benezet. The Benezets had their European roots in the Albigensian heresy of southern France, and their journey away from religious persecution and toward religious freedom and purity had passed, as it almost had to, through Rotterdam and London. Here they were thrown into the mix of fellow Camisards, German Anabaptist pietists, Quakers, and the English sect known as the "Philadelphia Society," who all shared the mystical "light" quest. Many of these seekers, helped along by William Penn's land agents, made their way to Pennsylvania, and the Benezets—whose son Anthony died in 1784 as the most beloved of eighteenth-century Philadelphians—were among them.[4]

There can be no doubt that Brown had this historical frame in mind for his novel, for he *literally* locates his fictional Wieland family estate, and their "temple," in the very place near Germantown where in the 1690s a renowned group of "Saxon" radical pietists had set up their own little "Philadelphia." In this regard, when Brown has the religious seeker and family patriarch, the elder Wieland, build "what to a common eye would have seemed a summer-house," but which was really his "temple," in the woods "on the top of a rock whose sides were steep, rugged, and encumbered with dwarf cedars and stony asperities," on a precipice "sixty feet above the river which flowed at its foot," he has him do it in the spot northwest of Philadelphia, near where Wissahickon Creek joins the Schuylkill River, where the so-called "Hermits of the Wissahickon," and their spiritual leader, Johannes Kelpius, had established their settlement and "tabernacle"—which to contemporaries looked like "a hall"—in 1694.[5]

Again, the Kelpius community, like the Benezets, were in a religious sense quintessential *ur*-Pennsylvanians. They had left Germany in 1693 for Rotterdam, where they fell in with Benjamin Furly, William Penn's land agent for Pennsylvania. Furly, a one-time Quaker and friend to Penn, Fox, and George Keith (as well as to the English Whig martyr Algernon Sidney, John Locke, and Locke's patron Shaftesbury), then helped move them along, via London, to Penn's colony. While in London, the Kelpius group fell in with the Philadelphia Society for the Advancement of Piety and Divine Philosophy, a band of seekers dedicated to the pietist ideal of a spiritual community of true believers. What the Kelpius group and the Philadelphia Society (and later the Camisards, who began arriving in London in 1706) had in common was an immersion in the mystical theosophist doctrines of the German cobbler Jacob Boehme, the Jewish Cabbala, and a dabbling in the occult of Rosicrucianism. In London, indeed, observers had trouble telling these groups apart. The Philadelphia Society and Quakers, in particular, appeared to be one and the same in their "visionary" doctrines and practices.[6]

Arriving in Philadelphia in June 1694, the forty members of Kelpius's group settled outside Germantown, on the ridge above the Wissahickon, and here they built a structure in which to live and worship which they called a "tabernacle." Their worship, like that of the London Philadelphia Society, combined celibacy, contemplative solitude, and scientific observations of the heavens. It was all designed to advance them on their quest toward *the light*, or what Kelpius himself called the spiritual *fire*. "It is necessary," he wrote, "in the beginning to kindle the fire by working; but afterwards, when once it is kindled, let it burn." As well, "whoso draws near to the fire will be warmed by it . . . [as] the nearer we approach the sun, the stronger and more powerful we find its heat." And as for "the Kingdom of God, which consists in the internal spiritual life," Kelpius described this as "a treasure hid in a field":

We find not this treasure always by such as pretend to be something above others and are in great repute; much rather is it the less there, the more it is exposed to danger. But this treasure is by them who keep themselves hidden and make not much show of themselves, since their fire is concealed inwardly.

Quaker-like in his call for social humility as in so much else, Kelpius pushes on to the plea "to [ascend the Mountain of the Spirit], the highest degree of contemplation, [where the undivided soul may break forth in a creative fire]."[7]

In 1690s Pennsylvania, Kelpius and his brethren were not an unusual group of mystic seekers. Skirting about the pietistic norm, they were representative. They mixed with other groups of religious seekers in the area, and in particular other German-Dutch pietists and Quakers, and just as typically, they split apart and generated new societies of seekers. The Kelpius community itself—known as the "Society of the Woman in the Wilderness" because the Germans identified themselves as the woman in Revelation 12 who had escaped into the wilderness to await her Bridegroom, Christ— underwent such a split in the late 1690s when one of its number, Henry Koster, withdrew with several others, some of whom were apparently Quakers, and formed the "Brethren in America," also known as the "True Church of Philadelphia, or Brotherly Love." This "True Church," in quest of an ever purer form of spirituality, moved to another wilderness spot near Germantown and built *its* own "tabernacle"; and its "brethren" went on to mix with other seemingly like-minded groups. Koster in particular involved himself with the cause of the Quaker schismatic George Keith—the two men had in common, like Kelpius, an interest in the Cabbala—and it was at this explosive time in the early history of Pennsylvania that the great-great-grandparents of Brockden Brown almost certainly came into contact with the Hermits of the Wissahickon.[8]

James and William Browne, the family immigrants, shared with Kelpius, Koster, and countless other early Pennsylvanians the "seeker" nature, and so it was not surprising that the brothers would be drawn into the Keithian controversy. Actually, as pious Quaker farmers in 1690s Chichester—a Keithian hotbed—it would have been hard for them to avoid entanglement. Here is how Brown family legend recorded this early context of "seeking":

Keith, who coming to their meeting at Chichester . . . spake or preached largely using some arrogant and lofty expressions, beyond the simplicity of the gospel; expressing that the hearers might know his doctrine was right by the power that attended it. After this meeting James and William had some conversation on the subject, wherein James expressed approbation. . . . William being a deep feeling man was doubtful and more cautious of joining with a spirit which he thought was leading some into a separation from the Truth, therefore replied to his brother, "I am satisfied, but it is in this, that he is in a wrong spirit:" which James rather took amiss and thereupon was about to leave his brother hastily, but William stop'd him or stepped after him, querying of him whether he did not remember how they used to feel at their meetings when in England, though they were but as lads; and so mentioned nearly to the following import concerning the love and melting seasons they were often sensible of under the powerful operation of the pure principle of Love and Light.

The family legend concludes with the two brothers urging themselves to "remember that the truth is still as precious as ever, and perhaps it is now time for us more fully to resume our former exercise of spirit."[9]

Historians have explained the perplexing Pennsylvania phenomenon of the 1690s Keithian Schism in terms of social-political conflict (with Keith, supposedly, advancing the "progressive" cause of small merchants, shopkeepers, artisans, and farmers against the policies and pretensions of an arrogant Quaker elite) and as a theological squabble (with Keith attempting to mute the implicit antinomianism of Quakerism by requiring of all Quakers an explicit confession of faith). But perhaps the Keith affair makes the most sense when it is viewed simply as a kind of free-flowing cultural ferment fed, willy-nilly, by the extreme spiritual energies of the time and place. In this context, what stands out about Keith is the farthest reach of his Gnostic quest for esoteric knowledge: his Hermeticism and Cabbalism.[10]

George Keith, a Scottish Presbyterian who was converted to Quakerism in the 1660s by William Dewsbury—the man who converted Richard Browne of Northamptonshire—and who thereafter belonged, along with Fox, Robert Barclay, Isaac Penington, and William Penn, in the group of leading Quakers, sought in the supposed pre-Mosaic writings of the Egyptian Hermes Trismegistus and in the Jewish Cabbala dimensions of knowledge and spiritual answers, or in a word *light*, unavailable to him elsewhere. What he found through these studies—the notions of the transmigration of souls and reincarnation—he made a central facet of his Quaker theology. Eventually this would bring him trouble with Quakerism's authorities, but in the 1670s and 1680s he was only doing what so many other Quaker seekers were doing: seeking knowledge and "truth." His friends and European traveling companions, Fox, Penn, Barclay, and Benjamin Furly, were doing the same, as, in the 1670s, was a charismatic Dutch-Flemish nobleman and seeker and Quaker-to-be, Francis Mercury van Helmont. Van Helmont, who called himself "a wandering eremite," was a devotee of the Cabbala, the theosophy of Jacob Boehme, Rosicrucianism, astrology, and other magic-Hermetic traditions. A friend to Locke, Leibniz, Robert Boyle, and Henry More, he met Fox, Barclay, Penn, and Keith and, impressed by their examples and especially by Keith, he converted to Quakerism.[11]

On the Continent in the 1670s, 1680s, and 1690s, van Helmont worked, as did Fox, Penn, and Furly, to convince spiritually compatible German pietists to migrate to Pennsylvania. One such German was a Lutheran deacon in Württemberg, Johann Jakob Zimmermann. Zimmermann, like van Helmont and Keith, was a student of the Cabbala and the mystic Boehme, and in 1685 he was condemned as "doctissimus Astrologus, Magus, and Cabbalista." Dismissed from his official church post, Zimmermann traveled though Germany and Holland. For a time he channeled his religiously based interest in mathematics and astronomy into a professorship in Heidelberg. But his ultimate goal was the colony promoted by William Penn, where he planned to realize a millenarian "Chapter of Perfection." Leaving Germany in 1693, Zimmermann, alas, never made it to Pennsylvania, for he died en route. But his disciple Johannes Kelpius, along with thirty-nine companions, did make it across the ocean, after first spending a season in London, where they mixed with the quasi-Quaker mystics, Rosicrucians, and Cabbalists of the Philadelphia Society. Consequently, in 1695–96, the energies and spiritual strivings of Kelpius, Zimmermann, van Helmont, Keith, and the pre-1680s William Penn and George Fox (the latter claimed to possess the power to effect miracles, and in particular miraculous cures), transpired in the humble Chester County village of Chichester.[12]

When Kelpius and his "Chapter of Perfection" built their "tabernacle" in 1694 above the Wissahickon, they built a structure said to be—after Rosicrucian calculations—forty feet square, with an observatory on the roof, where brethren would sit through the night with a telescope to search for celestial phenomenon, in millennial anticipation of the coming of the "Bridegroom." (By the late eighteenth century—when Brockden Brown would have had an opportunity to see it—this structure was mostly in ruins, except for the walls and "the large lower room, which was *circular* in form," where there were "remnants of an altar and a large iron cross fixed against the wall.") A year later, concerns about "Astrologors Magitions Southsayors Stargazers" had percolated down into Chester County, surfacing at the Concord Quarterly Meeting (which subsumed the Chichester Monthly Meeting). This can be seen, in part, as an application of Fox's warnings, first raised back in London in 1684, about van Helmont's Cabbalistic notions—some of which Keith shared. More generally the Meeting's admonitions simply registered the ongoing spiritual efflorescence of the Quaker experiment in Pennsylvania.[13]

In this context, it became the official task of the 1696 Yearly Meeting, held in Burlington, first to air and then, most important, to put down, to define as beyond the acceptable pale, these heterodox expressions of "Quakerism." At this gathering, which owing to the Keithian crisis was "considerably Larger than any heretofore in this Place," "Divers" of "the Adversaries of Truth"—as the clerk of the Meeting phrased it in the official minutes—"appear'd among us at this Time to give us Trouble, & disturb the Peace of our Meeting." Among these was one of the "Stargazers," Henry Koster, who appeared as a leading Keithian. To continue with the official minutes:

up steps divers Germans & others, who were very Fierce & violent Opposers, the Chiefest of them was one of those called Pietists, his Name—Henry Barnard Coster, whom Friends in London as we hear assisted in their Coming here which (if True) they [the German pietists] are very Ungrateful and Forgetful of their Kindnesses Receiv'd, For divers of them have given Friends here much Exercise & Trouble, but especially at this Meeting, where they brought divers Friends Books with them, Some of E[dward] B[urrough], Some of W[illiam] P[enn], & the Clamour that they made against us was, that We deny the Lord Jesus Christ & they were there to Prove it out of those Books.

It is likely that James and William Browne attended this Yearly Meeting (for aside from their status as committed Quakers, they were both from Burlington and still had relatives and friends there), and it is certain that they were aware of the spiritual cravings and religious strife, and the specific drama, that came to a head there. Also aware of this time and place, and its tendencies—by the evidence of *Wieland*—was James's great-great-grandson.[14]

Viewed generally, the mystical strivings of Johannes Kelpius, Henry Koster, and their "Saxon" cohorts were akin to the strivings of many of the early Quakers, among whom were Richard, James, and William Browne and John Churchman of Nottingham. The Wissahickon "hermits" wrote of the "conviction of being impelled by a power to live apart from the vices and temptations of the world, and to be prepared for some immediate and strange revelations which could not be communicated amid scenes of worldly life, strife and dissipation, but would be imparted in the silence and solitude of the wilderness to those who came out from iniquity." Brockden Brown's most noteworthy American ancestor, John Churchman, had heard this call too, to the point where he was once tempted to abandon his wife and family "to go into some remote place where I should not be known." John Churchman had first felt the "glorious light" when he was about eight, and as a mature man—*when he was Elijah Brown's minister*—he had counseled parents—*like Brockden Brown's grandfather James and grandmother Miriam*— that "by living in the pure fear of the Lord, and near the spirit of truth in their own hearts, they may be furnished with example, and precept to direct the minds of their offspring, to attend to the voice of him who called to Samuel in days of old, and remains to be the same teacher to his people in this age."[15]

Some such place as this, then, some such "wilderness" community marked by a burning piety and an ever-twisting spiritual striving, a place like Kelpius-Koster's Wissahickon or the Browne brothers' Chichester or the Browns-Churchmans' Nottingham, is the setting for *Wieland.* Brockden Brown calls it "Mettingen."

*   *   *

The Wielands come from Germany. The grandfather, a "native of Saxony" (6), was college educated and from a noble family. When he married the non-noble daughter of a Hamburg merchant, his family disowned him. Thereafter he lived in Hamburg, made a "scant" income composing sonatas and dramatic pieces, and died young, with his wife soon following him to the grave. Left behind was one son, from whose spiritual/psychological makeup would flow all the tragedies in the tale.

This Wieland—the "father" in the novel—is a seeker. Apprenticed to a merchant in London, he grew dissatisfied with his circumstances and gave in to "morose and gloomy reflection," and it was "in this state of mind" that he happened upon a book written by "one of the teachers of the Albigenses." Opening it, his eyes "lighted" upon the words, "'Seek and ye shall find.'" In this book he found an exposition of the French Camisard doctrine and a historical account of the Camisards' origins, and with this, "The craving which had haunted him was now supplied with an object" (7–8).

Wieland next passes through the familiar phases of the spiritual seeker. Beginning an ardent study of the Bible, he applied the mystical beliefs of the Camisards to its exegesis, and in the process he became what others would call a religious fanatic.

His constructions of the [biblical] text were hasty, and formed on a narrow scale. Every thing was viewed in a disconnected position. . . . Hence arose a thousand scruples to which he had hitherto been a stranger. He was alternately agitated by fear and by ecstacy. He imagined himself beset by the snares of a spiritual foe, and that his security lay in ceaseless watchfulness and prayer.

His morals, which had never been loose, were now modeled by a stricter standard. The empire of religious duty extended itself to his looks, gestures, and phrases. All levities of speech, and negligences of behaviour, were proscribed. His air was mournful and contemplative. He laboured to keep alive a sentiment of fear, and a belief of the awe-inspiring presence of the Deity. Ideas foreign to this were sedulously excluded. To suffer their intrusion was a crime against the Divine Majesty, inexpiable but by days and weeks of the keenest agonies. (8–9)

Wieland, feeling it "his duty to disseminate the truths of the gospel among the unbelieving nations," and helped along by the fact that "residence in England had . . . become almost impossible, on account of his religious tenets" (9), was now ready for the migration to America and a new, purified life. So he embarked for Philadelphia, and five miles outside that city, along the Schuylkill River, he bought a farm at a place called Mettingen.

Fourteen years now elapse in the life of Wieland, during which time he married, and, with the aid of African slaves, materially prospered. As a result he was afforded leisure time, and with this his thoughts returned to their old channel. "The reading of the scriptures, and other religious books, became once more his favorite employment. His ancient belief relative to the conversion of the savage tribes, was revived with uncommon energy. To the former obstacles were now added the pleadings of parental and conjugal love. The struggle was long and vehement; but his sense of duty would not be stifled or enfeebled, and finally triumphed over every impediment." That is, he left his family and went off into the forest as a missionary. Here, "the licence of savage passion, and the artifices of his depraved countrymen, all opposed themselves to his progress." He persisted though—until "at length" he returned to his family, with "a constitution somewhat decayed" (10).

So far Brown has recounted a generic "pilgrim's progress" undergone by the likes of Anthony Benezet, Richard Browne of Northamptonshire, and William and James Browne of Nottingham, among hundreds of others in Pennsylvania history. What he concocts next is an intensification of the seeking, as could be illustrated, say, by the examples of Johannes Kelpius and Henry Koster and the eccentric Finnish mystic Peter Schaffer (who did go off at one point as a missionary to the native Indians, and who, upon leaving the Kelpius community, entered upon a "death-fast," in which he received a revelation that he would arise and wander about at random), and—for a time—John Churchman.[16]

The seeker Wieland, *Wieland* reports, "allied himself with no sect, because he perfectly agreed with none. . . . He rigidly interpreted that precept which enjoins us, when we worship, to retire into solitude, and shut out every species of society. According to him devotion was not only a silent office, but must be performed alone." And so out in the woods he built the "temple of his Deity." The edifice was "slight and airy" (10–11), a circular area no more than twelve feet in diameter, edged by twelve Tuscan columns and covered by an undulating dome.[17]

Wieland's neighbors might call him "a fanatic and a dreamer, but they could not deny their veneration to his invincible candour and invariable integrity." Though a "sadness perpetually overspread his features," it was "unmingled with sternness or discontent. The tones of his voice, his gestures, his steps were all in tranquil unison. His conduct was characterised by a certain forbearance and humility, which secured the esteem of those to whom his tenets were most obnoxious" (11).

Wieland, in short, was and could have remained a valuable member of his Pennsylvania society—only he was doomed by the very intensity of his quest for purity. He became obsessed with a vague sense of failure, with what he deemed a personal "disobedience." That is, a "command," he believed, "had been laid upon him, which he had delayed to perform." "The duty assigned to him," then, "was transferred, in consequence of his disobedience, to another, and all that remained was to endure the penalty." These morbid thoughts fed upon themselves; and he became convinced of his imminent "end." About this, "His imagination did not prefigure the mode or the time of his decease, but was fraught with an incurable persuasion that his death was at hand" (12).

Wieland was "haunted" by the belief that "the kind of death that awaited him was strange and terrible" (12), and to be sure the manner of his death—spontaneous combustion—could be described in these terms. Yet it also carries a delicious appropriateness. After all, the seeker George Fox had written that "the Word of the Lord was like a fire in me"; and in William Penn's writings "God is light" and His "fire must come from heaven." John Woolman had once awoken in the night to see "a light in my chamber at the apparent distance of five feet, about nine inches diameter, of a clear easy brightness; and near its center the most radiant; and as I lay still without any surprise looking upon it, words were spoken to my inward ear." John Churchman had once dreamed of riding a horse and seeing "a light before me towards sun-rising, which did not appear to be a common light, but soon [I] observed the appearance of something therein, whereat the beast I rode was much affrighted and would have run from it, which I knew would be vain; for I took it to be an Angel, whose motion was as swift as thought, so [I] rather stopt and reined in my beast towards it; it was encompassed with a brightness like a rainbow." Churchman, in his *Account of the Gospel Labours, and Christian Experiences of a Faithful Minister of Christ*, a book published in Philadelphia in 1779, went on further to describe this "light":

it rather seemed to move even along than to walk, and then stood still in the midst of many curious stacks of corn, it was of a human form about seven feet high (as I thought,) and smiling on me, asked where I was going.

And another Pennsylvania seeker after "spiritual fire," Johannes Kelpius, wrote of the need to "kindle [it]" and "let it burn." So, in a sense, Brockden Brown *gives* his character, the elder Wieland, that which Churchman turned his terrified horse *toward* and that which Wieland himself craves. Which is to say, Brown has *this* happen to Wieland:

while engaged in silent orisons, with thoughts full of confusion and anxiety, a faint gleam suddenly shot athwart the apartment. His fancy immediately pictured to itself, a person bearing a lamp. It seemed to come from behind. He was in the act of turning to examine the visitant, when his right arm received a blow from a heavy club. At the same instant, a very bright spark was seen to light upon his clothes. In a moment, the whole was reduced to ashes. (17)[18]

This is Wieland's own "imperfect account" (17) of his "mysterious" demise. There are, in the novel, three other witnesses to the horrifying event, and they describe it not in the (as it were) "orthodox" mystical manner of Wieland himself, but in more empirical terms. Wieland's wife, for instance, who observed the event from across a clearing, describes what happened in the temple this way:

Suddenly it was illuminated. A light proceeding from the edifice, made every part of the scene visible. A gleam diffused itself over the intermediate space, and instantly a loud report, like the explosion of a mine, followed. . . . The gleams, which had diffused themselves far and wide were in a moment withdrawn, but the interior of the edifice was filled with rays. (15)

Wieland's wife's brother, likewise an eyewitness, "also imagined what he saw to be fire." According to this account,

a blazing light was clearly discernible between the columns of the temple. . . . Within the columns he [Wieland's brother-in-law] beheld what he could no better describe, than by saying that it resembled a cloud impregnated with light. It had the brightness of flame, but was without its upward motion. . . . No part of the building was on fire. This appearance was astonishing. He approached the temple. As he went forward the light retired, and . . . [then] utterly vanished. . . . Fear and wonder rendered him powerless. An occurrence like this, in a place assigned to devotion, was adapted to intimidate the stoutest heart. (16)

The third witness was—is—the novel's narrator. This is Wieland's daughter Clara, who was six years old at the time of the "mournful catastrophe" (13). In the opening section of the novel, she is recalling this pivotal traumatic event from her family's past. In this regard it is not clear, from what she says, whether Clara had been an actual *eye*witness to her father's combustion, but it is clear that she had been at Mettingen when the horror occurred, and that she has heard her uncle's version of events. Here's how Clara remembers "the end of my father":

None surely was ever more mysterious. When we recollect his gloomy anticipations and unconquerable anxiety; the security from human malice which his character, the place, and the condition of the times, might be supposed to confer; the purity and cloudlessness of the atmosphere, which rendered it impossible that lightning was the cause; what are the conclusions that we must form?

The prelusive gleam, the blow upon his arm, the fatal spark, the explosion heard so far, the fiery cloud that environed him . . . the sudden vanishing of this cloud at my uncle's approach—what is the inference to be drawn from these facts? (17)

It seems apparent that Brockden Brown modeled the elder Wieland's own sense of his immolation after Quaker testimonies about spiritual "illumination." (Brown had read the classic texts by Fox, Penn, Woolman, et al. at the Friends' Latin School, and if he had missed Churchman's *Account* there, he almost certainly would have read it at home, for his father had a special interest in Churchman. Brown also, at meeting, would have heard a bevy of testimonies about the coming of "the light.") But what about his three *witnesses*, those loved ones profoundly affected by the "mournful catastrophe"? Their accounts carry a different feeling, and it is indeed here where Brown invokes in *Wieland* the weight of a second historical experience: one which he didn't need to read or ask elders about, but which was simply, viscerally, a part of him.

The three witnesses associate what happened with disturbing noises, such as one would hear in wartime. "A loud report, like the explosion of a mine. . . . The first suggestion was that a pistol was discharged, and that the structure was on fire. . . . Piercing shrieks. . . . loud and vehement shrieks." Is *Wieland*'s author drawing on his own store of memories when *he* was six? There are unquestionably echoes here of 1777 Philadelphia. For instance, from a Philadelphia diary, March 4, 1777: "demonstrations of joy from the Mob, the Cannon fired & Bells rung . . . & in order to heighten the farce in the evening was fire rockets & Bonfires." July 4, 1777: "about 4 the fireing of Cannon began which was terible to hear . . . & in the evening were illuminations, & those people's windows were broke who put no Candles in . . . N[icholas] Waln 14 [windows broken]." And on *the day* that the six-year-old Charles Brown's father was carried away from Philadelphia, September 11, 1777: "a great fireing heard below [the town]." Which noise was the Battle of Brandywine.[19]

Curious, too, is that in relating the events surrounding "the end of my father," Clara gives special credence to "my uncle's testimony." When Charles Brown, in 1777, "witnessed" his own father's "catastrophe," the two people, other than his mother, who were best situated to try to explain to him what was going on were his uncles, Nicholas and Richard Waln. Uncle Nicholas, it can be presumed, was among the visitors to the Masonic Lodge—a kind of "temple," no?—during the week of September 5 to 11, 1777, when Elijah Brown was imprisoned there and all sorts of mysterious and terrifying things were happening, as for the ensuing eight months he would have been a frequent visitor at 117 South Second. Uncle Richard— who like the uncle in the novel had a "skeptical" temper and a "belief" "unalterably attached to natural causes"—for his part, was vital for Charles and his family, for during the winter of 1777–78, the Browns lived off his money.[20]

In any case, Brockden Brown, writing this opening section of *Wieland* in the spring and summer of 1798—at a time when the sounds of revolution and war had returned to the streets of Philadelphia and New York—has his narrator, who is writing in "the present" about past family traumas, remark: "Their resemblance to recent events revived them with new force in my memory, and made me more anxious to explain them." And Brown could not be clearer about the psychological dynamic, and its entanglement with family history and historical events, that lies at the core of his "tale." As Clara explains it: "I was at this time a child of six years of age. The impressions that were then made upon me, can never be effaced. I was ill qualified to judge respecting what was then passing; but as I advanced in age, and became more fully acquainted with these facts, they oftener became the subject of my thoughts" (17–18).[21]

*   *   *

In Brown's "American Tale," one generation's traits get passed down, transmogrified, to the next generation, which suffers accordingly.

In the years after Wieland's mysterious demise (conveniently, his wife dies soon after him), Wieland's two children Clara and Theodore grow up with a kindly maiden aunt, and they seem destined for happiness and fulfillment. And why not? The time is that of the enlightened American mid-eighteenth century. The dark, twisted, "European" mystical strains that had deranged their father would seem to have no claim on them. They were cultured and sociable Pennsylvanians. Clara in particular, along with her circle of friends, self-consciously molded herself within a pleasant, easygoing deism. In her words, "Our education had been modelled by no religious standard." Not that "we were without religion, but with us it was the product of lively feelings, excited by reflection on our own happiness, and by the grandeur of external nature." Unlike her father, "we sought not a basis for our faith, in the weighing of proofs, and the dissection of creeds" (21).

On the other hand, her brother Theodore, for all his rationalism, was not as lighthearted. His deportment, Clara says, "was grave, considerate, and thoughtful. . . . Human life, in his opinion, was made up of changeable elements, and the principles of duty were not easily unfolded." Moreover, Theodore had "a propensity to ruminate on these truths." His features and tone "bespoke a sort of thrilling melancholy." In this regard Clara has to admit "an obvious resemblance between him and my father." However, while "their characters were similar," "the mind of the son was enriched by science, and embellished with literature." Surely this, the novel posits—and "enlightened" late eighteenth-century American Revolutionaries would have readily concurred—makes all the difference in the world. Unlike the "Saxon" background of the elder Wieland, Theodore's roots, like Clara's, were in the wholesome soil and intellectual climate of eighteenth-century Pennsylvania. And so, where the father searched Camisard tracts for "the light," Theodore parses Cicero for the principles of right reason. And where the father visited his austere "temple" in quest of the sacred flame,

Clara, Theodore, and their friends go to that summer house-like structure, which they furnish with a bust of Cicero and a harpsichord, to enjoy themselves, to read poetry, to sing, and on occasion, to "banquet" (21–22).

The descent of Theodore Wieland into madness and murder takes place in the period between the French and Indian War and the American Revolution. During six years of "uninterrupted happiness" (25), Theodore has married and had four children, as well as adopted a daughter. His wife, Catharine, is Clara's best friend. His best friend, Henry Pleyel—a fellow Ciceronian, no less—is Catharine's brother and appears headed for marriage to Clara. In such an idyllic and enlightened and symmetrical setting as this, what could go wrong?[22]

Plenty. In the tale, Theodore is going to kill his wife and all five of his children, and he will attack his sister Clara (who has a particular fear about being raped). This is the novel's "tragedy." An interloper character, one Carwin, whose ventriloquistic talent sets off "voices" in Theodore's head, is going to be implicated in these events. But Carwin will not be their cause. The germ of the tragedy, as *Wieland* dramatizes it, is the very sensibilities of Theodore and Clara. Whatever their professions and the apparent auspicious circumstances of their "Mettingen," the experience of their father's catastrophe has had its profound effect. Because of *it*, and perhaps because of inherited family traits, neither of them is psychologically suited to confront life's complexities. Their continuing happiness, then, depends on life remaining calm, clear, straightforward, and unmysterious.

The Gothic spiral down into terror begins with a "voice" that Theodore hears one night as he walks to the "temple" to pick up, of all things, a Ciceronian text. The voice, which sounds like his wife Catharine's, says to Theodore: "'Stop, go no further. There is danger in your path'" (31). When Theodore, obeying it, returns to the main house, he discovers that, not only is Catharine in the house; she has been there the whole time he was away. Theodore, understandably, is confused by this. Pleyel, for his part, puts the whole incident off to "an auricular deception" (33). But Clara is not soothed. She is spooked, and she is spooked because *this* is the very thing she has always, secretly, feared. To the reader at least, Clara at this point seems to overreact ridiculously to this silly little conundrum—except that as events will prove, she knows what she's talking about.

Theodore's hearing of the "voice," she fears, "argued a diseased condition of his frame, which might show itself hereafter in more dangerous symptoms." With Clara's next line, Brown announces the philosophical moral that critics have rightly found in the novel. Thus Clara: "The will is the tool of the understanding, which must fashion its conclusions on the notices of sense. If the senses be depraved, it is impossible to calculate the evils that may flow from the consequent deductions of the understanding" (33).

This is for Brown to turn the philosopher John Locke, and the Enlightenment itself, on their side by highlighting the disturbing implications of the optimistic epistemology that had influenced so many of the Revolutionaries. People like Jefferson and Paine (and Godwin), working from a solid Lockean foundation, maintained that the corruptions of the past could be purged from society and that a new political order, grounded entirely upon right reason, could be erected from a fresh foundation, a tabula rasa. In line with this, a Pennsylvania Revolutionary in 1776 had exulted in the glorious opportunity of

forming a plan of Government upon the most just, rational, equal principles; not exposed as others have hitherto been to caprice or accident or the influence of some mad conqueror or prevailing parties or factions of men but full [of] power to settle our Government from the very foundation "de novo" by deliberate Council directed solely to the publick good, with wisdom impartiality and disinterestedness.

Another Pennsylvania Revolutionary, in the same Lockean spirit, had spoken of the need "to clear every part of the old rubbish out of the way and begin upon a clean foundation." But what Clara—and *Wieland*—is suggesting is that, in view of the ineluctable vagaries of the human mind, there can be no such "clean" start, for in the real world "the testimony of the senses" is necessarily cockeyed. Accordingly, to act self-consciously and self-exultantly in the cause of right reason, of "wisdom impartiality and disinterestedness," is to court not just hubris—but horror. And surely the son of Elijah Brown knew this as well as anybody.[23]

Reading the novel within its full eighteenth-century Pennsylvania Quaker context, it becomes clear that Clara's deepest fear is that her brother was now going to lapse into the gloomy "Saxon"—or mystic pietistic—mood that is the family's heritage. Whatever her joys in the society of her friends, she has always known that her brother "is in some respects, an enthusiast." He has been indelibly marked by the elder Wieland's catastrophe. "His father's death," Clara explains, "was always regarded by him as flowing from a direct and supernatural decree. It visited his meditations oftener than it did mine. The traces which it left were gloomy and permanent" (33–34). Without these "traces," the vocal games of Carwin would have had no effect. As it is, they destroy a family.[24]

With each subsequent appearance of the "voice," additional complications ensue. (Most centrally, Clara's relationship with Henry Pleyel is undermined, as his own senses deceive him into thinking she's sexually involved with Carwin.) With the fourth "aural" episode, all hell breaks loose, in both the novel's text and, seemingly, the novel's author. For *Wieland*, which begins amid the radical pietistic foundations of eighteenth-century Pennsylvania, works out its climax amid the memories and associations and emotions of a Philadelphia Quaker's Revolutionary experience.

With the fourth appearance of the "voice" comes the novel's first extensive associative exercise, which is to say, its first dream. This dream, structurally, prefigures the novel's tragic denouement. Simultaneously, it evidences the highly anxious condition of Clara. Hitherto it has seemed that Theodore was the neurotic one. Now, though, the reader sees how unsettled by the past, and perhaps by her congenital nature, Clara herself is. The whole Wieland clan, it now becomes plain, are given, in Clara's terms, to "chimeras of [the] brain" (60).

Clara is enjoying a favorite part of Mettingen, and as she sits on a bench, the "lulling sounds of the waterfall, the fragrance and the dusk" put her to sleep. And she dreams:

I . . . imagined myself walking, in the evening twilight, to my brother's habitation. A pit, methought, had been dug in the path I had taken, of which I was not aware. As I carelessly pursued my walk, I thought I saw my brother, standing at some distance before me, beckoning and calling me to make haste. He stood on the opposite edge of the gulph. I mended my pace, and one step more would have plunged me into this abyss, had not some one from behind caught suddenly my arm, and exclaimed, in a voice of eagerness and terror, "Hold! Hold!" (58)

The "voice" shakes her out of her dream. It says: "'I leagued to murder you. I repent. Mark my bidding, and be safe. Avoid this spot. . . . Mark me further; profit by this warning, but divulge it not. If a syllable of what has passed escape you, your doom is sealed. Remember your father, and be faithful'" (59).

Now past-present-future cohere in Clara's mind. Awake, but in a "state of uncertainty," Clara

perceived a ray flit across the gloom and disappear. Another succeeded, which was stronger. . . . It glittered on the shrubs that were scattered at the entrance, and gleam continued to succeed gleam for a few seconds. . . . The first visitings of this light called up a train of horrors in my mind; destruction impended over this spot; the voice which I had lately heard had warned me to retire, and had menaced me with the fate of my father if I refused. I was desirous, but unable, to obey; these gleams were such as preluded the stroke by which he fell. . . . I shuddered as if I had beheld, suspended over me, the exterminating sword. (59)

Clara, it becomes clear, has been affected by her father's death as much as Theodore. She is not then a fully dependable reporter of events. She is, as critics have noted, "unreliable"—which she herself admits. To the reader she writes: "You will believe that calamity has subverted my reason, and that I am amusing you with the chimeras of my brain, instead of facts that have really happened" (60).[25]

What gives these passages their power is their autobiographical energy. Through them and through Clara, Brown is bodying forth his own memories/emotions of a father's catastrophe. What was the "voice" saying to Clara? By her account,

He talked of my father. He intimated, that disclosure would pull upon my head, the same destruction. Was then the death of my father, portentous and inexplicable as it was, the consequences of human machinations? (62)

And again:

> I had been assured that a design had been formed against my life. The ruffians had leagued to murder me. Whom had I offended? Who was there with whom I had ever maintained intercourse, who was capable of harbouring such atrocious purposes? (61)

These are thoughts that no doubt plagued the young Brown in the wake of his father's disappearance. Now they are questions *Wieland* is designed to worry about, if not answer. Within the novel, they pose simple matters of Gothic plot. Who was behind the voice? Which people desired to hurt Clara and her family? However, conceived *outside* the novel, or rather when read as existential questions asked by one Brockden Brown in the 1790s United States, they are as interesting as any asked by a late eighteenth-century American about his or her society. They boil down to this: Given the moral reality that all actions, good and particularly bad, engender their own autonomous long-term consequences, how was the American Revolution, through its often inglorious not to say hypocritical means, going to bring into being the glorious and candid and *sincere* republic that the Revolutionaries themselves so rousingly proclaimed?[26]

By its midpoint *Wieland* has come to focus on "the state" of Clara's mind. Events have caused her to grow increasingly confused, and her budding passion for Henry Pleyel has only added to her mental instability. She herself worries about her discombobulation, and in so worrying, *she makes it worse.* Thus, the agitated state of her mind "naturally introduced a train of reflections upon the dangers and cares which inevitably beset an human being. By no violent transition was I led to ponder on the turbulent life and mysterious end of my father. I cherished, with the utmost veneration, the memory of this man, and every relique connected with his fate was preserved with the most scrupulous care" (78). Now a series of associations intervene, until finally Clara is whipped up into a veritable lather of Gothic frenzy:

> My fears had pictured to themselves no precise object. It would be difficult to depict, in words, the ingredients and hues of that phantom which haunted me. An hand invisible and of preternatural strength, lifted by human passions, and selecting my life for its aim, were parts of this terrific image. All places were alike accessible to this foe, or if his empire were restricted by local bounds, those bounds were utterly inscrutable by me. (79)

It is here where Brown's Revolutionary experience and his Gothic sensibility and literary expression can be seen to intersect and effloresce. For what Brown is doing—à la the "Romantic" or "visionary" method he shared in common with Coleridge and Wordsworth, among others—is invoking, at the core of his novel, *himself.* The sense of victimhood he indulged with friends like Wilkins and Bringhurst, the deceptiveness and indirection he exercised with Smith and Dunlap, the explanations he offered his family for not settling on a profession, they are all concentrated here—and they are being imaginatively interrogated, exploited, and finally given an autonomous life of their own. Ground zero in this exercise is the experience of a father's mysterious demise, and the emotional sense of a dangerous place where even the private precincts of one's home are open to one's "foes." In Brown's own life this place had been his childhood.[27]

American Gothicism, it thus turns out, has its origins in the same place where the American Enlightenment attained its apogee, and where the United States of America was created: Revolutionary Philadelphia. At 117 South Second Street.

*   *   *

Viewed formulaically, *Wieland* recasts the haunted castles and monasteries of *Otranto* and *Udolpho* and *The Monk* into the "picturesque beauties and rural delights" (188) of Mettingen, a locale of purling streams and waterfalls, of fragrant orchards and cornfields. (Leave it to its author to know the Gothic potential of such a place.) *Wieland* is inventive too in its handling of the Gothic hero/villain. For most of the novel this role seems to belong to the Irish interloper with the "lustrously black" eyes possessing "a radiance inexpressibly serene and potent," along with that "something in the rest of his features, which it would be in vain to describe, but which served to betoken a mind of the highest order" (50). When the first murder, that of Catharine, is revealed, Clara the narrator—and the trusting reader along with her—assumes Carwin to be the murderer, not least because he is linked to the crime scene by an object of his. As the litany of additional innocent victims is rolled out—the four natural children, the adopted Louisa ("*not a lineament*" of whose face remained after the bludgeoning [147])—Clara still thinks Carwin responsible. But eventually Clara learns the truth from her uncle, and all of a sudden a reconsideration of the hero/villain in the tale is required.

For if Theodore Wieland is the culprit, who then is Carwin? A more thorough look at this shifty figure ensues, and from this it becomes clear that while Carwin may be some sort of villain, there is nothing heroic about him. Carwin is just a mischievous wanderer with a special talent for projecting voices. He is out to have fun, to indulge his appetites (he pays Clara's servant for sex), and to satisfy his curiosity by prying into other people's private affairs. He is certainly irresponsible and probably destructive. But he is no hero/villain.

Then what about Theodore, the "grave, considerate, and thoughtful" Ciceronian? Nothing about him seems grand enough to place him on the level of the monk Ambrosia, the prince Manfred, or even the corrupt Montoni of *Udolpho* (much less Victor Frankenstein, or Ahab). Clara, understandably, is loath to view him as the prime agent of evil in the world of Mettingen. She wants to see him as a victim too: of Carwin's wiles. At worst, she wants to leave it an open question as to "whether Wieland was a maniac, a faithful servant of his God, the victim of hellish illusions, or the dupe of human imposture" (173–74).

But Theodore himself at his trial reveals his secret depths: the fact that, unbeknownst to everybody around him—like the real-life Brockden Brown he doesn't tell his intimates the most deep-seated things about himself—he has long been embarked on a heroic personal quest for absolute spiritual purity and certainty.

As Theodore testifies, the night he slaughtered his wife and children, "'emotions that were perpetual visitants . . . recurred with unusual energy.'"

"For a time, my contemplations soared above earth and its inhabitants. I stretched forth my hands; I lifted my eyes, and exclaimed, O! that I might be admitted to thy presence; that mine were the supreme delight of knowing thy will, and of performing it! The blissful privilege of direct communication with thee, and of listening to the audible enunciation of thy pleasure!

"What task would I not undertake, what privation would I not cheerfully endure, to testify my love of thee? Alas! thou hidest thyself from my view: glimpses only of thy excellence and beauty are afforded me. Would that a momentary emanation from thy glory would visit me! that some unambiguous token of thy presence would salute my senses!" (154)

Quiet, gloomy Wieland, it turns out, possesses the essential quality of the hero/villain: He deems himself above mere mortals. "'My deed was enjoined by heaven'" and "'[my] obedience was the test of perfect virtue, and the extinction of selfishness and error.'" He scoffs at his jury's limited purview: "'You say that I am guilty. Impious and rash! thus to usurp the prerogatives of your Maker!'" (163).

Yet in the final analysis he isn't the true source of evil, of the terror in the tale—not like Manfred and Ambrosia, or Frankenstein and Ahab are in theirs. This becomes clear when he describes the vision that prompted him to murder:

"I was dazzled. My organs were bereaved of their activity. My eye-lids were half-closed. . . . A nameless fear chilled my veins, and I stood motionless. This irradiation did not retire or lessen. It seemed as if some powerful effulgence covered me like a mantle.

"I opened my eyes and found all about me luminous and glowing. It was the element of heaven that flowed around. Nothing but a fiery stream was at first visible; but, anon, a shrill voice from behind called upon me to attend.

"I turned. It is forbidden to describe what I saw: Words, indeed, would be wanting to the task. The lineaments of that being, whose veil was now lifted, and whose visage beamed upon my sight, no hues of pencil or of language can pourtray.

"As it spoke, the accents thrilled to my heart. 'Thy prayers are heard. In proof of thy faith, render me thy wife. This is the victim I chuse. Call her hither, and here let her fall.'—The sound, and visage, and light vanished at once." (155)

Rather, the *terror* is that for the Wielands this basic vision just won't quit. This is the third time in the tale it has intruded. The first time was with the elder Wieland, the night he spontaneously combusted. The second was when Clara was alone in her bedroom and she sensed the presence of something threatening in the closet. Bravely, she moved "towards the closet. I touched the lock, but my fingers were powerless; I was visited afresh by unconquerable apprehensions. A sort of belief darted into my mind, that some being was concealed within, whose purposes were evil. . . . My fears had pictured to themselves no precise object. It would be difficult to depict, in words, the ingredients and hues of that phantom which haunted me." And then she imaged the Gothic vision already quoted: the "hand invisible and of preternatural strength, lifted by human passions, and selecting my life for its aim, were parts of this terrific image. All places were alike accessible to this foe, or if his empire were restricted by local bounds, those bounds were utterly inscrutable by me" (79).

The Wielands are haunted all right, and nothing—not enlightenment, not Cicero, not classical music—is going to make it go away.

Only Brockden Brown in the end tries to make it go away by burning down Clara's house—just as the castle in *Otranto* and the monastery in *The Monk* are destroyed. In *Wieland* this makes for a happy ending, for Clara, in her Wieland gloom, is not able to leave Mettingen absent such a conflagration. She wants to stay there and die like everybody else in her family. But when her house burns to the ground, she—unlike Poe's Ushers—is forced to leave, and as the novel closes she faces the prospects of a fresh start, in France, with Henry Pleyel as her husband.

It is a stab at fulfilling the optimistic, uplifting side of the book's epigraph—"From Virtue's blissful paths away / The double-tongued are sure to stray; / Good is a forth-right journey still, / And mazy paths but lead to ill"—but appended to a tale that denies the basis for such hope, not entirely convincing.[28]

Chapter 5

The Anti-Godwin

Wieland was Brockden Brown's first pure act of "unsanctified imagination," and it is the founding text of American Gothic. Brown would tap supremely into this aesthetic realm once more, with *Edgar Huntly* in 1799—and thereafter express regret if not embarrassment that he had ever done so. In the meantime he pursued another vein of fiction, for along with *Wieland*, in 1798 and early 1799 he also wrote "Memoirs of Carwin" and *Ormond* and completed *Arthur Mervyn—First Part*, three works less Gothic than Godwinian in character. Taken together, these "fictions of ideas" chart Brown's imaginative engagement not with the haunting sins of the past, but with American society in the 1790s, with the Friendly Club and Elihu Smith, and with a novel that touched him like no other.[1]

*   *   *

William Godwin was courageous to publish *Things as They Are; or, the Adventures of Caleb Williams* in 1794 England. The year before William Pitt's ministry had considered banning his *Political Justice* as seditious, as it had banned Paine's *Rights of Man*, but the prime minister decided to leave author and publisher alone because the book's high price and philosophical complexity would keep it out of the hands of "those who had not three shillings to spare." Godwin, though, desired to reach that very audience, and so—as he wrote in the preface to *Caleb Williams*, highlighting its political ambition—he invented "a single story" which comprehended "a general review of the modes of domestic and unrecorded despotism, by which man becomes the destroyer of man." On the day in May 1794 Godwin penned these words, his reformer friend Thomas Hardy was arrested in his home on charges of high treason. In the next few days other reformer friends— John Thelwall, Horne Tooke, and the dramatist and novelist Thomas Holcroft (who had been the one to suggest to Godwin that he write *Caleb Williams*)—were arrested and imprisoned in the Tower of London, and Parliament voted to suspend habeas corpus to help keep them there. In late May his publisher issued the novel, but without the reformist preface, which he feared too provocative for the times. He had a point. A week later a naval victory over the French fleet by Lord Howe (the brother of the

Godwin and Smith

General Howe whose invasion of Pennsylvania in 1777 had precipitated the arrest and deportation of Elijah Brown) inspired a government decree for "victory illuminations," which Tory mobs, armed with clubs, enforced in London by smashing unlit windows in the homes of citizens lacking sufficient patriotic enthusiasm.[2]

Godwin's novel is a surprisingly engrossing tale. Part murder mystery, part psychological thriller, part social and political exposé, *Caleb Williams* dramatizes how a corrupt political and economic system necessarily debases everyone within it, either through direct oppression or sinuous cooptation. In the story, a rich country squire, Falkland, carries the best virtues of his type. He is generous, refined, brave, compassionate, just. "The lower orders" can count on his solicitation and protection. In particular, he protects the humble farmers and servants and women of his district from the depredations of Barnabas Tyrrel, a rival squire who is "tyrannical to his inferiors," "insolent to his equals," and a muscular bully to boot. Unfortunately Falkland also carries the great flaw of his type: the honor code. Honor—and not virtue or justice or truth—is everything to him, and when at a gathering of fellow gentlemen he is surprised by the drunken Tyrrel and physically assaulted, his sense of humiliation, of lost honor, is so severe that he goes off and murders his rival, and then—not being able to countenance the dishonor of being known as a murderer—he frames a humble local farmer and son, the Hawkinses, for the crime, and allows them to be tried and hanged.[3]

This had all happened before the eighteen-year-old orphan, Caleb Williams, came into Falkland's employ as his secretary. As far as Caleb and the world know at this point, Falkland is simply the great local landowner. Caleb, though, hears the story of Falkland's charmed prior life, of the fate of Tyrrel and the Hawkinses, and of how Falkland, who used to be noted for his sociability, had changed overnight into a gloomy recluse. Caleb begins to sense in Falkland the workings of "a secret wound" and to suspect that his employer may be the actual murderer of Barnabas Tyrrel. So he decides "to be a spy upon Mr. Falkland." He observes him obsessively. He pries into his private possessions. Ultimately—Caleb's curiosity is "uncontrolable"—he breaks into a locked chest in the squire's private quarters and is discovered in the act. Falkland's reaction is to give the boy precisely what he desires: the truth. But first he exacts from Caleb a promise never to reveal it to anyone, before admitting: "I am the murderer of Tyrrel. I am the assassin of the Hawkinses." Then he adds the threat: "If ever an unguarded word escape from your lips, if ever you excite my jealousy or suspicion, expect to pay for it by your death or worse."[4]

Now the pursuit reverses. What had been Caleb's psychological quest for the truth about Falkland turns into Falkland's campaign to render Caleb harmless. Falkland utilizes all his wealth and power and prestige to isolate and silence Caleb, and when Caleb tries to flee, Falkland has him arrested and charged with theft. False evidence of the crime is produced, manufactured by Falkland. Caleb defends himself with the actual truth—and as a consequence people come to think of him as a robber *and* a vile slanderer of a great man. Not even his friends will stand by him now. Left to rot in prison awaiting trial, he escapes. The law tracks him. He seeks out the anonymity of London. Bounty hunters—paid by Falkland—locate him. He flees to an obscure village in Wales and, for a while at least, commences a new life. Taken in by a loving family, he glimpses the possibility of happiness. But one day a pamphlet appears in the village, "The Wonderful and Surprising History of Caleb Williams"—traceable, of course, to Falkland—which relates the sordid criminal tale of one "Caleb Williams." His new friends believe *it* and not him. "You are a monster, and not a man," he is told, and ordered to leave. His flight begins anew.[5]

"Things as They Are," as Caleb discovers, is that once you get on the wrong side of the powerful you are lost, for the law is their "weapon of tyranny" and not, as the official ideology would have it, "a shield to protect the humbler part of the community." In the world of *Caleb Williams*, what the decent folk have to look forward to is jail. Which is where its world and the world of Brockden Brown can be seen to mesh.[6]

Consider Caleb's first-time experience with prison:

> To me every thing was new, the massy doors, the resounding locks, the gloomy passages, the grated windows. . . . It is impossible to describe the sort of squalidness and filth with which these mansions are distinguished. . . . the dirt of a prison speaks sadness to the heart. . . . I was thrust into a day room in which all the persons then under confinement for felony were assembled, to the number of eleven. . . . The horse stealers were engaged in a game at cards, which was presently interrupted by a difference of opinion, attended with great vociferation.[7]

Godwin wrote this in London, in early 1794, two years after Brockden Brown had written to Joseph Bringhurst about a prison cell too, "an apartment defended by an iron door and grated windows" with "ten or twelve persons" in "this mansion." "Some of them are employed in conversation either mirthful or serious, either delicate and man[ner]ly or base and brutal. . . . another [is] at the Card table practicing with amazing skill and eagerness all the wiles and artifices of Piquet and whist." Godwin, in his novel, was recalling actual recent visits to a friend in London's Newgate prison. The friend stood convicted of seditious libel for being present at a dinner at which it was "Resolved," in good American Revolutionary fashion, "That law ceases to be an object of obedience whenever it becomes an instrument of oppression." His sentence was "transportation" to Botany Bay for fourteen years. Brown, in his 1792 letter, had been remembering his father's Walnut Street prison experience as a debtor in 1784 Philadelphia, which humiliation had culminated not just a seven-year period of unjust political persecutions (and mob-enforced illuminations) for the

Brown family, but Elijah Brown's twenty-seven-year quest to make it as a merchant in Philadelphia.[8]

In his own novel *Arthur Mervyn* Brockden Brown would replicate the essentials of *Caleb Williams* almost to the point of plagiarism: the "twinned," mutually persecuting relationship between Caleb and Falkland, the moral miasma of a "sick" society, the law as an instrument of abuse, the hard lot of the poor and powerless, the ever looming threat of jail. Yet in one key component Brown would depart from his literary model. *Caleb Williams* is a "plain and unadulterated tale" narrated by Caleb in an "artless and manly" way. There is never any doubt for the reader what "the truth" is—as there was never any doubt for William Godwin. *Arthur Mervyn*, on the other hand, in its tendency to draw attention to its own inconsistencies and contradictions, has been called the first "metafiction." Its essence is a lack of certainty about "truth." Arthur insists—like Caleb—that he is telling an unvarnished tale, but the careful reader will be quick to doubt it. Is Arthur a poor, innocent victim, or is he the villain? The narration credibly suggests both—or maybe something in between. Brockden Brown's "Philadelphia novel," then, patterned directly after *Caleb Williams* and written within the supporting enclave of the Friendly Club, breathes out a moral that "truth" may well be too complicated to divine.[9]

*   *   *

Arthur Mervyn—unlike *Wieland*—was long in gestation. The publication of *Caleb Williams* in Philadelphia in March 1795 seems to have galvanized Brown into work on a novel "equal in extent to Caleb Williams." This corresponds to the "Philadelphia novel" that Elihu Smith later said Brown had "fiercely undertaken" in the autumn of 1795 and then "recommenced" in early 1797. By the spring and summer of 1798, when Brown wrote *Wieland*, the first twelve chapters of his urban novel were in something like their final form. Brown would finish *Arthur Mervyn—First Part* in early 1799, and it was published in May. Thereafter the novel, and the main character, continued to evolve (as Brown wrote *Arthur Mervyn—Second Part* over the course of 1800), right down to Arthur's decision at the very end to dump the farm girl Eliza Hadwin as his intended and marry Achsa Fielding, an older Jewish woman who may have been a prostitute.[10]

As he is Brockden Brown's first successful literary persona—and a pre-*Wieland* creation—the "Arthur" in the opening section deserves close scrutiny. Appearing to be "no more than eighteen years old," the character explains that he comes from a small farm in Chester County. He had five siblings, all of whom, due to some "defect in the constitution of our mother," had died as they attained the age of nineteen or twenty. His mother had died the previous spring, leaving his father free to marry the family's milkmaid and market woman. This marriage had blasted Arthur's worldly prospects, leaving him "the most calamitous and desolate of human beings." Deprived in one stroke of his patrimony—upon which he "had built a thousand agreeable visions"—he set out for the city, where "I must build a name and a fortune for myself." Reaching the city at night, he immersed himself for a time in its "tumultuous sensations." But before long his wits returned, as did his sense of his actual situation. Here he was "a stranger, friendless, and moneyless."[11]

Walking forlorn through the city streets, he came upon a mansion. It made him think of his father's dwelling, which "might be easily comprised in one fourth of those buildings which here were designed to accommodate the menials" (271). His thoughts were on the evils of city life and the virtues of the country, but the sight of this magnificent building provoked an "unaccustomed . . . strain of reflection":

My books had taught me the dignity and safety of the middle path and my darling writer abounded with encomiums on rural life. At a distance from luxury and pomp I viewed them, perhaps, in a just light. A nearer scrutiny confirmed my early prepossessions, but at the distance at which I now stood, the lofty edifices, the splendid furniture, and the copious accommodations of the rich, excited my admiration and my envy.

His education had taught him to detest the luxury represented by this mansion, yet, "By some transition it occurred to me that the supply of my most urgent wants, might be found in some inhabitant of this house" (272).

He meets the proprietor of this house—one Thomas Welbeck—who hires him as his amanuensis, or copyist. He stays there for the night, and in the morning at breakfast he joins his new employer and a woman introduced to him as Welbeck's daughter. He fantasized about being adopted by Welbeck as a son and by this woman as a husband.

His involvement with Welbeck does not go well. Welbeck is given to radical mood shifts and "dissimulation" (294). Arthur begins to suspect a darker dimension to his benefactor. He even comes to wonder about Welbeck's actual relation to the supposed daughter, about his possible "depravity" (298). And he learns that Welbeck is "the subject of some fraudulent proceeding" (300). One night he hears a pistol shot in the house. Following the sound, he stumbles into a room where there is a dead body on the floor and Welbeck sitting in a chair. He feels, naturally enough, "confusion and terror" (304). Welbeck, though, explains the scene to him, but not before—Falkland-like—exacting from him a promise not to let "a syllable of what I tell you . . . ever pass your lips" (305).

Welbeck now launches into the story of his life, and from this Arthur learns that nothing is as it appears. Welbeck is not a rich citizen of the city. He is a bounder from Liverpool, a thief, and a libertine who ruins the lives of innocent girls. Arthur wants to go back to the country, "my sole asylum" (336).

What is aesthetically vital in *Arthur Mervyn*'s opening section is the *feel* of the place Brockden Brown conjures. The city, with its "perils and deceptions" (271), is "like a vision" (261). One negotiates it as if one were "walking in the dark and might rush into snares or drop into pits before [one] was aware of . . . danger" (292). It operates according to strange "ideas of floating or transferable wealth" (280). Knowledge of it had to be sought within "the interior of dwellings" and from "converse with their inhabitants" (286). "After viewing various parts of the city; intruding into churches; and diving into alleys," one is naturally brought into "conjecturing the causes of appearances" (284) Ultimately, it imparts experiences that seem "the monstrous creations of delirium" (334).

These opening twelve chapters patently take their inspiration from the experience of Elijah Brown's introduction to Philadelphia. Brockden Brown himself, it needs to be stressed, was a city boy, as his Quaker friend Thomas Cope captured in a description of Brown walking the streets of New York: "C[harles] seems to be in his element & I am glad to see him enjoy himself. He flutters & hops about like a bird & I don't know whether I shall be able to catch him again without salt." Pastoralism for him was something to be read about in books—while he was ensconced in a city chamber. To him, the moral dichotomy of country/city was an abstract and literary question. He could think about it, but only from *within* the encompassing city culture that was his world.

On the other hand, his father Elijah's life had profoundly embodied the country/city dichotomy. When Elijah Brown came to Philadelphia in the late 1750s—at the age of seventeen—he left behind him a childhood in Nottingham, the lessons of the East Nottingham meeting (and the moral voice of John Churchman), a father and stepmother, and five siblings. Entrance into the commercial world of North America's richest city, *for him*, would have been dizzying and exciting. What Elijah Brown found there— not over three days, but decades—were opportunities (including a promising connection with the wealthy Waln family), many pitfalls, and a general moral terrain that he was not, in the end, equipped to handle. Or in other words, the mix of equivocation and sincerity demanded by the "perilous precincts of private property"—the market environment of mid- to late eighteenth-century Philadelphia—were clearly skills Elijah Brown never mastered. Now in *Arthur Mervyn; or, Memoirs of the Year 1793* it is the protagonist's turn.[12]

Arthur is a fully imagined character—as he should be, considering that Brockden Brown had been thinking about him for much of his life. The other characters in the novel are not so complex. The hero/villain Thomas Welbeck is a melange of qualities. Part Falkland, he has been Americanized along the lines of that "contemptuous creature" in 1790s Philadelphia, the businessman and Jeffersonian turncoat politician John Swanwick. Welbeck seeks by any means possible, including—à la the "eel" Swanwick—schemes involving "counterfeit bills," to rise "to the pinnacle of affluence and honour" (310). He carries hints of Alexander Hamilton too, not least in his propensity to find himself drawn into duels. The gunshot scene in particular, which brings Arthur's employment with him to an end, echoes Hamilton's predicament in July 1795 New York, when James Nicholson had taunted him with the jibe that he had once "declined an interview." "No man could affirm that with truth" had been Hamilton's reply, along with a formal challenge. Welbeck attempts to avoid a duel with Captain Watson (whose sister he has ruined), but when Watson calls him "Coward!" Welbeck responds with "How much a stranger are you to the feelings of Welbeck! How poor a judge of his cowardice!" (325). In Brockden Brown's experience, Alexander Hamilton was the most notorious duelist, as he was renowned in Brown's circle for his "depraved appetites." Thus not only Welbeck's misadventure with Mrs. Villars's devious mercenary daughter— shades of Maria Reynolds—but Brown's very evocation of Mrs. Villars's Philadelphia house of prostitution calls to mind the famous men in Philadelphia who patronized such establishments. Of these Hamilton stood as *primus inter pares*. Welbeck, in any case, never achieves the sum of his parts. Nor are the heroine/victims in the tale any more complexly human, because in *Arthur Mervyn* Brown really isn't interested in them.[13]

What he cares about is the character Arthur, and in the end this is what lives about the novel, along with the highly original effect of a 1790s fiction that purposely casts doubt on itself. This last quality is implicit in the structure of having Dr. Stevens for the narrator (as opposed to following *Caleb Williams* and making it a first-person narrative), and Brown prepares for the later "trial" of Arthur Mervyn's tale by having his lead prosecutor, Dr. Stevens's good friend Mr. Wortley, appear in the first chapter to spread a vague suspicion about Arthur's good faith. Wortley will reappear in the opening chapter of the *Second Part* to accuse Arthur of being a "wily imposter" (433), and a Mrs. Althorpe will show up to challenge Arthur's whole account of his Chester County family background.[14]

In *Arthur Mervyn—Second Part* Arthur undergoes an additional development, with the slippery (and entertaining) earnestness of Elijah Brown hardening into the piously utilitarian (and boring) manner of Elihu Smith. This is always implicit in the Arthur of the first volume, as when he discovers $20,000 in a manuscript and debates with himself what he should do according to the dictates of utility. But as the novel progressively loses its energy in the second volume, it's in good measure because Arthur has become Godwin/Smith. He is now, unlike the earlier Arthur, fond of the city. And every situation is digested, and *re*digested, and *re*redigested, for its proper Godwinian tonic. For example, when Arthur needs to go to the

Villars house to find Clemenza Lodi—the woman who had first been introduced to him as Welbeck's daughter, but who was in reality Welbeck's pregnant lover—his brain snaps into overdrive.

Suppose I should enter Mrs. Villars' house, desire to be introduced to the lady,
accost her with affectionate simplicity, and tell her the truth? Why be anxious to
smooth the way; why deal in apologies, circuities and inuendoes? All these are fee-
ble and perverse refinements, unworthy of an honest purpose and an erect spirit.
To believe her inaccessible to my visit, was absurd. To wait for the permission of
those whose interest it might be to shut out visitants, was cowardice. This was an
infringement of her liberty, which equity and law equally condemned. By what right
could she be restrained from intercourse with others? Doors and passages may be
between her and me. With a purpose such as mine, no one had a right to close the
one or obstruct the other. Away with cowardly reluctances and clownish scruples,
and let me hasten this moment to her dwelling.

But what should he say to Mrs. Villars?

The truth. To faulter, or equivocate, or dissemble to this woman, would be wicked.
Perhaps her character has been misunderstood and maligned. Can I render her a
greater service than to apprize her of the aspersions that have rested on it, and
afford her the opportunity of vindication?

Ah, but "Perhaps she is indeed selfish and profligate; the betrayer of youth
and the agent of lasciviousness." Still, "Does she not deserve to know the
extent of her errors and the ignominy of her trade?" (513) And on and on
and on and on.[15]

Arthur is now out-Godwinning Godwin. Eventually Clemenza says to
him: "your language is so singular" (527), and it is. It is the language of that
American Godwin, E. H. Smith.

Arthur Mervyn—First Part was published in May 1799, and in September
it received its first review, written by . . . Brockden Brown, who, with the support of his Friendly Club friends, had become editor in 1799 of the New
York *Monthly Magazine and American Review.* Among his many contributions
to this start-up literary journal were a fragment of his novel *Edgar Huntly,*
"Memoirs of Stephen Calvert," "Thessalonica: A Roman Story," "Portrait of
an Emigrant," and "Walstein's School of History. From the German of
Krants of Gotha."

The latter, ostensibly about a school of historians in Jena, Germany, is a
thinly veiled allegory of the Friendly Club. The leader, Professor Walstein,
is Smith-like. "How men might best promote the happiness of mankind in
given situations, was the problem that he desired to solve." Among Walstein's nine "more assiduous" pupils (the Friendly Club commonly had ten
members) there is Engel, who sought—like Godwin specified in his preface

to *Caleb Williams*—a "mode by which truth could be conveyed to a great number," to "exhibit, in an eloquent narration, a model of right conduct." Engel's solution is his "fictitious history" of "Olivo Ronsica."

Olivo [Arthur Mervyn] is a rustic youth, whom domestic equality, personal independence, agricultural occupations, and studious habits, had endowed with a strong mind, pure taste, and unaffected integrity. Domestic revolutions oblige him to leave his father's house [Chester County farm] in search of subsistence. He is destitute of property, of friends, and of knowledge of the world. These are to be acquired by his own exertions, and virtue and sagacity are to guide him in the choice and the use of suitable means.

This youth "bends" his way to Weimar (Philadelphia), where he is involved, "by the artifices of others, and, in consequence of his ignorance of mankind, in many perils and perplexities." Here he "forms a connection with a man of a great and mixed, but on the whole, a vicious character" named Semlits (Welbeck). He faces a pestilence (the yellow fever). And so on.

And now Brockden Brown's review of *Arthur Mervyn—First Part*:

[The author] has certainly succeeded in producing a tale, in which are powerful displays of fortitude and magnanimity; a work whose influence must be endlessly varied by varieties of character and situation of the reader, but, from which, it is not possible for any one to rise without some degree of moral benefit, and much of that pleasure which always attends the emotions of curiosity and sympathy.[16]

*   *   *

In the spring and summer of 1798 Brockden Brown was busy and in love. Living in Philadelphia over the prior fifteen months he had written the second part of *Alcuin* while seeing the first part to press, written and published the "Man at Home" series, published the first chapters of *Arthur Mervyn*, finished a novel manuscript entitled "Sky-Walk," begun *Wieland*; and he had commenced a real-life romance. As described by a friend, his "mistress," Susan Potts, was "very interesting. . . . without being beautiful." To Brown's parents, on the other hand, one thing alone mattered about Susan Potts: she was not a Quaker. Brown chose this moment to move back to New York, arriving there on the eve of the Fourth of July celebrations. Staying first with William Dunlap, he eventually moved in with Elihu Smith, and it was at Smith's house at 45 Pine Street, over the next month or so, that he finished *Wieland* and began a new work based on the character Carwin.[17]

Meanwhile that same spring and summer, international events were bringing the precarious existence of the United States, and the vulnerability of the young nation's virtue, into sudden, sharp relief.

The Jay Treaty had temporarily defused tensions with England, but just as Great Britain ceased its attacks on American merchant shipping, France—which deemed the treaty a betrayal of the 1778 Franco-American alliance—commenced its own. President Adams, in response, sent a Jay-like peace mission to Paris in October 1797. His three envoys met with the French foreign minister, Talleyrand, who informed the Americans that a bribe of $250,000 was required before discussions could commence. Absent this tribute, the Americans were led to believe, there would be war. When news of the XYZ Affair reached the American capital in March 1798 (W, X, Y, and Z were the letters Adams used to refer to four French representatives involved in the shakedown attempt), John Adams and the Federalists contemplated war and initiated defense measures. Jeffersonian Republicans, in the context, could only grouse among themselves about the "insane" bellicosity of the "Tories" in power.[18]

By June and July, as the war hysteria intensified, Federalists in Congress felt brazen enough to propose and pass the Alien and Sedition Acts in an effort to silence, jail, and deport those who opposed Adams administration policy. The first of these partisan bombshells, the Naturalization Act of June 18, lengthened from five to fourteen years the residence requirement for citizenship. Then came the Alien Act of June 25, which empowered the president to expel on his own authority "dangerous" aliens, and the Alien Enemies Act of July 6, which additionally authorized the president, in time of declared war, to expel or imprison enemy aliens. Finally, on July 14, Congress passed the Sedition Act, which made it a crime to utter or publish "any false, scandalous, and malicious writing or writings against the Government of the United States, or either House of the Congress, with intent to defame . . . or to bring them . . . into contempt or disrepute." By the late summer, Vice President Jefferson was declaring this legislation unconstitutional and calling on the states to declare it null and void, and by the early fall Virginia Republicans—with the vice president among them—were contemplating the prospect of secession.[19]

The cultural anxiety and hysteria and the fear of French and Irish immigrants that the Alien and Sedition Acts registered found another expression during the summer of 1798 in the spread of a theory about who was to blame for all the ills of the advancing revolutionary era. The sources of this were two European books, the French Abbé Barruel's *Memoirs of Jacobinism* (1797–98) and the Scotsman John Robison's *Proofs of a Conspiracy against All the Religions and Governments of Europe, carried on in the Secret Meetings of the Free Masons, Illuminati, and Reading Societies* (1797). Written independently of each other, these two works traced all the turmoil of the revolutionary age to the machinations of a secret order, called the "Illuminati," that had been formed in Germany in the 1770s, and that was (they claimed) dedicated to the general destruction of government and religion, and that now (they further claimed) operated, through its covert agents, in all the nations of Europe and in the United States.

Ridiculed by Jeffersonian Republicans and discounted as absurd or over-blown by most non-New Englanders, the "Illuminati Conspiracy" nevertheless hung heavily in New York about the residence of 45 Pine Street. Not that Elihu Smith himself believed in it; only that its prime American advocates happened to be his best friends back in Connecticut, and what those friends were condemning, neither Smith nor his summer of 1798 house-mate could fail to notice, was Smith's Revolution.[20]

Elihu Hubbard Smith was an unusual product of the American Revo-lution in its New England incarnation. A moralistic and incredibly indus-trious scion of New England Puritans, Smith's liberty quest had led him into the purer realms of Godwinian rationalism. He was, proudly, a deist. In his own personal terms, he was a "disciple of truth," and it was as such a disciple that he tried to engage the frenzied politics of 1798.[21]

In the face of "the fearful outcries against democracy, & modern philos-ophy," Smith called for "frankness & courage." About France he had no ide-ological illusions. To a friend there he wrote: "When you are safe out of France, & dare to hazard opinions concerning the politics of that coun-try—I wish you to consider those inquiries as extended to that of Des-potism—mis-named Republic." On the subject of Thomas Jefferson, too, he was quite harsh. "Mr. Jefferson," he felt, "is jacobinical almost to lunacy." He was indeed critical of all partisan types, be they of the Federalist or Republican persuasion. Viewing "our french partizans" as "ranged . . . under the banners of terror," he saw "our english partizans under those [banners] of despotism; in short . . . they only differ in the sides they take, not in the principles by which they are actuated."[22]

This was for Smith to take an abstract political stand within the emerg-ing national party culture of 1790s America. But politics turned excruc-iatingly personal for Smith when he chose to return to Connecticut for a vacation. A deistic Daniel venturing into New England Puritanism's lion's den—otherwise known as the Connecticut River Valley—Smith spent late June and early July mixing with the people he loved and who loved him, and who, during the summer of 1798, were declaring their desire to make all America like Congregationalist Connecticut.

Thus New York City's purest Godwinian arrived in New Haven on June 17 at 8 P.M. and immediately called on his friend Noah Webster, who was preparing a Fourth of July oration on "the inevitable consequences of that false philosophy which has been preached in the world by . . . Godwin and other visionaries." Despite the late hour, Smith then stopped by the house of his old Greenfield teacher Timothy Dwight, who was now the pres-ident of Yale and nationally renowned for his sermons and publications on "Infidelity." Later this night, at his boardinghouse, Smith read a pamphlet Webster had given him, entitled *The Aliens: A Patriotic Poem*, which sought, in verse, to distinguish good from "malignant" immigrants in America.

(About the latter it advised: "Those who are, of guilt accused, / Examine, with strict formality; / And punish, if they've abused, / Republican [i.e., American], hospitality.") It was, Smith noted in his diary, "wretched." The next day he was off to his ancestral Litchfield home.[23]

However "wretched," *Aliens* was the appropriate aperitif for the cultural fare of the next two weeks. In Litchfield, where Smith stayed with his parents, he saw the fetching Susan Tracy (who had been "converted, by the French Revolution, to Christianity"), he visited with Oliver Wolcott (who had succeeded Alexander Hamilton as the Federalist administration's secretary of the treasury), and he met a Mr. Day, "the young gentleman who is to deliver the 4th of July Oration at Hartford." (In that oration Thomas Day would condemn Americans who, "For the benevolent principles of Christianity . . . substituted the wild dogmas of infidel philosophy, a philosophy originating in wickedness, founded in error, and subversive of the peace and happiness of society.") In nearby Hartford Smith spent much time with his old friend Theodore Dwight, who was preparing—what else?—his own oration for the Fourth.[24]

The "proposition" of Theodore Dwight's *Oration, Spoken at Hartford, in the State of Connecticut, on the Anniversary of American Independence,* was to be "that the United States are in danger of being robbed of their independence, by the fraud and violence of the French Republic." Tracing the potentially lethal threats to American liberty to "the characters, dispositions, and practices, of many of our own citizens," Dwight would attack Jefferson—whom he suspected of being an Illuminati agent—along with everybody else who had a connection, as he saw it, to the wicked doctrines and practices of the Jacobins. Prominent in this group were people with "enmity against religion." Dwight would identify what he termed "atheism" as a key element in the Jacobin and "Illuminati" assault on liberty and virtue, for—he would say—such people were "Sensible, that so long as any ideas of moral obligation should remain, and the doctrine of future accountability be believed, it would be impossible to introduce that universal system of depravity." For this reason "the Leaders of the Revolution early laid the axe at the root of Religion."[25]

At some point during his first two weeks in Connecticut someone gave Smith a copy of the first American edition of Robison's *Proofs of a Conspiracy*, which Smith began reading on July 3. So it was with Robison's words about *doctrines subversive of all our notions of morality—or all our confidence in the moral government of the universe—of all our hopes of improvement in a future state of existence* ringing in his head that Smith assumed his spot in the central village ritual of the summer, the Fourth of July. It was just as in the days of his village childhood—"The Independent Uniform Company, with a band of music went first, followed by the men in the order of age, & concluding by the Magistrates, Clergy, & the Orator of the day. We entered the Meeting-House, where the ladies &c. were assembled in reverse order"—

except that now when the "patriotic toasts were drunk," they were no doubt distinctly partisan Federalist, anti-French, and *anti*-anti-Christian.[26]

Smith "took leave of my friends" on July 6 and headed back to New York, stopping again in New Haven to see Theodore's older brother, Timothy Dwight, who had just delivered his own Fourth of July diatribe.[27]

In *The Duty of Americans at the Present Crisis*, Timothy Dwight, the man Smith deemed his "second intellectual father," had conjured the talismanic biblical words and Whig emotions so central to the New England Revolution:

We fight for the lives, the honor, the safety, of our wives and children, for the religion of our fathers, and for the liberty, "with which Christ hath made us free." "We jeopard our lives," that our children may inherit these glorious blessings, be rescued from the grinding insolence of foreign despotism, and saved from the corruption and perdition of foreign atheism.

Then, drawing liberally from Robison's *Proofs of a Conspiracy*, Dwight had defined the overarching summer of 1798 threat to American liberty and religion. It was, in Dwight's extended analysis, the ravages of rationalism itself. As Dwight viewed Illuminatism, "The secrecy, solemnity, mysticism, and correspondence of Masonry, were in this new order preserved and enhanced; while the ardour of innovation, the impatience of civil and moral restraints, and the aims against government, morals, and religion, were elevated, expanded, and rendered more systematical, malignant, and daring." The result was the creation of a new personality type which justified all actions in strictly rationalistic terms. About this "moral" development Dwight had noted: "Of the goodness of the end every man is to judge for himself; and most men, and all men who resemble the Illuminati, will pronounce every end to be good, which will gratify their inclinations."[28]

Elihu Smith left the company of Timothy Dwight on the evening of July 6—and it is hard to believe the two of them did not discuss *Proofs of a Conspiracy*—and boarded a packet boat for New York. Arriving back at 45 Pine late the next evening, before going to bed he noted in his diary the news that "C. B. Brown" was in town. The next morning Brown came by for breakfast, and Smith reported that "He looks as usual. His health is pretty well restored." A few days later Brown moved in.[29]

The summer of 1798 would profoundly alter many American destinies. For the High Federalists behind the Alien and Sedition legislation, it was the season to go for broke in trying to eliminate all meaningful opposition to Adams administration policy and Federalist principles—and then suffer the political consequences. For Jefferson and James Madison, it was the clarion call to formalize an opposition party and to aim for a Republican takeover of the national government in the 1800 elections. It was as well the occasion to write the Virginia and Kentucky Resolutions, which introduced to national political culture the "constitutional" principles of states rights and secession. For the Dwights and Tracys of Connecticut, it was the millennial time to proclaim a grand pending threat to American religion and liberty and rally the forces of Christianity and order. The summer of 1798 would serve to promote Timothy Dwight into the "Pope" of New England Congregationalism. Theodore Dwight and Uriah Tracy, less exalt-edly perhaps, were headed for leadership positions in New England's own future secessionist movement, the Hartford Convention. For the old members of the Friendly Club, the summer of 1798, and the yellow fever epidemic it generated, would prove fateful too in the way it challenged, bat-tered, provoked, infected. And killed.

Fellow deists William Dunlap and William Johnson good-humoredly stood their ground against the cultural and viral assaults. Dunlap, half tongue-in-cheek, reveled in thinking himself the "infidel" others would have him be. Thus Dunlap writes of a June evening he spent in New York, dis-cussing morality and religion with members of the Dwight family. "I could not help," Dunlap writes, "reflecting on the situation of the poor Infidel philos-opher"—he means himself—"combatting for virtue . . . with the brother in law, sister, & son of the President of Yale Colledge, the author of Sermons 'on the nature and danger of infidel philosophy.'" It was as an "Infidel philos-opher" too that Dunlap read *Proofs of a Conspiracy*, which struck him as "A strange mixture knowledge & prejudice, truth & error, and another proof of the avidity with which we make every circumstance bend to the favorite System." Johnson, living with Smith and Brown at 45 Pine, upheld the urbane traditions of the Friendly Club when, with the yellow fever spreading around him in early September, he wrote to Dunlap, then safely ensconced with his family in the New Jersey countryside: "You had better leave a dull uninteresting country scene & join us. The Town is the only place for ratio-nal beings. Under the shield of Philosophy what have we to fear?"[30]

Elihu Smith, by contrast, was a man feeling a burden. During his brief summer sojourn in Connecticut Smith had visited over 150 people, and the editor of his diary sees in this "social frenzy" evidence of some "advanced hysteria." What might be the nature of this "force," though, the editor can-not guess. Yet surely the force at work upon Smith was his desire to preserve that most cherished thing, friendships, amid the divisive politics of 1798. All these people he visited—his parents, his extended family, his friends, respected acquaintances—were the Illuminati Conspiracy's natural con-stituency, and the most prominent among them were in the process of using the political anxiety of the day to transform Connecticut into the citadel of High Federalism. Smith's response to this distressing ideological and cultural situation was not, as was his custom and personal dictate, to speak the "truth," but rather, in effect, to gather everybody up in a mutual, and desperate, social embrace. That was his "frenzy." His diary is conspicuous for the political comments he *doesn't* make. During this trip when the palaver about "infidelity" was unending, his only political comment is in reaction to the "wretched" *Aliens*. The rest of the time he is mute in his diary on all political matters. Robison's *Proofs of a Conspiracy*—the book everybody is reading and parroting in orations and sermons—cannot elicit from Smith a diary comment. For his two-and-a-half weeks in Connecticut, Smith evidently decided to tone down his vaunted "sincerity."[31]

The summer of 1798 had its effect on Brockden Brown too. If anything, his already astounding creative binge intensified, and William Johnson, for one, marveled at this. In early September Johnson recorded that "Charles feels all the joy and parental exultation of an Author having this day . . . been delivered . . . of an handsome duodecimo, the offspring of that fertile brain which already engendered, two more volumes. This borders upon the *prodigious!*—300 pages in a month! Yet he is neither in a delerium or a fever. What an admirable antidote is philosophy." The duodecimo was *Wieland*, and one of the new volumes was "the history of Carwin," which represented the beginning of Brown's own considered response to *Proofs of a Conspiracy* and the paranoid cultural moment.[32]

What William Johnson meant by "philosophy" was the calm rationalism of the Friendly Club, and indeed this was now at the heart of Brown's literary prodigality, only not in the way Johnson conceived. For Brockden Brown, while continuing to speak and function, around his New York friends at least, as a rationalist, had begun in his fiction a thoroughgoing examination and critique of rationalism. In effect *his friends* had become his subject. In his own terms, he was functioning as a kind of "secret witness." It was as back in the days of late 1780s Philadelphia and his first published effort, when he utilized the husk of a Quaker's anti-Franklinian poem, grounded in the Whig-caused horrors of his childhood, to generate an American Whig panegyric on Benjamin Franklin. Now his imagination, ever subversive, was playing with Godwinianism and the New York world of E. H. Smith.[33]

*   *   *

In "Memoirs of Carwin," written in August to early September, Brown fleshed out the shadowy protagonist from *Wieland*. William Dunlap, reading the manuscript in mid-September, noted that "C. B. Brown . . . has taken up the schemes of the Illuminati." By that time Brown had set his "Carwin" aside after some 16,000 words and had begun yet another partial work, "Stephen Calvert." In another month or so, though, Brown would set aside "Calvert" and return to the Illuminati inquiry, this time in a new novel, *Ormond; or the Secret Witness*, into which he would filter his thoughts and emotions from the summer of 1798, his general reflections about his 1790s New York experience, and a scathing rendition of contemporary Philadelphia. Central to the conception would be the Friendly Club and Elihu Hubbard Smith. Inspirational too would be Timothy Dwight's *The Duty of Americans* and John Robison's *Proofs of a Conspiracy*.[34]

Though Brown nowhere mentions it, reading *Proofs* must have been an uncanny intellectual experience, for the book treats of strange, arcane things that the author of *Wieland* knew in his bones. Indeed in a curious way, *Proofs of a Conspiracy* traces the historical link between the seeker Richard Browne of mid-seventeenth-century Northamptonshire and the Brockden Brown of 1798 New York City, in the process offering up a revelation that, in late 1790s America, was for Brown alone.

Robison's Gothic-like tale of the Illuminati begins amid the "zeal and fanaticism" of seventeenth-century Germany, and in a German Masonic Lodge "much disturbed by the mystical whims of J. Behmen [Boehme] and Swedenborg—by the fanatical and knavish doctrines of the modern Rosycrucians—by Magicians—Magnetisers—Exorcists, &c." Spreading out then into an examination of the Freemason movement throughout Europe, and especially in France, it works its way around to an understanding of Masonic fellowship as a means "for venting and propagating sentiments in religion and politics, that could not have circulated in public without exposing the author to great danger." In the tale, the "impunity" offered by this special fellowship "gradually encouraged men of licentious principles to become more bold, and to teach doctrines subversive of all our notions of morality—of all our confidence in the moral government of the universe—of all our hopes of improvement in the future state of existence— and of all satisfaction and contentment with our present life, so long as we live in a state of civil subordination." The highly select society of the Illuminati, which had developed within the Masonic Lodges but that now functioned as an autonomous enterprise outside of Freemasonry, was the result.[35]

For hyperorthodox New Englanders like Timothy Dwight, the Scots Presbyterian Robison's story offered up a host of familiar bugbears. After all, entwined in the far-reaching "conspiracy" are Jesuitical, House of Stuart plots to reimplant Catholicism in England, Hermetic-magico-Cabbalistic-deistic-atheistic threats to pure Protestant religion, and everything else Dwight—the grandson of Jonathan Edwards and the great-great-great-great-grandson of Puritan Connecticut's founder, Thomas Hooker—had been reared to maintain eternal vigilance against. Brockden Brown likewise—by the evidence of "Carwin" and *Ormond*—recognized something familiar in Robison's story. Only what he saw was not the enemy of the true and proper New England Reformed tradition, but rather his own extended Quaker heritage, his New York friends and the Friendly Club, and, ultimately, shades of his "unsanctified imagination."

Consider what Brown read. Robison's Illuminati, or their movement, began in Europe as "a mystical Society." They are noteworthy for their "sincerity," or at least for their constant professions of "sincerity." Over time, though, the fellowships developed into sophistical debating clubs. In these lodges, "Brother orator[s]" delivered "wire-drawn dissertations on the social duties, where every thing is amplified and strained to hyperbole."

Thus accustomed to allegory, to fiction, to finesse, and to a sort of innocent hypocrisy, by which they cajoled themselves into a notion that this child's-play had at bottom a serious and important meaning, the zealous champions of Free Masonry *found no inclination to check this inventive spirit or circumscribe its flights.* Under the protection of Masonic secrecy, they planned schemes of a different kind, and instead of more Orders of Chivalry directed against the enemies of their faith, *they formed associations* in opposition to the ridiculous and oppressive ceremonies and superstitions of the church. There can be no doubt, that *in those hidden assemblies, a free communication of sentiment was highly relished and much indulged.*

These lodges then "became schools of scepticism and infidelity" that specialized in "the slang of sentimental declamation on the topic of Brotherly love and Utopian felicity." And from here, writes Robison, "it is hardly a step" to rationalism's criticism of the "propriety" and "justice" of existing "civil society." A man who has reached this perspective, Robison concludes,

cannot avoid taking notice of the great obstructions to human felicity which we see in every quarter, proceeding from the abuses of those distinctions of rank and fortune which have arisen in the world: and as the mischiefs and horrors of superstition are topics of continual declamation to those who wish to throw off the restraints of religion; so the oppression of the rulers of this world, and the sufferings of talents and worth in inferior stations, will be no less greedily listened to by all whose notions of morality are not very pure.[36]

When the rationalist Elihu Hubbard Smith read *Proofs* during his summer visit to Connecticut, did he think about the Friendly Club? He had once described that most precious fellowship in his life as "a small association of men, who are connected by mutual esteem, & habits of unrestricted communication . . . of different professions & occupations; of various religious or moral opinions . . . [who] coincide in the great outlines of political faith." Smith, ever the intellectual literalist, probably would not have indulged the reflection. (But then again, he *was* uncharacteristically silent in his diary about the book. Perhaps the silence registered an agitation?) His more imaginative Quaker friend, on the other hand, did not fail to recognize the general spirit and practices of the Friendly Club and its Godwinianism in Robison's descriptions. It would be hard, in any case, for a member of the Friendly Club not to think of their purest Godwinian— their Herr Professor Walstein—when reading Robison's descriptions of the "illuminated."[37]

The Illuminati, according to Robison, taught that ends justify means, that "the preponderancy of good in the ultimate result consecrated every mean[s] employed; and that wisdom and virtue consisted in properly determining this balance." Elihu Smith advocated that

Every action, of consequence, should have a moral end in view; much more every system of conduct. In the proportion of our adherence to this axiom, do we deserve the character, & shall we feel the charms & blessings, of virtue.

The Illuminati, according to Robison, believe that "reason is the only light which nature has given to man," and they share with Freemasonry the notion that "Reason is the Sun that illuminates the whole, and Liberty and Equality are the objects of their occupations." According to Elihu Smith,

To enlighten one ignorant mind; to confer a superior degree of illumination on one already, considerably enlightened; is to promote the progress of knowledge, the extension of virtue. For knowledge & virtue have an inherent inseparable, & eternal, tendency, like light, to extend in every direction; and every virtuous being, like the planets which diffuse around them a portion of that splendor which they derive from the sun, becomes a new point in the universe of mind, a new & subordinate center of intellectual illumination, from whence originates a new diffusion of that truth & virtue, primarily derived from God, the Source of Animation, the imperishable spring & exhaustless fountain of knowledge, virtue, & happiness."[38]

Proofs of a Conspiracy offered Brown more than exaggerated Elihu Smith-like rationalist types to contemplate, though; it supplied a quirky glimpse into his own extended history. The "strange mixture of Mysticism, Theosophy, Cabalistic whim, real Science, Fanaticism, and Freethinking, both in religion and politics" that Robison identified behind "Illuminism"—this was Brown's cultural heritage. For a Quaker like Brown, the very word "Illuminati" was a term associated with the early Society of Friends. Other early Quaker-like groups too, such as the Hermits of the Wissahickon or the Camisards, were typically called "illuminists." And what was Brown's own creation, the elder Wieland, if not an "illuminist" who burned, as it were, a little too brightly?[39]

Finally, there are places in *Proofs* that evoke Brown himself, such as where Robison's Illuminati justify suicide in the very terms Brown had used in his suicide-justifying letters to Joseph Bringhurst. Most uncanny of all, there is a description of "Cosmo-political Brethern" who are consumed with their "Utopian plan of universal benevolence in a state of liberty and equality." On this score Brown had only to think of the many unrealized "plans and scraps of Eutopias" that *he* had hatched during the New York Friendly Club years, and of his stated grand ambition to write a political romance designed to expound a "new system of morality perfect in all its parts."[40]

In sum, *Proofs of a Conspiracy*, published in Scotland in 1797 and available in the United States in mid-1798, held out to Brown a weird sort of doppelgänger cultural and moral history. Deluded in its claims about an actual worldwide "conspiracy" and feckless in its use of evidence to bolster its case, the book does, from Brockden Brown's angle of vision at least, touch on some rather curious personal "truths." In "Memoirs of Carwin" and *Ormond*, Brown contemplates these.

*   *   *

In *Wieland*, Carwin had been an undeveloped character. His main attribute—beyond his ventriloquistic talent—had been mystery. Nobody knew
much about him, and what was said about him seemed contradictory.

When Henry Pleyel had met the man years before in Spain, Carwin was
"an adherent to the Romish faith, yet was an Englishman by birth and, perhaps, a protestant by education." Carwin's "garb, aspect, and deportment,
were wholly Spanish," and he was "indistinguishable from a native, when
he chose to assume that character." As for occupation, Pleyel recalled
that Carwin "pursued no profession, but subsisted on remittances from England." Pleyel's suspicion was that Carwin "counterfeited" his Roman faith
"for some political purpose," but what that might be Pleyel had no clue (63).

When Carwin wanders into the Pennsylvania action at Mettingen, he is
marked by rustic garb and "indisputably great" (66) intellectual endow-
ments. Also riveting was his strangeness. According to Clara, "The inscrut-
ableness of his character, and the uncertainty whether his fellowship tended
to good or to evil, were seldom absent from our minds" (71).

Midway in the story, another account of Carwin emerges, which comes
from Pleyel too. He sees in a newspaper a reward notice for the "apprehension of a convict under sentence of death, who had escaped from
Newgate prison in Dublin," and the criminal's name is Francis Carwin. The
description given of the man leaves no doubt in Pleyel's mind that this is
the same Carwin. In the newspaper account, he had been found guilty in
two indictments—"one for the murder of the Lady Jane Conway, and the
other for a robbery committed on the person of the honorable Mr. Ludloe"
(120–21).

At the end of the novel, Carwin offers his own version of himself. He is
an American by birth, but had left for Europe in his youth. There, he had
been "engaged in various scenes of life, in which my peculiar talent has
been exercised with more or less success. I was finally betrayed by one who
called himself my friend,"—the aforementioned Ludloe—"into acts which
cannot be justified, though they are susceptible of apology" (184). As for
the Irish prison, Carwin explains: "This was the work of an enemy, who, by
falsehood and stratagem, had procured my condemnation. I was, indeed, a
prisoner, but escaped, by the exertion of my powers, the fate to which I was
doomed, but which I did not deserve. I had hoped that the malice of my foe
was exhausted; but I now perceived that my precautions had been wise, for
that the intervention of an ocean was insufficient for my security" (196).

As Carwin presents himself and as the novel ultimately sees him, Carwin
is not evil—just overly proud. His sins are those of "credulity on the one
hand, and of imposture on the other" (196). His only true "crime," he avers,
is that of "curiosity" (190). *Wieland* closes with Carwin having run away to
"a remote district of Pennsylvania" (222) in order to escape the persecutions of his foe, Ludloe. About this Ludloe, *Wieland* says next to nothing.

Brown, in drawing these portraits during the summer of 1798, vaguely hints at an "Illuminati" connection, though he never uses the word. Instead there is reference to some mysterious "political purpose" (63). But that is it. *Wieland,* in any case, is about something else.[41]

What is vague or mysterious about Carwin in *Wieland,* Brown clarifies in "Memoirs of Carwin." Carwin is no more strange than Arthur Mervyn, except that he possesses an unusual talent. Unlike Mervyn, though, who is (seemingly) a well-intentioned country innocent (though he very well might not be) preyed upon by city society, Carwin is clearly the agent of his own troubles. His great trait is his "thirst of knowledge"; his moral flaw is that he seeks knowledge for its own sake and not to advance the happiness of others.[42]

Carwin is the second son of a very superstitious farming family in a "western district of Pennsylvania." (Nottingham would qualify.) About his family he remarks: "Apparitions had been seen, and voices had been heard, on a multitude of occasions. My father was a confident believer in supernatural tokens. The voice of his wife, who had been many years dead, had been twice heard at midnight whispering at his pillow." Carwin, wishing to get out of the farming life, decides to use his father's superstition to achieve his goal. He will counterfeit the voice of his dead mother and use it to convince his father to send him to the city. Other events intervene first, however—a thunderstorm, a barn fire—and his father decides on his own to send Carwin off to live with the aunt in Philadelphia.[43]

Carwin, at this point in his life, is mischievous and ambitious, but he is also capable of feeling guilt, as when he thinks about his plans to deceive his father. He has a conscience. In Philadelphia he meets Ludloe, a man of a different order. Ludloe is concerned first and last in the techniques of controlling others, in *power.* It is this Ludloe that now commands Brockden Brown's interest, and in exploring him Brown seemingly takes his cue from Timothy Dwight's analysis of the rationalist's personality in *The Duty of Americans.* Only with a difference: Dwight's people did not hear voices (at least, for their sake, they better not!); Brown's, typically, did. For Brown to write about this subject, then, was unavoidably to write about his people, and himself.

Ludloe had once seen a vocal demonstration—in the story he does not know about Carwin's own special ventriloquistic talent—and in telling Carwin about it he exhibits an horizon far beyond Carwin's ken. Mankind can be manipulated, Ludloe explains, *because they are religious.* "Men . . . believed in the existence and energy of invisible powers, and in the duty of discovering and conforming to their will. This will was supposed to be sometimes made known to them through the medium of their senses. A voice coming from a quarter where no attendant form could be seen would, in most cases, be ascribed to supernal agency, and a command

imposed on them, in this manner, would be obeyed with religious scrupu-
lousness. Thus men might be imperiously directed in the disposal of their
industry, their property, and even their lives. . . . If it were his desire to accu-
mulate wealth, or institute a new sect, he should need no other instrument." Here Brown moves beyond the quietist religious frame of *Wieland,*
which converts Carwin's playful mischief into murderous tragedy, and
enters the 1790s cultural world of the French Revolution and Robison's
Proofs of a Conspiracy.[44]

The corrosive moral effect of Ludloe on Carwin appears immediately.
Carwin is staying with his Philadelphia aunt, who is old, wealthy, and very
superstitious. Maybe, he thinks, the application of his vocal talent could
influence her decisions concerning her last will and testament. And now
Carwin justifies this thought in these startling moral terms:

> I considered this woman as the usurper of my property. In [her and her husband's]
> hands, money was inert and sterile, or it served to foster their vices. To take it from
> them would, therefore, be a benefit both to them and to myself; not even an imag-
> inary injury would be inflicted.

Anticipating Dostoevsky's Raskolnikov and the rationalistic nihilists in *The
Possessed* and Turgenev's *Fathers and Sons,* with this passage Brockden Brown
begins his philosophical assault on radical rationalism.[45]

Ludloe is a man totally in control of himself. He's no Thomas Welbeck
or Theodore Wieland. "There were no vicissitudes in the deportment or
lapses in the discourse of my friend. . . . He was regular and temperate in
all his exercises and gratifications. Hence were derived his clear perceptions and exuberant health." Just what *type* of man Ludloe is Brown indicates when he has Ludloe offer to send the impecunious Carwin to Europe
and pay for the trip. Carwin tries to thank his benefactor, but Ludloe
responds that "generosity had been expunged from his catalogue as having
no meaning or a vicious one. It was the scope of my exertions to be just.
This was the sum of human duty. . . . If it were my due, I might reasonably
demand it from him and it was wicked to withhold it." Ludloe, the reader
sees, in his disdain for the play of "inefficient" emotions like generosity or
gratitude, is a Godwinian.[46]

In certain ways he is like his creator. For instance, when it came to necessary labor, Ludloe recommended the "choice of a pursuit" with the
"fewest inconveniences. He dwelt on the fewness of our actual wants, the
temptations which attend the possession of wealth, the benefits of seclusion
and privacy, and the duty of unfettering our minds from the prejudices
which govern the world." Ludloe's advice to Carwin could well have been
Brown's own self-advice at the age of eighteen. "You want [lack] knowledge," Ludloe observes. Well,

Means, for this end, are within your reach. Why should you waste your time in idleness, and torment yourself with unprofitable wishes? Books are at hand . . . books
from which most sciences and languages can be learned. Read, analise, digest; collect facts, and investigate theories; ascertain the dictates of reason, and supply yourself with the inclination and the power to adhere to them.

Ludloe might as well have been talking to the teenage Brown who said similar things to Philadelphia's Belles Lettres Club back in the late 1780s.
What Carwin is now going to learn, though, is what the summer of 1798 was
doing to Brown.[47]

Ludloe sends Carwin to Spain for as yet unclear purposes. By this point
Carwin has discovered Ludloe to be, like Godwin and Elihu Smith, a glut-
ton for "sincerity." "My friend," Carwin writes,

was the eulogist of sincerity. He delighted to trace its influence on the happiness of
mankind; and proved that nothing but the universal practice of this virtue was necessary to the perfection of human society. His doctrine was splendid and beautiful.
To detect its imperfections was no easy task.

No easy task, yet this was the assignment Brown had set for himself in examining the reigning philosophy of the Friendly Club. The passage continues:

to lay the foundations of virtue in utility, and to limit, by that scale, the operation
of general principles; to see that the value of sincerity, like that of every other mode
of action, consisted in its tendency to good, and that, therefore the obligation to
speak truth was not paramount or intrinsical; that my duty is modeled on a knowledge and foresight of the conduct of others; and that, since men in their actual state,
are infirm and deceitful, a just estimate of consequences may sometimes make dissimulation my duty, were truths that did not speedily occur. The discovery, when
made, appeared to be a joint work. I saw nothing in Ludloe but proofs of candour,
and a judgment incapable of bias.

Here Brown has Carwin naively regurgitating Ludloe's teachings, but
Brown's point is anything but naive. It is that Godwinianism, E. H. Smith-
ianism, in its all-out insistence on "sincerity," paradoxically amounted to a
self-serving call to *in*sincerity. Again, Carwin summarizes the philosophy
he's learned from Ludloe:

If to act upon *our conceptions of right, and to acquit ourselves of all prejudice and
selfishness* in the formation of our principles, entitle us to the testimony of a good
conscience, I might justly claim it.

Carwin proclaims this with the innocent pride of a Ludloeian acolyte;
Brown offers it up as a moral horror.[48]

Gradually, Carwin finds out from Ludloe about the existence of a
special "fraternity," and the reader learns that this man with the Godwinian philosophy is a member of an Illuminati-like organization. Brown, in

describing this fellowship, dresses it up variously with Freemason and Illuminati aspects, and a heavy dash of Gothic sensation. (Thus, if any member of the fraternity ever divulges its secrets, he is to be killed: not for reasons of "vengeance"—a most irrational, un-Godwinian emotion—but utility.) The ultimate target, however, is not Illuminatism, for Brown was not "political" in the way, say, of the New England Dwights. Nor, given who he was and given the nature of his intellectual sophistication, would he have believed in an actual wide-ranging Illuminati conspiracy. But he did nevertheless espy what he deemed a profound human truth during the summer of 1798 concerning the psychological and moral implications of rationalism, which he knew to be a doctrine with a rich European—and Pennsylvanian—heritage. Godwin and George Fox, he might have said, had more in common than either would have recognized. Both were lowercase "illuminists" and both followed an "inner light," though one called it "reason." As a result both touted systems vulnerable, at the extreme edges, to the dictates of unbounded egotism. As Carwin addresses the reader: "Your notions of duty differ widely from mine. If a system of deceit, pursued merely from the love of truth; if voluptuousness, never gratified at the expense of health, may incur censure, I am censurable." But of course Carwin, the novitiate Godwinian, is saying this to "minds ordinarily constituted," and so his ironic meaning is that he is, in the higher view, *not* censurable for his deceit and voluptuousness. The author of "Memoirs of Carwin"—and the former Rousseauean solipsist of the Henrietta Letters—on the other hand, means to say that he is.[49]

Brown stopped writing "Carwin" during the first week of September. Perhaps inherent plot difficulties played their part in this, as a story begun in the prosaic farming districts of Pennsylvania was careening away into European Gothic vagaries, but most likely Brown put "Carwin" aside, unfinished, because of events unfolding at 45 Pine Street. He obliquely made reference to this context a few years later when he explained that he had ceased the work "from a persuasion that the narrative was of too grave and argumentative a cast to be generally amusing." "Grave" must be a Brownian pun, for in early September the dear friend who had brought Brown into the Godwinian world of the Friendly Club, and who had inspired the central character in the story, had contracted a fatal case of yellow fever.[50]

Elihu Smith noted in his diary on August 25 that the "sickness increases in town." On August 27 he recorded his "more than ordinary fatigue" and his inability to sleep owing to "the musquitoes." On September 5–6 he "Passed a restless and perturbid night, tormented with musquitoes & incongruous dreams." A week later he remarked the "increasing" sickness again and "the desertion of the city." On September 14 Smith hailed the publication of *Wieland;* and two days later he entered the crisis phase of his disease. Three days after that he died. By this time, Brockden Brown too showed early signs of the fever. After attending his friend's funeral, Brown recuperated for a few days at a doctor friend's house, and then left the city for Perth Amboy, New Jersey, where William Dunlap had a farm.[51]

If Brown had contracted yellow fever, he recovered from it quickly, for on September 28 he walked with Dunlap the five miles from Perth Amboy to Woodbridge. Dunlap records in his diary: "Conversation on French politics, Atmospheric air, Animal heat, respiration. Brown tells me the manner in which his mother breaks off his connection with Miss Potts." (So much for Brockden Brown's first real romance with a non-Quaker.) That evening, Dunlap received a letter from Uriah Tracy, who had been asked by Elihu Smith's parents to inquire into the specifics of their son's demise. What the parental Smiths really wanted to know, though, was one specific, the only one that ultimately mattered to them. Did their son die a Christian? Uriah Tracy, suspecting the answer, put the matter delicately to Dunlap: "Did Smith die a Diest? if you require, the answer will be kept secret."[52]

*   *   *

Written in the immediate wake of the death of Elihu Smith and the collapse of the New York cultural world centered upon Smith, *Ormond; or, The Secret Witness* is the most "contemporary" and topical fiction Brown ever attempted. The story is set in 1780s to 1790s New York, 1790s Philadelphia, and Perth Amboy, New Jersey, and for the first time in his fiction Brown uses real, undisguised places and people. Thus there is "112 Walnut Street," the "Indian Queen Tavern" at Market Street and Fifth, a German emigrant farm tenant named "Laffert" (a private joke: Laffert, an immigrant who lived just outside Philadelphia, was a friend of Smith, Dunlap, and Brown), the French writer Volney (whom Brown's circle knew), "a new theater . . . lately . . . constructed" (the Chestnut Street Theater opened in February 1794), and so on.[53]

Interwoven in the story are the 1793 Philadelphia yellow fever epidemic, French revolutionary plots and subplots involving, variously, the Brissot-Marat (or Girondin-Jacobin) contest in Paris and French émigrés in Philadelphia. Finally, bound up with the realistic settings and politics is a conventional literary seduction tale, with Ormond—the Ludloe-like character—craving the body of one Constantia Dudley unto death.

Ormond is a valentine to the Friendly Club: a Brownian valentine. There is a lot of William Dunlap in the story. The Perth Amboy farm which the heroine gains legal possession of and where, in the penultimate scene, she is almost raped, must be Dunlap's own Perth Amboy farm, which Brown often visited and where he convalesced after Smith's demise. And the heroine Constantia's father—Stephen Dudley—is, like Dunlap, a New Yorker who studied painting in Europe. (Stephen Dudley "enjoyed the instructions of Fuzeli and Bartolozzi"; William Dunlap studied with Benjamin West.) Stephen Dudley, whose name echoes the name of Dunlap's father, Samuel Dunlap, lives in New York on Queen Street, which is where the young William Dunlap worked in his father's retail shop. These elements in the story, and the character Laffert, must have amused Dunlap. The spirit of Elihu Smith also pervades the book. For while the protagonist Ormond is in part patterned after such literary villains as *Caleb Williams's* Falkland, *Clarissa's* Lovelace, *The Mysteries of Udolpho's* Montoni, and *The Monk's* Ambrosia, he also embodies transmogrified facets of the recently departed Smith. Ormond, that is to say, is not E. H. Smith. But then again he is.[54]

Through this character Brown finishes the analysis of a 1790s Godwinian rationalist that he had pursued in "Memoirs of Carwin." Ormond is a Godwinian and an Illuminati (though, again, Brown uses neither term), and through him Brown seeks to illustrate the moral/psychological lesson highlighted in "Carwin." In "Carwin" Brown had argued the case concerning rationalism; in *Ormond* he seeks to dramatize it novelistically.

About Ormond we are told that "No one could entertain loftier conceptions of human capacity." He is an idealist. On the other hand, Ormond was a deep cynic who "carefully distinguished between men in the abstract, and men as they are." His political machinations were grounded in both perspectives. "The principles of the social machine must be rectified, before men can be beneficially active." When he is introduced he seems all benevolence. "That in which he chiefly placed his boast was his sincerity . . . . He *affected* to conceal nothing." What the story will illustrate is the special crux borne by that word "affected." In its double meaning lies Brockden Brown's critique of rationalism—and the philosophy of Elihu Smith.[55]

Brown signals Ormond's Godwinianism in his evocation of Ormond's views concerning marriage. As Godwin notoriously argued in *Political Justice*, marriage is an irrational and unnecessary institution, and Ormond will have none of it. He will have none of it, that is, *unless* it is the only way to get what he wants. *Then*, according to his "higher views," even an absurd institution like marriage could become an acceptable means to an end. Standard Godwinian arguments work for Ormond with his current mistress, Helena Cleves (a name curiously suggestive of Henrietta Chew), but when his desires fix on the novel's heroine, Constantia Dudley, his arguments fall flat. True to her name, Constantia has a mind of stronger stuff. She cannot be facilely reasoned into immorality with Ormond, nor, when Ormond holds out to her the prospect of marriage, can she be tempted into treachery against her friend Helena. All the while, Constantia's fineness, intelligence, and "moral constitution" bestir Ormond into desiring her *more.*[56]

Brown's target in *Ormond* is not the indisputably good and moral Elihu

Smith—or the decent William Godwin for that matter—but the psychological/moral dynamic he views as intrinsic to the rationalist way. Timothy Dwight, in *The Duty of Americans*, had highlighted this in his assertion that "most men, and all men who resemble the Illuminati, will pronounce every end to be good, which will gratify their inclinations." It is that transition, from the Ormond at the story's beginning—a quite impressive, learned, and reasonable man who desires to make the world a better place—to the rapacious lunatic at the novel's end, that Brown seeks to explore in *Ormond*.[57]

The twisted depths of Ormond's personality are revealed only when he is finally denied something he absolutely wants: in this case, Constantia. What now surfaces is that in his Godwinian sincerity, in *affecting* to conceal "nothing," he in reality is concealing everything of importance. Beneath his logic and persuasive rhetoric is the reality of a self-obsessed monster. In the American summer of 1798 cultural terms Brown employs for the story, Ormond's corruption, his viciousness, is expressed through his involvement with the Illuminati. On this level, Ormond's "schemes" "depended on their secrecy." And in fact, "Ormond aspired to nothing more ardently than to hold the reins of opinion—to exercise absolute power over the conduct of others, not by constraining their limbs or by exacting obedience to his authority, but in a way of which his subjects should be scarcely conscious. He desired that his guidance should control their steps, but that his agency, when most effectual, should be least suspected."[58]

Ultimately, the rationalist Ormond is driven to the madness and criminality of attempted rape, all the while justifying his actions in "rational" Godwinian terms. First, to get to Constantia, he murders her father, proclaiming that "My motive was benevolent; my deed conferred a benefit." Her father's death, he tries to convince her, "was a due and disinterested offering on the altar of your felicity and mine." (The "logic" here is that Stephen Dudley was going to take his daughter away on a trip, and thereby, Ormond tells Constantia, "snatch you from the influence of my arguments.") And as for his claims on Constantia's body: "I am not tired of well-doing. . . . I have come hither to possess myself of all that I now crave, and by the same deed to afford you an illustrious opportunity to signalize your wisdom and fortitude." He is offering Constantia a Panglossian best of all worlds. Rationally, he can get what he wants—her body; and she can get what her nature craves—an opportunity to show the depth of her virtuous character and her ability to triumph over adversity. Voltaire's Pangloss, though, is a deistic fool; Brown's Ormond is clearly beyond all bounds and indeed insane. Alas, there is nothing in his Godwinian system that can help bring him back under control. The logic only subserves—and thereby further incites—the cravings. This is where Brown, in *Ormond*, traces the psychological and moral arc of "rationalism." By itself, he is saying, rationalism as a system leads to the nightmare of unchecked egotism.[59]

*   *   *

In its plot turns and dialogue, then, *Ormond* is a novel of ideas about the rationalistic dangers inhabiting the Revolutionary era. Yet in its literary textures, its animating emotion, it amounts to quite another book, one addressed to what it calls "the state of manners . . . and the endless forms which sickness and poverty assume in the obscure recesses of a commercial and populous city." But not just any commercial and populous city, for through *Ormond* Brown makes a visit to the place he knows best of all: William Penn's City of Brotherly Love and Benjamin Franklin's City of Philanthropy, which during the summer of 1793 also served as the capital of the American republic.[60]

Brown had been here before, in the first part of *Arthur Mervyn*. On that occasion, he had imagined Philadelphia through the experience of his father, working his way around into his own peculiar sense of the "perils and deceptions" of city life. The narrator of that work was "Dr. Stevens," who pieces Arthur's story together from a number of different sources. In *Wieland*, Brown next imagined the interrelated worlds of himself and his ancestors, and for the purpose he utilized "Clara" as his narrator. In *Ormond*, Brown again chose to narrate a familiar Pennsylvania world through the persona of a female, one Sophia Westyn, and the decision highlights what might be termed the "feminine" dimensions of his imagination.

In his nonfiction writings of 1798–99, published in the Philadelphia *Weekly Magazine* and New York's *Monthly Magazine and American Review*, Brown maintained an insistently "masculine" pose. Trying to fashion himself as a professional literary journalist in 1790s America, he invariably begins his essays with an authoritative "To ascertain the tendency of plays is by no means difficult. . . ," or an informed "Among English writers of history, common consent seems to have assigned the first place to Hume, Robertson, and Gibbon. . . ," and the like. But in the fiction he was concurrently writing, Brown assumed feminine perspectives and personae. He had first done this, inspired by the epistolary novels of Richardson and Rousseau, in the Henrietta Letters and in his letters to William Wilkins, to whom he had written that "I will willingly become a pupil to you and be taught, by my amorous friend, the art and mystery of a Lover." No doubt, too, his Quaker upbringing had its influence here, for Quaker men, like Quaker women, were trained to degrees of passivity, as they were reared to be attentive to, and comfortable with, the subtle feelings teased out by "silence." Yet the poignancy of *Wieland*'s Clara, and *Ormond*'s compelling evocation of Constantia's Philadelphia circumstances, point to a depth of specific personal experience in Brown that was, in its fundamental attributes, "feminine." Nor is this surprising, in view of Brown's biography. For outside the oracular literary journalism he could produce by virtue of being a magazine editor, little in Brown's existence allowed him to feel "masculine" mastery of anything. He couldn't even romance Susan Potts without his mother stepping in to spoil it.[61]

In *Ormond*, Philadelphia is a cruel, heartless place, and not because of yellow fever. The contagion merely serves to reveal *the plague* of what's already there, or more to the point, what's *not* really there.

The economic descent of Stephen Dudley from successful New York apothecary to embarrassed bankrupt to makeshift Philadelphia conveyancer, exposes him and his daughter to the unlovely practices and procedures of late eighteenth-century market society. With Dudley's bankruptcy, accordingly, "It was his lot to fall into the grasp of men who squared their actions by no other standard than law, and who esteemed every claim to be incontestably just that could plead that sanction." His creditors, in the event, "did not indeed throw him into prison." No. "When they had despoiled him of every remnant of his property, they deemed themselves entitled to his gratitude for leaving his person unmolested." In his new life as a conveyancer, too, humiliations mount. The one-time respected and independent merchant now had to associate "with sordid hirelings, gross and uneducated, who treated his age with rude familiarity, and insulted his ears with ribaldry and scurril jests. He was subject to command, and had his portion of daily drudgery allotted to him, to be performed for a pittance." As a hopeful and proud young man Stephen Dudley had felt "a certain species of disgrace" for "every employment of which the only purpose was gain." Now, though, his daily routine consisted of "one tedious round of scrawling and jargon; a tissue made up of the shreds and remnants of barbarous antiquity, polluted with the rust of ages." Most vexingly, he had to worry about money for the basic necessities of rent and food. In one scene Dudley advises his daughter not to squander their remaining cash on rent—they need it for food—and to await instead the "agent of the law." His reasoning is that "the debt will be merely increased by a few charges," and that "in a state like ours, the miserable remnant is not worth caring for." Constantia, however, views and feels the situation differently. Whatever the consequences, it was "wiser" to pay the rent than "to exasperate their landlord, to augment the debt, *and to encounter the disgrace accruing from a constable's visits.*"[62]

In *Arthur Mervyn* Brown had purposely left his Philadelphia settings vague and ambiguous. Arthur visits "a house," walks down "a street," crosses "a river." The city where the action takes place is never identified; it could be anywhere. The effect is dreamlike, phantasmagoric. In *Ormond* Brown summons a most precise Philadelphia, and the novel's settings are readily recognizable to anybody familiar with the city. Thus when Stephen Dudley and his daughter arrive in Philadelphia—where they move after he has been financially ruined in New York by the defalcations of his trusted apprentice Thomas Craig—they first "hired a small house in the suburbs of the city." Subsequently, the two move to a small house "near the center of the city, in a quiet, cleanly, and well-paved alley." This locale turns out to be, come the summer heat and the yellow fever, "at no great distance from the seat of the malady." Their next door neighbor, a cooper, worked in a shop "near the water, and at a small distance from the scene of original infection." This cooper lived with a sister, and she is the first person on their street to be infected with the disease. Thereafter the fever spreads rapidly through the Dudleys' neighborhood.[63]

This is to situate Stephen and Constantia Dudley in the area of Philadelphia adjacent to North Water Street, where the first cases of yellow fever had appeared in early August 1793. This was in reality "the scene of original infection," and it was in this quarter, in the blocks north of Arch Street between the Delaware River and Third Street, where the contagion in reality killed the highest percentage of residents. Known to Philadelphians as "Helltown," here lived and congregated the city's alcoholics, vagrants, prostitutes, escaped servants and slaves, and other down-on-their-luck unfortunates—like the fictional Dudleys.[64]

Brockden Brown has this father and daughter pair move into what they deem a "quiet, cleanly, and well-paved alley." But when the plague hits, the neighborhood changes guise.

In alleys and narrow streets, in which the houses were smaller, the inhabitants more numerous and indigent, and the air pent up within unwholesome limits, it raged with greatest violence. Few of Constantia's neighbors possessed the means of removing from the danger. The inhabitants of this alley consisted of three hundred persons. . . . two hundred were destroyed in the course of three weeks. Among so many victims, it may be supposed that this disease assumed every terrific and agonizing shape.

Constantia, meanwhile, found it impossible

to shut out every token of a calamity thus enormous and thus near. Night was the season usually selected for the removal of the dead. The sound of wheels thus employed was incessant. . . . The shrieks and laments of survivors, who could not be prevented from attending the remains of a husband or child to the place of interment, frequently struck her senses. Sometimes, urged by a furious delirium, the sick would break from their attendants, rush into the streets, and expire on the pavement, amidst frantic outcries and gestures. By these she was often roused from imperfect sleep, and called to reflect upon the fate which impended over her father and herself.

Her despair seemed unrelievable, for

To preserve health in an atmosphere thus infected, and to ward off terror and dismay in a scene of horrors thus hourly accumulating, was impossible. Constantia found it vain to contend against the inroads of sadness. Amidst so dreadful a mortality, it was irrational to cherish the hope that she or her father would escape.[65]

This is the emotional core of *Ormond*. From this geographical quarter and from this down-and-out experience flow the sufferings and the plot turns of the story. Ormond himself appears on the scene as a potential savior for Constantia, as one capable of rescuing her from the hells of poverty, from Helltown . . . from a Philadelphia like that the Browns got to know in the early 1790s.

After Elijah Brown's imprisonment for debt in 1784, he tried to make a living as a "conveyancer," and the family rented a house on Pear Street between Third and Dock Streets. Though not far from Charles Brown's grandmother's town house, Pear, in the language of *Ormond*, would qualify as a "narrow street," and in marked contrast to Elizabeth Armitt's South Second Street, it was a distinctly laboring-class neighborhood, comprising brewers, bookbinders, coachmen, sail makers, house carpenters, flower sellers, and coopers.[66]

When the Elijah Brown family next shows up in public records, it is in the 1790 federal census. They are living in Northern Liberties, a suburb abutting the northern edge of Philadelphia. In the household are listed three free white females (undoubtedly Charles's mother and two sisters), one free white male under sixteen (Charles's younger brother Elijah), and two white males over sixteen—no doubt Elijah, Sr. and Charles. In the 1791 city directory Elijah Brown, now a "broker," is listed at 159 Vine Street. This was four blocks away from North Water Street, where on the night of August 3, 1793, an English lodger in a boardinghouse died of what Philadelphians would learn two weeks later was the yellow fever. It was next door to 161 Vine, where James and Maria Reynolds, flush (for them) with funds blackmailed from the secretary of the treasury, lived in 1792. In a 1792 letter to Joseph Bringhurst, written at 159 Vine, Charles had fantasized himself at "The Cocoa Tree. Pall Mall. London," in love, and planning a trip to Switzerland, before shifting to the "Vine Street Sunday Morn" reality and the comment: "With what regret do I percieve that all this is the painting of my fancy only! And yet why may not imagination supply the place of reality?" Elijah Brown next appears in the 1795 city directory, listed as a "Land Broker," living at 117 South Second Street, a place, an asylum, he and his wife would never again leave.[67]

Juxtapose these facts to the "fictions" of *Ormond*. The bankrupt turned conveyancer Stephen Dudley struggles to find a secure, safe place for himself and his daughter. Along the way he must deal with heartless landlords and the ever-present threat of eviction. After his bankruptcy he moves to a suburb of Philadelphia—like Northern Liberties—and then into the city proper, into a small alley dwelling not far from "the scene of the contagion"—and not far from Vine Street. Stephen Dudley moved to this place because he was embarrassed by his misfortune and too proud to live amid his old associates. In the Brown family case, it cannot be known why after

the war Elijah moved his family out of his mother-in-law's house. The bare
record is that this father who had once pridefully refused to accept the
advice and aid of the Philadelphia Meeting had sought, in the wake of his
own humiliating bankruptcy, to make his living as a conveyancer and in this
pursuit had moved his family from rented house to rented house. Unlike
Stephen Dudley, though, who deemed himself friendless in Philadelphia,
Elijah Brown always had mother-in-law Elizabeth Armitt to fall back
upon—if, that is, she was in fact willing to help *him*, and if he was prepared
to swallow his pride. In *Ormond*, the Dudleys must deal with the unsympathetic landlord M'Crea, who, returning to the city after the end of the epidemic, immediately duns the Dudleys for their accumulated back rent. The
narrator notes that "Some proprietors, guided by humanity, had remitted
their dues" at this trying time, when no one had been able to make a living
for several months. M'Crea, though, "was not one of these." *Ormond* goes
on to render M'Crea with exquisite detail and animosity.

According to his own representation, no man was poorer than himself, and the
punctual payment of all that was owing to him was no more than sufficient to afford
him a scanty subsistence.
    He was aware of the indigence of the Dudleys, and was therefore extremely
importunate for payment, and could scarcely be prevailed upon to allow them the
interval of a day for the discovery of expedients.

Did the Elijah Brown family have its own dealings with M'Creas, "men who
squared their actions by no other standard than law"? What is certain is that
at least once Elijah "fell into the grasp" of someone who used the law to put
him in jail for unpaid debts. Equally certain is that *Ormond* literarily captures
the desperation of a family caught up in these impossible circumstances.[68]
    What did the actual 1793 epidemic mean to Brockden Brown? How
much of it did he experience? The evidence indicates that when Mrs.
Parkinson of North Water Street was treated by a physician on August 3 for
a strangely violent malignant fever, Brown was on his way home from his
summer sojourn in Connecticut with Elihu Smith. He was back in the city
by August 16, three days before physicians concluded that the numerous
cases of deadly fever in the Water Street area were related and signified a
yellow fever outbreak. The severity of the situation did not become apparent until the second week of September, when thirty to forty people a day
were being buried. (On an average August day Philadelphia might expect
five burials.) The worst of it hit the second week of October, when over a
hundred corpses a day were being buried.
    The Elijah Browns had few resources of their own, and around this time
Charles complained of "want" of money as "the first of miseries." "Present
circumstances," he wrote, deprived him of "tranquility of mind and disembarrassment of views" (a curious phrase). On the other hand, the Browns
had extended family who could help: in particular Mary Brown's sister

Elizabeth Waln, who lived north of the city on a country estate in Frank-ford, New Jersey. This would have made an ideal refuge. According to William Dunlap, Brown and his family "fled in time" from 159 Vine Street to avoid the pestilence. Did the Browns remove to Walnford? If so, it was the second time Uncle Richard had stepped in to help the Elijah Browns through peril. In any case what is later evident about Brockden Brown is that he carried no fear of the yellow fever. In the summer of 1797, when the fever returned to Philadelphia, as it had in 1796, he reported himself entering the city as "carriages . . . loaden with families and furniture" fled the other way. From the afflicted city he wrote to a friend: "Alarms are prevalent and removals into the country numerous and incessant. The obnox-ious vicinity is a desert." Again in the summer of 1798, when the yellow fever hit Philadelphia and New York, he wrote unfearfully from Elihu Smith's house in New York: "the yellow fever has kept at a respectful dis-tance from Pine Street, and I hope will continue so." This time, though, the contagion caught up with him, and it killed his friend Smith. In the after-math he wrote *Ormond*, and thereby his imagination necessarily took a return trip to the frightful Philadelphia of 1793.[69]

Yet *Ormond* is not really about the 1793 outbreak, per se. Other books had been published about that: Matthew Carey's *A Short Account of the Malig-nant Fever* (1793), William Currie's *A Description of the Malignant Infectious Fever* (1793), Benjamin Rush's *An Enquiry into the Origins of the Late Epidemic Fever in Philadelphia* (1793), Absalom Jones and Richard Allen's *A Narrative of the Proceedings of the Black People, during the Late Awful Calamity in Philadelphia. In the Year 1793* (1794). *They* are about the events of August–October 1793. *Ormond* is about something larger (as too was Jones and Allen's *Narrative*). It is about post-Revolutionary Philadelphia society and, in par-ticular, about what an unfeeling, heartless place it was for those truly in need. It is about the divergence between rhetoric and reality, between a society's stated moral codes and the actual way people behave. It's about hypocrisy.

This is underlined by the failure of people in the book to keep promises. Thomas Craig lies to Stephen Dudley (and ends up ruining him), M'Crea breaks his promise to the Dudleys (and they end up out on the street, homeless), a doctor fails to honor his promise to visit a sickhouse (and the patient dies). Only the most humble in this story bother to keep their word, like the black wood-carter who promised Constantia he would remove the dead body of Mary Whiston from her house and who subsequently "faith-fully performed his promise"; and Constantia herself, whom Ormond crit-icises precisely because she keeps her promises. To his way of thinking, this is her weakness, her error. A tacit reference here is Godwin's *Enquiry Con-cerning Political Justice*, which denigrated the philosophical basis of prom-ises, and the practice of making decisions based on "feeling." But Brown, clearly, needs no help from books to create his picture.[70]

Those who meet the human sympathy test—who behave, that is, the way they are *supposed* to behave—are preeminently Constantia and her friend, Sophia Westyn, the narrator. These two possess the actual sensibility, and the values, that the religious and moral codes of the time—the Age of Sensibility—call for. Ormond denies the possibility of "sympathy." Constantia and Sophia exhibit how it does and should work. Indeed they, the "female sex," embody the proper values of "sympathy"—and in a way Brown lets "justice" reign, for when the story ends Thomas Craig and Ormond and M'Crea and all the other hypocrites are dead, while Constantia and Sophia endure. They endure, but they choose to live out the rest of their lives in Europe.[71]

That these humane sentimental values are for women alone is refuted by the figure of Melbourne, who also is a paragon of charity and fellow feeling. He uses money the way it should be used: he lends it to those who need it most, like the Dudleys. That these values are naturally female is perhaps refuted by the figure of Martinette—Ormond's sister—who is heralded for her "masculine attainments." Educated, brave, intrepid, Martinette has played the part of an actor in the trans-Atlantic revolutionary drama of the age. A figure of accomplishment, she is not an appealing figure for Brown, as her name indicates. In a cruel world all too lacking in the play of basic sympathy, of fellow feeling, her proud boast that, in Paris, when it came time to cut the throats of her former friends in the cause of "liberty," she did it easily is not a recommendation coming from Brockden Brown. She, like her brother Ormond, is a moral horror, but a horror differentiated from the majority of other characters in the story merely by degree.[72]

*   *   *

Ormond has one other vital biographical quality, for within it echoes a fateful debate that Brown, as an imaginative artist, circa late 1798, was having with himself. Brown's protagonist is artist-like in his talents. "In listening to his discourse," the narrator observes, "no one's claim to sincerity appeared less questionable." Yet a "somewhat different conclusion would be suggested by a survey of his actions." This would reveal "a remarkable facility in imitating the voice and gestures of others. His memory was eminently retentive, and these qualities would have rendered his career, in the theatrical profession, illustrious." Again, Ormond is described as having had earlier in his life an "aversion to duplicity" owing to his having been a "victim" of its evils. Subsequently, however, he found himself in a situation where the "usual mode of solving his doubts he deemed insufficient, and the eagerness of his curiosity tempted him, for the first time, to employ, for this end, his talents at imitation. He therefore assumed a borrowed character and guise, and performed his part with so much skill as fully to accomplish his design." The ultimate consequence, for Ormond, was a mature character too easily given to hypocrisy and licentiousness.[73]

Was Brown thinking about himself? With his first published novel, *Wieland*, he had skirted the orthodox Quaker taboo against "fiction." Addressing this in the novel's preface, he had averred that his "purpose is neither selfish nor temporary, but aims at the illustration of some important branches of the moral constitution of man," and that it was his business, as a "moral painter," to "exhibit [his] subject in its most instructive and memorable forms." Yet was that what the visionary indulgence of *Wieland* amounted to? In *Ormond* Brown states the case for the morality of his fiction in more detail. "It is above all things necessary," his narrator writes,

that we should be thoroughly acquainted with the condition of our fellow-beings. Justice and compassion are the fruit of knowledge. The misery that overspreads so large a part of mankind exists chiefly because those who are able to relieve it do not know that it exists. Forcibly to paint the evil, seldom fails to excite the virtue of the spectator and seduce him into wishes, at least, if not into exertions, of beneficence.

But how about his imaginative evocation of Ormond's lasciviousness and the lurid rape scene. Was there perhaps hypocrisy and licentiousness at play here too—in addition to the "excitement" of virtue?[74]

Certainly *Ormond* draws an opposite moral to that exhibited in "Carwin" (and *Wieland*). In "Carwin," it was those who were religious who could be easily manipulated; in *Ormond*, Constantia is in danger because she was "unacquainted with religion" and as a result vulnerable to powerful reasoned argument. (On the other hand, as her name implies and her ultimate actions prove, she is the strongest character in the story.) This change reflects the impact of the summer of 1798 on Brown, and it presages the profound turn Brown was destined to take in the near future. This transformation would express itself not as a rejection of rationalism and a return to his Quaker religious heritage, but as a renunciation of his New York present and Philadelphia past-present altogether. In the event Brown would cease to write Gothic fiction. Instead he would manufacture sentimental domestic dramas with happy endings. He would also churn out partisan Federalist political pamphlets, one of which would advocate the American takeover of Louisiana "by forceful means, if need be." And he would choose to leave the Quaker fold.[75]

To anticipate, then: Brockden Brown's visionary days were about to end. But not before he took one last great visionary leap.

Chapter 6

The Return of the Present . . . and Past

Brockden Brown invented American Gothic with *Wieland,* a grisly tale that, willy-nilly, just flowed out of his imagination. With *Edgar Huntly; or, Memoirs of a Sleep-Walker* he set out determinedly to write a Gothic novel, American style. His preface announces this. The tale will not involve the "Puerile superstition and exploded manners; Gothic castles and chimeras" of the Walpole-Radcliffe-Lewis school. Rather, Brown informs, "It is the purpose of this work . . . to exhibit a series of adventures, growing out of the condition of our country." The reader is then told that this special American condition involves "the incidents of Indian hostility, and the perils of the western wilderness." "For a native of America to overlook these," says Brown, "would admit of no apology." *Apology?* Brown's words here have to be closely attended to, for he was never writing with more precision, or deadlier irony. *The incidents of Indian hostility. The perils of the western wilderness.* Brockden Brown's most violent "fictional" vision of all is precisely about this.[1]

* * *

One night in mid-1780s Pennsylvania, Edgar Huntly throws himself on his bed in his uncle's cottage and falls asleep. The next thing he knows he is "supine upon a rugged surface and immersed in palpable obscurity," wondering "what dungeon or den had received me, and by whose command was I transported hither?" All around him is space and darkness. The setting effects in him "a species of delirium." His thoughts are "wildering and mazy . . . and disconnected with the loco-motive or voluntary power. . . . I existed as it were in a wakeful dream."

And things get weirder still. Walking in the featureless darkness, he, unbelievably, comes across an Indian tomahawk. He picks it up and walks on. He notes of his state of consciousness that with "nothing to correct my erroneous perceptions, the images of the past occurred in capricious combinations, and vivid hues." He sees two "glowing orbs" which turn out to be the eyes of a panther. Heaving the tomahawk, he kills the animal. Famished, he devours the raw carcass and drinks its blood. Later he will with "loathing and horror" think back to this scene as "some hideous dream."

He comes across a fire with men around it. He discovers them to be

"Two Savages, disputing which should deliver Miss McRea into her Lover's hands and obtain the promised reward; one of them struck his Tomahawk into her scull and killed her." *Philadelphia Magazine*, 1797.

Indians—"four brawny and terrific figures"—and is mystified. "Had some mysterious power snatched me from the earth, and cast me, in a moment, into the heart of the wilderness? Was I yet in the vicinity of my paternal habitation, or was I thousands of miles distant?" He tries to account for this spectacle. It is the 1780s, after all, and he lives in a farming district thirty miles north of Philadelphia, on the edge of an area called Norwalk that was long since cleared of native Indians. He remembers, though, that "during the last war," "notwithstanding the progress of population . . . a band of them had once penetrated into Norwalk, and lingered long enough to pillage and murder some of the neighbouring inhabitants."

Now Edgar's thoughts drift back to the time of the Revolutionary War and "that event" when "eight of these assassins assailed [my father's house] at the dead of night. My parents and an infant child were murdered in their beds; the house was pillaged, and then burnt to the ground." He reflects:

Most men are haunted by some species of terror or antipathy, which they are, for the most part, able to trace to some incident which befel them in their early years. You will not be surprised that the fate of my parents, and the sight of the body of one of this savage band, who, in the pursuit that was made after them, was overtaken and killed, should produce lasting and terrific images in my fancy. I never looked upon, or called up the image of a savage without shuddering.

As Edgar, in hiding, observes the Indians and thinks about getting away from this dangerous spot, he notices that they have a captive, a young girl. He must not only effect his own escape; he must save her too. So he contrives to grab a musket and hatchet from one of the Indians who is asleep. But what next? Should he, who had "never before . . . taken the life of an human creature," try to kill these savages? "Let it be remembered," he reasons,

that I entertained no doubts about the hostile designs of these men. This was sufficiently indicated by their arms, their guise, and the captive who attended them. Let the fate of my parents be, likewise, remembered. I was not certain but that these very men were the assassins of my family, and were those who had reduced me and my sisters to the condition of orphans and dependants.

Edgar hatchets one of the Indians and flees with the girl.

Now the really uncanny intrudes. Edgar notices that the gun he has taken from the Indian is *his own gun*, which he had left in his uncle's house. With this discovery his "teeth chattered with horror." He can only conclude that "My uncle and my sisters had been murdered; the dwelling had been pillaged, and this had been a part of the plunder." He faults himself for not having been there to protect them. With this he contemplates a new explanation for the events of the last night: "Had not the cause of my being cast into this abyss some connection to the ruin of my family? Had I not been dragged hither by these savages, and reduced, by their malice, to that breathless and insensible condition? Was I born to a malignant destiny never tired of persecuting? Thus had my parents and their infant offspring perished, and thus completed was the fate of all those to whom my affections cleaved, and whom the first disaster spared."

At this point Edgar's emotions undergo a transformation. Hitherto he had contemplated violence with "remorse"; now the desire for "vengeance" overtakes him. "It was the scope of my wishes to kill the whole number of my foes; but that being done, I was indifferent to the consequences." And by the time Edgar finally succeeds in exiting "the abyss" and returning home to his uncle's cottage, he has killed five Indians.[2]

Brown wrote *Edgar Huntly*, at the heart of which beats this "bloody and disastrous tale" (809), in early to mid-1799. It had been seven years since he had described for Joseph Bringhurst his visionary literary method. On that occasion Brown had evoked a childhood place, "an apartment," "a *Jail*," where he had been "woken by the clanking of chains and bolts & iron doors," where his "ears were continually assailed by blasphemies or obscenities," where there had been "a continual Suspicion of Inhabitants, of various and opposite characters, associated by Calamity." He had then asked his friend to "Suffer your imagination to connect with this incident all the Circumstances by which it is accompanied," to tell him "how thou wouldst have acted in similar circumstances or what emotions would the recollection produce." In *Edgar Huntly* Brown applies this method. Through the medium of his sleepwalking protagonist, he pursues the circumstances and emotions of his childhood, and his heritage, to their infernal Pennsylvanian depths.[3]

There are markers to his method. In one of the subplots, the character Weymouth, who leaves $8,000 with his friend Waldegrave for safekeeping when he departs on business for Europe, gives—quite gratuitously—the date of his embarkation from Philadelphia as "the tenth of August 1784" (772). Now why would Brockden Brown have picked, of all possible dates, a time when his own father was incarcerated in Philadelphia's Walnut Street prison? In this same subplot, Edgar describes Waldegrave as one whose "religious duty compelled him to seek his livelihood by teaching a school of blacks" (764). Why would Brown thus unmistakably invoke Anthony Benezet, who had for fifteen years famously run Philadelphia's "Negro school" (and who had died in 1784). Brown had used the "great good Man" before, in *Wieland*, when he gave the Wielands a Benezet-like Camisard past. Now in a tale in which the eponymous hero lives "near the *Forks* of the Delaware," he resurrects him again. Why?

Because once upon a time—*and not just any time*—Anthony Benezet had been there. At the Forks. That is, *Edgar Huntly* tells of things—dark, murderous, despicable things—that Anthony Benezet, and other Philadelphia *and Nottingham Quakers*, had a privileged relation to. And it explores these things through a Gothic aesthetic. Which is why Brown evokes early August 1784, one of the darkest times of his life, as throughout the novel he evokes a host of his own Revolutionary memories. For to write this "memoir of a sleep-walker," Brown needs to become like a sleepwalker, to induce in himself the "unsanctified" visionary state, and in that state he channels his way right *through* the Revolutionary period, back into the darkest Pennsylvanian episode of all, for which "apology" was indeed in order.[4]

*   *   *

Edgar Huntly has many subplots, but when these are discounted, what remains is the central tale of Edgar's voyage, his odyssey, into "Norwalk."

The action proceeds from the town of Solebury. From this home base, Edgar ventures north and west into an area, Norwalk, that is described variously. It is "uncultivated," a "desert tract"; it is "in the highest degree, rugged, picturesque and wild" (655). Initially this region is defined as "a space, somewhat circular, about six miles in diameter, and exhibiting a perpetual and intricate variety of craggy eminences and deep dells." It has "mists" and "chasms," "caves" and "caverns." A "sort of continued vale, winding and abrupt, leads into the midst of this region and through it" (723).

Edgar thinks he knows this region well. Years before he had traveled and explored it extensively with a man named Sarsefield. But in the central adventure in the novel, Edgar discovers that he does not know Norwalk—that there's a boundary he can pass through, "along the edge of this cavity," and on the other side he enters a wild and violent world where "it seemed as if I was surrounded by barriers that would forever cut off my return to air and to light" (727).

It is in this "subterranean prison" that Edgar wakes up one day, wearing only trousers and a shirt, not knowing how he got there. His first thought: "I endeavoured to recall the past." (*Be careful what you wish for!*) What happens to him next is incredible. He finds that "Indian tom-hawk" (780). Kills and devours the panther. Sees the "swarthy band" of savages sitting around the fire, and their young captive, whose "features denoted the last degree of fear and anguish" (793–94). The two whites escape. And now the surreal action continues.

Edgar comes upon a hut, a dwelling that "was suited to the poverty and desolation which surrounded it" (800). Its owner is not at home; so Edgar and the girl settle in. She lies down on the bed. Edgar decides to step outside, and "at the farther end of the field" (804) he detects three figures. Indians again. They are tracking him! They approach and enter the cottage, while Edgar hides behind a sandbank, and listens through the wall.

Presently I heard an heavy stroke descend. I shuddered, and my blood ran cold at the sound. I entertained no doubt but that it was the stroke of an hatchet on the head or breast of the helpless sleeper.

It was followed by a loud shriek. . . . I waited to hear it repeated, but the sounds that now arose were like those produced by dragging somewhat along the ground. The shrieks, meanwhile, were incessant and piteous. (806–7)

Edgar watches one of the Indians drag the girl from the hut and across a field, and as the Indian is about to shoot her, Edgar fires and kills him. He shoots another Indian above the ear. Another rushes at him. Edgar kills him.

A band of ten or twelve white men arrives, the girl's anguished father among them. They ask the bleeding Edgar "who I was, whence I had come, and what had given rise to this bloody contest" (811)? He faints from loss of blood. When he awakes the men and girl are gone, and his head is resting on one of the slain Indians. The other two dead Indians lay close by. Edgar gets up and resumes his wilderness travail.

His eye catches something moving in the forest and he assumes it is an animal. But he's in such a strange place, he decides to scrutinize "the beast" closely. And a good thing too, because it's yet another Indian, moving "upon all fours." "His disfigured limbs, pendants from his ears and nose, and his shorn locks, were indubitable indications of a savage." Edgar shoots him, with gruesome effect, for the man "rolled upon the ground, uttering doleful shrieks, and throwing his limbs into those contorsions which bespeak the keenest agonies to which ill-fated man is subject. Horror, and compassion, and remorse, were mingled into one sentiment, and took possession of my heart." Edgar bayonets the man to death for mercy's sake. He picks up the Indian's tomahawk and heads east, toward the reddish hue of the rising sun, in search of food and repose, and home. Yet "the spots of cultivation, the *well-pole*, the *worm-fence*, and the hay-rick, were no where to be seen" (814–18).

Finally, he chances upon a house. Inside he finds a white woman with two children. She feeds him and supplies him with recent news. White men, she tells him, had just passed by in search of someone from Solebury who, three days before, had rambled into the mountains and lost his way. The night before, she adds, this "tall, slender" person wearing "nothing but shirt and trowsers" (820) had been sighted in the wilderness—eight miles away— at a hut inhabited by an old Indian woman known as Old Deb or Queen Mab.

Old Deb. Edgar knew this Indian woman. She used to live in Norwalk and visit Solebury. In fact, Edgar had been the one in Solebury who had, sardonically, given her the nickname "Queen Mab," on account of her pretensions to royalty. He relates her story:

This woman originally belonged to the tribe of Delawares or Lennilennapee. All these districts were once comprised within the dominions of that nation. About thirty years ago, in consequence of perpetual encroachments of the English colonists, they abandoned their ancient seats and retired to the banks of the Wabash and Muskingum.

This emigration was concerted in a general council of the tribe, and obtained the concurrence of all but one female.

The one female, of course, was Old Deb. Edgar adds one more bit of information: "The village inhabited by this clan was built upon ground which now constitutes my uncle's barn yard and orchard. On the departure of her countrymen, this female burnt the empty wigwams and retired into the fastnesses of Norwalk" (820).

Edgar can now deduce where he is. He is thirty miles from home. From Solebury. Apparently the world of Norwalk was much vaster than he had thought.

*   *   *

"Norwalk." North Walk.

In September 1737, starting about seven miles southwest of the Bucks County township of Solebury, three young woodsmen employed by the chief justice of Pennsylvania, James Logan, began the "walk" north that resulted in the most notorious land fraud in Pennsylvania history. Using an unfinished draft of a 1686 deed, Logan, acting in the interest of the cash-starved sons of William Penn—and in his own interest (Logan had years before purchased a small property from the Delaware Indians for an iron-works, and he now needed the surrounding forests to power its furnace)—claimed that the Delawares had sold land to William Penn in 1686, but that the tract had never been surveyed. Logan then showed the Delawares a doctored map, with creeks and rivers purposely misrepresented. What the illiterate Delawares *saw* was a map of the country south of Tohickon Creek (which runs east to west starting about two miles north of Solebury Township). These lands the Delawares had in fact sold to William Penn. What the map *said*, though, in written English, was that it represented lands "north" of Tohickon Creek. Four Delaware chiefs, including one Nutimus, were induced to sign a confirmation of the supposed "contract." By its terms—in the customary phrase used by the Delawares in the time of William Penn—the purchase conveyed an extent of land that could be leisurely walked, with due stops for meals and rest, in "a day and a half," or about twenty miles. Nutimus's lands, which extended from Tohickon Creek north to the Lehigh River, in any case, were not involved in the 1686 transaction.[5]

As far as the Delawares were concerned, then, James Logan was going to carry out a survey that would confirm the prior sale of Indian lands south of Tohickon Creek to the Penns. But Logan had prepared for the walk weeks earlier by clearing the brush along *his* intended path, and at dawn on September 19, his three "walkers," paced by horses carrying their provisions, headed off, and over the next thirty-six hours they traversed sixty-four miles, advancing some forty-seven miles above Tohickon Creek. Logan had netted for the Penns all of Nutimus's land, plus the Lehigh Valley between the Lehigh and Delaware Rivers, and a large tract beyond the Blue Mountain.[6]

The problem now was to evict the Forks Delawares from their tribal territory. To this end Logan struck a deal with the militarily powerful Iroquois of New York. In exchange for recognition by the colony of Pennsylvania of Iroquois suzerainty over the Delawares (and Delaware lands)—which the Iroquois had no historical right to—the Iroquois were to see to the removal of their unwarlike "nephews" from the region in question.[7]

The scheme culminated in 1742, in Philadelphia, at a treaty conference where the Iroquois relayed to the Delawares, as Godwin would have put it, "things as they are." The Iroquois chief Canasatego, leading a large Six Nations contingent, first verbally abused and intimated the Forks Delaware chief Nutimus. Then, in language that curiously anticipated the biblical curse which would hang over the head of the usurping Manfred in the first Gothic novel, the pagan Canasatego said to the Delawares: "This string of Wampum serves to forbid You Your Children and Grand Children to the latest Posterity for ever medling in Land Affairs neither you nor any who shall descend from You are ever hereafter to presume to sell any Land for which Purpose you are to Preserve this string in Memory of what your Uncles have this Day given You in Charge."[8]

In the next year the Forks Delawares were cleared from their tribal lands. Some moved northwest to the Susquehanna River region, some west to the Ohio, and some stayed up north above the Walking Purchase territory, on land now claimed by the Iroquois. In the bargain Pennsylvania gained upper Bucks and the new county of Northampton, with its seat, the town of Easton, founded in 1751.[9]

Yet the Forks Delawares never forgot the episode, and in 1755, when General Braddock with his army of British Regulars lost to a small force of French Indians near Fort Duquesne, and in the aftermath the frontiers exploded into violence, the formerly peaceful Delawares began attacking white Pennsylvania settlements. First, on October 16, 1755, at Penn's Creek, on the left bank of the Susquehanna River, a small Delaware war party murdered and scalped thirteen men, women, and children. Five days later, at a hamlet called Great Cove, children's brains were smashed against door posts and trees; women were tied to trees and made to watch as their husbands were trussed and burned alive. It took another month before the warriors crossed over into Northampton County. At the village of Gnadenhütten, eleven whites were shut in their houses and burned to death. Of that December 1755, the Pennsylvania Council recorded: "During all this Month the Indians have been burning or destroying all before them in the County of Northampton, and have already burnt fifty houses here, murdered above one hundred Persons, & are still continuing their Ravages, Murders and Devastations, & have actually overrun and laid waste a great part of that Country, even as far as within twenty miles of Easton, its chief Town." In Easton, at the spot where the Delaware and Lehigh Rivers converge which the Lenni Lenape called "the Forks"—this is twenty miles north of Solebury—a panicked militia major wrote a confidential communication to the Pennsylvania governor: "Your honour will be pleased to consider the Defencelessness of this little Town, which stands upon the very Land which the Indians claim, and is upon that Account alone much more in danger of an Attack from the Savages than any other place."[10]

Nottingham's John Churchman duly heard the news of "The Indians having burnt several houses on the frontier, of this Province, also at Gnadenhutten in Northampton County, and murdered and scalped some of the inhabitants," and he was in Philadelphia in May 1757 when Northampton settlers—people whose farms had been purchased, from the Penns, from the domains of the Walking Purchase—brought "two or three of the dead bodies . . . in a waggon, and with an intent as was supposed to animate the people to unite in preparations of war to take vengeance on the Indians, and destroy them." Churchman's eyewitness account was published in his 1779 autobiography:

[The white corpses] were carried along several of the streets, many people following, cursing the Indians, also the Quakers because they would not join in war for destruction of the Indians. The sight of the dead bodies and the outcry of the people, were very afflicting and shocking to me: Standing at the door of a friend's house as they passed along, my mind was humbled and turned much inward when I was made secretly to cry; *What will become of Pennsylvania?* For it felt to me that many did not consider, that the sins of the inhabitants, pride, profane swearing, drunkenness with other wickedness were the cause, that the Lord had suffered this calamity and scourge to come upon them; the weight of my exercise increasing as I walked along the street; at length it was said in my soul, *This Land is polluted with blood, and in the day of inquisition for blood, it will not only be required at the frontiers and borders, but even in this place where these bodies are now seen.*[11]

In response to the frontier outrages—which were slowly but surely mapping their way from the western and northern fringes of the colony toward and through the Walking Purchase settlements of Gnadenhütten, Bethlehem, Nazareth, Fort Allen, and Easton—Pennsylvania declared war on the Delawares and decreed a "bounty" for Delaware scalps. The government would pay $130 for the scalp of each Delaware male over the age of ten, $50 for any Delaware woman's scalp. Horrified Quakers sought other avenues to peace. Rather than simply respond to Indian violence in excessive bloody kind, they advocated trying to talk to the Delawares. Before anything else, they at least wanted to ask the Delawares why they, who hitherto had always maintained peaceful relations with Penn's colony, were murdering white settlers.[12]

In 1756, in large part due to Quaker efforts—the official government policy of building forts and killing Indians was failing to promote the cause of security—a series of treaty conferences was arranged with a leader from Nutimus's tribe, Teedyuscung, who chose the symbolic town of Easton, at the Forks, for this "council fire." The first conference, which met in July,

opened up a dialogue, and afterward Teedyuscung returned home to consult with his people. The second conference, in November, was intended
for the actual peace treaty. But here Teedyuscung dropped a bomb. On
November 13, before an audience which included the Pennsylvania government in the person of its governor, members of the council, assembly-
men, the colonel of militia Benjamin Franklin, and some forty-five to fifty
Quakers who had *not* been invited, who were in fact not wanted there by
certain interested parties, but who had come anyway to look after the fair-
ness of the proceedings—before this audience Teedyuscung, when asked by
the governor why he warred on the English, stunningly replied:

this very Ground that is under me (striking it with his Foot) was my Land and
Inheritance, and is taken from me by Fraud. When I say this Ground, I mean all the
Land lying between Tohiccon Creek and Wioming, on the River Susquahannah.[13]

Which included the region Edgar Huntly knows as Norwalk.[14]

*   *   *

So when Edgar travels north and west into Norwalk, he is traveling into a
place where the past hangs heavy, where its energies, its angers, its terrors
from "about thirty years ago" still haunt. Yet the historical incidents that
personally shadow Edgar in the time-warp tale that is *Edgar Huntly*, are not
from 1755 to 1757; they are all from the Revolutionary period. This was
when, according to Edgar, "savages" and "assassins" had murdered his family. But, historically speaking, no such "savagery" prevailed during the Revolution, at least not *here*. At least not in Solebury. In another place, though,
in the region around South Second Street, in Philadelphia, "savages" had
rampaged, and a boy did see his family and their friends "massacred."
    Edgar Huntly is Brown's only novel in which the core violence is bodied
forth *through* the narrator. In *Arthur Mervyn*, Welbeck cheats and kills; and
Dr. Stevens, who is at times relating Arthur's words, narrates the tale. In
Wieland, Theodore kills and Clara narrates. In *Ormond*, Ormond murders
and attempts rape, before being accidently killed by Constantia in self-
defense. Meanwhile the tale is told by Constantia's friend, Sophia Westwyn.
    In *Edgar Huntly*, by contrast, the main violence is projected through
Edgar and thereby through the very consciousness of the novel as a whole.
To be sure violent acts are splayed throughout the story. In the background
Ireland frame, as Edgar learns from Clithero, Clithero's patroness's
brother, Wiatte, tried to kill Clithero, who—à la Constantia—killed him
instead in self-defense. And the consequently deranged Clithero then tried,
unsuccessfully, to stab to death Mrs. Lorimer, in the crazed hope that
he would save her from the fatal anguish of learning about her dead, and
therefore eternally unredeemable, brother. (Shades of Poe.) And in the
foregrounded Pennsylvania frame Waldegrave has been killed—though the

event is not depicted. Indians too kill—but are not seen to kill. Their deeds either took place in the Revolutionary past, or are discovered secondhand, by Edgar, in the present. In the mid-1780s context of the novel, the depicted violence is Edgar's alone, and it is violence directed not at the presumed killer of his friend Waldegrave—Clithero—but, curiously, at "Indians."

To return again to the novel's visionary core: Prefigured by the primal killing and devouring of the panther—surely the most memorable scene Brown ever wrote—this main sequence involves Edgar facing up to Indians. Initially Edgar, reasonably, is trying just to escape them, but his reasonableness is undermined by vagrant reflections—more signs of a "mind sorely wounded" (650)—on "the fate of my parents." That phrase is invoked *twice* (792, 796), and it is the second invocation that launches Edgar into his first deadly assault on a fellow human being—the hatchet attack on an Indian. Before he's done, though, his anger and craving for vengeance will be further roused by the influx of other memories. Here is Edgar's mind at work:

My uncle and my sisters had been murdered; the dwelling had been pillaged. . . . Defenceless and asleep, they were assailed by these inexorable enemies, and I, who ought to have been their protector and champion, was removed to an immeasurable distance, and was disabled, by some accursed chance, from affording them the succour which they needed.

For a time, I doubted whether I had not witnessed and shared this catastrophe. I had no memory of the circumstances that preceded my awaking in the pit. Had not the cause of my being cast into this abyss some connection with the ruin of my family? Had I not been dragged hither by these savages, and reduced, by their malice, to that breathless and insensible condition? Was I born to a malignant destiny never tired of persecuting? Thus had my parents and their infant offspring perished, and thus completed was the fate of all those to whom my affections cleaved, and whom the first disaster had spared. (803)

At this point Edgar's "emotions were totally changed." Now he desires to kill the "savages." And he does.

*   *   *

Brockden Brown was born too late to take in the common pre-Revolutionary sight of Indian diplomats coming to Philadelphia to confer with the Friendly Association for Regaining and Preserving Peace with the Indians by Pacific Measures led by Israel Pemberton; though he undoubtedly saw the delegations of Iroquois sachems who came to the nation's capital in the 1790s to negotiate with the American government and to consult with Quaker well-wishers and the new Quaker "Indian Committee." Yet these were not "savages." More likely than not, they were houseguests of Quaker leaders like the Pembertons and Drinkers and Parrishes. The only *personal* and deeply emotional memory Brown would have carried of "savage" Indians traced back to 1777–78, when his father was "in jail" on the Virginia frontier. At that time the exiles' families feared the prospect of a native Indian assault on the white villages of Winchester and Staunton, or as the young Philadelphia Quaker Phineas Pemberton wrote to his exiled father, "the thought of the Indians committing Hostilities not far from [you] . . . has much afflicted my Mind." But in that context, from Brockden Brown's perspective, the native Indians weren't the "savages." The Revolutionaries were.[15]

Nor was Brown brought up to think of Indians as savages. In the diaries and letters and published writings of his people, of that enclosed Quaker cultural world in which he spent his first seventeen years, only one group qualified, at times, as "savages," and that was the Scots-Irish or "Irish." Brown's cousin, George Churchman, had given anguished expression to this back in 1763 when he learned of "that bloody Transaction in Lancaster town, The murder of peaceable Indians!" by "a Banditti of cruel Unmerciful men, in number about 120, from Pextang, Dunnagall & elsewhere." The dominant ethnic hue of these murderers, which is conveyed implicitly through the village names, Churchman stated explicitly two months later in his diary notation on the Paxton Boys episode: "a Company of Rioters (somewhat similar to those who murder'd the Indians at Lancaster . . .) from the western part of the Province, principally of Irish Extraction, made their Appearance . . . marching to Philadelphia to fall upon some friendly Indians who had been removed thither. . . . The Noise of the Rioters . . . & their wicked design against the Indians seemed to raise indignation in the Breasts of many who were Friendly to those poor Natives."[16]

The Philadelphia Meeting, and its leaders like Israel Pemberton and George Churchman and John Woolman and Henry Drinker, and Anthony Benezet, and William Brown, worked during the years leading up to the Revolution to preserve, or restore, the harmonious relations that had once existed between Pennsylvania's native Indian population and its white European settlers. The Pennsylvania Revolution signified the death knell of this vision, for it brought the political ascendancy of a new sort of people with their own characteristically aggressive and sometimes brutal ways.[17]

Here is a dream datelined "late in the Spring 1775," recorded in a Philadelphian's commonplace book:

an almost innumerable Herd of the most feirce & savage Beasts appeared, some of them foreign to this part of America, and the Terror they spread on the minds of the People was great. . . . they left one horrid scene of desolation behind them, broke down all Enclosures, levell'd the grain to the Earth, and tore up the Ground like the violent shocks of an Earthquake with dreadfull which [sic] echoed far. No refuge appeared from their fury.

The late spring chronology—the battles at Lexington and Concord occurred in April 1775—might suggest a portentous vision of invading

British armies and the destruction they were destined to bring, except that this is not an American Whig dream. It is a Quaker dream, and it continues:

their rage & roarings encreased as they advanced to one Particular spot and they were just on the point of seizing a Person, when a door of Refuge was instantly opened, and a Keeper was then perceived (but not before) who had the direction of the Herd, & beyond his Permission they could not go. All of a sudden as in a moment, at the Divine Word of Command, they stopp'd their career stood still and ceased their fury: the influence of Heaven covered them, changed their brutal natures & tears dropped from their rough faces, and it was said, "They were then under the Influence of the Most High."

In this dream it is "the restraining Hand of the Almighty" that intervenes to "humble" the "savage Beasts." Who these "savages" might be is not clearly indicated. Who they *aren't*, though, can be easily determined. They are not British Redcoats, because the issue with them was never about proper Christian principles. Nor are they Indians, as 1770s Quakers did not fear Indians as "an almost innumerable Herd." In that capacity, they feared somebody else.[18]

The Quaker exiles, Elijah Brown among them, in their 1777 published account of their situation and plight, referred repeatedly to "our enemies" and "our adversaries." In that publication designed to effect their release, the jailed Quakers politicly forbore specifying further who these people were, but in the private journal of the affair kept by the Pemberton brothers, the list of the men held responsible for the arrests left no doubt as to their cast: Revolutionaries all, a conspicuous number of this "set of men" were Scots-Irish Revolutionaries.[19]

These memories and emotions, which served to reinforce more general Quaker cultural velleities and biases, did not disappear in the 1790s, a decade that saw a massive new influx of "Irish" immigrants into the city, along with continuing efforts by American whites, both through military campaigns and peaceful negotiations, to resolve the "Indian problem." After 1791, indeed, the Washington administration, realizing the special relationship obtaining between Quakers and native Indian tribes, actually encouraged Quaker participation in the peace-making process; and native groups like the Iroquois, for their part, expressly requested that "some Friend, or Quaker" accompany government commissions. The Philadelphia Meeting itself, in March 1792, weighed in on the Indian question with a determination that

when any of the Natives of the Wilderness comes to the City to transact business with the Government, it is thought advisable to continue the Custom that has long subsisted of shewing our friendly regard to them, to inculcate on their minds the value and benefit of a peaceable disposition, and to remind them of the Cordiality and friendship which early commenced between their Ancestors & ours on the first settlement of Pennsylva, and continued uninterrupted through many years; on which occasions they have always expressed their pleasure & Satisfaction.

In the same year the Philadelphia Quaker James Emlen, after meeting with Timothy Pickering, the Federalist administration's commissioner for Indian Affairs, noted favorably "the contrast between those who formerly executed Government in Pennsylvania," who were "impelled by that selfish jealousy which a dark & covetous policy inspires," and "the present rulers of the United States."[20]

Which is to say the past's echo perdured for Quakers in 1790s Philadelphia. It was, for them, a poignantly contrapuntal place. Thus to return again to the Drinker house on North Front Street: Elizabeth Drinker records in her diary the political developments of 1798–99. She notes the "violent party work" that accompanies the February 1798 elections, the news that "the troubles in Ir[e]land have increased—more inserrections there" and the "many secrets . . . relative to the conspericies of the French &c." She worries about the appearance in Philadelphia of one Henry Cox, a supposed Quaker who "is very plain in his dress, has no pockets in his Coat, speaks the plain language, very sinsiable," but who also carries "No letters from any of our Society—some suspect him as being a Demo. [N]ot a united Irishman we hope," and in October 1799 she notes the election of the Republican Thomas McKean as governor, adding the haughty exclamation: "had the real worth and respectability of the voters carried the Election things would have been different." At the same time, that "mob fashion" February election with its "croud with lighted Candles" prompts her to reread the "Address to the Inhabitants of Pennsylvania by our Friends and others who were then prisoners in the Masons Lodge, 20 years ago," and in May 1798, when rumors spread of "a Mobb riseing" in an Irish enclave in north Philadelphia, she rereads, apparently for the first time in thirty-four years, "A Narrative of the late Massacres in Lancaster county of a number of Indians . . . dated 1764," with its descriptions of "cruel" "barbarous Men" who "fired upon, stabbed and Hatcheted to Death," who "scalped, and otherwise mangled" the "little Common-wealth" of "defenceless Indians" at Conestoga. And while Thomas McKean is objectionable because of his Republican politics and constituency, she well knows too that he had been a central figure in the exile ordeal of her husband.[21]

Henry and Elizabeth Drinker, in late 1790s Philadelphia, were good Quakers of a generally Federalist persuasion. Though socially snobbish, they were not given to the habit of being divisive or invidious about different ethnic-religious-racial groups. Peace and harmony were still their ideal. And to be sure no one ever specifically asked them the question, "In your experience, and in eighteenth-century Pennsylvania history as a whole, who were the true 'savages': the native Indian tribes or the Scots-Irish and their ilk who played such a vital part in the Paxton Boys affair, the Revolutionary militias of the 1770s, the Constitutionalist governments of the 1780s, and the Republican advance of the 1790s?" But if they *had* been asked, Elizabeth and Henry Drinker, under the obligation of the truth testimony, would have answered: "the Irish."

As, in his own imaginative way, did Brockden Brown. Consider the line of his fictional villains. Clithero is "an emigrant from Ireland." Ormond carries an Irish name, though he is in fact a mysterious deracinated European of (if his sister Martinette is to be believed) mixed Greek-"Sclavonian" parentage. Ludloe, Ormond's first incarnation, is Irish. Carwin, in *Wieland*, is thought to be Irish, but he turns out to be from a farming district in western Pennsylvania. While Thomas Welbeck exhibits "foreign lineaments," he doesn't appear to be Irish, for he says his father was a "trader of Liverpool." On the other hand, Brown modeled Welbeck after the Philadelphia politician John Swanwick, whose father was an Irishman who had emigrated to Pennsylvania from Liverpool, where he was a trader. And then there is the earliest of all Brown villains. Brown created this character, his *ur*-villain, in a 1793 letter to Joseph Bringhurst, at a time when he lived in the ethnically diverse—and immigrant-rich—neighborhood of Vine Street.[22]

"Jackey Cooke" was an Irishman who arrived in Philadelphia "some five or six months ago" with a wife and four daughters. "This wretch was the slave of drunkenness." His wife was "a woman of good family and excellent education, and the fear of exposing her husband was a sufficient motive with her to abstain from all public complaints." And she had ample cause to complain, for her husband "would return [to his house] late at night, seldom less than three times a week, raised by intoxication into a fit of madness, and exercise the most brutal cruelties on his innocent and helpless family." Neighbors—and the narrator writes that the Cookes moved into a house "opposite to us"—could hear the commotions, and on one night was heard "a faint screem and an indistinct cry of murder and help." When a neighbor approached the Cookes' kitchen door to check out the commotion, he "heard there the sound of a lash. Every stroke was accompanied with a weak and stifled cry of anguish from some unhappy sufferer, who, at every interval exclaimed . . . 'Oh Jackey, dont expose yourself. Have pity on me for the sake of your own reputation. Oh Mother, Mother. Had you lived to see this . . . treatment from one whom your charity saved from starving[.] For God sake Jackey don't expose yourself!'" Entering the house, the inquisitive neighbor found Mrs. Cooke kneeling before her husband, who had her by the hair and who was inflicting on her, with a horsewhip, "the most dreadful severities on her back and sho[u]lders from which he had torn away all covering. The four daughters were standing in different parts of the room weeping and wringing their hands." Before the tale ends, "Jackey Cooke" beats his wife to death and takes to whipping his eldest daughter.[23]

Jackey Cooke, without doubt, is a real savage. Might he have a connection to the "savages" in *Edgar Huntly*, a novel whose explicit moral is that "Most men are haunted by some species of terror or antipathy, which they are, for the most part, able to trace to some incident which befel them in their early years" (791)?[24]

The savages in *Edgar Huntly* are integrally linked to the sad fate that is Edgar's experience. They had first traumatized his family "during the last war" when "a band of them" had "pillage[d] and murder[ered]" in the Huntlys' neighborhood. Moreover, "Eight of these assassins" had "assailed . . . at the dead of night" "my father's house" (791). In the "malignant destiny" Edgar was born to, this was "the first disaster" (803)

When Edgar next runs into savages, he is an adult, and he wonders whether "these very men were the assassins of my family, and were those who had reduced me and my sisters to the condition of orphans and dependants" (796). Fearing that this contemporary band of savages has struck his family again, that they have killed his uncle and surviving sisters, he concludes: "Thus had my parents and their infant offspring perished, and thus completed was the fate of all those to whom my affections cleaved" (803).

Edgar, throughout the novel, is given to fantastic, obscure, self-pitying states of mind. When he first wakes up in the cave and in the confusing darkness is subjected to "images of the past" occuring in "capricious combinations," he feels like "the victim of some tyrant who had thrust me into a dungeon . . . and left me no power to determine whether he intended I should perish with famine, or linger out a long life in hopeless imprisonment." "Sometimes," he reports, "I imagined myself buried alive. Methought I had fallen into seeming death and my friends had consigned me to the tomb, from which a resurrection was impossible" (781). Later, when he imagines that savages have killed his uncle and sisters, he comments: "For a time, I doubted whether I had not witnessed and shared this catastrophe. . . . Had not the cause of my being cast into this abyss some connection with the ruin of my family" (803)?

For Brockden Brown, surely, the question was a profound one. For certain in his world, two "savages" named James Loughead and James Kerr had come to the Brown-Armitt residence at 117 South Second Street on September 5, 1777, and arrested his father. Before that, militiamen had warned and threatened his father against making a living. Afterward, Revolutionary rioters had stormed through his neighborhood, breaking windows, knocking down doors, smashing interiors. Later patently alluding to those riots in a letter, Brown had evoked the sense of being "in a *Jail*. . . . in an apartment in which my chambers were hourly woken by the clanking of chains and bolts & iron doors." Certainly too, by the mid-1780s—the time frame for *Edgar Huntly*—the "fate" of being Quakers in Revolutionary Philadelphia had led to his father's economic ruin, social embarrassment, and imprisonment, and hard times for the Brown family. As a child,

Brockden Brown, like Edgar, had been unable to protect his family from the "savages," and as an adult Brown well might have exclaimed, with Edgar, "I, who ought to have been their protector and champion . . . was disabled . . . from affording them the succour which they needed" (803). For Edgar Huntly, the consequences of his Revolutionary childhood were a confusing host of "lasting and terrific images in my fancy" (792). For Brockden Brown the consequence had been the visionary sensibility that he had first indulged in his letters to Wilkins and Bringhurst and the "Henrietta" manuscript, that had found its novelistic rhythm in the opening section of *Arthur Mervyn*, that attained its fullest and strangest power in *Wieland*, and that culminated in the violence of *Edgar Huntly*.[25]

Edgar Huntly, this is to suggest, is Brown's deepest and final imaginative reckoning with *his* Revolution. Like *Wieland* it is an idiosyncratic family allegory. *Wieland* evokes the Brown-Churchman saga writ large, tracing it back to its seventeenth-century European mystical wellsprings. *Edgar Huntly* is grounded in the direct Revolutionary experience and pressing memories of Brockden Brown himself, and it pushes back *through* these to the historical seedtime of the Pennsylvania Revolution, to 1755 to 1763, that period when angry men began their fierce campaign to overturn the Quaker commonwealth, and to the primal fraud of 1737, perpetrated by the Quaker James Logan and the children of William Penn.[26]

*   *   *

This is *Edgar Huntly*'s "subject." Its *meaning*, though—biographical and historical—lies elsewhere.

In its violence, the novel enacts the desires of another Quaker exile's son, Robert Morton, who addressed his Revolutionary oppressors with the words, "the day must come when the Avenger's hand shall make thee suffer for thy guilt, and thy Rulers shall deplore thy Fate." Morton wrote that in September 1777 Philadelphia, in the midst of the Quaker community's pain and hurt. Brown wrote *Edgar Huntly* in 1799, in New York, as an act of memory and vision, and family tradition.[27]

Brockden Brown was the last in the line of Brown-Churchman Quaker visionaries. The first had been Richard Browne of Northamptonshire, who had embraced the Quaker vision to start with. As a result his children and grandchildren had suffered persecution, and spiritual "trial," and "great terror." In Nottingham, Pennsylvania, the Browns had merged through marriage with the Churchmans, and the greatest visionary of all in the family—before Brockden Brown himself—had been John Churchman.

Churchman's mightiest visions had been called forth by the atrocities of 1755 to 1757. It had been during his trip to the treaty conference with Teedyuscung at Easton when Churchman had seen "a light before me towards sun-rising, which did not appear to be a common light, but soon observed the appearance of something therein . . . it was encompassed with a brightness like a rainbow." At Easton, "remembering my dream very fresh, when I had seen the Indians at the treaty, and had heard some matters remarkably spoken by some particulars of them, I was made to believe it was not unreasonable to conclude, that the Lord was in them by his good spirit, and that all colours were equal to him."[28]

This was the time too when Churchman "said within myself, 'How can this be? Since this has been a Land of peace, and as yet not much concerned in war;' but as it were in a moment mine eyes turned to the case of the poor enslaved Negroes: And however light a matter they who have been concerned with them may look upon the purchasing, selling, or keeping those oppressed people in slavery, it then appeared plain to me, that such were partakers in iniquity, encouragers of war and the shedding of innocent blood, which is often the case, where those unhappy people are or have been captivated and brought away for slaves: The same day I went to the Pine-Street meeting under an exercising mournful state of mind, and thought I could be willing to sit among the people undiscovered."[29]

In December 1756, a month after Teedyuscung accused the colony of land "fraud," Churchman was in the East Nottingham meeting, when he heard "a voice" which was "attended (I thought) with Divine authority." It said to him: "I will bow the inhabitants of the earth, and particularly of this land, and *I will make them fear and reverence me, either in mercy or in judgment*," whereupon, Churchman later recalled,

a prospect immediately opened to my view of a day of calamity and sore distress which was approaching, and in which the careless and stupid professors, who are easy, and not concerned to properly worship and adore the almighty, and have not laboured to witness their foundation to be laid on him the immoveable Rock, will be greatly surprised with fearfulness; and on the behalf of such, a piercing cry and lamentation ran through me, thus, *Alas for the day! Alas for the day! Woe is me!*[30]

This was the sixteen-year-old Elijah Brown's minister and uncle speaking—and Elijah clearly wanted none of it. Two months later he moved to Philadelphia to pursue a career as a merchant. Elijah was not a visionary. His fourth child though was, and that son's last vision, *Edgar Huntly*, stands in diametrical contrast to the visionary world and values of his ancestors, and John Churchman in particular. For after calling forth all the terrifying "perils of the wilderness" and "incidents of Indian hostility"—and the very historical events that had set off John Churchman's "inner light"—Edgar can sit and contemplate a native Indian writhing in pain and have these thoughts:

Why should he be suffered to live? He came hither to murder and despoil my friends; this work he has, no doubt, performed. Nay, has he not borne his part in the destruction of my uncle and my sisters? He will live only to pursue the same sanguinary trade; to drink the blood and exult in the laments of his unhappy foes, and of my own brethren. Fate has reserved him for a bloody and violent death. For how long a time soever it may be deferred, it is thus that his career will inevitably terminate. (815)

Edgar, facing up to this "task of cruel lenity" (816), decides to kill him.

*   *   *

It is hard to avoid the judgment that the writing of *Edgar Huntly* served its author as a psychological purgative, for after killing off his "Indians," the creator of Welbeck, of the murderer Theodore Wieland, of Ludloe, Ormond and Clithero never wrote another Gothic scene. Up until this juncture Brockden Brown had never written a happy ending; henceforth, he would only write happy endings.

In 1800 he wrote and published the second part of *Arthur Mervyn*, and that novel, begun in the phantasmagoria of a Philadelphia marked by "the monstrous creations of *delirium*," ends in the domestic haven of a happy marriage. In 1800 and 1801 he wrote his last two novels, *Clara Howard* and *Jane Talbot*. In these Brown's protagonists learn the meaning of true love and find the happiness of marriage and family. Not burdened like their novelistic predecessors with personal demons, they are free to make the conventional, sentimental choices. And, unlike those predecessors, who tend in the end to flee to Europe, they make those choices, significantly, in America.

Brown summed up his own sense of personal evolution and his post-*Edgar Huntly* intellectual and emotional state in the central drama of his last novel: the struggle of Jane Talbot and Henry Colden to find each other and to persuade Jane's guardian of the rightness of their relationship.

Mrs. Fielder (the guardian) is convinced that Colden is "a zealot: a sectary." "Contemplative and bookish" and "vaguely described as being somewhat visionary and romantic," this man, Mrs. Fielder fears, is dangerous to Jane. A "poet" who "had imbibed that pernicious philosophy which is now so much in vogue," he promised only to encourage and exacerbate Jane's worst qualities. For this reason Mrs. Fielder prohibits any further contact between the two. Indeed, if Jane decides to marry Colden, Mrs. Fielder makes clear, Jane will never see her "mother" again.

Of course, Mrs. Fielder is totally mistaken about Henry. Yes, as a youth he had fallen under the spell of Godwin's *Political Justice*. Yes, he had written to an intimate friend as "the advocate of suicide; a scoffer at promises; the despiser of revelation, of Providence and a future state." But that was in the past. The present was different. "[A]re not remorse and amendment adequate atonements," he asks Jane, "For past faults and rectified errors"? Has not his life been, whatever its flaws, an honest quest, earnest and self-correcting, after truth? And would not union with her virtue and religion make "*my mind whole*"? Through Jane, that is to say, he has seen a new kind of light.

I have awakened from my dreams of doubt and misery, not to the cold and vague belief, but to the living and delightful consciousness, of every tie that can bind man to his Divine Parent and Judge.

Which scarcely leaves Mrs. Fielder any choice. In the end, she sanctions the marriage.[31]

Part III
A Lie,
1800–1804

Charles Brockden Brown

Conclusion
Charles Brown, American

In late 1800, as editor of the New York *Monthly Magazine and American Register*, Charles Brown reviewed one of the American Revolutionary era's strangest productions. In *Letter from Alexander Hamilton Concerning the Public Conduct and Character of John Adams, Esq., President of the United States*, one great Federalist tried to destroy the public reputation of another great Federalist, in the hope of inducing Federalist electors to choose Charles Pinckney of South Carolina over Adams in the upcoming 1800 presidential election—and in the exchange helped the Republican Thomas Jefferson become the next president.

Brown approached this publication, in which—as he puts it—"a man of known discernment and eminent abilities, and an important actor in the great scene of political affairs, has undertaken to arraign a most distinguished leader in the revolution, and the chief magistrate, of the United States, before the bar of the people," in the spirit of "the impartial spectator of public events." First noting Hamilton's "favourable" mention of Adams's "patriotism and integrity" and "high claims upon the public gratitude," he then summarized the devastating indictment of President Adams: "a sublimated and eccentric imagination; unsoundness of judgment; want of perseverance; a boundless vanity; extreme egotism; impatience of inferiority even to Washington; disgusting arrogance; distempered jealousy; ungovernable indiscretion; indecent irrascibility; absolute unfitness for the post of chief magistrate." Brown's task, meanwhile, was "to scrutinize the picture before us, and to weigh the credit it deserves as a faithful copy of nature." On the one hand, there's the question of "our own knowledge of the original," namely John Adams; on the other hand, there's the matter of "the genius, knowledge, and impartiality of the artist," namely Alexander Hamilton.[1]

Brown in the exercise does not say much on the subject of "our knowledge" of John Adams. In quoting extensively from the text, he does publicize the particulars of Hamilton's version of Adams, but at no point does he accept the portrait as "truth." Indeed he quite explicitly criticizes the *Letter* for its perverse one-sidedness. "Every man has vanity," Brown reminds his readers, after citing one of Hamilton's cheap shots, "and the difference, as to merit, between vain men, lies in the degree and the objects of their vanity." It is this broader, fairer context that Brown finds lacking in the *Letter*, and on these grounds Brown disparages Hamilton's "perplexed and obscure" performance with the ironic praise: "No one will withhold his tribute of admiration from the ingenuity and skill, *at least*, of the commentator." Brown's substantive judgment on Hamilton is that "the motives of the man were complicated; that personal resentment has had a considerable share in guiding and invigorating the pencil, but that he has likewise designed the benefit of his country."[2]

Now what is remarkable about this review is its balanced, confident, even Olympian character. Brown had always possessed this side. It's how he sounded in the late 1780s in the Belles Lettres Club, and probably in the discussions of the Friendly Club in the mid-1790s. This was the "rational," nonmysterious Brown so prized by friends like Elihu Smith and William Dunlap. It's the tone of the essays he submitted in 1798 to the Philadelphia *Weekly Magazine of Original Essays, Fugitive Pieces, and Interesting Intelligence*, and the other essays and reviews he published in the Friendly Club-inspired *Monthly Magazine*, which he edited in New York in 1799 and 1800. In a 1799 review of a new history of Pennsylvania, for example, Brown opens with the omniscient (and, for the reviewee, ominous) line: "The value of this book lies not in the elegance of its style, the profoundness of its reflections, or the accuracy of its method." Brown in this instance decrees that "We are not to look, in this work, for any traces of the genuine historian." Instead he finds the "path of the humble, honest, and industrious compiler." The historian so judged and categorized was Brown's former schoolmaster Robert Proud, whom Brown had outdistanced in so many ways since their Friends' Latin School days together back in mid-1780s Philadelphia. Yet Brown writes with the same brio and confidence in judging Alexander Hamilton's public literary performance and in discussing the public character of John Adams, and he does so in a clear sense of service to the republic. As a public man and citizen, Brown, in 1800 America, evidently felt himself to be anybody's equal, even *theirs*.[3]

It had not always been so. Lieutenant Colonel Hamilton, with other "armed men," on General Washington's orders, had once roamed through Brown's neighborhood and "forcibly" broken into the storerooms of Quaker merchants to take away "a large quantity of goods" for the use of Continental troops. (Hamilton and his men had also, Quakers noticed, "very unwillingly let any [clothes] be taken out for the family use.") And Delegate Adams, who for a time boarded just down Second Street from the Browns—as, for that matter, did Hamilton—had had a notable run-in with the Quaker leaders of the Philadelphia Meeting, as he had been one of the three Revolutionaries to start the arrest list that came to include the name of Elijah Brown, as, in his various official capacities in the Continental Congress, he had been involved in the fate of the exiles.[4]

In Brown's review of *Letter from Alexander Hamilton*, though, there is no indication whatsoever, in theme or style, of this private tribal context. Nor would Brown ever again explore that experience in anything else he wrote. No longer a practicing "visionary," he had joined as a full-fledged citizen the republic that Adams and Hamilton, along with the McKeans and Bradfords and Delanys and Bryans and Cannons, and the Kerrs and Lougheads and others of 1770s Philadelphia, had helped to create.

Brown entered the arena of American partisan politics in 1803 with *An Address to the Government of the United States, on the Cession of Louisiana to the French*, a pamphlet advocating the Federalist party position on the issue of Louisiana. Settled by the French, the Louisiana Territory had been ceded in 1763 to Spain, a weak European power of little threat to post-1783 Americans. But in 1800 First Consul Napoleon Bonaparte arranged for the territory's retrocession back to France, in anticipation of its use as a North American French imperial base. When President Jefferson received unofficial word of this deal in 1801, he sent a minister to France to convince the French either to cancel the retrocession or to sell New Orleans and its environs to the United States, which needed to control the Mississippi delta in order to safeguard the economic interests of its western settlers. Short of one of these concessions, Jefferson informed France, the United States would necessarily become England's ally and France's enemy. In 1803 Napoleon, who had problems of his own, came back with the counteroffer of selling all of Louisiana outright to the United States, which sale would be completed as the Louisiana Purchase.[5]

The Federalists in 1802 and 1803 were unaware of the secret diplomatic developments and the Republican administration's adroit maneuverings. All they knew was that they did not trust the unmilitaristic Jefferson to look after America's national interests. Brown's *Address to the Government* took this party line. It is not mere hack work, however, for Brown—writing anonymously as "an obscure citizen"—cleverly invents a secret report that has come into his hands. This document, "the production of a [French] counsellor of state," is addressed to First Consul Bonaparte and it offers, in its advocacy of French imperial expansion into North America, a candid assessment of American national vulnerabilities. Brown, that is, presents a fiction as fact, so that he can view the young American republic through the eyes of an unsympathetic French government official. In this guise, Brown can say some unsettling and offensive things about the United States. Thus:

They call themselves *free*, yet a fifth of their number are slaves. . . . They call themselves *one*, yet all languages are native to their citizens. All countries have contributed their outcasts and refuse to make them a people. Even the race of Africa, a race not above, or only just above, the beasts, are scattered every where among them, and in some of the districts of their empire are nearly a moiety of the whole . . . . The only aliens and enemies within their borders, are not the blacks. They indeed are the most inveterate in their enmity, but the INDIANS are, in many respects, more dangerous inmates. Their savage ignorance, their undisciplined passions, their restless and warlike habits, their notions of ancient right, make them the fittest tools imaginable for disturbing the states. . . . This is a nation of pedlars and shop-keepers. Money engrosses all their passions and pursuits. For this they will brave all the dangers of land and water; they will scout the remotest seas, and penetrate the rudest nations. Their ruling passion being money, no sense of personal or national dignity must stand in the way of its gratification. . . . The peculiar colour of their factions is, also, extremely favourable to the designs of a powerful and artful neighbour.[6]

The disunity, the materialism that Brown here decries was at the heart of the Federalist critique of Jeffersonian America. Beyond the intrinsic violence and chaos they associated with Jeffersonian "mobocracy," Federalists feared the societal self-indulgence and crassness that they thought must follow from Jeffersonian principles of limited government and limitless expansionism. In Brown's "counsellor"'s rendition: "Was there ever a people who exhibited so motley a character; who have vested a more . . . precarious authority, in their rulers; who have multiplied so much the numbers of those that govern; who have dispersed themselves over so wide a space; and have been led by this local dispersion, to create so many clashing jurisdictions and jarring interests, as the States of America?"[7]

For Federalists, everything wrong with the nation lay with the "faction" in power—and its leader. "If," Brown's counselor conveniently warns Napoleon, "the powers of this rising nation were intrusted to the hands of one wise man; . . . if the *founder* of the nation was still its *supreme magistrate* and *he* had no wills to consult but *his* own," well then the United States could fulfill the true promise of the Revolution and rise to its proper destiny. But the Federalist dilemma was that George Washington was dead, and there was no one, save the great but hubristic (and soon to be dead) Alexander Hamilton to take up the mantle. In Washington's dominant place there was now, almost inexplicably, Thomas Jefferson. The man was a hypocrite, a slaveholding aristocrat, who bamboozled the electorate with his rhetoric about "liberty." How did he do it? In the Federalist cosmos Jefferson was, in the worst sense of the word, a "philosopher," a projector of airy schemes, a *visionary* in the way of Condorcet, Godwin, and Wollstonecraft. Brown invokes this Jefferson by having his French counselor mock "the visionary notion, that the conduct of nations is governed by enlightened views."[8]

In response to the supposed delusions of Jeffersonian "philosophy" and the mystifications of Jeffersonian rhetoric, Federalists—and Brown in his pamphlet—posited "real world" national self-interest. Brown is startlingly brutal in this regard. "[N]o wise man will think a renewal of all the devastations of our last war, too great a price to give for the expulsions of foreigners [he means the French and Spanish] from this land; for securing to our own posterity, the possession of this continent." "We have a *right* to the possession."[9]

Brown's "secret document" device is ultimately calculated to anger American readers into demanding that their government stand up for *American* rights, interests, and glory and immediately seize Louisiana. Or as the pamphlet's concluding line reads: "*The iron is now hot,* command us to rise as one man, and STRIKE!"[10]

It could be said that Brown was merely invoking the *realpolitik* that Edgar Huntly summons when, as a "task of cruel lenity," he kills injured Indians. Or that he was implementing the anti-visionary animus of *Wieland* and *Ormond*'s critique of Godwinian rationalism. In any case, in his *Address to the Government* he sounds and reasons like the Federalists Oliver Wolcott and Theodore Dwight and the arch-Federalist Hamilton himself, and no doubt he sincerely believed his cogent arguments about history, the nature of power, and America's true national interests. Again, this can be seen as consistent with his extended life experience and the running moral of his Gothic novels.

This, though, is not the biographically poignant aspect of the *Address*. That sits elsewhere in the pamphlet, for to make these Federalist arguments about the need for the American people to look beyond their day-to-day material self-interests and take on the burdens, some of them military, of national destiny and glory, Brown has to subscribe to a particular version of the American Revolution. Charles Brown, the American of 1803, needs to inspire his readers, his fellow citizens, with a vision of Americans banding together gloriously in a great liberty crusade. And so to his French counselor of state's cynical and belittling appraisal of the American character, the author of the *Address* responds in his own voice:

The American [Revolutionary] war supplies us with an eternal confutation of the slander. It was then evident that the ploughman and mechanic at either end of the continent, could recognize a common interest with each other; could sacrifice their ease, their fortunes, their lives, to secure a remote and general benefit; that the passion for gain could not deter us from repelling encroachments on our *liberty*, at the cost of every personal advantage; that all the biasses in favour of the nation we sprung from; the sense of internal weakness; the want of forts, armies, and arms[,] of unity of government and counsels, slackened not the zeal of our resistance. . . . Mutinous slaves in the heart of our country; hostile garrisons and fortresses on one side; numerous and tumultuous savages around us; the ocean scoured by the fleets of our enemy; our sea ports open to their inroads; a revenue to create out of paper; the force of an established government . . . all these affrighted not the men of that day from the pursuit of an end most abstracted from personal ends; from the vulgar objects of gain; an end which only a generous spirit, a mind that makes the good of posterity and distant neighbours its own, that prefers liberty and all its hardships to servitude.[11]

This was Brown speaking as a "Federalist" in the broadest sense—welcoming all who had sacrificed and who would sacrifice for the "true" American Whig ideals. Yet to do so he had to sign on to a lie. He had to deny his past. For *his* Revolution was nothing like this. Charles Brockden

Brown, in post-Revolutionary America, could in all honesty embrace the Federalist critique of Jeffersonian America. The Republicans presented themselves as the party of "liberty." Brown instinctively sensed holes and fraudulence in the rhetoric. It was natural for him to align with the Federalists. But Brown could not in all honesty embrace the Federalist Whig myth about a golden age under Washington, about a time—the Revolution, and then the Washington presidency—when all Americans had struggled as one and civic virtue had reigned. After 1800 Federalists saw themselves as the vanguard to lead the nation back to the saner, more organic, more virtuous republican ideals of the heroic Revolutionary past. Yet if Brown was to be true to his experience, to his family's experience, to his people's experience, he had to admit that that past was not a place of safe retreat.[12]

Or he could, in the American way, reinvent himself. For a politician like Jefferson, self-refashioning was an empowering expedient, as it would be for a philosopher like Emerson, a poet like Whitman, or any commercial person in pursuit of the main chance. But for a Gothic artist to deny the weight of the past was to cut himself off from the source of his power. It was to cease to be an artist.[13]

Yet that's what Charles Brockden Brown did. At the age of thirty-one, he positively chose to become a generic American, and he only deepened that identity in 1804 when he married the Presbyterian Elizabeth Linn. For this act the Philadelphia Meeting formally disowned him.[14]

Brockden Brown and the American Gothic Tradition

> . . . I the LORD thy God *am* a jealous God, visiting the iniquity of the fathers upon the children unto the third and fourth *generation* of them that hate me.
>
> —Exodus 20:5

> . . . *the sins of fathers are visited on their children to the third and fourth generation.*
>
> —Horace Walpole, *The Castle of Otranto*

> . . . you ought to be taken by the Hair and shak'd severely till you recover your Senses and become Sober you don't know what Ground you stand on nor what you are doing. . . . This string of Wampum serves to forbid You Your Children and Grand Children to the latest Posterity for ever medling in Land Affairs neither you nor any who shall descend from You are ever hereafter to presume to sell any Land for which Purpose you are to Preserve this string in Memory . . .
>
> —Canasatego to the Delawares, Philadelphia, 1742

A friend observed the sad demise of Charles Brown in 1810.

Thomas Cope had not always known Brown. A Quaker from Lancaster County, Pennsylvania, Cope had first moved to Philadelphia in the mid-1780s. But he had known Brown for a long time—dating back to the youthful literary clubs of the late 1780s. He last saw Brown on the fifteenth of February, 1810, six days before Brown's death at the age of thirty-nine. Brown, during their final half-hour together, "spoke with difficulty but great composure." As the two separated, Cope wrote that night in his diary, "he pressed me with his cold hand & bid me, I fear, a last adieu."[1]

"Poor fellow!" Cope added, and the successful Philadelphia merchant went on to tally up the ledger of his dying friend's life. On the assets side, Cope listed "learning, genius & a mind capable of grasping the whole store of knowledge," and "an amiable heart & almost unequalled candor in weighing the conduct & opinions of others." For debits, Cope counted Brown's abandonment of law study "without applying to be admitted to practice in the courts," along with this most especial "error": "for several years after he attained the age of 25, his time was spent not absolutely in listless idleness but without that regular application to business which is necessary to the acquirement of steady habits & to the formation of a settled character." Cope recalled this time in detail:

His hours were spent in seclusion from the world & were principally devoted to reading & the society of a few select friends. He was poor, nor had his parents the means of conferring on him anything beyond a bare subsistence in their family. . . . In this very embarrassing situation he became unhappy & often, to shake off importunities with which he thought he could not comply . . . he wandered from home & gave himself up to gloomy reflections. While in this state of mental perplexity he became acquainted with the poisonous writings of the celebrated Godwin.[2]

Such was Cope's rendition of the concentrated period after 1796 when Brown wrote *Alcuin*, "The Man at Home," "Sky-Walk," *Arthur Mervyn, Wieland, Ormond, Edgar Huntly*, when Brown conjured out of himself an American genre that in its time would nourish Poe, George Lippard, Hawthorne, Melville, Twain, Faulkner, Flannery O'Connor, Toni Morrison, Stephen King, and Wes Craven.

Brown's endearing personal side, and the quality of his friendship, shine through Cope's reminiscence. Noting what everybody saw in Brown—his "extensive knowledge," his "ingenuity," his "force of eloquence" and "command of language"—Cope admits that, intellectually, he was no "match" for his friend. (In 1801, after visiting Brown in New York, Cope wrote in his diary, with patent pride, that "my friend C.B.B. . . . lived there in fields of literary clover" with companions who "are all learned Doctors," and that "Chas. is equal to any of them.") Cope remembers too that in their discussions, "I sometimes lost my patience so far as to treat him with considerable personal asperity, yet he never resorted to abuse or lost his temper, even when loaded with invective." More to the point, Cope writes that "Amid all these warm disputes we never lost our friendship for each other & his visits were continued as usual."[3]

As Brown invariably treated the pious Cope and his beliefs with patience and respect—and this was a quality many people remarked in Brown— so Thomas Cope responded to the gloomy circumstances of 1810 with "mourn[ing]" for "my much loved companion & friend" and appropriate concern for Brown's surviving wife and children. After his marriage to Elizabeth Linn in 1804, Brown had had four children, whom he supported in part by engaging with his brothers in commercial ventures, but mostly through editorial work. Cope was well informed about the financial details of his friend's situation, and indeed a good part of their final talk had concerned the matter of money. Through his various incarnations as a magazine editor Brown had been able "to acquire by his pen a very sufficient competency." The problem, though, said Cope, was that Brown "has amassed nothing, but has lived in abundance." At the time of their last talk, Brown was receiving $1,500 a year for editing *The American Register, or General Repository of History, Politics, and Science*, and "what seemed most to press on his mind . . . was to engage my friendship in soliciting from the proprietor a continuance of the editorship to his widow." Cope, realizing the futility of this hope, could not forbear remarking in his diary that "It had been my uniform advice to him so to economize as to lay by one third of his income. This was not done & I greatly fear he will leave his family very destitute." So in the end, Charles Brown's wife and children would have to make do with the same resources Elijah Brown and his family had always fallen back upon: the residual assets of that early to mid-eighteenth-century Philadelphia Quaker joiner, Joseph Armitt.[4]

Thomas Cope was a true and dear friend, but in many ways he did not know Charles Brown. In his diary entry, for instance, Cope no doubt got the $1,500 income figure correct, but he doesn't seem to know the names of Brown's novels, which he refers to as "*William Ormond* &c." The same could be said of William Dunlap, selected by the Brown family to write Charles Brockden Brown's biography. Dunlap had first met Brown in New York in the mid-1790s. He was familiar with Brown's general activities from that juncture on, and he had the benefit of conversations with Brown through the years when Brown was writing his novels. Still Dunlap never fathomed the special and eventful place Brown came from. Nor, interestingly, did Brown's surviving family—his mother, his sisters and brothers (his father died in August 1810)—choose to enlighten Dunlap on any of the vital family facts from the 1770s and 1780s.

As a result, the two-volume *Life of Charles Brockden Brown*, published in 1815, tells a story oblivious of the context of Revolutionary Quaker Philadelphia and unaware of the deepest experiences in Brown's life. Dunlap, like Cope, harps on 1793 and Brown's abandonment of a law career as the unfortunate turning point in Brown's life. His portrait of Brown amounts to a Romantic era cliché about "Charles," the sensitive, sickly, bookish child who grows up to write "'poetical effusion[s]'" marked by "'wild and excentric brilliance.'" Dunlap's Brown becomes a writer because he is too "frail" to participate in the competitive tumble of post-Revolutionary American society. In Dunlap's estimation, "Had [Brown] been furnished with the nerves and muscles of his comrades, it was very far from being impossible that he might have relinquished intellectual pleasures. Nature had benevolently rendered him incapable of encountering such severe trials." Dunlap remarks about this decision that Brown "was dissatisfied with his own conduct in relinquishing his profession, and . . . the disappointment of his friends, and their anxiety for his future preyed upon his spirits."[5]

The period around 1793, as we have seen, was indeed in many respects a depressing one for Brown, in part because he was aware of disappointing his family, in part because he lived in depressingly impecunious circumstances. But the evidence is clear that he was *not* dissatisfied with his choice of career. To the contrary. At this time he wrote to William Wilkins precisely on the point, making the observation that "The approbation of anxious and affectionate parents and relations is cheaply purchased by the sacrifice of the most impetuous inclination." In this letter he does speak of "guilt" and "a sentiment of self-contempt and self-abhorence." But he ends with this affirmation of his decision to become a writer of fiction: "The indefensable tenor of my conduct has not weaken[ed] or obscured my sense of right and wrong. [I]t has rather strengthened and confirmed them." Quite simply, Charles Brockden Brown had a tale to tell.[6]

*   *   *

If friends and family felt he had wasted his talents, and if contemporary Americans failed to buy and read his novels, Percy Bysshe Shelley was "captivated" by Brown's fiction. Indeed the great English visionary poet had a veritable obsession with the "temple" summer-house in *Wieland* where the elder Wieland was illuminated unto death, and when Shelley looked at country houses "he always examined if he could find such a summer-house, or a place to erect one." Shelley's friend Thomas Peacock went so far as to claim that of the six literary works "which took the deepest root in [Shelley's] mind," one was Schiller's *Robbers*, one Goethe's *Faust*, and the other four were Brockden Brown's Gothic novels. Shelley's wife too, Mary Godwin, was drawn to the dark qualities in Brown's fiction, both before and after she wrote *Frankenstein.*[7]

Edgar Allan Poe paid Brown the high Poeian compliment of plagiarizing from him, directly in "A Tale of the Ragged Mountains," and indirectly in numerous wilderness scenes and perhaps in selective renditions of the insane imagination. Nathaniel Hawthorne went so far as to place Brown in his "Hall of Fantasy," where all "who have affairs in that mystic region, which lies above, below, or beyond the Actual, may . . . meet, and talk over the business of their dreams." In Hawthorne's grand hall stand "the statues or busts of men, who, in every age, have been rulers and demi-gods in the realms of imagination": the "grand old countenance of Homer," "the dark presence of Dante," "Rabelais's smile of deep-wrought mirth," "the all-glorious Shakespeare," Spenser and Milton and Bunyan and Fielding and Richardson and Scott, and in "an obscure and shadowy niche was reposited the bust of our countryman, the author of Arthur Mervyn."[8]

Brockden Brown is the only American to make it into Hawthorne's "Hall," and the fact underscores the special feeling Hawthorne had for his Quaker predecessor. Hawthorne certainly possessed a deep appreciation of

Brown's historical world, as evidenced by his short story, "The Gentle Boy." This is about the persecution and execution of Quakers by Puritans in 1650s Boston—the very incidents Israel Pemberton threw into John Adams's face in Carpenter's Hall in 1774, and that the twelve-year-old Charles Brown, in 1783, obliquely referenced in his school essay "Liberty of Conscience." In Hawthorne's history-saturated tale, a "not more than six years old" boy, whose father "was of the people whom all men hate," is orphaned when that father is executed by the Massachusetts Puritans for his beliefs and his mother is "carried into the uninhabited wilderness, and left to perish there by hunger or wild beasts." Taken in by a Puritan couple, the Quaker boy—who possessed "a faculty which he had perhaps breathed in with the air of his barbaric birthplace": "that of reciting imaginary adventures, on the spur of the moment, and apparently in inexhaustible succession"—suffers abuse at the hands of adults and fellow children alike.[9]

Hawthorne could not have been thinking specifically about Brockden Brown when he wrote "The Gentle Boy," for he could not have known the relevant details of Brown's life. But he was most definitely thinking about "the author of Arthur Mervyn" when he wrote his great early short story, "My Kinsman, Major Molineux," for it is patently patterned after the very novel that qualified Brown, in Hawthorne's eyes, for the "Hall of Fantasy." "My Kinsman," like *Mervyn*, is a coming-of-age story. More precisely, it is an American-country boy-travels-to-the-city-and-happens-upon-*history* story. Hawthorne flags his literary inspiration in his opening description of Robin, who "was a youth of barely eighteen years, evidently country-bred, and now, as it should seem, upon his first visit to town." Never mind that when Hawthorne wrote this it had been some eighty years since a country boy completely unknown to him, Elijah Brown, had moved from Nottingham to Philadelphia, and never mind that what Robin happens upon in the city are not the machinations of Thomas Welbeck and the strange "ideas of floating or transferable wealth" of mid-eighteenth-century Philadelphia (though he does get "entangled in a succession of crooked and narrow streets" and suffers an "evening of ambiguity and weariness"), but rather the tar- and featherings of soon-to-be Revolutionary Boston. Robin, in the architecture of the tale, is Arthur.[10]

Brockden Brown hovers about another early Hawthorne tale, "Roger Malvin's Burial." In this story about the ravages of guilt and the psychological roots of the uncanny, the action unfolds when the protagonist, overwhelmed with "strange reflections," becomes "rather like a sleep-walker." It is a common enough expression, but when the scene involves a wilderness locale and a man wracked by remorse who is about to expiate with tragic violence what is a sin to his mind alone, and when it is used by a great artist in the making who had seen fit to accord a "niche" to a single countryman in his "Hall of Fantasy," an unmistakably loaded one. Hawthorne was reprising *Edgar Huntly*.[11]

It was in his two greatest novels, though, and most particularly in *The House of the Seven Gables*, that Hawthorne codified for American literature Brockden Brown's Gothic legacy. The point can be made by a comparison of wall portraits. In *The Castle of Otranto*, there is a picture in the castle's gallery of "the good Alfonso," the former rightful prince, and in the tale Manfred's daughter is accustomed to look on it with "adoration," persuaded that "somehow or other my destiny is linked with something relating to him." In *The House of the Seven Gables*, there is a looming portrait too. "Colonel Pyncheon's picture—in obedience, it was said, to a provision of his will—remained affixed to the wall of the room in which he died."[12]

The good Alfonso, whose death led to the usurpation of Manfred and whose spirit reigns as judgment on the corrupt goings on in the principality, dates to thirteenth-century Italy, as does the tale itself, which alludes to the travails of the medieval Hohenstaufen emperor Frederick II, his successor Conrad, and Frederick's illegitimate son, Manfred of Taranto. The question is: What relevance might this context have to the mid-eighteenth-century English world of *Otranto*'s author, Horace Walpole? In psychological terms, certainly, the good Alfonso and the bad Manfred, in their power, in their force, could be seen, in one way or another, as projections of Walpole's own father, who really *was* the most powerful man, not just in his son's world (à la Freudian theory), but in just about everybody's world save King George's. To be the youngest legitimate child of the great Robert Walpole was no doubt quite a burden. But in historical terms the Alfonso portrait in *The Castle of Otranto* offers little but antiquarian interest.[13]

The Colonel Pyncheon on the wall in Hawthorne's novel carries an entirely different quality. The name itself conjures up an actual early Massachusetts settler family that moved out to Springfield in the 1640s and—dispossessing native Indians and gobbling up great tracts of land—turned themselves into western Massachusetts's greatest and richest family. Yet the portrait holds additional weight, for in Hawthorne's tale, Colonel Pyncheon is clearly a stand-in for the real-life characters that the tale's history and moral emotion revolve around: Major William Hathorne and Colonel John Hathorne. The first had come to Massachusetts with John Winthrop on the *Arbella*, and he had earned his military title in Indian wars. In the 1650s too, as a magistrate, he had issued warrants calling for the persecution of Quakers. The second was the first's son, and he had been a presiding judge at the Salem witchcraft trials. Major William Hathorne was Nathaniel's great-great-great-grandfather; Colonel John Hathorne was his great-great-grandfather—and as Hawthorne wrote in the introduction to *The Scarlet Letter*, the heritage "still haunts me."[14]

Which is to say, the point of difference between European Gothic and American Gothic is that in the latter, the ancestral portrait on the wall is a figure whose deeds have a direct and inevitably tragic connection to the foregrounded action. In American Gothic, history still haunts the present *in reality*.

*   *   *

Dozens and dozens of portraits hung on the walls of Monticello—but not, it seems, ancestral portraits. Along with buffalo-hide hangings (one of which depicted a battle between Panis and Osage tribes, another a map of the territory of Missouri) and the mounted heads of elk, deer, buffalo, and mountain rams, Jefferson interspersed such sentimental religious subjects as *A Flagellation of Christ, Jesus bearing his Cross, A Crucifixion, The Sacrifice of Isaac,* with *David with head of Goliath* and *Jesus driving the money changers from the temple.* (Did he think of these as 1790s political allegories?) Then he had a gallery of paintings or prints of the Revolutionaries Washington, John Adams, Franklin, Madison, Lafayette, along with Paine, and assorted other contemporaries like Bonaparte, Kosciuszko, and Volney. Finally, and perhaps most meaningful to him, were the portraits of his intellectual heroes, Bacon, Newton, and Locke. In all, "the strange furniture on its walls," as one visitor described this interior vertical aspect of America's inimitable neo-classical castle, conveyed Thomas Jefferson's belief that the earth and all its things belong to the living, that the past could be transcended.[15]

It took a cheeky twenty-seven-year-old Philadelphia Quaker to send the great Revolutionary a Gothic novel, the American republic's first, which strongly suggested otherwise.

Notes

Introduction

1. David Lee Clark, *Charles Brockden Brown: Pioneer Voice of America* (Durham, N.C., 1952), 163–64; Thomas Jefferson, *Writings* (New York, 1984), 148; Douglas L. Wilson, "Jefferson vs. Hume," *William and Mary Quarterly* 46 (January 1989): 49–70; Alf J. Mapp, Jr., *Thomas Jefferson: A Strange Case of Mistaken Identity* (New York, 1987), 97, 185, 415.

2. On country Whig republicans and the "specter" of Robert Walpole, see Drew R. McCoy, *The Elusive Republic: Political Economy in Jeffersonian America* (Chapel Hill, N.C., 1980), 136–65.

3. Horace Walpole, *The Castle of Otranto* (Oxford, 1998), 7; Jefferson, *Writings*, 959.

4. Dumas Malone, *Jefferson and the Rights of Man* (Boston, 1951), 6, 207; Joseph Ellis, *American Sphinx: The Character of Thomas Jefferson* (New York, 1998), 108.

5. Matthew G. Lewis, *The Monk* (New York, 1952), 241–44.

6. Ibid., 268, 320–21, 368, 385, 296–97, 374–75, 108, 236, 266, 366–67.

7. Simon Schama, *Citizens: A Chronicle of the French Revolution* (New York, 1990), 391.

8. André Parreaux, *The Publication of* The Monk: *A Literary Event, 1796–1798* (Paris, 1960), 43–44, 71–73; *Diary of Elizabeth Drinker*, ed. Elaine Forman Crane (Boston, 1991), 2:1052.

9. Clark, *Charles Brockden Brown*, 163.

10. Peter Wagner, *Eros Revived: Erotica of the Enlightenment in England and America* (London, 1988), 49–54; Lewis, *The Monk*, 345.

11. Stephen King, *The Shining* (New York, 2001), 281, 565–66, 625.

12. Ibid., 28–29, 269, 485, 231–32.

13. Mark Edmundson, *Nightmare on Main Street: Angels, Sadomasochism, and the Culture of Gothic* (Cambridge, Mass., 1997), 51.

14. For this 1790s context and its imaginative possibilities, see Annette Gordon-Reed, *Thomas Jefferson and Sally Hemings: An American Controversy* (Charlottesville, Va., 1997), 59–66; William Howard Adams, *The Paris Years of Thomas Jefferson* (New Haven, Conn., 1997), 219–22; Joshua D. Rothman, "James Callender and Social Knowledge of Interracial Sex in Antebellum Virginia," in *Sally Hemings and Thomas Jefferson: History, Memory, and Civic Culture*, ed. Jan Ellen Lewis and Peter S. Onuf (Charlottesville, Va., 1999), 87–108; Francis Sergeant Childs, *French Refugee Life in the United States, 1790–1800: An American Chapter of the French Revolution* (Baltimore, 1940), 103–59. One French philosophe in particular who knew Jefferson in Paris

and at Monticello (where he noted, in 1796, slaves "as white as I am") *and* the young Charles Brown in Philadelphia, was the Comte de Volney, whose *Ruines, ou Méditations sur les révolutions des empires* Jefferson started to translate in the early 1790s and Brown later did translate. Rothman, "James Callender and Social Knowledge," 87–88; Adams, *Paris Years of Thomas Jefferson*, 154–55; Charles Brockden Brown to J. Bringhurst, October 10, 1795, in the Charles Brockden Brown Papers, George J. Mitchell Department of Special Collections and Archives, Bowdoin College Library, Brunswick, Maine. The Frenchman La Rochefoucauld-Liancourt, who visited Monticello in 1796, wrote in his journal: "In Virginia mongrel negroes are found in greater number than in Carolina and Georgia; and I have even seen, especially at Mr. Jefferson's, slaves, who, neither in point of colour nor features, shewed the least trace of their original descent; but their mothers being slaves, they retain, of consequence, the same condition." *Travels through the United States of North America, the Country of the Iroquois, and Upper Canada, in the Years 1795, 1796, and 1797* (London, 1799), 82. A clearinghouse for high- and low-level gossip in 1790s Philadelphia was Moreau de St. Méry's bookshop on Front Street, which the bookish Brown, who was improving his French in these years, inevitably would have visited. Here, in addition to Volney and the proprietor, who was quite a gossip (see *Moreau de St. Méry's American Journey (1793–1798)*, trans. and ed. Kenneth Roberts and Anna M. Roberts [Garden City, N.Y., 1947]), were to be met dozens of Parisian émigrés, and in particular the great roué Charles-Maurice de Talleyrand-Périgord, who was a friend and admirer of Alexander Hamilton—and who thereby would naturally have been a connoisseur of juicy *Jeffersonia*. He also, in the mid-1790s, lived within a block of the Brown family home on South Second Street.

15. Gordon-Reed, *Thomas Jefferson and Sally Hemings*, 32. For the actual aspiring novelist Brown in 1790s Philadelphia (and New York), see Chapter 3 below.

Prologue: "the Horrors of the night"

1. *Journals of the Continental Congress, 1774–1789* (Washington, D.C., 1907), 8: 688–89, 694; Thomas Gilpin, *Exiles in Virginia: With Observations on the Conduct of the Society of Friends during the Revolutionary War* (Philadelphia, 1848), 35–39, 84, 259–66; John William Wallace, *An Old Philadelphian, Colonel William Bradford, the Patriot Printer of 1776: Sketches of his Life* (Philadelphia, 1884), 144–47, 392–97; "Journal of the transactions of a number of the inhabitants of Philadelphia who were arrested on the second, third, fourth, and fifth days, of the 9th month 1777 under the Authority of a General Warrant," Pemberton Family Papers (no. 484A), vol. 31, pp. 79–84, the Historical Society of Pennsylvania (hereafter cited as HSP). On page 3 of the journal manuscript are listed the order and times of the arrests.

2. *Exiles in Virginia*, 38–41, 71–73; Wallace, *An Old Philadelphian*, 146–47, 388–95; (John Pemberton), "Observations on the Proceedings of Congress and Executive of Pennsylvania against Friends Sent into Banishment," Pemberton Family Papers, vol. 31, pp. 85–89. At least one on the list avoided arrest by being sick and in the country. See "Letters of Robert Proud," *Pennsylvania Magazine of History and Biography* (hereafter cited as *PMHB*) 34 (1910): 67. William Drewet Smith took the test oath—yet was exiled nonetheless. See H. Drinker to E. Drinker, December 13, 1777, in "Henry Drinker Correspondence, 1777–1778" (typescript), Quaker Collection, Haverford College, Haverford, Pa.

3. *Exiles in Virginia*, 111–12, 130–33; Wallace, *An Old Philadelphian*, 405–10; "Journal of the Transactions," Pemberton Family Papers, vol. 31, p. 84.

4. "Journal of the Transactions," p. 79.

5. For example of Matlack's violence, see Sarah Logan Fisher "Diaries" (no. 1923), vol. 7, pp. 44–46, HSP, where he is recorded as beating Thomas Fisher on the head with "a large Hicory Stick."

6. See note 1 in *Letters of Delegates to Congress, 1774–1789*, ed. Paul H. Smith (Washington, D.C., 1981), 7: 573; for sightings of Howe's fleet, 7: 528, 532, 551, 554. *Exiles in Virginia*, 57–62.

7. John Adams's account of this meeting is in *Diary and Autobiography of John Adams*, ed. L. H. Butterfield (New York, 1964), 2: 152–53, 3: 311–13. See "Journal of the Transactions," Pemberton Family Papers, vol. 31, p. 5, for Joseph Fox's good fortune in getting removed from the list.

8. *An Address to the Inhabitants of Pennsylvania, By Those Freemen of the City of Philadelphia, who are now confined in the Mason's Lodge, by Virtue of a General Warrant* (Philadelphia, 1777), 3–5, 9, 18–20, 23, 10.

9. Ibid., 26, 20, 2.

10. "Journal of the Transactions," Pemberton Family Papers, vol. 31, p. 84.

11. *Exiles in Virginia*, 133–56; Wallace, *An Old Philadelphian*, 407–28; "Journal of the Transactions," Pemberton Family Papers, vol. 31, p. 84; H. Drinker to "Beloved wife, Sister & Child," September 13, 1777, and to E. Drinker, September 18, 1777, "Henry Drinker Correspondence, 1777–1778." The Whig Christopher Marshall in Lancaster notes the "report," in his "Diary," September 15, 1777, in Christopher Marshall Papers (no. 395), HSP.

12. James Pemberton, "Diary, 1777–1778," September 28, 1777, Pemberton Family Papers; "Journal of the Transactions," Pemberton Family Papers, vol. 31, p. 83. For the obfuscations of who was in authority, see Pemberton "Diary, 1777–1778," January 12, 1778; *Exiles in Virginia*, 40; and H. Drinker to E. Drinker, January 30, 1777, and April 14, 1778, "Henry Drinker Correspondence, 1777–1778." The instruction from Congress is in R. H. Lee to Patrick Henry, September 8, 1777, *Letters of Delegates to Congress*, 7:637.

13. James Pemberton "Diary, 1777–1778," September 30, 1777; Israel Pemberton to Mary Pemberton, October 2, 1777, Pemberton Family Papers, vol. 30, p. 154. John Adams order printed in *Exiles in Virginia*, 161–62. For two accounts of the exiles' experiences in Winchester, see Robert F. Oaks, "Philadelphians in Exile: The Problem of Loyalty During the American Revolution," *PMHB* 96 (July 1972): 298–325; and James Donald Anderson, "Thomas Wharton, Exile in Virginia, 1777–1778," *Virginia Magazine of History and Biography* 89 (October 1981): 425–47.

14. *Exiles in Virginia*, 41–42, 177; H. Drinker to E. Drinker, April 14, 1778, "Henry Drinker Correspondence, 1777–1778." For the complicated machinery behind the release, see Oaks, "Philadelphians in Exile," 322–24; and Anderson, "Thomas Wharton," 444–445. The "broken . . . old man" was Edward Penington. See Israel Pemberton to Mary Pemberton, March 3, 1778, Pemberton Family Papers, vol. 32, p. 11; the "speechless" man was Thomas Wharton. See Anderson, "Thomas Wharton," 447.

15. Sarah Fisher reminisces about her love for Thomas on their fifth wedding anniversary, Fisher "Diaries," vol. 4, pp. 11–12. Quotes from vol. 3, pp. 62, 63. See also "'A Diary of Trifling Occurrences,' Philadelphia, 1776–1778," ed. Nicholas B. Wainwright *PMHB* 87 (October 1958): 411–14, 419n.

16. Fisher "Diaries," vol. 3, pp. 67, 73–75. The omission(s) after "my" in the September 13 entry are Fisher's.

17. I. Pemberton's "Account of arrest, 9 mo. 3, 1777," Pemberton Family Papers, vol. 30, pp. 84–85; "Essay toward an account of my being arrested," ibid., vol. 30, p. 86; and James Pemberton to Phineas Pemberton and Hannah Pemberton, September 10, 1777, vol. 30, p. 99.

18. Hannah Pemberton to Hannah Lloyd, September 8, 1777, Pemberton Family

Papers, vol. 30, p. 97; Phineas Pemberton to James Pemberton, September 10, 1777, ibid., vol. 30, p. 100; Hannah Lloyd to James Pemberton, December 29, 1777, ibid., vol. 31, p. 76.

19. *Diary of Elizabeth Drinker*, ed. Elaine Forman Crane (Boston, 1991), 1: 226–27.

20. Ibid., 228.

21. "Journal of the Transactions," Pemberton Family Papers, vol. 31, pp. 83–85; *Diary of Elizabeth Drinker*, 1: 228–29.

22. *Diary of Elizabeth Drinker*, 1: 229.

23. *Exiles in Virginia*, 39–40; "Remonstrance of the Prisoners at the Lodge," dated September 8, 1777, "Quaker Exiles in Virginia" file (no. 951), Quaker Collection, Haverford College; C. Marshall "Diary," August 23, 1777; *Journals of the Continental Congress*, 9: 942–44; Phineas Pemberton to James Pemberton, September 23, 1777, Pemberton Family Papers, vol. 30, p. 142. On these Quakers' views of native Indians, see Chapter 6 below.

24. H. Drinker to E. Drinker, September 8, December 19, 1777, and February 16, 1778; and E. Drinker to H. Drinker, November 5, 1777, "Henry Drinker Correspondence, 1777–1778"; Fisher "Diaries," vol. 4, 54, 67, 70; *Diary of Elizabeth Drinker*, 1: 276; Mary (Molle) Pemberton to James Pemberton, February 2, 1778, Pemberton Family Papers, vol. 31, p. 102.

25. *Exiles in Virginia*, 210–16; Phineas Pemberton to James Pemberton, April 5, 1778, Pemberton Family Papers, vol. 32, p. 23; Hannah Lloyd to James Pemberton, dated February 3, 1778, but it seems to be an unsent letter, for it has this entry for "4 mo. 1st": "Last Sixth day a more melancholy scene was disclosed, the loss of T: Gilpin, most of you ill, J. Hunt is wrote of in very doubtful terms"; Pemberton Family Papers, vol. 31, p. 104; *Diary of Elizabeth Drinker*, 1: 291, 294–95.

26. *Diary of Elizabeth Drinker*, 1: 299. The decision to bring the prisoners to Lancaster was apparently made the day before the wives arrived there. See Oaks, "Philadelphians in Exile," 323.

27. John Adams to Abigail Adams, August 23 and 24, 1777, in *Letters of Delegates to Congress*, 7: 533, 538; *Diary of Elizabeth Drinker*, 1: 235–36.

28. Fisher "Diaries," vol. 3, pp. 81–83—recounting events of "two Nights ago." I have emphasized "Children Crying" for reasons which will become clear below. See also vol. 4, p. 2; *Diary of Elizabeth Drinker*, 1: 234–35. The image on this book's cover, of the "FEU TERRIBLE A NOUVELLE YORCK," was the image Philadelphia Quakers carried in their imaginations this night—as they knew all about the great fire that had engulfed New York City in September 1776, set, it was rumored, by Revolutionary arsonists—and they feared a similar conflagration breaking out in their city.

29. The quiet could be startling—see *Diary of Elizabeth Drinker*, 1: 257, where that evening's explosions induce the comment: "till now, we have experience'd great quiate since the English came in, I have heard the Noise of a Drum, but twice since they came." For subsequent developments, see ibid., 263–65; and Fisher "Diaries," vol. 2, pp. 15–17, vol. 5, p. 21. Fisher olfactorily—and snobbishly—reacts to the Virginia riflemen in her entry for January 23, 1777, vol. 2, pp. 15–17.

30. Fisher "Diaries," vol. 5, pp. 32–35; Israel Pemberton, Pemberton Family Papers, June 3, 1778, vol. 32, p. 76.

31. Fisher "Diaries," vol. 5, p. 43; *Diary of Elizabeth Drinker*, 1: 312.

32. Fisher "Diaries," vol. 5, pp. 43, 50–51. For the general Philadelphia context experienced by these Quakers and a number of Tory families, see Judith Van Buskirk, "They Didn't Join the Band: Disaffected Women in Revolutionary Philadelphia," *Pennsylvania History* 62 (Summer 1995): 306–25.

33. *Diary of Elizabeth Drinker*, 2: 1050, 1424; 3: 1664. "The glorious 4th July 1777—Commemorated by H. Griffitts," Pemberton Family Papers, vol. 30, p. 58.

34. M. Brown to Israel Pemberton, December 12, 1777, Pemberton Family Papers, vol. 31, p. 70.

35. Fisher "Diaries," vol. 4, pp. 28–30.

36. "The Diary of Robert Morton," *PMHB* 1 (1877): 5.

37. Rachel Parke, "Dream," 1777, Pemberton Family Papers, vol. 31, p. 90, HSP.

38. Mary Pemberton to James Pemberton, November 24, 1777, Pemberton Family Papers, vol. 31, p. 46.

39. *Diary of Elizabeth Drinker*, 1: 242; E. Drinker to H. Drinker, November 5, 1777, in "Henry Drinker Correspondence, 1777–1778."

Chapter 1. Children of the Light

1. William Brown's account of early family history, "taken down from the relation of William Brown" by George Churchman and read at Nottingham Monthly Meeting, January 28, 1786, exists in two forms in the Brown family envelope at the Chester County Historical Society, West Chester, Pennsylvania. A typescript of a document entitled "The Browns of Nottingham" contains an afterword by Gilbert Cope, dated February 6, 1864. There is a printed version of this document, which I will call "Account Concerning William Brown"; quotes are from the printed version, pp. 1–4. Cope used this "Account" earlier to write an article on the Brown family which he published in *The Friend: A Religious and Literary Journal* 23 (1850): 243, 251–52.

2. Mary Williams Smith, "The Browns of Nottingham, Penna. and Related Families" (1969), 2–3, 5–7, 10–11, 24–25, manuscript at the Chester County Historical Society; and letter from Nancy P. Speers to Mary Sue Francis, dated October 30, 1988, in "Brown Family" folder, PG 7, Friends Historical Library, Swarthmore College, Swarthmore, Pennsylvania.

3. Smith, "Browns of Nottingham, Penna. and Related Families," 1–4; J. Smith Futhey and Gilbert Cope, *History of Chester County, Pennsylvania* (Philadelphia, 1881), 195–96.

4. These events will be covered below.

5. John Woolman, *Works of John Woolman in Two Parts* (Philadelphia, 1800), 37.

6. James T. Lemon, *The Best Poor Man's Country: A Geographical Study of Early Southeastern Pennsylvania* (New York, 1972), 59; Futhey and Cope, *History of Chester County*, 195–97.

7. Lemon, *Best Poor Man's Country*, 39–41, 65–67, 88–89, 168, 186–88, 207.

8. I calculate "average yields per taxpayer" from Lemon, *Best Poor Man's Country*, 168, 164. For example of villagers' "pious" pride, see "Journal of George Churchman, 1759–1813" (no. 975c), vol. 1, pp. 24, 62, in Quaker Collection, Haverford College.

9. *The Journal of George Fox*, ed. Rufus M. Jones (Richmond, Ind., 1983), 176–77; William Penn, *The Peace of Europe, The Fruits of Solitude, and Other Writings*, ed. Edwin B. Bronner (London, 1993), 229; J. William Frost, *The Quaker Family in Colonial America* (New York, 1973), 10–26.

10. Robert Barclay, *An Apology for the True Christian Religion* (Aberdeen, 1678), 40; Frost, *Quaker Family*, 22.

11. Frost, *Quaker Family*, 10–26; H. Larry Ingle, *First Among Friends: George Fox and the Creation of Quakerism* (New York, 1994).

12. Frost, *Quaker Family*, 48–61; Barry Levy, *Quakers and the American Family: British Settlement in the Delaware Valley* (New York, 1988), 53–85; Ingle, *First Among Friends*, 102–6, 150–52, 251–65; Richard Bauman, *For the Reputation of Truth: Politics, Religion, and Conflict Among the Pennsylvania Quakers, 1750–1800* (Baltimore, 1971), 231–34.

13. See Jack D. Marietta, *The Reformation of American Quakerism, 1748–1783* (Philadelphia, 1984), 98–110. Quote from 306–7 n. 8.

14. Smith, "The Browns of Nottingham, Penna. and Related Families," 3; John Churchman, *An Account of the Gospel Labours, and Christian Experiences of a Faithful Minister of Christ, John Churchman, Late of Nottingham in Pennsylvania, deceased* (Philadelphia, 1779), 29, 43; Marietta, *Reformation of American Quakerism*, 32–39.

15. Churchman, *Account*, 57, 2–6, 9–10, 27.

16. Churchman, *Account*, 34, 85–166; Marietta, *Reformation of American Quakerism*, 35–39.

17. Bauman, *For the Reputation of Truth*, 12–17.

18. Churchman, *Account*, 69–71.

19. Ibid., 71–72.

20. Ibid., 167–68, 186–87.

21. Smith, "The Browns of Nottingham, Penna. and Related Families," 6, 10. David Lee Clark, in *Charles Brockden Brown: Pioneer Voice of America* (Durham, N.C., 1952), 14, prints a portion of CBB's certificate of removal from East Nottingham, which mentions that Elijah "hath been sometime at school" in Philadelphia. Clark also prints part of the Philadelphia Arch Street Meeting marriage certificate for Elijah and Mary Armitt Brown's 1761 wedding. The list of witnesses begins: "William, Susanna, Sarah, William, Jr., and Susanna Brown, Elizabeth and Sarah Armitt, . . ." The last two names are the bride's mother and sister—that is, her extant family. The first five names are the nuclear William Brown family and constitute, it seems clear, the groom's Philadelphia family. Aside, therefore, from the logic that the young Elijah Brown would board in Philadelphia with his uncle's family, here is evidence of the priority of that family in the young Elijah's life. See also Nottingham Monthly Meeting Minutes, February and March 1757, film MR-B 179, p. 14, in Friends Historical Library, Swarthmore College.

22. Alice L. Beard, *Births, Deaths and Marriages of the Nottingham Quakers, 1680–1889* (Westminster, Md., 1989), 125, 7.

23. Smith, "The Browns of Nottingham, Penna. and Related Families," 11.

24. Gary B. Nash, *The Urban Crucible: Social Change, Political Consciousness, and the Origins of the American Revolution* (Cambridge, Mass., 1979), 407–11, 178–82; Billy G. Smith, *The "Lower Sort": Philadelphia's Laboring People, 1750–1800* (Ithaca, N.Y., 1990), 81–84; *Burnaby's Travels Through North America*, ed. Rufus Rockwell Wilson (New York, 1904), 89, 91; Carl Bridenbaugh, *Cities in Revolt: Urban Life in America, 1743–1776* (New York, 1955), 13–16.

25. Bauman, *For the Reputation of Truth*, 8–24.

26. Fred Anderson, *Crucible of War: The Seven Years' War and the Fate of Empire in British North America, 1754–1766* (New York, 2001), 86–107, 160–65; Theodore Thayer, *Israel Pemberton: King of the Quakers* (Philadelphia, 1943), 74–131; Francis Jennings, *Benjamin Franklin, Politician: The Mask and the Man* (New York, 1996), 100–121.

27. Thayer, *Israel Pemberton*, 113–94; Bauman, *For the Reputation of Truth*, 19–33; Robert Middlekauff, *Benjamin Franklin and His Enemies* (Berkeley, Calif., 1996), 55–76.

28. *Works of John Woolman*, 69.

29. Churchman, *Account*, 186. Churchman, 181, gives the date July 1756—but he could be referring to November 1756 or even 1757, as in his *Account* he (understandably) conflates somewhat the three Easton conferences held in 1756–57. See too the 1757 "Dream of a Young Man" in "Commonplace Book of Samuel Garrigues" (no. 975a), Quaker Collection, Haverford College. Interestingly and no doubt not coincidentally, western Pennsylvania and Ohio River Valley native Indians were experiencing an outbreak of prophetic dreams at exactly the same time. See Gregory Evans Dowd, *A Spirited Resistance: The North American Indian Struggle for Unity, 1745–1815* (Baltimore, 1992), 25–36.

30. Churchman's "vision" is recorded in the "Journal of George Churchman, 1759–1813" (no. 975a), vol. 1, pp. 27–28 (entry for "11th mo. 19th, 1761"), Quaker Collection, Haverford College. On Edward Brown's disownment, see "Nottingham Monthly Meeting (Baltimore Yearly Meeting): Transcript of Births, Deaths, Marriages and Removals Excerpted from the Records," typescript in Friends Historical Library, Swarthmore College.

31. William Wade Hinshaw, *Encyclopedia of American Quaker Genealogy* (Ann Arbor, Mich., 1938) 2: 332; Clark, *Charles Brockden Brown*, 14; copy of Joseph Armitt will in Charles Brockden Brown Manuscripts (no. 84), vol. 8, HSP; Nicholas Waln Family Papers, "Waln Family Genealogical Chart," Waln Collection (no. 966), box 1, folder 16, Quaker Collection, Haverford College. The witness list for Elijah and Mary's marriage contains an impressive collection of Philadelphia's most prominent Quakers, including Israel and James Pemberton, Anthony Benezet, Charles Brockden, Nicholas and Richard Waln, along with assorted Fishers, Mifflins, Joneses, and Morrises, and of course Armitts. One suspects these were all family and friends attending on the "Armitt side." It is harder to identify the guests from the Elijah Brown "side." Elijah's father—who died in 1772—did not attend, nor—it seems— did any of his Nottingham siblings. From his Nottingham past, as far as I can tell, only his Aunt Susanna Churchman Brown and Uncle William Brown, their daughters Sarah and Susanna, and another "Brown" whose first name reads something like "John," attended. What this list indicates, in sum, is that Elijah Brown was most definitely marrying into opportunities. See "Elijah Brown and Mary Armitt Marriage Certificate, July 9, 1761," Henry A. Brown Collection (no. 1341), HSP. For business ventures with Richard Waln, see "Richard Waln Account Books, Ledgers, 1761–1800," box 11, ledger A; and "Richard Waln Letterbook, 1762–66," box 1, letters from Richard Waln to John Cummins, October 30, 1762, and Richard Waln to Robert Wilson, November 21, 1764, in Richard Waln Papers (no. 1651), HSP.

32. Arthur J. Mekeel, *The Relation of the Quakers to the American Revolution* (Washington, D.C., 1979), 20, 30, 186; 1767 Tax Record—Philadelpia & Adjoining Counties, p. 216 b, in Special Collections, Van Pelt Library, University of Pennsylvania, Philadelphia; Thomas Doerflinger, *A Vigorous Spirit of Enterprise: Merchants and Economic Development in Revolutionary Philadelphia* (New York, 1987), 17, 55.

33. Doerflinger, *Vigorous Spirit of Enterprise*, 179, calculates Waln's profits for 1763–68. Philadelphia Monthly Meeting (Arch St.) Minutes, January 29 and March 25, 1768, microfilm at Friends Historical Library, Swarthmore College.

34. Richard Waln to Elijah Brown, Phila., May 26, 1770, "Richard Waln's Letterbook, 1766–1794," box 1; Elijah Brown to Richard Waln, Cape Henlopen, May 27, 1770, in Richard Waln Domestic Correspondence, 1762–1799, box 6, folder 4— both in Richard Waln Papers. One "Richard Somers," a Quaker merchant, lived in Egg Harbor, New Jersey, in the 1770s, and Richard Waln's brother, Nicholas, had contacts there. See Leah Blackman, *History of Little Egg Harbor Township, Burlington County, N.J.* (Tuckertown, N.J., 1963), 411.

35. The "Fifteenth Eighteen Penny Provincial Tax" list for the City and County of Philadelphia, from March 1772, Tax Lists (no. 1101), HSP, lists Elijah Brown in the Dock Ward. He had no property to assess and was apparently living in the house of his widowed mother-in-law. By 1774 he was more or less in the dry goods retailing business again, receiving from brother-in-law Waln shipments of flour and wheat, which he would try to sell. He also helped his "Esteemed Brother" Waln load his ships—on one occasion in February 1775 with flour and other goods lacking the proper invoices. The leitmotif of his business correspondence for 1774–75 was that he was devoid of money and that the price of "flour very dull, now falling. . . ." See Elijah Brown to Richard Waln, Philadelphia, October 18, October 29, 1774; January 31, April 11, May 20, July 8, 1775 ("Robert Morris told me this day he did not expect

the Congress would stop trade before the 10th September"), and Jacob Shoemaker to Richard Waln, Philadelphia, July 31, 1775—all in Richard Waln Domestic Correspondence, 1762–1799, box 6, Richard Waln Papers.

36. Elijah and Mary Brown would have ten children in all. Their first, James, died (apparently) at birth, in 1762. Three others—apparently at or soon after birth— would die during CBB's infancy and adolescence: William (buried in February 1773), Elijah (buried in July 1774), and Mary (buried in December 1782). Smith, "The Browns of Nottingham, Penna. and Related Families," 10–11; and see Philadelphia Monthly Meeting (Southern District) files, Swarthmore College.

37. William Smith, *A Brief State of the Province of Pennsylvania* (1755, reprint New York, 1865), 8, 40, and passim; Jennings, *Benjamin Franklin*, 161–67; Brooke Hindle, "The March of the Paxton Boys," *William and Mary Quarterly* 3 (October 1946): 461–86; Bauman, *For the Reputation of Truth*, 103–25, especially 113–16; "Journal of George Churchman," vol. 1, pp. 68–71; *Address of the People Called Quakers, in the Province of Pennsylvania, to John Penn, Esquire, Lieutenant-Governor of the said Province, &c.* (Philadelphia, 1764).

38. For context, see Jennings, *Benjamin Franklin*, 160–67; Nash, *The Urban Crucible*, 283–90. For examples of rhetoric, see *A Declaration and Remonstrance of the Distressed and Bleeding Frontier Inhabitants of the Province of Pennsylvania* (Philadelphia, 1764). The three Quaker signers who would become exiles were Israel and James Pemberton, and Owen Jones.

39. See Chapter 2 below for CBB's place in this society. For the deaths of William and Elijah, see Philadelphia (Southern District) Meeting files, Friends Historical Library, Swarthmore College. William was buried February 2, 1773, and Elijah was buried July 30, 1774. The Browns would have three more children who survived into adulthood: another son Elijah, and two daughters, Elizabeth and Catherine. See Smith, "The Browns of Nottingham, Penna. and Related Families," p. 11.

40. Thayer, *Israel Pemberton*, 186–90.

41. Ibid., 208–14; Marietta, *The Reformation of American Quakerism*.

42. Elijah Brown notes the existence of these "committees" in E. Brown to Richard Waln, Philadelphia, April 22, 1775, "Richard Waln Domestic Correspondence, 1762–1799," Richard Waln Papers. On general context, see Richard Alan Ryerson, *The Revolution Is Now Begun: The Radical Committees of Philadelphia, 1765–1776* (Philadelphia, 1978), 117–246; Mekeel, *Relation of the Quakers to the American Revolution*, 129–69. For the feeling inside the city's Quaker community see *An Epistle from Our Yearly-Meeting, Held at Philadelphia, for Pennsylvania and New Jersey, by Adjournments, from the 24th Day of the 9th Month, to the 1st of the 10th Month, Inclusive, 1774* (Philadelphia, 1774); *An Epistle from the Meeting for Sufferings, Held in Philadelphia, for Pennsylvania and New-Jersey, the 5th Day of the First Month 1775* (Philadelphia, 1775); *The Testimony of the People Called Quakers, Given Forth by a Meeting of the Representatives of Said People, in Pennsylvania and New-Jersey, Held at Philadelphia the Twenty-fourth Day of the First Month, 1775* (Philadelphia, 1775); and "To the Monthly Meeting of Friends in Philadelphia for the Southern District," datelined Philadelphia, July 28, 1777, and "An Account of the Sufferings of Friends belonging to the Monthly Meeting," datelined Philadelphia, April 28, 1779, both in Philadelphia Yearly Meeting for Sufferings, Miscellaneous Papers, roll 29, Friends Historical Library, Swarthmore College. The A. Hamilton identification is in "'A Diary of Trifling Occurrences,' Philadelphia, 1776–1778," ed. Nicholas B. Wainwright, *PMHB* 82 (October 1958): 449.

43. (Thomas Gilpin), *Exiles in Virginia: With Observations on the Conduct of the Society of Friends during the Revolutionary War* (Philadelphia, 1848), 38ff; Robert F. Oaks, "Philadelphians in Exile: The Problem of Loyalty During the American Revolution," *PMHB* 96 (July 1972): 299–325; James Donald Anderson, "Thomas

Wharton, Exile in Virginia, 1777–1778," *Virginia Magazine of History and Biography* 89 (October 1981): 425–47; Anne M. Ousterhout, "Controlling the Opposition in Pennsylvania during the American Revolution," *PMHB* 105 (January 1981): 3–34; Henry J. Young, "Treason and Its Punishment in Revolutionary Pennsylvania," *PMHB* 90 (July 1966): 287–313. The "Tory" opinions and style of such as Drinker, Wharton, Fisher are evident in their letters, and in the case of Fisher, in the diary of his wife. For the special concern of the influence of leaders upon Quaker youth, see John William Wallace, *An Old Philadelphian: Colonel William Bradford, the Patriot Printer of 1776* (Philadelphia 1884), 387–88, and the astonishing incident recorded in Sarah Logan Fisher's diary, where in March 1779 the lapsed Quaker and local Revolutionary leader Timothy Matlack attacked her husband "with a large Hicory Stick on his Head, then followed [him] out of the House, repeating his Blows with all his might for a considerable distance." What had her husband Thomas Fisher done? He had come to the Matlack house "to wait on Timothy Matlacks son to deal with him for his departure from Friends principles"; Sarah Logan Fisher Diaries, vol. 7, pp. 44–46, HSP. Elijah Brown to Richard Waln, April 28, 1775, Richard Waln Domestic Correspondence, 1762–1799, Richard Waln Papers.

44. Mekeel, *Relation of the Quakers to the American Revolution*, 160–69; *Complete Writings of Thomas Paine*, ed. Philip S. Foner (New York, 1945), 1: 91, 94, 83, 100.

45. Fisher Diaries, vol. 2, p. 72. For context of "selling," see Mekeel, *Relation*, 166–69; Anne Bezanson, "Inflation and Controls, 1774–1779," *Journal of Economic History, Supplement* 8 (1948): 1–20; and Doerflinger, *A Vigorous Spirit of Enterprise*, 197–223. For examples (from mid-1776) of the written penances sometimes required of merchants who "sold," see Thompson Westcott, *Names of Persons Who Took the Oath of Allegiance to the State of Pennsylvania, between the Years 1777 and 1789* (1865; reprint Baltimore, 1965), ix–x. Elijah Brown's absorption in trying to sell flour, and his trouble making any money at it, are evident in his 1774–75 letters to Richard Waln, cited above in note 34.

46. "Richard Waln Account Books, Ledgers 1761–1800," box 11, ledger B, p. 48, Richard Waln Papers; *Exiles in Virginia*, 72–73; James Pemberton, "Diary, 1777–78," Pemberton Family Papers, HSP. Brown lived five miles from Winchester, with the two Quaker artisans Thomas Affleck and Charles Jervis.

Chapter 2. From Terror to Terror to Terror

1. Charles Brockden Brown, *Wieland*, in *Three Gothic Novels* (New York, 1998), 17–18 (my emphasis).

2. Sarah Logan Fisher "Diaries," vol. 3, pp. 81–83, vol. 5, pp. 50–51, HSP. E. Drinker's diary entry for April 27, 1777—she is in Lancaster—notes: "Israel Pemberton, Thos. Wharton, Thos. Afflick, Charles Jervis, Charles Eddy, the 3 Fishers, Owen Jones, and Elijah Brown, left us, and went homewards." *Diary of Elizabeth Drinker*, ed. Elaine Forman Crane (Boston, 1991), 1: 303. Edmund Hogan's *The Prospect of Philadelphia* (Philadelphia, 1795), locates 117 South Second Street—the Armitt-Brown residence—on the east side of Second Street, three houses south of Dock Street.

3. "Richard Waln Account Books, Ledgers 1761–1800," box 11, ledger B, p. 48, Richard Waln Papers, HSP; *Diary of Drinker*, 1: 259; Fisher "Diaries," vol. 4, pp. 27, 47. I say Waln was "certainly a Tory" on the basis of a 1789 letter in which he still laments the "radical Evil in the loss of British Community" and writes that "I am not without Hope of seeing Things restored to their old State." See Richard Waln to Joseph Galloway, March 29, 1789, "Richard Waln's Letterbook, 1766–1794," box 1, Richard Waln Papers, HSP. I base my comment about the social divide between the Elijah Brown family and such families as the Drinkers and Fishers on the fact that

the Browns are not mentioned in the latter families 1770s to 1780s diaries except during the 1777–79 episode. This is especially noteworthy with regard to Fisher's diary, as she was a close neighbor of the Browns. These diaries indicate quite clearly, as does that of Anna Rawle, that while Armitts, Walns, and William Brown were in the diarists' social circle, the Elijah Browns were not. This "class" dimension of his life will be a component of CBB's first epistolary fiction, the "Henrietta Letters," and his two urban Philadelphia novels, *Arthur Mervyn* and *Ormond*.

4. Fisher "Diaries," vol. 4, pp. 27, 63; *Diary of Elizabeth Drinker*, 1: 248, 253, 259, 280, 293; Philadelphia Monthly Meeting (Arch Street) Minutes, February 26, 1779—held at the Fourth Street meetinghouse—p. 117, and March 1779, p. 125, at Friends Historical Library, Swathmore College. There are two bits of evidence that suggest that Elijah Brown—even as a disowned Friend, and thereby as someone whose name would never appear in the official Quaker records—still attended meeting. One is an entry in Elizabeth Drinker's diary, for September 27, 1779, which records that a Quaker visiting from out of town took ill at the Pine Street Meeting, and went home with Elijah Brown; *Diary of Elizabeth Drinker*, 1: 360. On that one occasion, apparently, he was at meeting. Another is the letter of advice he composed for his children in the mid-1780s, which included the admonition to attend meeting. Though, as I will discuss later, Elijah, Sr., was not always the most consistent of fathers, I don't believe he would have tendered this particular piece of advice if he himself didn't attend meeting. In the end, it is my sense that Elijah was a seventeenth-century type of Quaker. Eccentric, independent, and prickly when it came to what he deemed principles, he didn't have to officially belong to a congregation to bear witness to Quaker "truth."

5. "Journal of Samuel Rowland Fisher," *PMHB* 41 (1917): 168–70; *Diary of Elizabeth Drinker*, 1: 361; John K. Alexander, "The Fort Wilson Incident of 1779: A Case Study of the Revolutionary Crowd," *William and Mary Quarterly* 31 (October 1974): 601–4. There is a glimpse of the Elijah Brown family amid this pending ominous event in Elizabeth Drinker's September 27, 1779 entry, cited above. September 27 was the day Samuel Rowland Fisher recorded the rumor about the militia "about to take up all the Tories & Quakers." Drinker's diary entry: "this Evening [John Willis] was taken ill at the pine-street meeting and went to Bed at Elijah Browns— where I expect he must stay all night"; *Diary of Elizabeth Drinker*, 1: 360. The Pine Street meetinghouse, which was now the cynosure of all official Quaker activity because the Arch Street meetinghouse had been taken over by the Revolutionaries as a hospital, was just down the street from the Brown residence at 117 South Second Street.

6. Alexander, "Fort Wilson Incident," 602–6; Charles Page Smith, *James Wilson, Founding Father, 1742–1798* (Chapel Hill, N.C., 1956), 130–39; "Journal of Samuel Rowland Fisher," 169–72. Fisher notes, in his October 24 entry, 170, that "I heard the noise & could see part of the Mob from the Goal Window." That jail at Market and Third, was a block farther away from the action than was the Brown residence at Second near Walnut. "Terrible to hear" quote is from Sarah Logan Fisher "Diaries," vol. 8, p. 75.

7. [Anna Rawle], "A Loyalist's Account of Certain Occurrences in Philadelphia after Cornwallis's Surrender at Yorktown: Extracted from the Diary of Miss Anna Rawle," *PMHB* 16 (1892): 104–7; *Diary of Elizabeth Drinker*, 1: 393. For the three-phased nature of this riot, with one mob succeeding another succeeding another, see Hannah Moore to her sister (Milcah Martha Moore), in Edward Wanton Smith Collection (no. 955), "Additions, 1971," box 5, no. 55, Quaker Collection, Haverford College. Though this letter is not dated, its subject is clearly the October 25, 1781, riot. That the rioters made it to the Browns' precise neighborhood is indicated by Sarah Fisher's "Diaries," vol. 10, p. 79. Fisher lived a couple of houses away from the Browns.

8. Douglas McNeil Arnold, "Political Ideology and the Internal Revolution in Pennsylvania, 1776–1790" (Ph.D. dissertation, Princeton University, 1976); John N. Shaeffer, "Public Consideration of the 1776 Constitution," *PMHB* 98 (October 1974): 415–37.

9. For a description of the difficulties faced by dry goods merchants in postwar Philadelphia, see the letter from Alexander Wilcocks—CBB's future mentor in the law—to Phineas Bond, dated August 26, 1785, in Society Collection, HSP. See, too, Thomas Doerflinger, *A Vigorous Spirit of Enterprise: Merchants and Economic Development in Revolutionary Philadelphia* (New York, 1987), 242–50; and Arnold, "Political Ideology and the Internal Revolution," 105–9. Richard Waln to Nicholas Waln, July 22, 1784, and Sarah Richardson Waln to Nicholas Waln, July 23, 1784, Waln Collection, "Additions," box 3, folder 24, Quaker Collection, Haverford College. (These letters are published in Mary Harrison, *Annals of the Ancestry of Charles Custis Harrison and Ellen Waln Harrison* [Philadelphia, 1932], 93–94.) As for citizenship, Elijah Brown remained a nonjuror—and thereby a noncitizen—at least until 1789, when the Pennsylvania Assembly finally abolished all test laws. See Thompson Westcott, *Names of Persons Who Took the Oath of Allegiance to the State of Pennsylvania, Between the Years 1777 and 1789* (1865; reprint Baltimore, 1965) xvi–xlii, and the index, where Elijah Brown is not listed.

10. CBB to Joseph Bringhurst, n.d. (Bennett Census no. 9—Charles E. Bennett, "The Letters of Charles Brockden Brown: An Annotated Census," *Sources for American Literary Study* [Autumn 1976]: 164–90), in Charles Brockden Brown Papers, George J. Mitchell Department of Special Collections and Archives, Bowdoin College Library, New Brunswick, Maine (hereafter cited as CBB Coll., Me.). CBB would later draw upon this experience in *Arthur Mervyn—Second Part*, chapter 4, for Dr. Stevens's visit to his friend Carlton in the Prune Street Debtors' Apartments: "The apartment was filled with pale faces and withered forms. The marks of negligence and poverty were visible in all; but few betrayed, in their features or gestures, any symptoms of concern on account of their condition. Ferocious gaiety, or stupid indifference, seemed to sit upon every brow. The vapour from an heated stove, mingled with the fumes of beer and tallow that were spilled upon it, and with the tainted breath of so promiscuous a crowd, loaded the stagnant atmosphere. At my first transition from the cold and pure air without, to this noxious element, I found it difficult to breathe. . . . Almost every mouth was furnished with a segar, and every hand with a glass of porter. . . . Sundry groupes, in different corners, were beguiling the tedious hours at whist." *Three Gothic Novels*, 458.

11. Not least among the strange aspects of this "advice"—this soul-felt knowledge—is that Elijah Brown apparently abstracts it from a formal address written by somebody else! The document is in Charles Brockden Brown Manuscripts (no. 84), vol. 3, pp. 53ff, HSP.

12. Ibid.

13. Francis White, *Philadelphia Directory* (Philadelphia, 1785), 4. For an example of Mary Brown's conventional Quaker devoutness, see Charles Brockden Brown Manuscripts, vol. 3, HSP, where she copies out "Some Account of the Convincement Christian Experiences and Travels of Jane Hoskins, deceased." The strongest evidence of her piety is the fact of her—and her children's—membership in the Meeting, which membership she maintained in the face of all her husband's difficulties. For the children's sense of Mary Brown's "economy," see Charles Brockden Brown Manuscripts, vol. 5, HSP, where Elijah Brown records "A part of my Son C B Browns Diary" from June 1788: "brother Armit came down in the morning [brr?] Elijah gave me a 20:d piece which he had gotten that morning for Cherries which he laid claim to upon the merit of having picked them. I have bought the Death of Abel with it for him, though I now repent having done so as my Mother

214 Notes to Pages 46–47

may think it thrown away." A strong indication of Armitt family feeling about Elijah Brown—or at least about his "responsible" side—is Mary's mother's 1798 will, in which grandmother Elizabeth Armitt names as executors the "son-in-law" Richard Waln (that is, the husband of her elder daughter Elizabeth) and Charles Brockden Brown. Her other son-in-law, Elijah Brown, is not mentioned in the will. See "Elizabeth Armitt's Will, 1798," Charles Brockden Brown Collection (no. 6349), Clifton Waller Barrett Library, Special Collections, University of Virginia Library (hereafter cited as CBB Coll., Va.).

14. White, *Philadelphia Directory* (1785), 4. For Elijah Brown's notebooks, see Brown Family Manuscripts, HSP. See vol. 9 for the Godwin and Wollstonecraft material, along with a digest of "A Confession of Faith—Containing 23 Articles—of the People called Quakers," and Elijah Sr.'s 1797 admonition to his children to marry within the faith, which includes—"[how?] truly astonishing to me it is, that the members of this Society will not all of them religiously conform to their mode in this respect rather than forfeit their right of communion by departing from it." Vol. 9 also contains, among many silly "anecdotes," this "pun," which Elijah wrote down in 1797: "Some persons broke into the Stables of a Troop of Light-horse and cut of[f] all their tails. A brother Officer advised the troop to sell them by Wholesale, for, says he, you can never retail them." The poem, entitled "My Father," which contains the information about Elijah, Sr. that "Not on insect would he tread," is in vol. 8. This volume is a "Book of Selections," written down by Elijah Brown between 1806 and 1808 from papers and scraps he had no doubt saved. The "My Father" poem is annotated by Elijah: "By C.B.B. esq. I believe." Whether it was indeed written by a youthful CBB—which seems likely—is not as interesting to me as the fact that it is the production of one of Elijah Brown's sons, and therefore records *their* sense of him as a father. In this regard, among Elijah's other traits, he was clearly entertaining. Thus: "Who from each flow'r and verdant stalk / *Gather'd a honey'd store of talk*, / And fill'd the long delightful walk? / My Father" (my emphasis). The quote from "H.D.," from a "series of original letters" published in the *Weekly Magazine* in 1798, is in *The Rhapsodist and Other Uncollected Writings by Charles Brockden Brown*, ed. Harry R. Warfel (New York, 1943), 110. For the general context of being a bankrupt male in late eighteenth-century Philadelphia, see Toby L. Ditz, "Shipwrecked; or, Masculinity Imperiled: Mercantile Representations of Failure and the Gendered Self in Eighteenth-Century Philadelphia," *Journal of American History* 81 (June 1994): 51–80.

15. An uncle on the Armitt side, the merchant Henry Lisle, "let Joseph and James Brown"—the two eldest—"take one Eighth" interest in "a Bermudan built Brig about 4 years old" in 1783–84. See Henry Lisle to Richard Waln, Philadelphia, December 19, 1783, in Richard Waln Domestic Correspondence, 1762–1799, Richard Waln Papers. Thomas Woody, *Early Quaker Education in Pennsylvania* (New York, 1920), 58–60, 172–74, 190–99; John Merrill Beeson, "Robert Proud (1728–1813): A Biography" (Ph.D. dissertation, Pennsylvania State University, 1974), 51–52, 62; Jean S. Straub, "Teaching in the Friends' Latin School of Philadelphia in the Eighteenth Century," *PMHB* 91 (October 1967): 434–56, and "Quaker School Life in Philadelphia Before 1800," *PMHB* 89 (October 1965): 447–58. For CBB's classmates, see Robert Proud School Account Book, 1759–1792, in the Robert Proud Collection (no. 529), HSP. On p. 65 of the manuscript, under the year 1786, is the notation that "22 10—" were received for four years of CBB's "learning."

16. Beeson, "Robert Proud," 30–122.

17. "Autobiography of Robert Proud, the Historian," *PMHB* 13 (1889): 430–39, quotes from 436 (and n. 1); Beeson, "Robert Proud," 107, 115, 119, 121–35. For an especially good example of Proud's whining, see 132. Proud's unsent letter to the exiles is in Robert Proud Letterbook, Robert Proud Collection.

18. Here, in an 1811 letter to his sister, is Proud's own assessment of the impact of the Revolution on himself: "at the time of what is called the *Revolution* of this Country, tho' more properly the *Revolt* of it, I suffered greatly in my circumstances, & otherwise, by its Effects, while the Lives of divers of my near Frds & Acquaintances were much shortened thereby;—some in Banishment & others by the difft Consequences, or sad Catastrophe of that Time, from which I escaped, I may say, with my life alone; but from certain Experience, I have sufficient Reason to know & believe that I have never yet entirely recovered from the Blow"; Robert Proud Letterbook, 1770–1811, Robert Proud Collection. In the mid-1780s the Latin School's two trustees were James Pemberton and Owen Jones—both exiles. See Beeson, "Robert Proud," 135. Proud's comment, from 1782, about "rebel foes" is on 125. Beeson notes Proud's "martyr-wish" on 115 and 89. CBB's review of Proud's *History*, in the *Monthly Magazine* (June 1799), is printed in Charles Brockden Brown, *Literary Essays and Reviews*, ed. Alfred Weber and Wolfgang Schäfer (Frankfurt am Main, 1992), 25–27.

19. CBB to Joseph Bringhurst, n.d. (Bennett Census no. 20), CBB Coll., Me.

20. CBB's "Liberty of Conscience" essay—from 1783—is in CBB Coll., Va. On his literary ambitions, see Paul Allen, *The Late Charles Brockden Brown*, ed. Robert E. Hemenway and Joseph Katz (Columbia. S.C., 1976), 11–14. CBB mentions that he had written in 1787 what he terms a "Journal of a Visionary," in a letter to Bringhurst, May 20, 1792 (Bennett Census no. 21), CBB Coll., Me.

21. On Wilcocks, who was a member of Philadelphia's non-Quaker elite both before and after the war, see Richard Alan Ryerson, *The Revolution Is Now Begun: The Radical Committees of Philadelphia, 1765–1776* (Philadelphia, 1978), 129–31, 140, 171–73, 221–23, 241; and Stephen Brobeck, "Changes in the Composition and Structure of Philadelphia Elite Groups, 1756–1790" (Ph.D. dissertation, University of Pennsylvania, 1973), 150–51, 205–8, 218–20. On CBB and the law, see Robert A. Ferguson, *Law and Letters in American Culture* (Cambridge, Mass., 1984), 129–49.

22. On Waln, see Henry Simpson, *Lives of Eminent Philadelphians* (Philadelphia, 1859), 925–27. Burton Alva Konkle, *Benjamin Chew, 1722–1810* (Philadelphia, 1932), 117, notes that in 1769 Nicholas Waln had the first practice in the colony. In Sarah Logan Fisher's "Diaries," vol. 18, pp. 18–20, there is a glimpse of Nicholas Waln, at meeting in March 1790, referencing his past in the law for the present-day cause of spiritual truth. Thus, Fisher evokes Waln as he talked about his giving up the law—"he might have had great prospects—no doubt he meant of enriching himself, & being popular & great in this World"—and as he "lay as at the Feet of Jesus, bewailing himself."

23. Allen, *The Late Charles Brockden Brown*, 15–16, 31–39; Charles Brockden Brown Manuscripts, vol. 5 (under rubric "A part of my Son C B Browns Diary"), printed in Robert Hemenway, "Charles Brockden Brown's Law Study: Some New Documents," *American Literature* 39 (1967): 200–201.

24. Little is known about the Belles Lettres Club and its apparent successor, the Society for the Attainment of Useful Knowledge. For an analysis of the record, see Wolfgang Schäfer, *Charles Brockden Brown als Literaturkritiker* (Frankfurt am Main, 1991), 41–47. For the type of topics discussed in the club, see the correspondence of CBB with William Wilkins and Joseph Bringhurst—cited in note 43 below. See also Thomas P. Cope, "Minute Book" for the "Philomathian Society, 1787–1788" (no. 975a), Quaker Collection, Haverford College, which was a coterminus liberal arts society with an overlapping membership. CBB quotations in Allen, *The Late Charles Brockden Brown*, 21–31. Wilkins's entry into the club in 1790 (or perhaps late 1789) can be inferred from CBB to Joseph Bringhurst, May 20, 1792 (Bennett Census no. 21), CBB Coll., Me.

25. CBB's poem was apparently submitted to the newspaper by his older brother,

Joseph Armitt Brown, who did business in Edentown, North Carolina. See Harry R. Warfel, *Charles Brockden Brown: American Gothic Novelist* (Gainesville, Fla., 1949), 32, and A. Owen Aldridge, "Charles Brockden Brown's Poem on Benjamin Franklin," *American Literature* 38 (1966): 230–35.

26. Aldridge, "Charles Brockden Brown's Poem on Benjamin Franklin," 233, believes the loyalist Jonathan Odell "a much more likely author" of the piece. I am less interested in who wrote it than that the poem came out of the persecuted Quaker-Tory community of mid-1770s Philadelphia (in the heart of which, at 117 South Second Street, lived the Browns), that some attributed it to Hannah Griffitts and Deborah Norris, and that CBB—unlike his non-Quaker 1789 American readers—would have known this. For the attribution of authorship to Griffitts and for a rich collection of Quaker anti-Revolutionary poems, see *Milcah Martha Moore's Book: A Commonplace Book from Revolutionary America*, ed. Catherine La Courreye Blecki and Karin A. Wulf (University Park, Pa., 1997), 280–81 and passim. Griffitts's "Horrors of the Night" poem is in Pemberton Family Papers, vol. 30, p. 58, HSP.

27. Warfel, *Charles Brockden Brown*, 32. To my mind, this example of CBB's irony, indulged in this very early publication, refutes Michael Warner's entire chapter on CBB ("The Novel: Fantasies of Publicity") in *The Letters of the Republic: Publication and the Public Sphere in Eighteenth-Century America* (Cambridge, Mass., 1990), 151–76, which is premised on the assumption that CBB was not ironical.

28. See Konkle, *Benjamin Chew*. Wilcocks had married Chew's eldest daughter, Mary, in 1768.

29. David Lee Clark, *Charles Brockden Brown: Pioneer Voice of America* (Durham, N.C., 1952), 53–55, 55–107 (where Clark prints the Henrietta Letters—as I refer to them in my text—under the rubric "The Journal Letters"; all Henrietta Letters quotes are from this edition); Eleanor M. Tilton, "'The Sorrows' of Charles Brockden Brown," *Publications of the Modern Language Association* 69 (1954): 1304–7. That his apprenticeship with Wilcocks brought CBB into social contact with Henrietta Chew is established by a July 22, 1786, journal entry written by another aspiring lawyer from the Chew-Wilcocks circle, William Rawle: "Dined at A. Wilcock's where were Henrietta Chew, B. Chew jun, J. Galloway, Lewis, Ingersol, W. Hamilton, Mifflin & Swanwick"; "Journals of William Rawle, 1782–1826," Rawle Family Papers (no. 536), HSP. Interestingly, two of the guests at this party would make it into CBB's fiction as characters: Henrietta Chew, as "Henrietta G.," and John Swanwick, as "Thomas Welbeck" in *Arthur Mervyn*. See Chapters 3 and 5 below. CBB's quote about the "amiable Henrietta G." is in CBB to Bringhurst, May 20, 1792, CBB Coll., Me. On clues from the Henrietta Letters, see Clark, *Charles Brockden Brown*, 62, 78 (where "the additional ceremony"—marriage between the two—is described as "absolutely prohibited"), 85 (where "our union" is described as "impossible, but that, if it were possible to take place, it would be an instance of the most inexcusable impudence and temerity that ages of repentance would be bought by moments of pleasure"), 56, matched against the situation of the real Henrietta Chew in Konkle, *Benjamin Chew*, 81–82, 192. I am indebted to John R. Holmes for bringing to my attention facts that caused me to revise my understanding of when the "Letters" were composed.

30. Clark, *Charles Brockden Brown*, 63. Jean-Jacques Rousseau, *Julie; ou, La Nouvelle Héloïse*, part 1, letter 54 (N.B.: All but the first ellipsis are in Rousseau's text), part 2, letter 7. CBB wrote about reading *Eloisa* with Henrietta back in 1788, in CBB to Bringhurst, May 20, 1792, CBB Coll., Me. Of course, CBB could have been making up this 1788 detail.

31. On Henrietta and Harriet Chew, see Konkle, *Benjamin Chew*, 125–26, 145–46, 192–93, 285–88; *Letters of Mrs. Adams, the Wife of John Adams*, ed. Charles Francis Adams (Boston, 1840), 408–10; Charles Merrill Mount, *Gilbert Stuart: A Biography*

(New York, 1964), 201. Harriet Chew was a star in 1790s Philadelphia high society who married a rich and prominent man, whereas Henrietta was an apparent homebody who never married. She died in 1848.

32. Clark, *Charles Brockden Brown*, 83; CBB to Bringhurst, n.d. (Bennett Census no. 20)—but by internal evidence 1792, as Brown says he is twenty-one years old—and May 15, 1792 (Bennett Census no. 18), CBB Coll., Me.

33. Clark, *Charles Brockden Brown*, 55–59.

34. Letters 8, 9, ibid., 75, 77.

35. Letter 10, ibid., 79, 81. For other examples of CBB employing this distinctive diction, see CBB to James Brown, April 19, 1795, and CBB to Wilkins, (1790–1795?), both in CBB Coll., Va. Interestingly, CBB the literary critic notices this shift—even if CBB the artist did not bother to fix it. Thus he has Henrietta at the end of letter 10 (p. 82) write: "Consider before you write, whether the language which you are about to use be reconcilable with the dialect of former letters."

36. Clark, *Charles Brockden Brown*, 65, 75, 101 (letter 14). G. J. Barker-Benfield, *The Culture of Sensibility: Sex and Society in Eighteenth-Century Britain* (Chicago, 1992).

37. Clark, *Charles Brockden Brown*, 83.

38. Ibid., 83; CBB to Bringhurst, May 15, 1792, CBB Coll., Me. In 1792 CBB excavates an old "specimen of an amorous correspondence" to show Bringhurst, which seems clearly to be the Henrietta Letters, and in rereading it in this context—when the then eighteen-year-old Harriet Chew reigned as Federalist Philadelphia's belle—CBB would have experienced a new set of erotic pleasures that were tied in with his "fiction." (Or so I would imagine.) See CBB to Bringhurst, May 5, 1792 (Bennett Census no. 12), CBB Coll., Me.

39. Clark, Charles Brockden Brown, 104–5.

40. Rousseau, *The Confessions of J.J. Rousseau: With the Reveries of the Solitary Walker* (Dublin, 1783), 2:180. For the availability of the *Confessions* in Philadelphia, see *Catalogue des livres qui se trouvent Chez Boinod & Gaillard* (Philadelphia, 1784), 13.

41. *The Rhapsodist and Other Uncollected Writings*, 5, 6.

42. Ibid., 7, 13. On this sentimental/Romantic cultural strain in Europe, see Rupert Christiansen, *Romantic Affinities: Portraits from an Age, 1780–1830* (New York, 1988), esp. chaps. 1, 2, 4; Jay Fliegelman, *Prodigals and Pilgrims: The American Revolution against Patriarchal Authority, 1750–1800* (Cambridge, 1982), 131–32.

43. On Wilkins, see "A Sketch of the Life of William Wood Wilkins, Esq." by "Jos. Bringhurst Jun." in Charles Brockden Brown Manuscripts, vol. 8, HSP. CBB to Wilkins, "Thursday Night," n.d., CBB Coll., Va.; CBB to Bringhurst, May 20, 1792, CBB Coll., Me.; "Unpublished Letters of Charles Brockden Brown and W. W. Wilkins," *Studies in English* 27 (1948): 86.

44. CBB to Wilkins, n.d., CBB Coll., Va.; "Unpublished Letters of Charles Brockden Brown and W. W. Wilkins," 88; CBB to Bringhurst, June 9, 1792 (Bennett Census no. 26), CBB Coll., Me. The CBB-Wilkins friendship bears comparison to the highly intimate late eighteenth-century friendships existing between the young Philadelphians John Fishbourne Mifflin, James Gibson, and Isaac Norris III, documented by Caleb Crain in "Leander, Lorenzo, and Castelio: An Early American Romance," *Early American Literature* (1998): 6–31. Crain reads these "romances" as "tell[ing] a story of affection between American men at a crucial moment: at the acme of the culture of sentiment and sensibility, when individuals first considered following the unruly impulse of sympathy as far as it would go" (6). In this context, a key element of the CBB and Wilkins friendship (and CBB's and Bringhurst's as well) is that while it took shape within what cultural historians have dubbed the "culture of sensibility," it lacked Crain's dynamic of "following the unruly impulse of sympathy *as far as it would go*." For unlike the Princeton-educated John Mifflin, who (Crain tells us) wore his "powdered hair . . . at the rear into a fashionable

queue," and the Princeton-educated Gibson, who, coming from a family that was "genteel but no longer wealthy," also "had a 'taste for old fashioned queues,'" and Isaac Norris III, scion of one of the great and wealthy Quaker families and whose finishing education came by way of a grand tour of Europe (during which he converted to Catholicism!)—CBB, Wilkins, and Bringhurst were from pious Quaker families and their habits and manners (if not always, in CBB's case, his thoughts) reflected it. Thus, though educated, they weren't "genteel" in the manner of Mifflin, Gibson, Norris; and indeed their upbringings were calculated to make them suspicious of such self-indulgent "worldly" gentility. Keeping to Quaker tradition, their pious families did not send them to college, and it's inconceivable that, in their teens and twenties, they would powder and queue their hair. Indeed, among the traits that that post-Puritan moralist Elihu Hubbard Smith found most unusual and engaging about CBB and Bringhurst, was their "bald-face stile"—namely, their utter Quaker simplicity and manner of dress. See *The Diary of Elihu Hubbard Smith*, ed. James E. Cronin (Philadelphia, 1973), 248, and Chapter 3 below, where I discuss CBB's relationship with Smith in depth. In short, an *un*-advantaged Quaker background and a natural respect for pious actions and Quaker morality, separated CBB and his friends from the society of Mifflin, Norris, and Co. In this, the two different coteries occupied different worlds, and their friendships reflected it.

45. "Unpublished Letters of Charles Brockden Brown and W. W. Wilkins," 96–101; Fliegelman, *Prodigals and Pilgrims.*

46. "Unpublished Letters of Charles Brockden Brown and W. W. Wilkins," 81, 79, 88–89.

47. On the "visionary" culture of Quakerism, see, for example, Phyllis Mack, *Visionary Women: Ecstatic Prophecy in Seventeenth-Century England* (Berkeley, Calif., 1992). For example of CBB dreaming within a mixed literary and Quaker religious "visionary" frame, see CBB to Bringhurst, n.d. (Bennett Census no. 42), CBB Coll., Me. In this dream, which I present below in Chapter 3, CBB and Bringhurst begin in the "region of Romance: In Spensers fairy land," but soon they are "Pilgrims . . . going to perform our devotions: at the temple of some divinity." I consider CBB's "visionary" family heritage in Chapter 4 below, in conjunction with my analysis of *Wieland.* Coleridge's clan came from Devon, Wordsworth's from Cumbria, and CBB's from Northamptonshire, England.

48. Stephen Gill, *William Wordsworth: A Life* (Oxford, 1989), 13–175; William Wordsworth, *1805 Prelude*, book 10, lines 692–93, in *The Prelude: The Four Texts (1798, 1799, 1805, 1850)*, ed. Jonathan Wordsworth (London, 1995).

49. Wordsworth, *1805 Prelude*, book 1, lines 149, 275–76; 4:392–95; 11:333–35; "Was It For This," lines 127–28; *1799 Prelude*, 1:460–65; *1805 Prelude*, 1:67; 12:320, 13:185, 12:282–83.

50. Richard Holmes, *Coleridge: Early Visions* (New York, 1990), 1–38; "Frost at Midnight" (1798), lines 28–30, in *The Portable Coleridge*, ed. I. A. Richards (New York, 1950), 128–29.

51. Holmes, *Coleridge*, 14, 16–17.

52. Ibid., 21–134. Quotes in Holmes, *Coleridge*, 22, 66, 62; Gill, *Wordsworth*, 119; and Coleridge, "Frost at Midnight," lines 51–53.

53. Holmes, *Coleridge*, 162; Coleridge, "Kubla Khan," lines 12–14, 29–30; and "Rime of the Ancient Mariner," part 7, lines 582–90, both in *Portable Coleridge.*

54. *The Rhapsodist and Other Uncollected Writings*, 6; Wordsworth, *1805 Prelude*, book 1, lines 64–65.

55. Gill, *Wordsworth*, 56–121; Nicholas Roe, *Wordsworth and Coleridge: The Radical Years* (Oxford, 1988); *1805 Prelude*, book 9, lines 70–71; 10:48, 62–66 (my emphasis).

56. CBB to Bringhurst, August 9, 1792 (Bennett Census no. 30), CBB Coll., Me.

57. CBB to Bringhurst, n.d. (Bennett Census no. 9), CBB Coll., Me. For signatures

of Joseph Bringhurst Sr. (the uncle) and James Bringhurst (the father), see "To the President and Council of Pennsylvania," datelined "Philada. 5th 9mo: 1777," "Quaker Exiles in Virginia" file (no. 951), Quaker Collection, Haverford College. Joseph Bringhurst Sr. was also visiting with the exiles at the Mason's Lodge prison on September 11, 1777 (see above, Prologue, for the scene), and presumably witnessed their heartbreaking exit, under armed guard and in the face of much abuse from the patriot citizenry, from the city on that day. See "Journal of the Transactions of a Number of the Inhabitants of Philadelphia Who Were Arrested," Pemberton Family Papers, vol. 31, p. 21.

58. Edmund Burke and Thomas Paine, *Reflections on the Revolution in France and The Rights of Man* (Garden City, N.Y., 1973), 84.

59. See Prologue above.

60. CBB to Bringhurst, n.d., CBB Coll., Me.

61. The scold among his friends was Elihu Smith. See *Diary of Elihu Hubbard Smith*, 164.

62. *Papers of Thomas Jefferson*, ed. Julian Boyd et al. (Princeton, N.J., 1950-   ), 25: 95, 661; 26: 444. On Genet, see Conor Cruise O'Brien, *The Long Affair: Thomas Jefferson and the French Revolution, 1785–1800* (Chicago, 1996), 156–57, and Harry Ammon, *The Genet Mission* (New York, 1973).

63. Simon Schama, *Citizens: A Chronicle of the French Revolution* (New York, 1990), 793–820; Jared Sparks, *Life of Gouverneur Morris, with Selections from His Correspondence and Miscellaneous Papers* (Boston, 1832), 2:361, 369; James Roger Sharp, *American Politics in the Early Republic: The New Nation in Crisis* (New Haven, Conn., 1993), 85–89; J. H. Powell, *Bring Out Your Dead: The Great Plague of Yellow Fever in Philadelphia in 1793* (1949; reprint Philadelphia 1965), 8–119.

Chapter 3. Revolutionary Reverberations

1. CBB to Bringhurst, October 30, 1795 (Bennett Census no. 64), CBB Coll., Me. On Godwin's influence, see William Hazlitt, *Spirit of the Age* (Oxford, 1989), 31–36.

2. Charles Brockden Brown Manuscripts, vol. 9, HSP.

3. The daughter, named Mary, would forge the great intellectual partnership of the next generation when she ran off with the married poet Percy Bysshe Shelley, and as Mary Shelley she would write the most successful Gothic novel of all time, *Frankenstein, or the Modern Prometheus*, which she would dedicate "to William Godwin." William St. Clair, *The Godwins and the Shelleys: A Biography of a Family* (New York, 1989), 1–58, 168–78, 502, 163; *Diary of Elihu Hubbard Smith (1771–1798)*, ed. James E. Cronin (Philadelphia, 1973), 386.

4. Henry F. May, *The Enlightenment in America* (New York, 1976), 172–73, 225, 231, 233–35, 246, 249, 250–51; Chandos Michael Brown, "Mary Wollstonecraft; or, The Female Illuminati: The Campaign against Women and 'Modern Philosophy' in the Early Republic," *Journal of the Early Republic* 15 (Fall 1995): 389–424; Marcelle Thiébaux, "Mary Wollstonecraft in Federalist America: 1791–1802," in *The Evidence of the Imagination*, ed. Donald H. Reiman, Michael C. Jayne, and Betty T. Bennett (New York, 1978), 195–235; Susan Branson, *These Fiery Frenchified Dames: Women and Political Culture in Early National Philadelphia* (Philadelphia, 2001), 38–46, 49–52; Mary Wollstonecraft and William Godwin, *A Short Residence in Sweden, Norway and Denmark* and *Memoirs of the Author of "The Rights of Woman"*, ed. Richard Holmes (London, 1987), 250, 234, 240, 258. A note of caution about *These Fiery Frenchified Dames*: Branson assumes, based on a not very authoritative 1935 article entitled "A Speculation," that CBB was the editor of the Philadelphia *Lady's Magazine* in

1792–93 (see 28, 39). While this is not impossible, it seems to me unlikely, as CBB was but twenty-one at the time and a law apprentice. In any case, there are no allusions in any of CBB's extant writings to such an editorial connection, and during this period CBB was stretching to claim credit for any kind of literary endeavor—even imaginary ones.

5. *The Complete Writings of Thomas Paine,* ed. Philip S. Foner (New York, 1945), 1: 252.

6. Albert Goodwin, *The Friends of Liberty: The English Democratic Movement in the Age of the French Revolution* (Cambridge, Mass., 1979), 170–207; George Rudé, *The Crowd in History* (New York, 1964), 139–47; R. B. Rose, "The Priestley Riots of 1791," *Past and Present* 18 (November 1960): 68–84; St. Clair, *Godwins and the Shelleys,* 52, 66–68.

7. St. Clair, *Godwins and the Shelleys,* 102–14; Isaac Kramnick's introduction to William Godwin, *Enquiry Concerning Political Justice,* ed. Isaac Kramnick (New York, 1985), 7–54; and William Godwin, *Enquiry Concerning Political Justice, and Its Influence on General Virtue and Happiness* (Dublin, 1793), 1: 129–73.

8. Godwin, *Political Justice* (Dublin, 1793), 2: 237–97, 129–227.

9. I am following Godwin here, *Political Justice,* from his book 2 ("Principles of Society") to book 3 ("Principles of Government") to book 4 ("Miscellaneous Principles").

10. Ibid., 1: 193, 120, 170.

11. Godwin, *Enquiry Concerning Political Justice, and Its Influence on Morals and Happiness* (Philadelphia, 1796), 1: 233, 236, 234, 218.

12. Ibid., 141.

13. Ibid. For this incident with John Churchman, quoted from Churchman, *An Account of the Gospel Labours, and Christian Experiences of a Faithful Minister of Christ, John Churchman, Late of Nottingham in Pennsylvania, deceased* (Philadelphia, 1779), 70–71, see Chapter 1 above. For CBB's familiarity with the Churchman family, see his essay on John Churchman's grandson and namesake, in *Literary Magazine and American Register* 2 (July 1804): 257, which I discuss in a note in Chapter 4 below. Godwin also shared with John Churchman the extreme utopian and Gnostic impulse to transcend the corruptions of "mere animal function" into a life of pure spirit and truth. For Godwin, who was a thirty-year-old virgin when he published *Political Justice,* as for Churchman once when he was a young married man, this meant the temptations of a life beyond the ties of family and the lowly pleasures of sex. How, for Godwin, would mankind then propagate itself? His principle of "perfectibility" contemplated the possibility that man could perfect himself to the point of physical immortality. (Churchman contemplated immortality as well, but of the *after death* Christian variety.) On the weirdly "utopian" Godwin, see Gertrude Himmelfarb, *Marriage and Morals Among the Victorians* (New York, 1987), 144–62.

14. I am paraphrasing Godwin's instructions in "Of the Mode of Excluding Visitors," *Political Justice* (Philadelphia, 1796), 1: 284–86; *Diary of Elihu Hubbard Smith (1771–1798),* ed. James E. Cronin (Philadelphia, 1973), 164, 100–101, 170–71.

15. CBB to Bringhurst, n.d. (Bennett Census no. 42), CBB Coll., Me.

16. I borrow the phrase about "exile" from Joseph Bringhurst's uncle, also named Joseph, who wrote to his niece, Elizabeth Foulke, on November 15, 1798, about "the real pleasures of being & conversing with my own People, after a time of trying exile amongst Aliens & Strangers." See "Bringhurst Manuscripts (J), 1785–1811," box 1, Friends Historical Library, Swarthmore College. On Smith, see *Diary of Elihu Hubbard Smith,* 6–12, 17–35 (quote from 20), 88, 213, 247–52 (quote from 249), 258–66, 465–68. Smith was related to the first Puritan settlers of Massachusetts Bay and Hartford through his mother's side of the family, the Hubbards. *Diary of William Dunlap (1766–1839)* (New York, 1931), 1: 343.

17. *Diary of Elihu Hubbard Smith,* 48; see xi–xiii for brief biographies of Smith's friends. CBB to Bringhurst, May 22, 1793 (Bennett Census no. 43), CBB Coll., Me.

18. *Diary of Elihu Hubbard Smith*, 43, 146, 164, 74, 244. For a close reading of the Brown-Smith friendship with different emphases, see Caleb Crain, *American Sympathy: Men, Friendship, and Literature in the New Nation* (New Haven, Conn., 2001), 88–96.

19. James E. Cronin, "Elihu Hubbard Smith and the New York Friendly Club, 1795–1798," *Publications of the Modern Language Association* 64 (June 1949): 471–79; *Diary of Elihu Hubbard Smith*, 48, 247–52, 46, 124, 143.

20. CBB to Bringhurst, May 22, 1793, CBB Coll., Me.

21. CBB to Bringhurst, July 25, 1793 (Bennett Census no. 47), CBB Coll., Me.

22. J. H. Powell, *Bring Out Your Dead: The Great Plague of Yellow Fever in Philadelphia in 1793* (1949, reprint Philadelphia, 1993), 8–18, and 8–66 passim (quote from 72); William Currie, *A Description of the Malignant Infectious Fever* (Philadelphia, 1793), 25–29; Matthew Carey, *A Short Account of the Malignant Fever* (3rd ed., Philadelphia, 1793), 26–28; *Federal Gazette*, August 23, pp. 2–3, August 24, p. 3, August 26, p. 3, September 10, p. 1. For Brown family whereabouts, see Clement Biddle, *Philadelphia Directory* (Philadelphia, 1791), 15; Philadelphia Southern District Meeting files, pp. 304–12, dated August 25, 1790, Friends Historical Library, Swarthmore College. See discussion of *Ormond* below, in Chapter 5, for a further exploration into the Browns early 1790s circumstances.

23. CBB to Bringhurst, July 29, 1793 (Bennett Census no. 48), August 16, 1793 (Bennett Census no. 49), CBB Coll., Me. The latter letter is dated "Friday 16th Aug. 1793—Franklin's Office," which I take to be the office of his Latin School friend, William Franklin. William Dunlap, in *The Life of Charles Brockden Brown* (Philadelphia, 1815), 2: 3, recalled that CBB's "father's family, his brethren and himself were among those who fled in time to avoid [the yellow fever's] influence, and to escape the necessity of witnessing those scenes of loathsome misery which distinguished that disease."

24. CBB to Bringhurst, August 16, 1793, CBB Coll., Me. For "Helltown," see Billy G. Smith, *The "Lower Sort": Philadelphia's Laboring People, 1750–1800* (Ithaca, N.Y., 1990), 21–27. I closely follow Smith's wording here.

25. CBB to Bringhurst, August 16, 1793, CBB Coll., Me.; CBB to James Brown, April 19, 1795, CBB Coll., Va. CBB's brother, Armitt, in 1792 at least, was a clerk in the Treasury Department, making $500 a year doing this job: "Makes the Blotter Enteries and journalizes the Accots. of the late Government"; *Papers of Alexander Hamilton*, ed. Harold C. Syrett (New York, 1966–87), 11:392. CBB's mother—but not her three children—switched in June 1794 from the Northern District to the Southern District Monthly Meeting, indicating that that was when she and her husband moved back to the South Second Street Armitt house. CBB is listed, in 1794, in James Hardie's *Philadelphia Directory and Register*, 17, as "master of the friends grammar school 117 No. Second St." The "north" is clearly a mistake for "South." His brother Elijah, "clerk in the treasury department" (17), is also listed at 117 South Second Street. While this indicates that the whole family had moved back to Grandma Armitt's house by late 1794, it could mean too that CBB and brother Elijah had been living there, off and on, over the prior year. There is mystery surrounding CBB's youngest sister Catherine. Her birth date is unknown (see Mary Williams Smith, "The Browns of Nottingham, Penna. and Related Families," 11), and strangely she is never listed with the other members of the family in the Quaker Meeting records. Yet the federal census of 1790 has three white females living in the Elijah Brown household—no doubt his wife Mary, and daughters Elizabeth and Catherine—and a still-living Catherine is mentioned in Mary Brown's "Last Will," dated November 11, 1822 (see Society Collection, HSP). The implication is that there was something "special" about Catherine—that is, she was perhaps seriously handicapped in some way.

26. See [Joseph Bringhurst] to Debby Ferris, March 12, 19, and May 28, 1795; and CBB to Bringhurst, October 24, 1795 (Bennett Census no. 62) and December 29, 1795 (Bennett Census no. 67), CBB Coll., Me. For example of Debby Ferris's piety, see D. Ferris to Fanny Canby, March 1, 1795, box 1, Ferris Family Collection, Friends Historical Library, Swarthmore College.

27. *Diary of Elihu Hubbard Smith,* 147, 199.

28. *Moreau de St. Méry's American Journey,* trans. and ed. Kenneth Roberts and Anna M. Roberts (Garden City, N.Y., 1947), 146–47, 149; Arthur F. Young, *The Democratic Republicans of New York: The Origins, 1763–1797* (Chapel Hill, N.C., 1967), 469; Sidney I. Pomerantz, *New York: An American City, 1783–1803* (Port Washington, N.Y., 1965), 389–90; *Diary of Elihu Hubbard Smith,* 75, 81; Michael Kammen, *Colonial New York: A History* (White Plains, N.Y., 1987), 239–40.

29. *Diary of Elihu Hubbard Smith,* 147, 152, 164, 171. CBB's statement is in Smith's comment that "You have acknowledged that you once thought yourself at liberty to vary circumstances, in the narration." On Smith's attempt to "convert" Mrs. Tracy, see below.

30. CBB to Bringhurst, June 11, 1793 (Bennett Census no. 46), October 24, 1795 (Bennett Census no. 62), October 30, 1795 (Bennett Census no. 64), CBB Coll., Me.

31. *Diary of Elihu Hubbard Smith,* 248, 117–18.

32. [Debby Ferris] to Bringhurst, March 12, 13, 19, April 21, May 28, 1795; CBB to Bringhurst, October 24, 1795—all in CBB Coll., Me.; Philadelphia Monthly Meeting (Southern District) minutes, April 27, 1796, microfilm at Friends Historical Library, Swarthmore College.

33. Ibid.; Benj. Ferris to D. Ferris, Philadelphia, January 21, 1797, box 1, Ferris Family Collection, Friends Historical Library, Swarthmore College.

34. *Diary of Elihu Hubbard Smith,* 163–64.

35. Ibid., 164.

36. Ibid., 170.

37. CBB to Bringhurst, May 11, 1796 (Bennett Census no. 73), CBB Coll., Me.

38. *Diary of Elihu Hubbard Smith,* 18, 86, 87.

39. Ibid., 103–5 (my emphasis).

40. Ibid., 122.

41. Ibid., 448.

42. Cronin, "Elihu Hubbard Smith and the New York Friendly Club," 474, writes that "Charles Adams, for some unknown reason, attended no meetings after October 28, 1795." On the context, see Paul C. Nagel, *Descent from Glory: Four Generations of the John Adams Family* (New York, 1983), 78–79.

43. *Diary of Elihu Hubbard Smith,* 268.

44. Ibid., 268.

45. Ibid., 197–98, 146.

46. Ibid., 171; Honoré Riouffe, *Revolutionary Justice Displayed, or, An Inside View of the Various Prisoners of Paris, under the Government of Robespierre and the Jacobins* (Philadelphia, 1796), 22, 25, 58–61. Consider in this regard, too, a visit Smith made to Philadelphia in May 1797 to attend a Manumission Society convention. Smith was spending much time with CBB, but on the afternoon of May 5 he dined at "Dr. Wistar's, with Genl. Bloomfield & Mrs. Coxe, of Burlington, (N.J.) members of Convention, & Blair McClenechan." Of these four names, it is the last that would have piqued CBB's memory, for McClenachan, in the 1770s, was a Scots-Irish Presbyterian Revolutionary, and he took advantage of Henrietta Chew's father's exile and resulting disarranged business affairs to purchase Cliveden, the Chews' beloved country estate in Germantown. *Diary of Elihu Hubbard Smith,* 315–16. On Benjamin Chew and Cliveden, see Burton Alva Konkle, *Benjamin Chew, 1722–1810* (Philadelphia, 1932), 145–46, 189; and Roger W. Moss, *Historic Houses of Philadelphia* (Philadelphia, 1998), 116–20.

47. Stanley Elkins and Eric McKitrick, *The Age of Federalism: The Early American Republic, 1788–1800* (New York, 1993), 336–41; *Papers of Thomas Jefferson*, 25:469, 26:62, 545; James Roger Sharp, *American Politics in the Early Republic: The New Nation in Crisis* (New Haven, Conn., 1993), 87–88, 92–112.

48. The document Jay signed in London in November 1794 obligated Great Britain to fulfill the terms of the 1783 Peace of Paris and evacuate British troops from the American northwest, granted to American ships circumscribed trading rights in the British East and West Indies, granted Great Britain most-favored-nation status in American trade, conceded the duty of American citizens to pay off their prewar debts to British merchants, but gained no compensation for American slaveholders whose slaves had run off during the war with British troops. Elkins and McKitrick, *Age of Federalism*, 396–403; Sharp, *American Politics in the Early Republic*, 117–37.

49. Jefferson calls Hamilton a "colossus" in this context. See *Papers of Alexander Hamilton*, 18:476 n. 5.

50. *Papers of Alexander Hamilton*, 18:475–89, and esp. nn. 31–33 on 484–88; Young, *Democratic Republicans of New York*, 449–53; Seth Johnson quote on 451. Joanne B. Freeman, *Affairs of Honor: National Politics in the New Republic* (New Haven, Conn., 2001), xiii–xiv.

51. *Papers of Alexander Hamilton*, 18:471–72, and n. 1; Freeman, *Affairs of Honor*, xiii–xiv.

52. I follow Freeman's account here, *Affairs of Honor*, xiii–xiv.

53. *Papers of Alexander Hamilton*, 18:559–60. During the 1796 election season, one of the Federalist newspapers that attacked John Swanwick was the New York *Minerva*, edited by Elihu Smith's close friend Noah Webster. See James T. Callender, *American Annual Register; or, Historical Memoirs of the United States. For the Year 1796* (Philadelphia, 1797), 270–74.

54. *Papers of Alexander Hamilton*, 18:316 n. 3, 20:324; *Memoirs and Letters of James Kent, LL.D.*, ed. William Kent (Boston, 1898), 312–18; *Diary of Elihu Hubbard Smith*, 65, 139.

55. *Diary of Elihu Hubbard Smith*, 271.

56. Ibid., 272. Seeing as the Federalist Watson was a friend of Smith's, and he dined at his house on November 9, 1796 (244–45), it seems likely he would have voted for him.

57. On Swanwick see Roland M. Baumann, "The Democratic-Republicans of Philadelphia" (Ph.D. dissertation, Pennsylvania State University, 1970), 315–16, 328–41, 447, 460, 488–511, 518–23, 527–28, 535–37, 549–59; and "John Swanwick: Spokesman for 'Merchant-Republicanism' in Philadelphia, 1790–1798," *PMHB* (April 1973): 131–82. For Armitt Brown and George Remsen as Hamilton's clerks, see *Papers of Alexander Hamilton*, 11:390; 13:107. CBB's younger brother, Elijah, served as a clerk in the treasury department too, at least in 1794. See Hardie, *Philadelphia Directory*, 17. On the New York Remsens, see Phoenix Remsen, *Family Record of the Remsen Ancestry* (New York, 1878), esp. 11, 22–23, 35–36. Richard Waln did business with the "grocer" William Remsen and his son Jacob. Henry and George Remsen were their cousins. For a glimpse of Swanwick socializing with Alexander Wilcocks, Henrietta Chew, et al., see "Journals of William Rawle, 1782–1826," entry for July 22, 1786, Rawle Family Papers, HSP.

58. Baumann, "John Swanwick," 172, 178–80.

59. *Three Gothic Novels*, 429.

60. *Diary of Elihu Hubbard Smith*, 372; Alexander Hamilton, *Writings* (New York, 2001), 888; Broadus Mitchell, *Alexander Hamilton: The National Adventure, 1788–1804* (New York, 1962), 399–422.

61. If Hamilton had given James Reynolds the job, his co-worker would have been

Armitt Brown. Or perhaps he would have been given Charles's brother's job! Hamilton, *Writings*, 894–96.

62. Unfortunately, the Library of America edition of Hamilton's *Writings* does not include these appended letters—which Hamilton's journalist nemesis, James Callender, thought too good to have been written by Maria. That is, Callender thought Hamilton had composed "the Maria letters" too. See "Introductory Note" in *Papers of Alexander Hamilton*, 22:121–44. Reynolds's quotes from *Works of Alexander Hamilton*, ed. Henry Cabot Lodge (New York, n.d.), 423–34.

63. The Reynoldses moved to 161 Vine St. between June and August 1792. See ibid., 440–41. Thus the active sexual part of the affair, with Hamilton sometimes sneaking into Maria Reynolds's house, and more often Maria visiting Hamilton's house (while his wife was away in New York), took place when she lived elsewhere in Philadelphia, but the latter part of the sting operation was run out of 161 Vine.

64. At least it appears he began to write *Alcuin* at this juncture. On the context and dating of *Alcuin*, and its various guises, see the "Historical Essay" by Robert D. Arner in *Alcuin: A Dialogue; Memoirs of Stephen Calvert* (Kent, Ohio, 1987), 273–98.

65. Rosemarie Zagarri, "The Rights of Man and Woman in Post-Revolutionary America," *William and Mary Quarterly* 40 (April 1998): 203–30. On Paine's significance in the emergence of the first American party system, see Michael Durey, "Thomas Paine's Apostles: Radical Emigrés and the Triumph of Jeffersonian Republicanism," *WMQ* 44 (October 1987): 661–87.

66. *Alcuin*, 5–6.

67. Ibid., 17, 15, 14.

68. On these issues in general within the 1790s British-American cultural world, see G. J. Barker-Benfield, *The Culture of Sensibility: Sex and Society in Eighteenth-Century Britain* (Chicago, 1992).

69. *Alcuin*, 23, 28. John Adams most explicitly stated the underlying assumptions of the era's "Whig Science of Politics" in a letter to John Sullivan. See *Papers of John Adams*, ed. Robert J. Taylor (Cambridge, Mass., 1983), 4:208–13. See too Elaine Forman Crane, "Political Dialogue and the Spring of Abigail's Discontent," *WMQ* 56 (October 1999): 745–74, and Zaggari, "Rights of Man and Woman."

70. *Alcuin*, 23–24.

71. Ibid., 24–25.

72. See Chapter 2 above.

73. The second part of *Alcuin* was not published until 1815, five years after CBB's death. Charles E. Bennett, "The Charles Brockden Brown Canon" (Ph.D. dissertation, University of North Carolina, 1974), 182–86.

74. On Coleridge, see *Diary of Elihu Hubbard Smith*, 229, 296.

75. *Alcuin*, 34.

76. Ibid., 38–41. On Fox and the Quaker heritage in this regard, see Phyllis Mack, *Visionary Women: Ecstatic Prophecy in Seventeenth-Century England* (Berkeley, Calif., 1992).

77. *Alcuin*, 44–45 (my emphasis).

78. St. Clair, *Godwins and the Shelleys*, 141–44, 172.

79. *Alcuin*, 52, 60.

80. Ibid., 65.

81. *Diary of Elihu Hubbard Smith*, 239, 238, 268.

82. "The Man at Home" appeared in the *Weekly Magazine* from February 3 to April 28, 1798. The setting (Philadelphia suburb) and date (1797) are established in installments 1 and 2. See *The Rhapsodist and Other Uncollected Writings by Charles Brockden Brown*, ed. Harry R. Warfel (New York, 1943), 27–39. All subsequent quotes are from this edition, 27–98.

83. The "tribunal" Brown is alluding to here was the Pennsylvania Supreme Executive Council. See the Prologue above for the 1777–78 context. See also the

Quaker exiles' own contemporaneous published account of their experience, *An Address to the Inhabitants of Pennsylvania* . . . (Philadelphia, 1777), which Elijah Brown signed; and "Journal of the transactions of a number of the inhabitants of Philadelphia who were arrested on the second, third, fourth, and fifth days, of the 9th month 1777 under the Authority of a General Warrant," Pemberton Family Papers, vol. 31, pp. 79–84, HSP.

84. N.B.: *Address to the Inhabitants of Pennsylvania*, 18, refers to the soldiers who came to arrest Quakers as "messengers" too.

85. Brown, *The Rhapsodist*, 81–83. Two of the exiles, Thomas Gilpin and John Hunt, did die, and the wife of Israel Pemberton died soon after the ordeal, as did the elderly Israel himself.

Interlude

1. Richard G. Miller, *Philadelphia—The Federalist City: A Study of Urban Politics, 1789–1801* (Port Washington, N.Y., 1976), 53–61; George Gibbs, *Memoirs of the Administrations of Washington and John Adams, Edited from the Papers of Oliver Wolcott* (1846, reprint New York, 1971), 1: 160.

2. Stanley Elkins and Eric McKitrick, *The Age of Federalism: The Early American Republic, 1788–1800* (New York, 1993), 581–618; Miller, *Philadelphia*, 71–72; *Diary of Elizabeth Drinker*, ed. Elaine Forman Crane (Boston, 1991), 1: 581, 699–700, 741. In the 1790s too, as in the 1770s, young Quakers were being drafted into the militia—this time to fight the Whiskey Rebels. *Diary of Elizabeth Drinker*, 588.

3. *Diary of Elizabeth Drinker*, 2: 893, 901, 903, 905, 907, 908, 910, 913. See also 1027, 1036.

4. Ibid., 795, 783, 810, 694, 1052; 1: 654, 746; 2: 1001, 1004, 1012, 1031–32, 1037.

5. Ibid., 2: 1034, 1076, 1111–12; Miller, *Philadelphia*, 86, 115; Edward G. Carter II, "A 'Wild Irishman' Under Every Federalist's Bed: Naturalization in Philadelphia, 1789–1806," *PMHB* 94 (July 1970): 332–33, 339–43; Maurice J. Bric, "Ireland, Irishmen, and the Broadening of the Late-Eighteenth-Century Philadelphia Polity" (Ph.D. dissertation, Johns Hopkins University, 1990), 396–97, 438–45, 487–505. My Quaker figures come from Professor Susan Klepp (personal communication, March 1999).

6. Roland M. Baumann, "The Democratic-Republicans of Philadelphia: The Origins, 1776–1797" (Ph.D. dissertation, Pennsylvania State University, 1970), 315–16, 328–41, 488–511, 518–23, 527–28, 535–37, 549–59; Bric, "Ireland, Irishmen, and the Broadening of the Late-Eighteenth-Century Philadelphia Polity," 487–89; *Diary of Elizabeth Drinker*, 2: 1006–7.

7. *A Further Salutation of Brotherly Love, from the Monthly-Meetings of Friends of Philadelphia, to the Members of Our Religious Society, in and near the Said City* (Philadelphia, 1795), 4–7; *An Epistle from the Three Monthly-Meetings of Philadelphia, to the Members of Our Religious Society, in the City and Neighbourhood* (Philadelphia, 1799), 5.

8. *Diary of Elizabeth Drinker*, 2: 917, 916.

9. CBB, along with his mother, brother Elijah, and sister Elizabeth, formally "removed" to the Northern District Monthly Meeting in 1790, where he remained until January 1801, when he moved to the Southern District Monthly Meeting. See Philadelphia (Northern District) Meeting files, October 26, 1790 and January 27, 1801, Friends Historical Library, Swarthmore College. *Diary of Elihu Hubbard Smith (1771–1798)*, ed. James E. Cronin (Philadelphia, 1973), 315–16. A letter from Uriah Tracy in Philadelphia to his good friend Alexander Hamilton in New York, written six weeks earlier (March 23–24, 1797), conveys the rhetorical scurrility and violence typical of this time, and the persisting motif of "Swanwick": "I foresee a struggle

now in our Councils to send [James] Maddison or [Albert] Gallatin, or possibly John Swanwick or Ned Livingston, Envoy Extraordinary to the Cut-throat Directory. The United States, for fear of being subject to G. Britain will struggle hard, to be so to France. God in his infinite mercy grant, that we may be sunk in an Asphaltic Lake rise, where once stood the States—rather than subject ourselves to that nest of Assassins." *Papers of Alexander Hamilton*, ed. Harold C. Syrett (New York, 1974), 20:547–48.

10. Drinker places the crowds on Second Street, *Diary of Elizabeth Drinker*, 2: 916.

Chapter 4. Sins of Fathers

1. On CBB and the Yates murder, see Alexander Cowie's "Historical Essay" in *Wieland; or the Transformation: An American Tale—Memoirs of Carwin the Biloquist*, vol. 1 of *The Novels and Related Works of Charles Brockden Brown, Bicentennial Edition*, ed. Sydney J. Krause et al. (Kent, Ohio, 1977–87), 319–21. I have taken the quotes from Carl Van Doren, "Early American Realism," *Nation*, November 12, 1914, 577–78.

2. Cowie, "Historical Essay," 319–22.

3. Ibid., 427–33.

4. For Anthony Benezet, see George Brookes, *Friend Anthony Benezet* (Philadelphia, 1937), 1–18; and see Sarah Logan Fisher "Diaries," vol. 13, p. 26, HSP, for quite typical Philadelphia Quaker expression of feeling for "that great good Man Anthony Benezet." See "Elijah Brown and Mary Armitt Marriage Certificate, July 9, 1761," Henry A. Brown Collection, HSP, for Benezet's attendance at CBB's parents' wedding. On the Camisards or "French Prophets," and the London context of the late seventeenth and early eighteenth centuries, see Hillel Schwartz, *The French Prophets: The History of a Millenarian Group in Eighteenth-Century England* (Berkeley, Calif., 1980), 11–112. For the Quaker side of this context, see William I. Hull, *William Penn and the Dutch Quaker Migration to Pennsylvania* (Philadelphia, 1935). See also C. E. Whiting, *Studies in English Puritanism from the Restoration to the Revolution, 1660–1688* (New York, 1931), 295–310.

5. The text is from Charles Brockden Brown, *Three Gothic Novels* (New York, 1998), 10–11. I will use this text for all *Wieland* quotations. On Kelpius, see Elizabeth W. Fisher, "'Prophesies and Revelations': German Cabbalists in Early Pennsylvania," *PMHB* 109 (July 1985): 299–331; Julius F. Sachse, *The German Pietists of Provincial Pennsylvania* (Philadelphia, 1895), 70–73, 205–15; Stephen L. Longenecker, *Piety and Tolerance: Pennsylvania German Religion, 1700–1850* (Metuchen, N.J., 1994), 27–32. To link the "Mettingen" of *Wieland* with the Wissahickon locale of Kelpius (and Henry Koster—see below), some footwork is necessary. In the novel, Mettingen is sited "five miles" outside Philadelphia, on the Schuylkill River (*Three Gothic Novels*, 123). This turns out to be where the Schuylkill meets the Wissahickon, and is where the Kelpius community lived. In reference to CBB's world, the spot is within easy walking distance of Cliveden, the country home of the Benjamin Chews, and it abuts land owned in the late eighteenth century by the Bringhurst family (Sachse, *German Pietists*, 424). The illustration introducing this chapter is a 1999 photograph taken by me at this spot.

6. Sachse, *German Pietists*, 13–19; Fisher, "German Cabbalists," 319–22; Hull, *William Penn and the Dutch Quaker Migration*, 253–54, 328–39; and William I. Hull, *Benjamin Furly and Quakerism in Rotterdam* (Lancaster, Pa., 1941); Whiting, *English Puritanism*, 295–310; Schwartz, *French Prophets*, 47 n. 31, 52–54, 86–87, 204.

Consider, in relation to CBB's text, the Philadelphians' leader of the time, Jane Leade, and her description of the four types of "revelation" of the Holy Spirit: (1) *visions*, which are heavenly shapes or images spiritually perceived by the inner sense of man; (2) *illuminations*, which occur when a ray of divine light "falls" upon the soul and makes some hidden things clear; (3) *immediate translations*, through which the spirit is carried up into the kingdom of God to behold the mysteries therein; (4) *the descent of the Holy Spirit into the soul*, when the soul gains complete regeneration and illumination; Whiting, *English Puritanism*, 300.

7. Sachse, *German Pietists*, 15–16, 70–71; Johannes Kelpius, *A Method of Prayer*, ed. E. Gordon Alderfer (New York, 1951), 91, 117–18, 122, 127. The bracketed text represents where the editor has surmised mangled text in the manuscript.

8. Jon Butler, "Into Pennsylvania's Spiritual Abyss: The Rise and Fall of the Later Keithians, 1693–1703," *PMHB* 101 (April 1977): 151–70; Dietmar Rothermund, *The Layman's Progress: Religious and Political Experience in Colonial Pennsylvania, 1740–1770* (Philadelphia, 1961), 1–15; Sachse, *German Pietists*, 79–80, 84–92; "The Missive of Justus Falckner, of Germantown, Concerning the Religious Condition of Pennsylvania in the Year 1701," trans. Julius F. Sachse, *PMHB* 21 (1897): 218–19.

9. "Account Concerning William Brown," pp. 4–5. See Chapter 1 note 1 above for a description of this document. The "Account" also records this exchange between Keith and James Browne: "Keith had a meeting at the house of Henry Reynolds, who lived near, and he knowing that James Brown had rather favoured him, on his way to the meeting called at James's house and asked if he was going to meeting; at which James hesitated; whereupon George Keith alighted and went in, intimating that if he began to be dissatisfied he would satisfy him; and though he used many words, all did not avail, for James went not to meeting and was favoured with preservation from further harm by that wily, separating spirit." There is also a record, from 1688, of Honour Brown—James's wife, and CBB's great-great grand-mother—running into problems with the Chichester Monthly Meeting. See Concord Quarterly Meeting minutes, 1684–1767, pp. 7–8, microfilm at Friends Historical Library, Swarthmore College. What the "matter concerning Honour Brown" entailed—did it involve heterodox beliefs, or just un-Quakerly decorum?—is not recorded. What the records state is that Honour Brown was visited by a committee of Friends, and subsequently she "doth acknowledged her faults tenderly & is Sorry for the same, & hath given a publick paper from under her hand to the Satisfaction of Friends, and for the Clearing of truth."

10. Gary Nash, *Quakers and Politics; Pennsylvania, 1681–1726* (Princeton, N.J., 1968), 144–61; Jon Butler, "Into Pennsylvania's Spiritual Abyss," 151–70; J. William Frost, *The Keithian Controversy in Early Pennsylvania* (Norwood, Pa., 1980), i–xx.

11. Fisher, "'Prophesies and Revelations,'" 313–16; Allison Coudert, "A Quaker-Kabbalist Controversy: George Fox's Reaction to Francis Mercury Van Helmont," *Journal of the Warburg and Courtauld Institute* 39 (1976): 171–89; and Hull, *Benjamin Furly and Quakerism in Rotterdam*, 105–23.

12. Fisher, "'Prophesies and Revelations'"; Coudert, "A Quaker-Kabbalist Controversy"; H. Larry Ingle, *First Among Friends: George Fox and the Creation of Quakerism* (New York, 1994), 64, 246; Richard Bailey, *New Light on George Fox and Early Quakerism: The Making and Unmaking of a God* (San Francisco, 1992); Sachse, *German Pietists*. While Zimmermann never made it to Pennsylvania, part of his library did—into James Logan's collection. See Edwin Wolf II, *The Library of James Logan of Philadelphia, 1674–1751* (Philadelphia, 1974), 578. On James Logan's place in CBB's tale, see Chapter 6 below.

13. Sachse, *German Pietists*, 70–72 (my emphasis). The description of the late eighteenth-century tabernacle ruin (71–72 n. 105), I should specify, comes from Sachse, whose information comes from someone—unnamed—who knew some-one—also unnamed—who "had in his youth frequently seen and been about the ruins of the old structure." Sachse, in this context, refers to the nineteenth-century Philadelphia novelist George Lippard, who was an admirer of CBB, and who indeed wrote a novel about, in part, the Wissahickon mystics—*Paul Ardenheim, the Monk of*

Wissahikon (Philadelphia, 1848)—which was clearly inspired, in part at least, by *Wieland*. Concord Quarterly Meeting minutes, 1684–1767, December 12, 1695, pp. 19–21.

14. Philadelphia Yearly Meeting minutes, July 7, 1696, pp. 58–59, microfilm at Friends Historical Library, Swarthmore College. The Brown family memoir ("Account") indicates that sometime before Keith's 1694 departure for England, James Browne had been first attracted by Keith's doctrines and then talked out of this heterodoxy by his brother William. The deep and continuing communal saga of Keithianism, however, is indicated by the fact that one of the witnesses at the marriage of James and Honour (Clayton) Brown in Burlington in 1679, Thomas Budd, was in the early to mid-1690s a leading Keithian. Eventually, Budd would not return to the Quaker fold, but move on to the Baptists. See Mary Williams Smith, "The Browns of Nottingham, Penna and Related Families," ix, manuscript at Chester County Historical Society; Frost, *Keithian Controversy*, 127–32, 134; and Butler, "Into Pennsylvania's Spiritual Abyss," 163, 168.

15. Sachse, *German Pietists*, 73; John Churchman, *An Account of the Gospel Labours, and Christian Experiences of a Faithful Minister of Christ* (Philadelphia, 1779), 34, 2, 34, 6. Churchman, elsewhere in his memoir, 46, notes that "Having a concern on my mind to visit the meetings of friends on the Eastern shore in Maryland," he asked the Nottingham Meeting for a certificate to travel there, and he received it. On the spiritual trip, he further records, "my brother in law James Brown [that is, Elijah's father and CBB's grandfather] bearing me company."

16. Sachse, *German Pietists*, 78–83, 141–43.

17. Why does CBB have Wieland build a circle-shaped "temple"? One possibility is that he is basing the shape on the remains of Kelpius's "tabernacle," as it existed in CBB's own day (See note 13 above). Why does he have Wieland choose *twelve* columns? Perhaps CBB is referencing the eschatology and the central biblical text of Kelpius and Koster's "Society of Woman in the Wilderness," Revelation 12: "And there appeared a great wonder in heaven; a woman clothed with the sun, and the moon under her feet, and upon her head a crown of twelve stars: . . . And the woman fled into the wilderness, where she hath a place prepared of God."

18. *The Journal of George Fox*, ed. Rufus M. Jones (Richmond, Ind., 1983), 132; William Penn, *The Peace of Europe, the Fruits of Solitude and Other Writings* (London, 1993), 292, 259; John Woolman, *Works of Woolman in Two Parts* (Philadelphia, 1800), 68–69; Churchman, *An Account*, 185–86; Kelpius, *A Method of Prayer*, 91. That Elijah Brown was intensely interested in his uncle John Churchman is established by the Churchman-William Brown letters that Elijah himself transcribed into one of his notebooks. See Charles Brocken Brown Manuscripts, vol. 1, HSP. In this context, it seems to me, it is highly unlikely that Elijah, and his bookish son CBB—and indeed the whole Brown family—wouldn't be familiar with Churchman's published "testimony."

19. The rhetoric of "illumination" and "light" was, of course, the distinctive language of CBB's people. Here is an example of Elijah Brown's cousin, George Churchman, employing the rhetoric in a letter to the recently liberated exile John Pemberton in May 1778: "Tho' I do not expect that either you there [in Philadelphia] or we that live in the Country [in East Nottingham], will be exempted from such a Portion of Difficulties of various kinds, as may be suffer'd or allotted unto us for our Refining, believing that to be a principal End for which the late, & present Adversities are permitted to come upon us & may it have the happy Effect of refining, on us the present Professors of the Pure Truth; then may we as availingly as our Predecessors minister Light & Instruction to many of our Neighbours, who have long sat in Darkness, & some of them (perhaps) waiting for Benefit herein from us heretofore. . . . I humbly hope there will be a Brightening with many under

the Trials, both in town & Country, & sometimes have that I did perceive a Glimpse of the Attention that would arise from it, as Divine Brightness comes to be more Visible"; Pemberton Family Papers, vol. 32, p. 72, HSP. There would have been much talk like this, too, around the Brown house and the Meeting in May 1778 and beyond. For CBB's curious 1804 essay on George Churchman's son, see note 28 below. For quotes: Sarah Logan Fisher "Diaries"—the Fishers lived just down the street from the Browns—vol. 2, pp. 51–52, vol. 3, pp. 23–24; *Diary of Elizabeth Drinker*, 1: 228–29. Another literary offshoot of this context was Hannah Griffitts' poem "The glorious 4th July 1777—Commemorated by H. Griffitts":

What Times are these:— a perfect Riddle
Whence fled, the Scenes of former Quiet
Bless us! When Patriots hum a fiddle
And Generals form, and head the Riot

The unarmed Quakers— & the Tories
Sustained the Horrors of the night. . . .

Still as a Foil, Ye new Law Makers,
"To former Happiness" remain
Blunderers, go on, despise thee Quakers
You men shall their height attain
The Wisdom of their gentle Ruling
"Can bear the retrospective View"
And this with all your boasted School[in]g
Is more— than will be said of you.
In Pemberton Family Papers, vol. 30, p. 58.

20. Nicholas Waln signed "To the President and Council of Pennsylvania," Philadelphia, September 5, 1777, Quaker Collection, Haverford College. As the Philadelphia Meeting's most prominent "minister," it is inconceivable that he wasn't among the many visitors to the Masonic Lodge. As a Second Street neighbor, it is also a near certainty that he visited the Browns often during this traumatic period. His presence is certainly recorded in the extant diaries of other exiles' families. See, for example, *Diary of Elizabeth Drinker*, 1: 230 (September 15, 1777), 259 (November 22, 1777). Richard Waln's temper and pragmatism are on view in his letterbooks at the HSP, and nowhere more so than in his May 26, 1770, letter to Elijah Brown; in "Letterbook 1766–1794," Richard Waln Papers, HSP. For the Walns' support during Virginia exile period, see Chapter 1 above. Richard Waln was exiled to New York in October 1777.

21. For a sense of CBB's environment in 1798, consider Thomas Jefferson's description of a political riot in Philadelphia, in early May: "A fray ensued, the light horse were called in, and the city was so filled with confusion from about 6 to 10 o'clock last night that it was dangerous going out." A New Yorker's description of New York City in mid-July, one week after CBB moved there from Philadelphia to finish *Wieland*: "Our city resembles a camp rather than a commercial port. Volunteer companies of horse and infantry are raising; and meetings of the old officers of the army and navy—and of the citizens, in the different wards have been had to concert measures for the defence of our port." Both quotes in James Roger Sharp, *American Politics in the Early Republic: The New Nation in Crisis* (New Haven, Conn., 1993), 175, 180.

22. The context: "The Indians were repulsed on the one side, and Canada was conquered on the other. Revolutions and battles, however calamitous to those who occupied the scene, contributed in some sort to our happiness, by agitating our

minds with curiosity, and furnishing causes of patriotic exultation"; *Three Gothic Novels*, 25.

23. See, for example, Larzer Ziff, "A Reading of *Wieland*," *Publications of the Modern Language Association* 77 (March 1962): 51–57; William Hedges, "Charles Brockden Brown and the Culture of Contradictions," *Early American Literature* 9 (Fall 1974): 107–63; Jay Fliegelman, *Prodigals and Pilgrims: The American Revolution Against Patriarchal Authority, 1750–1800* (Cambridge, 1982), 237–45. The first Pennsylvania Revolutionary quote comes from William Shippen, cited in Douglas McNeil Arnold, "Political Ideology and the Internal Revolution in Pennsylvania, 1776–1790" (Ph.D. dissertation, Princeton University, 1976), 57; the second from Thomas Smith, cited in Paul Selsam, *The Pennsylvania Constitution of 1776* (Philadelphia, 1936), 205. CBB has Theodore refer to "the testimony of my senses" on 30, *Three Gothic Novels*.

24. It seems to me that the literary critic Christopher Looby invokes the wrong "Saxony" in his discussion of *Wieland* in *Voicing America: Language, Literary Form, and the Origins of the United States* (Chicago, 1996), 149–58, as he inappropriately involves CBB in the civic humanist dialogue of the Revolutionaries. CBB simply did not share, as Looby assumes—and, for that matter, as Michael Warner assumes in *The Letters of the Republic: Publication and the Public Sphere in Eighteenth-Century America* (Cambridge, Mass., 1990)—a common Whig culture with the likes of James Wilson, James Madison, Thomas Jefferson, or Benjamin Franklin, and it is nonsensical to assert that "Brown's fixation on Saxony is determined by this prevalent political myth"—the Whig notion of pre-eighth-century Anglo-Saxon England as a special land of liberty—"and by its problematic relevance to American society. It is [Brown's] anxiety concerning the apparent groundlessness of American political legitimacy that makes him at once wish for a connection to a determinate and authoritative Saxon origin, and at the same time despair of reclaiming it" (Looby, 157). *Charles Brown?* Looby has the wrong guy.

25. See, for example, Nina Baym, "A Minority Reading of *Wieland*," in *Critical Essays on Charles Brockden Brown*, ed. Bernard Rosenthal (Boston, 1981), 95.

26. I believe the associational process here was conscious or at least semiconscious, as it clearly was in CBB's installment 11 of the "Man at Home." On the other hand, it could have been "unconscious" in the sense that CBB might have been able to write out of a "visionary" state that he neither examined nor analyzed, but just accepted—and nurtured—as the fount of his art. Perhaps a sign of the latter case would be his peculiar use of the word "treason" on 61 (*Three Gothic Novels*), through which Clara means to connote the threat she feels pending against her life. While this is solid eighteenth-century usage, its appearance at this particular place in the novel is a little unusual—though in terms of the experiential basis of the material, entirely appropriate. Did the word just innocently flow from CBB's pen, or was he being wickedly ironic? In either case, in the American 1790s CBB operated at a rare level of artistic density and sophistication.

27. He is also radically "ironizing" the resulting literary text, for if Clara's narration is, as she concedes, "invaded by inaccuracy and confusion" because "what but ambiguities, abruptnesses, and dark transitions, can be expected from the historian who is, at the same time, the sufferer of these disasters?" (*Three Gothic Novels*, 137), what can be said of CBB's own narration?

28. One final note needs to be added to this account of *Wieland* as family biography and tribal allegory. In CBB's family, the Churchman strain was the most radically visionary. John Churchman (1705–75) had had his visions, and so had his son George (1730–1814), whom CBB inevitably would have known. This George Churchman, who in the 1750s was clerk of the Philadelphia Yearly Meeting and who was a leader of Quaker "reform" throughout the late eighteenth century, was Elijah

Brown's cousin. (George's mother was the daughter of James Browne the immigrant, who in 1690s Chichester, amid all the ferment about astrologers and stargazers and magicians, had talked his brother James—CBB's great-great-grandfather—out of Keithianism.) This George Churchman's son John was CBB's cousin. So this John Churchman's line ran directly back to William Browne the immigrant, as CBB's line ran back to James Browne the immigrant—with the two lines intersecting many times along the way through Churchman-Brown marriages—and both lines ultimately uniting in Richard Browne of Northamptonshire, that "seeking, religious man" who was the family's *ur*-Quaker.

In 1804, CBB published a curious article on his cousin John Churchman (1755–1805), a surveyor, geometrician, and nautical mapmaker. This short piece appeared in Philadelphia's *Literary Magazine and American Register*, which CBB edited. "This singular man," CBB wrote about his cousin John, "is one of those examples of self-instructed genius, with which America abounds more than any other part of the world. His family were farmers, and the intimations and suggestions of his own mind, as he guided the plough or loaded the stack, led him to the study of arithmetic and astronomy. He has been distinguished, all his life, by an enterprising and indefatigable zeal. Without any external grace or liberal acquaintance with any branch of knowledge but mathematics, with a most obscure and imperfect elocution, ungainly person, and rustic manners, he has made vigorous efforts, both in Europe and America, to set himself at the head of maritime expeditions of great national expense and importance. He has made himself known to all the philosophers of Europe."

Now for most of CBB's readers in 1804 (and since), this portrait of a "self-instructed genius" no doubt evoked (and evokes) the figure of Benjamin Franklin. But almost certainly CBB himself had other models in mind. The "Churchman" lineage, the rusticity and ungainly person (by which CBB means that John Churchman grew up in Nottingham), *the arithmetic and astronomy*—these elements tie the second John Churchman not to Franklinian tinkerers but to the tradition of Kelpius (whose very tabernacle was designed according to astronomical considerations and a mystical theory of numbers), Zimmermann (mathematician and onetime professor of astronomy), van Helmont, and perhaps—who knows?—to William (really Richard) Browne himself, that seeking man who was accused of "witchcraft" back in Northamptonshire, and to whom CBB and John Churchman were in the exact same degree related. As with the Wielands, the visionary knack just seemed to flow in Brown-Churchman veins, and it was a quality CBB monitored in other family members, and proclaimed and nurtured—and with *Wieland*, perhaps, began to worry about—in himself. *Literary Magazine and American Register* 2 (July 1804): 257.

Chapter 5. The Anti-Godwin

1. I borrow the term "fiction of ideas" from Warner Berthoff, "'A Lesson on Concealment': Brockden Brown's Method in Fiction," *Philological Quarterly* 37 (January 1958): 45–57. Berthoff means to apply it to all of CBB's fiction. I want to make a distinction between CBB's truly "Gothic" line of fiction—*Wieland* and *Edgar Huntly*—and his Godwinian "fiction of ideas" line—which includes the works under consideration in this chapter.

2. William Godwin, *Caleb Williams*, ed. David McCracken (based on 1794 edition; New York, 1977), 1–2; William St. Clair, *The Godwins and the Shelleys* (New York, 1989), 85, 119–26; Albert Goodwin, *The Friends of Liberty: The English Democratic Movement in the Age of the French Revolution* (Cambridge, Mass., 1979), 332–34.

3. *Caleb Williams*, 77, 17.

4. Ibid., 109, 107, 108, 135–36.

5. Ibid., 300.

6. Ibid., 73.

7. Ibid., 177–78.

8. St. Clair, *Godwins and the Shelleys*, 118–19, 112–14, 110; CBB to Joseph Bring-hurst, n.d. (Bennett Census no. 9), CBB Coll., Me.

9. *Caleb Williams*, 323, 324; Cathy N. Davidson, *Revolution and the Word: The Rise of the Novel in America* (New York, 1986), 253. Davidson's section on *Arthur Mervyn* is masterful.

10. On the writing of *Arthur Mervyn*, see S. W. Reid's "Historical Essay" in *Arthur Mervyn*, vol. 3 of *The Novels and Related Works of Charles Brockden Brown*, ed. Sydney J. Krause ([Kent, Ohio], 1980), esp. 449–58, 450, 469.

11. Charles Brockden Brown, *Three Gothic Novels* (New York, 1998), 237, 244, 256, 247, 251, 253, 254. All quotes will be from this edition.

12. *Philadelphia Merchant: The Diary of Thomas P. Cope, 1800–1851*, ed. Eliza Cope Harrison (South Bend, Ind., 1978), 65.

13. On Swanwick and Hamilton, and Welbeck, see Chapter 3 above. Richard Godbeer quotes the Frenchman Moreau de St. Méry on Philadelphia brothels, and "a certain well-known gentleman" who left "his horse tied to the post outside one of these houses, so that everyone knows when he is there and exactly how long he stays." Godbeer, *Sexual Revolution in Early America* (Baltimore, 2002), 303. Could this have been Hamilton? Moreau, who knew Hamilton, is too much the gentleman him-self to "out" the individual he has in mind. But by Henry Remsen's account of Hamilton's "licentious & indiscriminate indulgence" in "the most common houses" of Philadelphia, it's clear the treasury secretary would fit the bill for the "well-known gentleman." *Diary of Elihu Hubbard Smith (1771–1798)*, ed. James E. Cronin (Philadelphia, 1973), 271.

14. On the trial-like aspect of *Arthur Mervyn*, see Davidson, *Revolution and the Word*, 240, 247, and 236–53 in general.

15. On Arthur and the city, contrast 494 and 370, *Three Gothic Novels*.

16. Charles Brockden Brown, *Literary Essays and Reviews*, ed. Alfred Weber and Wolfgang Schäfer (Frankfurt am Main, 1992), 33, 31, 35, 37, 39.

17. On CBB's relationship with Susan Potts and its quasi-furtive nature, see *Diary of Elihu Hubbard Smith*, 440.

18. James Roger Sharp, *American Politics in the Early Republic: The New Nation in Crisis* (New Haven, Conn., 1993), 163–84. Quotes from 173 and 174.

19. Stanley Elkins and Eric McKitrick, *The Age of Federalism: The Early American Republic, 1788–1800* (New York, 1993), 590–92; Sharp, *American Politics in the Early Republic*, 188–207.

20. Vernon Stauffer, *New England and the Bavarian Illuminati* (New York, 1967), 142–287. On the historical context of the Illuminati, see as well James H. Billington, *Fire in the Minds of Men* (New York, 1980), 88–123; and Larry E. Tise, *The American Counterrevolution: A Retreat from Liberty, 1783–1800* (Mechanicsburg, Pa., 1998), 326–97.

21. *Diary of Elihu Hubbard Smith*, 349.

22. Ibid., 418, 390. These quotes are not from the summer of 1798 but from January 1798 and November 1797.

23. Ibid., 449; Noah Webster, *An Oration Pronounced before the Citizens of New-Haven on the Anniversary of the Independence of the United States, July 4th, 1798* (New Haven, Conn., 1798), 13; Humphrey Marshall, *The Aliens: A Patiotic Poem* (Philadelphia, 1798), 11, 18.

24. *Diary of Elihu Hubbard Smith*, 450–52, 448; Thomas Day, *An Oration on Party Spirit, Pronounced before the Connecticut Society of Cincinnati, Convened at Hartford, for the Celebration of American Independence, on the 4th of July, 1798* (Litchfield, 1798), 15.

25. Theodore Dwight, *Oration, Spoken at Hartford . . . on the Anniversary of American Independence* (Hartford, 1798), 4, 12–19, 25, 30 (n. 4).

26. *Diary of Elihu Hubbard Smith*, 454; John Robison, *Proofs of a Conspiracy against All the Religions and Governments of Europe, Carried on in the Secret Meetings of Free Masons, Illuminati, and Reading Societies* (4th ed.; New York, 1798), 10.

27. *Diary of Elihu Hubbard Smith*, 454.

28. Ibid., 259; Timothy Dwight, *The Duty of Americans, at the Present Crisis, Illustrated in a Discourse, Preached on the Fourth of July, 1798* (published at New Haven, 1798), in *Political Sermons of the American Founding Era, 1730–1805*, ed. Ellis Sandoz (Indianapolis, 1991), 1388, 1374.

29. *Diary of Elihu Hubbard Smith*, 455.

30. *Diary of William Dunlap (1766–1839)* (New York, 1931), 1: 292, 324, 336.

31. See *Diary of Elihu Hubbard Smith*, 449 n. 42. Smith did evidence that "sincerity" in regard to the Illuminati, in January 1798, in response to an article he read about the Abbé Barruel's *Memoirs of Jacobinism*. On that occasion, he had logically wondered how Barruel could have known such horrible things as he attests about "the highest order of Freemasons" without being one himself, in which case "he could not have exposed their secrets." Smith further noted in his diary, commonsensically: "It is desirable to discover whence has arisen this strange belief respecting the agency of Freemasonry in the overthrow of Kings and priests. It is certainly very singular—especially as the general conviction is to the contrary; as the Free Masons are supposed, as far as they profess any sentiment, to be friendly to Xtianity, as the Illuminated, are deemed the most superstitious of men; & as many of the Philosophers here charged with favoring & directing the movements of these sects & societies, have been most active in writing, & otherwise influencing the public mind against them." Ibid., 412. Significantly, I think, with and after his summer trip to Connecticut, Smith does not offer this type of reasoned analysis of Robison's *Proofs*, a work every bit as illogical in its connections as Barruel's *Memoirs*.

32. *Diary of William Dunlap*, 1:335–36.

33. An example of CBB speaking in the Friendly Club "rationalist manner" is in a letter written jointly by CBB, Johnson, and Smith to Dunlap, in which CBB asks Dunlap, "Why are your Christian allusions so frequent?"—which is paraphrased by, "let us have no allusions to the Vulgar cant of the religionists"; ibid., 335–36.

34. Ibid., 338–39.

35. Robison, *Proofs of a Conspiracy*, 10–11, 14.

36. Ibid., 18–19, 30–33 (my emphasis).

37. *Diary of Elihu Hubbard Smith*, 438.

38. Robison, *Proofs of a Conspiracy*, 87, 84, 48; *Diary of Elihu Hubbard Smith*, 148.

39. Robison, *Proofs of a Conspiracy*, 39. The Quaker-Illuminati analogue was drawn out by a New England critic of Robison. See Stauffer, *New England and the Bavarian Illuminati*, 262–63. The mystical underpinnings of Freemasonry, and indeed the vital part played by the Hermetic tradition in the making of the pre-Enlightenment European intellectual and cultural world, has been brilliantly suggested by Frances A. Yates in her *Giordano Bruno and the Hermetic Tradition* (Chicago, 1964), esp. 398–455. This rich cultural world, which the early Quakers—and many other "seekers" in seventeenth-, early eighteenth-century England and Germany—were variously immersed in, was an embarrassment to eighteenth-century American Quaker leaders, who wrote it out of their histories, even as CBB was writing it *back* into his "fictions." See, for example, the Philadelphia Meeting-subsidized *History of Pennsylvania* by CBB's teacher, Robert Proud. Modern historians too have for the most part omitted this mystical component from the story of early American thought and culture, until, that is, the recent suggestive work by David D. Hall and Jon Butler; John L. Brooke's revelatory *The Refiner's Fire: The Making of Mormon Cosmology,*

1644–1844 (New York, 1994), Leigh Eric Schmidt's *Hearing Things: Religion, Illusion, and the American Enlightenment* (Cambridge, Mass., 2000), and the recent essays by Susan Juster.

40. Robison, *Proofs of a Conspiracy*, 79–87; William Dunlap, *Memoirs of Charles Brockden Brown, an American Novelist* (London, 1822), 46; see, too, Charles E. Bennett, "The Charles Brockden Brown Canon" (Ph.D. dissertation, University of North Carolina, 1974), 163–82.

41. Carwin is described as "engaged in schemes, reasonably suspected to be, in the highest degree, criminal, but such as no human intelligence is able to unravel: that his ends are pursued by means which leave it in doubt whether he be not in league with some infernal spirit: that his crimes have hitherto been perpetuated with the aid of some unknown but desperate accomplices: that he wages a perpetual war against the happiness of mankind, and sets his engines of destruction at work against every object that presents itself." *Three Gothic Novels*, 122.

42. *Wieland; or The Transformation: An American Tale—Memoirs of Carwin the Biloquist*, vol. 1 of *The Novels and Related Works of Charles Brockden Brown*, ed. Sydney J. Krause et al. (Kent, Ohio, 1977), 247.

43. Ibid., 247, 254.

44. Ibid., 263–64.

45. Ibid., 265.

46. Ibid., 268, 266.

47. Ibid., 269, 271.

48. Ibid., 273–75 (my emphasis).

49. Ibid., 283, 281–82, 275, 280. Dietmar Rothermund, in his preface to *The Layman's Progress: Religious and Political Experience in Colonial Pennsylvania, 1740–1770* (Philadelphia, 1961), xiv, makes this point. "Rationalism and mysticism are not contradictory approaches: they spring from the same source, the reliance on inner light and [inner] experience rather than on authority and tradition." Rothermund further notes, at xv, in a reference to early Pennsylvania history that links the worlds of *Wieland* and "Carwin"/*Ormond*: "The common background of religious speculation and scientific interest could be demonstrated by numerous individual examples. Thus the leader of the first pietist group migrating to Pennsylvania was the minister and mathematician Zimmermann; Zinzendorf, the imaginative revivalist, carried Pierre Bayle's dictionary in his pocket on most of his travels."

50. See *Diary of Elihu Hubbard Smith*, 463; *Diary of William Dunlap*, 1: 335; "Historical Essay," in *Wieland—Carwin*, 335–37 (CBB quote is on 336), and esp. n. 36. CBB later returned to "Carwin" manuscript in 1803–5, and wrote additional installments.

51. *Diary of Elihu Hubbard Smith*, 462–64.

52. *Diary of William Dunlap*, 1: 343.

53. See Sydney Krause's "Historical Notes" on the 1790s context of *Ormond*, in *Ormond; or The Secret Witness*, vol. 2 of *The Novels and Related Works of Charles Brockden Brown*, 389–478.

54. Charles Brockden Brown, *Ormond*, ed. Ernest Marchand (New York, 1937), 5. All quotes from the novel will be from this edition. Joseph Ellis, *After the Revolution: Profiles of Early American Culture* (New York, 1979), 121–26. CBB may have patterned another figure in the book after Samuel Dunlap, too: the "nightly watchman," Baxter, who had been "an English grenadier at Dettingen and Minden." *Ormond*, 52.

55. *Ormond*, 92, 93, 94 (my emphasis).

56. Ibid., 104, 112.

57. Dwight, *Duty of Americans*, 1374. See note 28 above.

58. *Ormond*, 146, 147.

59. Ibid., 231, 232.

60. Ibid., 203.

61. Brown, *Literary Essays and Reviews*, 4, 14; on letter to Wilkins, see Chapter 2 above.

62. *Ormond*, 14, 16, 6, 33 (my emphasis).

63. Ibid., 16, 25, 28, 35.

64. Billy G. Smith, *The "Lower Sort": Philadelphia's Laboring People, 1750–1800* (Ithaca, N.Y., 1990), 21.

65. *Ormond*, 47.

66. Francis White, *Philadelphia Directory* (Philadelphia, 1785), 4.

67. *Heads of Families at the First Census of the United States Taken in the Year 1790— Pennsylvania* (Washington, D.C., 1908), 199; Clement Biddle, *Philadelphia Directory* (Phila., 1791), 4, 15; CBB to Bringhurst, May 15, 1792 (Bennett Census no. 18), CBB Coll., Me.; Edmund Hogan, *The Prospect of Philadelphia* (Philadelphia, 1795), 119. The fact that Mary Brown, in June 1794, "removed" from the Northern District Monthly Meeting to the Southern District Monthly Meeting indicates that the Browns moved from Vine back to South Second Street at that time. See Southern District Meeting files, p. 19–3, Friends Historical Library, Swarthmore College. In 1795—to set the social ambiance of the Browns' Vine Street neighborhood—a "Sea Captain" resided at 159 Vine, a "Hairdresser" rented James and Maria Reynolds's 161 Vine, and along the block lived a bricklayer, a "huckster," a "labourer," a painter, a "Dealer in fruit," a blacksmith with his shop, a cabinet maker, shoemaker, tobacconist, and a "French watch-maker." There were also two boardinghouses on what had been the Browns' side of the street. See Hogan, *Prospect of Philadelphia*, 21.

68. *Ormond*, 60.

69. See Chapter 3 above, and J. H. Powell, *Bring Out Your Dead: The Great Plague of Yellow Fever in Philadelphia in 1793* (New York, 1965). William Dunlap, *The Life of Charles Brockden Brown* (Philadelphia, 1815), 2: 3; CBB to Bringhurst, August 18, 1797 (Bennett Census no. 88), in CBB Coll., Me.; CBB to Maria Nicholson, "circa August 1798," CBB Coll., Va. For CBB and yellow fever, see also CBB to James Brown, October 25, 1796, printed in David Lee Clark, *Charles Brockden Brown: Pioneer Voice of America* (Durham, N.C., 1952), 156–57.

70. *Ormond*, 44.

71. See, for example, ibid., 89, 75, 76, 127, 97, 139, 155.

72. Ibid., 157. Julia Stern, in *The Plight of Feeling: Sympathy and Dissent in the Early American Novel* (Chicago, 1997), turns Martinette into a full-throated heroine of liberty. Not that an intelligent, cross-dressing, throat-cutting eighteenth-century woman of the world isn't a noble thing: it just wasn't for CBB. Stern similarly wants *Ormond* to be an incisive analysis and critique of race relations in 1790s America, which it most definitely is not. Nor, painful truth be told, was CBB overly interested in, or perceptive about, the plight of African Americans. He thought, like most Delaware Valley Quakers, their situation was wrong. Unlike some Quakers, though— like his ancestor John Churchman (see Chapter 6 below)—he never evinced any effort in doing or even saying much about it. (See, for example, his April 19, 1795, letter to his brother James Brown in Edenton, North Carolina, about his "formidable prejudices" regarding "the Realities of Edenton," and how "I am still inclined to moralize, but should, I fear, be seduced into reflections of too sable a complexion for the occasion"; in CBB Coll., Va.) Sometimes literary "absence" is just absence.

73. *Ormond*, 95.

74. *Three Gothic Novels*, 3; *Ormond*, 203.

75. *Ormond*, 148; on CBB's *An Address to the Government of the United States, on the Cession of Louisiana to the French* (Philadelphia, 1803), see Conclusion below.

Chapter 6. The Return of the Present . . . and Past

1. Charles Brockden Brown, *Three Gothic Novels* (New York, 1998), 641. All subsequent quotes are from this edition. For CBB's attitude about the English Gothic tradition, see his essay on "Terrific Novels," in Charles Brockden Brown, *Literary Essays and Reviews*, ed. Alfred Weber and Wolfgang Schäfer (Frankfurt am Main, 1992), 143–45.
2. *Three Gothic Novels*, 779–803.
3. On the writing of *Huntly*, see Sydney Krause's "Historical Essay" in *The Novels and Related Works of Charles Brockden Brown*, ed. Sydney J. Krause et al. vol. 4, (Kent, Ohio, 1984), 297–316. For CBB's description of method, see Chapter 2 above.
4. Elijah Brown is recorded as "confined in Jaile" on July 23, 1784 (Sarah Waln to "My Dear Nicholas," in Mary Harrison, *Annals of the Ancestry of Charles Custis Harrison and Ellen Waln Harrison* (Philadelphia, 1932), 94. I'm making the assumption here that he was still in jail two and a half weeks later. I would bet, given the way CBB operated, that the financial data he gives relative to Weymouth on 772, *Three Gothic Novels*, corresponds to financial particulars of Elijah Brown's predicament in 1784—though I have been unable to discover the details of that predicament. Sarah Logan Fisher refers to "that great good Man Anthony Benezet" in her "Diaries," vol. 13, p. 26, HSP. It was a universal sentiment among Philadelphia Quakers. For Benezet, see George Brookes, *Friend Anthony Benezet* (Philadelphia, 1937), 45–52 (for the Philadelphia Negro school) and 115 (for his presence in Easton in July 1756). Benezet, upon his death in 1784, bequeathed his modest estate to the Negro school. Benezet was at the wedding of Elijah and Mary Brown, in 1761, as were at least five other Quakers who had been present at the treaty conferences in Easton in 1756 and 1757.
5. Francis Jennings, *The Ambiguous Iroquois Empire* (New York, 1984), 330–34; Anthony F. C. Wallace, *King of the Delawares: Teedyuscung, 1700–1763* (Syracuse, N.Y., 1990), 23–26.
6. Wallace, *King of the Delawares*, 26; Jennings, *Ambiguous Iroquois Empire*, 336–39.
7. Jennings, *Ambiguous Iroquois Empire*, 314–24.
8. Quoted in Paul A. W. Wallace, *Conrad Weiser, 1696–1760: Friend of Colonist and Mohawk* (Philadelphia, 1945), 131; Jennings, *Ambiguous Iroquois Empire*, 342–46.
9. C. A. Weislager, *The Delaware Indians: A History* (New Brunswick, N.J., 1996), 191–94, 204–8.
10. Fred Anderson, *Crucible of War: The Seven Years' War and the Fate of Empire in British North America, 1754–1766* (New York, 2001), 108, 160–65; A. D. Chidsey, Jr., *A Frontier Village: Pre-Revolutionary Easton* (Easton, Pa., 1940), 24–28; *Minutes of the Provincial Council of Pennsylvania* (Harrisburg, Pa., 1851), 6:766–68; Wallace, *Conrad Weiser*, 409–10, and 472 for the militia major quote.
11. John Churchman, *An Account of the Gospel Labours, and Christian Experiences of a Faithful Minister of Christ, John Churchman, Late of Nottingham in Pennsylvania, deceased* (Philadelphia, 1779), 175. Churchman, in his memoir, conflates events that happened across late 1755 to mid-1757 under the rubric "1756." The frontiersmen brought their corpses to Philadelphia in May 1757. See *Minutes of the Provincial Council*, 6: 538, and Theodore Thayer, *Israel Pemberton: King of the Quakers* (Philadelphia, 1943), 137.
12. Thayer, *Israel Pemberton*, 97–107; Wallace, *King of the Delawares*, 93.
13. *Minutes of the Provincial Council*, 7: 324; Wallace, *King of the Delawares*, 133–36; Francis Jennings, *Benjamin Franklin, Politician: The Mask and the Man* (New York, 1996), 123–45. Among the Quakers who on November 2, 1756, contributed to the fund that established the Friendly Association for Regaining and Preserving Peace with the Indians by Pacific Measures, which money was used to underwrite the Easton conference and provide gifts to Teedyuscung and the Delawares, were

William Brown (Elijah's uncle, and with whom, most likely, Elijah Brown lived when he moved to Philadelphia in early 1757), Anthony Benezet, Israel and James and John Pemberton, and James Bringhurst. These individuals almost certainly were among the group of forty-five to fifty Quakers who took in Teedyuscung's performance, and they were present at a Friendly Association conference after the event which discussed what should be done next. First and foremost, after Teedyuscung's speech, the Quakers of the Friendly Association wanted to examine all the secret deeds from the past through which the Penns had acquired Indian land. See Samuel Parrish, *Some Chapters in the History of the Friendly Association for Regaining and Preserving Peace with the Indians by Pacific Measures* (Philadelphia, 1877), 18, 20, 24, 34–35, and passim; and Thayer, *Israel Pemberton*, 129–35.

14. Sydney Krause, in his "Historical Essay" (cited above) on *Edgar Huntly*, remarks that a link between "Sky-Walk"—CBB's first name for what he renamed Norwalk—and the Walking Purchase, "is independently worthy of consideration" (304–5 n. 12). He could not have been more right. William Dunlap reports CBB exploring the Walking Purchase region on what very well may have been a research outing—"he had visited Bethlehem and Nazareth, and rambled on foot over the adjacent country"—in the early 1790s. *Life of Charles Brockden Brown* (Philadelphia, 1815), 1: 57–58.

15. Sydney James, *A People among Peoples* (Cambridge, 1963), 298–315; Richard Bauman, *For the Reputation of Truth* (Baltimore, 1971), 210–15. For Phineas Pemberton and the 1777–78 Philadelphia context, see Prologue above (and note 23 for Pemberton quote). On general 1780s to 1790s context, see Daniel K. Richter, "Onas, the Long Knife: Pennsylvanians and Indians, 1783–1794," in *Native Americans and the Early Republic*, ed. Frederick E. Hoxie, Ronald Hoffman, and Peter J. Albert (Charlotteville, Va., 1999), 125–61.

16. "Journal of George Churchman, 1759–1813," vol. 1, pp. 68, 71–72 (entries for December 27, 1763, February 7 and 20, 1764), Quaker Collection, Haverford College; *An Address to the Inhabitants of Pennsylvania* . . . (Philadelphia, 1777), 10, 21, 26; "Journal of the Transactions," Pemberton Family Papers, vol. 31, p. 79, HSP. See Prologue above too.

17. It is *not* a historical coincidence that the list of "traitors" to be exiled made up by Pennsylvania Revolutionaries in 1777 Philadelphia contained so many of the 1756 founders of the Friendly Association for Regaining and Preserving Peace with the Indians—including its leaders Israel Pemberton, James Pemberton, John Pemberton, Henry Drinker, Owen Jones, and Abel Jones.

18. This dream, by an anonymous female "friend," is recorded in the "Commonplace Book of Samuel Garrigues," pp. 85–87, Quaker Collection (no. 975a), Haverford College. I take it to be a Delaware Valley dream, though Garrigues does not specify it as such. It is Garrigues, a Philadelphia Quaker, who dates it to "late in the Spring 1775."

19. See Prologue above.

20. Bauman, *For the Reputation of Truth*, 203–4, 208.

21. *Diary of Elizabeth Drinker*, 2: 1006, 1076, 1111–12, 1230, 1232, 1012, 1037; *Narration of the Late Massacres, in Lancaster County, of a Number of Indians, Friends of the Province, By Persons Unknown*, in *Papers of Benjamin Franklin*, ed. Leonard W. Labaree (New Haven, Conn., 1967), 2: 50, 52, 53.

22. *Three Gothic Novels*, 651, 280, 306. On Swanwick, see Chapter 4 above; and [John Swanwick], *British Honour and Humanity; or The Wonders of American Patience* (Philadelphia, 1796), 51–54.

23. CBB to Bringhurst, July 29, August 1, 1793 (Bennett Census no. 48), CBB Coll., Me.

24. Sydney Krause, who has described the character Huntly as "Indian-haunted,"

has noted CBB's excessive and—in view of how CBB characterized Indians in his translation of Volney's *View of the Soil and Climate of the United States of America* (1804)—downright strange use of the term "savage" to define his Indians. ("On the one hand, [Brown] chastized Volney for insisting on the technicality that North American Indians should properly be called savages to distinguish them from East Indians, yet in *Edgar Huntly* Brown almost never calls *his* Indians anything other than savages.") Krause also notes the "phantom-like quality" that other literary critics, like Leslie Fiedler, have seen in CBB's Indians. See Krause, "Historical Essay," 367, 358, 369–70. Norman Grabo, in *The Coincidental Art of Charles Brockden Brown* (Chapel Hill, N.C., 1981), 68, describes CBB's Indians as deriving "from some nightmare without words." What all three critics agree on is that, wherever they come from, CBB's Indians seem more symbolic than "real."

25. Wilkins was surprised at first by CBB's writing, by "the grief that preys upon your spirits and the melancholy that seems to enshroud your soul." CBB *the person*, i.e., the nonwriter, Wilkins described as "an example of equanimity and fortitude." But when Wilkins read what CBB wrote, what came out of CBB's *imagination*, he was shocked to find a "fancy" "entirely employed in conjuring up phantoms of imaginary midnight and apparitions of unreal horror." CBB, for his part, explained the apparent strangeness of his "fiction" with the comment that "a visionary is not answerable for his sentiments or actions"—which is not unlike what Edgar Huntly says when he gives free rein to his "vengeance": "It was the scope of my wishes to kill the whole number of my foes; but that being done, I was indifferent to the consequences." "Unpublished Letters of Brown and Wilkins," *Studies in English* 27 (1948): 84, 81; *Three Gothic Novels*, 805.

26. Two interesting names show up in the early history of Solebury. James Logan came to Pennsylvania in 1699, and according to a historian of Solebury, he "was to have much to do with laying out Solebury Township." William Penn initially granted Logan six hundred acres in Solebury. Then in 1703 the township was formally organized, being divided into twenty-eight tracts. In 1716 among the property owners in Solebury are "Richard Walln and Ann his wife." These are the patriarch and matriarch of the Waln clan, which Elijah Brown would marry into. The other name is "Charles Brockden, of Philadelphia, gent."—whose son Elijah Brown would name his own son after. Charles Brockden in this 1716 deed is conveying his land to Richard Walln. Which means that on the morning of September 19, 1737, when Logan's three walkers headed north from their starting point, for the first ten miles or so they were technically clearing title to land claimed by CBB's Uncle Richard's family. (Which puts a curious gloss on Edgar Huntly's statement, 820, *Three Gothic Novels*, that "The village inhabited by this clan"—Old Deb's Delawares—"was built upon ground which now constitutes my uncle's barn yard and orchard.") John Richardson, *Solebury Township, Bucks County, Pennsylvania* (Philadelphia, 1958), 8–9; *Early Settlers of Solebury Township, Bucks County, Pa.*, compiled by Eastburn Reeder (Doylestown, Pa., 1971), 9–10.

27. "Diary of Robert Morton," *PMHB* 1 (1877): 5. Or consider the apparent running fantasy—or "prospect," as she calls it—of one Martha Harris. In September 1778 Sarah Fisher and Nancy Emlen visited Harris, and Fisher afterward recorded in her diary: "[Harris] was glad to see us, & told us of the prospect she had uniformly had for this 7 Years, of a Famine coming on this Land, that then there would be a Pestilence & a Fire, & all this to humble the People & bring down their arrogance & vain boasting." Fisher additionally noted that "the visit was attended with a sweet solemnity, & left an agreable composure on [my] mind"; Fisher "Diaries," vol. 6, no page number (entry for September 19, 1778), HSP.

28. Churchman, *An Account*, 185–86.

29. Ibid, 175–76.

30. Ibid., 187.

31. Charles Brockden Brown, *Jane Talbot* (New York, 1970), 67–70, 109, 234.

Conclusion. Charles Brown, American

1. Charles Brockden Brown, *Literary Essays and Reviews*, ed. Alfred Weber and Wolfgang Schäfer (Frankfurt am Main, 1992), 103–10.

2. Ibid., 104, 109, 105.

3. Ibid., 25–27.

4. "'Diary of Trifling Occurrences,' Philadelphia, 1776–1778," ed. Nicholas B. Wainwright *PMHB* 82 (October 1958), 449; *Writings of George Washington*, ed. John C. Fitzpatrick (Washington, D.C., 1933), 9:245, 248–49.

5. On the politics of the Louisiana Purchase, see Alexander DeConde, *This Affair of Louisiana* (New York, 1976).

6. (C. B. Brown), *An Address to the Government of the United States, on the Cession of Louisiana to the French; and on the Late Breach of Treaty by the Spaniards: Including the Translation of a Memorial, On the War of St. Domingo, and Cession of the Mississippi to France, Drawn up by a French Counsellor of State* (Philadelphia, 1803), 37, 45, 39, 43.

7. Ibid., 37. On the Federalists view of Jefferson and "his" America, see Linda K. Kerber, *Federalists in Dissent: Imagery and Ideology in Jeffersonian America* (Ithaca, N.Y., 1970), 3–14 ("Mobocracy" on 14), 173–93; and especially William C. Dowling, *Literary Federalism in the Age of Jefferson: Joseph Dennie and* The Port Folio, *1801–1812* (Columbia, S.C., 1999), 8, 15, 23–32.

8. *Address to the Government*, 36–37. CBB would examine Jefferson's character further in this Federalist vein in his 1807 party pamphlet, *The British Treaty* (n.p., n.d.). See especially 10–13.

9. *Address to the Government*, 49.

10. Ibid., 56

11. Ibid., 47.

12. On the Federalists' "golden age," see Kerber, *Federalists in Dissent*, 4–7; and Dowling, *Literary Federalism*, 30–31, 70–73.

13. For a cultural history of post-Revolutionary American "refashioners," see Joyce Appleby, *Inheriting the Revolution: The First Generation of Americans* (Cambridge, Mass., 2000), and especially 239–66.

14. See Philadelphia (Southern District) Meeting files at Swarthmore College. Charles Brockden Brown was disowned on "1804–12–26"—the day after Christmas. See too the Philadelphia (Southern District) Monthly Meeting's "testimony" of February 20, 1805, in CBB Coll., Va.

Epilogue

1. *Philadelphia Merchant: The Diary of Thomas P. Cope*, ed. Eliza Cope Harrison (South Bend, Ind., 1978), 248.

2. Ibid., 248.

3. Ibid., 248–49, 79.

4. Ibid., 249. David Lee Clark, *Charles Brockden Brown: Pioneer Voice of America* (Durham, N.C., 1952), 330–33, prints the inventory of CBB's property at the time of his death. It records that CBB had $451.83 in the bank, no real estate, and personal property—consisting mostly of household goods—worth $1,187.50. Most of the valuable household articles he had no doubt inherited from his grandmother, Elizabeth Armitt—the daughter of the well-to-do Joseph Armitt who had died in

1747. Elizabeth Armitt's will is in the CBB Coll., Va. For an example of CBB's father and mother still milking the Armitt assets in the early 1800s, see Richard Waln to Richard Stockton, March 13, 1806, in the Society Collection, HSP, and the Elijah Brown and Richard Waln "Indenture," August 31, 1808, in the H. A. Brown Collection, HSP.

5. The Brown family first contracted with Paul Allen to write CBB's "life." Allen, a Rhode Islander who seems to have met CBB in early 1800s Philadelphia, produced a thin manuscript, "Life of the Late Charles B. Brown," which was taken up by Dunlap and expanded. See introduction to Paul Allen, *The Late Charles Brockden Brown*, ed. Robert E. Hemenway and Joseph Katz (Columbia, S.C., 1976). In regard to William Dunlap's published *Life of Charles Brockden Brown*, consider this biographical analysis of Dunlap by the historian/biographer Joseph Ellis: "Dunlap's desire to make himself useful was all-consuming; it extended to his personal history and included a willingness to manipulate the facts of his early life to fit a fabricated, lesson-laden pattern. The central lesson of Dunlap's story was that excessive freedom, especially at an early age, led inevitably to habits of indolence and a selfish, aimless character. His various autobiographies are all morality plays designed to dramatize the danger of self-indulgence and the importance of self-control and discipline." Joseph E. Ellis, *After the Revolution: Profiles of Early American Culture* (New York, 1979), 117. It would seem that Dunlap, with his *Life of Charles Brockden Brown*, endeavored to fabricate yet another morality play in this vein. Subsequent biographies of CBB—Harry R. Warfel's *Charles Brockden Brown: American Gothic Novelist* (1949), David Lee Clark's *Charles Brockden Brown: Pioneer Voice of America* (1952), Steven Watts's *The Romance of Real Life: Charles Brockden Brown and the Origins of American Culture* (1994)—and the literary studies dependent upon them, have all followed in Dunlap's footsteps.

6. CBB to Wilkins, [1790–95?], CBB Coll., Va.

7. Richard Holmes, *Shelley: The Pursuit* (New York, 1975), 221, 274, 371–76; Eleanor Sickels, "Shelley and Charles Brockden Brown," *Publications of the Modern Language Association* 45 (1930): 1116–28.

8. G. R. Thompson, *Poe's Fiction: Romantic Irony in the Gothic Tales* (Madison, Wisc., 1973), 151–52; Nathaniel Hawthorne, *Tales and Sketches* (New York, 1982), 735.

9. Hawthorne, *Tales and Sketches*, 111, 114, 127.

10. Hawthorne, *Tales and Sketches*, 68–69, 70, 80.

11. Ibid., 103–4.

12. Horace Walpole, *The Castle of Otranto* (Oxford, 1998), 40–41; Nathaniel Hawthorne, *Collected Novels* (New York, 1983), 369.

13. Martin Kallich, in his *Horace Walpole* (New York, 1971), offers such psychological interpretations of *Otranto*.

14. Edwin Haviland Miller, *Salem Is My Dwelling Place: A Life of Nathaniel Hawthorne* (Iowa City, 1991), 16–23; Hawthorne, *Collected Novels*, 126. On the Pyncheons, see Stephen Innes, *Labor in a New Land: Economy and Society in Seventeenth-Century Springfield* (Princeton, 1983).

15. See Jack McLaughlin, *Jefferson and Monticello: The Biography of a Builder* (New York, 1988), 356–64. Monticello's full catalogue of paintings is printed in *Antiques* 59 (April 1951): 308–9, 311.

Index

Acknowledgments

Without Mike Zuckerman, this book would not have been written (and I pray this will not be held against him). He made it possible for me to work under the aegis of the McNeil Center for Early American Studies, where I did the bulk of my research. He has been an enthusiastic supporter of the project all along the way, and has read and commented on much of the text. Mike, in this latter capacity, is simply the best *reader* I've ever known.

I would also like to thank the then director of the McNeil Center, Richard S. Dunn, for making me feel at home at the Center, and Wayne Bodle and Ed Larkin for their comments on various chapters. Other individuals who have read and improved parts of the book are Mary Maples Dunn, Chuck Callanan, Lisa Weinsten, J. William Frost, and Paula O'Malley. I thank as well the staff of the *William and Mary Quarterly*, in particular Philip Morgan and Ann Gross, for their rigorous vetting of an early chapter. And I thank the interlibrary loan department at the Chester County Public Library. You can live in the sticks and still get your hands on dusty, scholarly tomes about the Albigensian heresy.

To the late Kenneth Lynn my account stands, sadly, permanently in arrears. I owe him for first teaching me how to read literary texts for the purposes of history and biography, and for the idea—exemplified by his own writings—that history and biography could be fun to read.

John Holmes read most of the manuscript and has saved me from so many errors that I am of a mind to blame him for all that remain. Edwin Saeger, whom I met many years ago in New Brunswick, Maine, was kind enough back then to allow me to use his personal transcription of the Charles Brockden Brown Papers at Bowdoin College. Charles Brown's father was a professional copyist who wrote with a clear and elegant hand. Alas, Charles did not follow the example. Access to Ed's transcriptions was of great use in helping me to decipher Brown's cramped scribblings. I look forward to the coming publication of the definitive Holmes and Saeger edition of the Brown letters.

At the University of Pennsylvania Press I've been blessed with two fine editors, Bob Lockhart and Alison Anderson. Bob saw things in a manuscript that I thought were there but a shocking number of other editors didn't, and he has encouraged me to expand and sharpen the work. In all areas where he was insistent, his instincts proved true. Alison, for her part, has given me a long overdue tutorial on the English language. I owe special thanks to a stranger I've never spoken to (though I once sat across the table from him at Zorba's in Philadelphia), Thomas Slaughter, who, as an outside reader for the Penn Press, gave an incredibly generous—and softly suggestive—reading of my manuscript. Every hint he gave of where things could be improved bore fruit, nowhere more so than in his assertion that he thought *Edgar Huntly* was about "liminality." Initially that sounded a bit mumbo-jumboey to me, but as I reworked my *Huntly* chapter, and as I correlated the "fiction" with all the historical and geographical material I had gathered, damn if it didn't turn out to be a novel about *liminality*.

Finally, to Arlene Newman I owe the central insight that powered this life and times study. Long ago I made an idle comment to her, apropos of a certain United States senatorial primary election in the American heartland, that it was outrageous the way out-of-state right-wing money was being channeled in to defeat the moderate incumbent at any cost. Her response surprised me: "Good riddance." "Good riddance?" I asked. "Yea," she said. "That lovely senator of yours, he's a"—and I paraphrase here——"a particular kind of bigot." "You're kidding," I said. "How do you know that?" To which she took a moment to think, before responding, "I'm not sure. I just do."

Forget the politics. For me this was a revelation about the underworld of tribal knowledge. We all have it. I had no doubt that if I investigated the voting record of the senator in question, I would indeed discover a certain leaning, unsuspected by me, on certain issues relating to a certain small country located halfway around the world. This thought proved the key to my unlocking the textures of Charles Brockden Brown's eighteenth-century Philadelphia world. Brown came from a tight-knit and self-consciously under-assault tribe. They spoke and wrote in English, but what they said to each other carried special nuances. I had to tune into the code. Luckily, while this Quaker tribe often kept silent in meeting, they loved writing letters to each other and keeping diaries—which they and their families made a point of preserving, and which reside today in the collections of the Historical Society of Pennsylvania and Swarthmore and Haverford Colleges. In these documents the subjective history, the ideology, the mythologies, the special emotions and fears of Charles Brown's family, friends, and community are in evidence; from these documents the day-to-day ambiance of Charles Brown's world can be reconstructed. Brockden Brown grew up to be the novelist of this Philadelphia, which was a special slice of the American Revolution, much as Franz Kafka was the novelist of his

Prague, which itself was a special slice of late nineteenth- and early twentieth-century Europe. Arlene's inadvertent inspiration reoriented me for my quest after Brown, and *Charles Brockden Brown's Revolution* is the result. Thank you.

Permission is gratefully acknowledged to reprint illustrations from the following sources.

Charles Brockden Brown, attributed to Ellen Sharples after James Sharples, 1810. Courtesy National Park Service, Independence National Historical Park.

Map of Philadelphia, 1777. Courtesy Historical Society of Pennsylvania.

Harriet Chew (Mrs. Charles Carroll), by John Trumbull. Yale University Art Gallery, Trumbull Collection.

Broad Street and Federal Hall, 1797, engraving from Samuel Hollyer's views of New York. Collection of the New-York Historical Society.

Frigate *United States*, by Thomas Clarke. *American Universal Magazine*, July 24, 1797. Courtesy Library Company of Philadelphia.

William Godwin, by J. W. Chandler, 1798. Tate Gallery, London, N01208. Courtesy Tate Enterprises.

Dr. Elihu Hubard Smith, B.A. 1786, by James Sharples. 1797. Yale University Art Gallery. Gift to Yale Medical Library through Dr. Herbert Thoms by Mrs. Frances G. Cold; accepted by Acceptance Form 11/30/1959.

"Two Savages, disputing which should deliver Miss McRea into her Lover's hands." *Philadelphia Magazine*, 1797. Courtesy Historical Society of Pennsylvania.

Portrait of Charles Brockden Brown, by James Sharples. Courtesy Worcester Art Museum, Worcester, Massachusetts.